WALKING SHADOWS

WALKING·SHADOWS

Shakespeare

in the National Film and Television Archive

EDITED BY LUKE MCKERNAN AND OLWEN TERRIS

BRITISH FILM INSTITUTE

bfi

BFI PUBLISHING

First published in 1994 by the
British Film Institute
21 Stephen Street
London W1P 1PL

The British Film Institute exists to encourage the development of film, television and video in the
United Kingdom, and to promote knowledge, understanding and enjoyment of the culture of the
moving image. Its activities include the National Film and Television Archive; the National Film
Theatre; the Museum of the Moving Image; the London Film Festival; the production and
distribution of film and video; funding and support for regional activities; Library and Information
Services; Stills, Posters and Designs; Research; Publishing and Education; and the monthly *Sight and
Sound* magazine.

British Library Cataloguing-in-Publication Data.
A catalogue record for this book is available
from the British Library.

ISBN 0–85170–414–X
 0–85170–486–7 pbk

Design by Altius Design Associates

Cover illustration:
Jean Simmons as Ophelia in HAMLET (1948),
courtesy of Rank Film Distributors

Typeset by
Method Limited, Epping, Essex
Printed in Great Britain by
The Trinity Press, Worcester

Contents

Foreword

I am very pleased to be able to recommend this book to lovers of Shakespeare and the screen alike. As the reader will discover, film has served not only as a means to preserve the performances and productions of the past, but has expanded our understanding of how Shakespeare may be presented. Shakespeare's plays were written for the stage, but they will become nothing if they do not remain popular. Through the media of film and television millions have learnt to appreciate the poetry, the drama and the sheer entertainment value of the greatest plays ever written.

Thanks, therefore, to the invaluable work of the National Film and Television Archive, we can witness again those great Shakespeareans of the past, from Herbert Beerbohm Tree to Laurence Olivier, and treasure almost a century of Shakespeare on film. Future generations will inherit an ever richer body of interpretations, as Shakespeare continues to inspire and entertain us.

Kenneth Branagh

Acknowledgments

For Bridget and Elizabeth   *Luke*

For my parents   *Olwen*

We would like to thank each of the following for their help and advice: Stephen Bottomore, the British Universities Film & Video Council, Linda Briggs, Steve Bryant, Elaine Burrows, Ed Buscombe, June Elvy, Anne Fleming, Roma Gibson, Nicholas Hiley, Timothy Holmes, Claire Hudson, Clyde Jeavons, Dawn King, Pam Logan, David Meeker, David Peterson, Markku Salmi, John Smoker, Veronica Taylor, Mark van den Tempel and Paul Willemen. A special thank you to the contributors Robert Pearson, William Uricchio and Tise Vahimagi, to John Thompson who oversaw the project, to Bridget McKernan for her sound critical assessments and to Mary Cowden Clarke for her invaluable concordance. Most of all we would like to thank past members of the NFTVA's Cataloguing Department and our present colleagues there, who all contributed greatly to the production of the catalogue: Simon Baker, Ros Cranston, James Griffith, Graham Melville and Emilio Monserrate.

Photographs are courtesy of BFI Stills, Posters and Designs, BBC, Channel Four and the Nederlands Filmmuseum.

We would like to give a special mention to the late Sam Wanamaker, for his wholehearted commitment and enthusiasm in bringing Shakespeare to the stage and screen. The encouragement and support he gave to this project throughout are gratefully acknowledged.

Luke McKernan
Olwen Terris

Note

Throughout this book, when a play is referred to it is given in italics (*Hamlet*); when a film is referred to it is given in capitals (HAMLET).

Introduction

'Look here, upon this picture, and on this' (*Hamlet*)

'It's wonderful – you wouldn't know it was Shakespeare'
(Anonymous studio executive commenting on Olivier's HAMLET, 1948)

Why, it is valid to ask, choose Shakespeare as the subject for a thematic trawl through the holdings of the National Film and Television Archive?

One reason is contained in the simple but surprising fact that it is possible to find more than 400 references to Shakespeare and his plays and characters among the films and television programmes preserved by the NFTVA. Another is reflected in the seemingly endless supply of researchers who appear to want to do just that: look up 'Shakespeare' in the Archive's catalogues. Our aim, therefore, is to provide what everyone wants, in one handy volume.

This is not, however, just an arid list of versions, variations and Shakespearean plot summaries, but a purposely critical, anything-goes anthology of ninety years of parodies, borrowings, quotations, homages, documentaries, operas, ballets, newsfilms, home movies and comic sketches – all the way from cinema's first stab at the Bard in Beerbohm Tree's KING JOHN (1899) to Richard Griffiths's hamming of Hamlet in WITHNAIL & I (1986) and Dustin Hoffman's study of Shylock on the *South Bank Show* (1989).

Nor is 'Walking Shadows' merely an indulgence of 'trivial fond records'. As film historian Roger Manvell wrote in 1971: 'The history of the adaptation of Shakespeare's plays for the screen is also the history of the adaptation of the screen to Shakespeare's plays.' What our catalogue reveals is not only how widely Shakespeare has infiltrated the moving image, but how great and varied is the range of material represented by this broad theme. Simply by using Shakespeare as the key, one can test new avenues of research and discover fresh nuggets of information and creative imagination scattered among the Archive's eclectic holdings.

Yet Shakespeare is, for all that, the heart of the matter, and those who seek to learn how the youngest of the arts has dealt with and fed off the man and his works will find a satisfaction of answers among these essays and annotations. 'But the poetry – shall we ever get the poetry upon the screen ...?' once complained Graham Greene rather unpoetically. That is for the critic and researcher to decide: meanwhile, we can offer plenty of entertaining prose among the 'abstracts and brief chronicles of our time' which make up this original and, we hope, useful and informative book.

Clyde Jeavons, Curator, NFTVA
January 1994

The Real Thing at Last

Luke McKernan

> Shakespeare, had he written for the screen,
> would have done his work differently.
>
> *Micheál MacLiammóir*

> I don't believe in an essential reverence for the original
> material – it's simply part of the collaboration.
>
> *Orson Welles*[1]

Filmed Shakespeare began in the third week of September 1899, on the Thames embankment, close by the Tivoli Theatre. The film was of Herbert Beerbohm Tree's forthcoming production of *King John* at Her Majesty's Theatre. The production company were the British Mutoscope and Biograph Company, who took films both for Biograph film shows, notably at the Palace Theatre in London, and for the sets of Mutoscope cards that were used in 'What the Butler Saw' machines in resorts and amusement parlours up and down the country. Four scenes were taken in the Biograph's open-air studio: King John (played by Tree) encouraging Hubert to kill Arthur; Queen Constance (Julia Neilson) lamenting in the French King's tent; the death agony of King John; and the crowning of his successor Henry (Dora Senior). Each scene was taken in a single shot and the overall film lasted about four minutes. It was premiered on the same night as the play, 20 September 1899, at the Palace Theatre, where the spectacular 68mm presentations of Biograph films were a considerable draw. Today, a one-minute fragment of the third scene survives, King John writhing in his chair while Pembroke, Bigot and the young Prince Henry look on.[2]

There are basically two critical approaches to Shakespeare on film. One looks for faithful reproductions of the text, judging such films by the standards of theatrical performance or literary criticism. The other looks at the phenomenon of Shakespeare on film, and is the approach taken by this history and catalogue. The emphasis is not on faithfulness to Shakespeare (though that has usually been of importance to the film-makers), but on the demands of the medium. KING JOHN was a poor record of both the production and the play, but then it was intended as neither. It was silent, it was made at a time before there was any notion of narrative cinema, it was produced in the studio to the dictates of the film-makers. The intention was to adapt the stage production to the requirements of the screen, to

Herbert Beerbohm Tree in KING JOHN (1899)

provide what amounted to an advertisement for Tree's production, or better still a news report, for the Biograph company were making their reputation with actuality coverage. It is not *King John* the play; it is KING JOHN the film.

Other noted Shakespeareans were recorded in a manner similar to Tree at the turn of the century. In 1900 Sarah Bernhardt was filmed in the duel scene from *Hamlet*.[3] The remarkable compilation film PARIS 1900 (France 1948) includes footage from this period of Mounet-Sully as Hamlet and Firmin Gémier as Julius Caesar and Shylock. But these were isolated examples at a time when films happily captured anything that moved. There was no Shakespearean cinema as yet.

Such a phenomenon emerged when the cinema first had need of it. As the public appetite for films grew, so special theatres for their exhibition came to be constructed, so more producers entered the market, so there was an ever increasing demand for source material, making literary and dramatic properties an obvious choice. At the same time, the film trade had become sensitive to its lowly reputation, and though grateful for its predominantely working-class audience, yet sought to elevate films by showing their close connections with the theatre: emulating theatre furnishings in the cinemas, employing stage stars, but most of all adapting plays as films, including the occasional Shakespeare. Only the occasional, because it was learned early on that the Bard was poison at the box office and would have to be variously disguised if he was to sell any tickets, but enough to create a lasting trend. Shakespeare was the stamp of social acceptability; he also provided some good stories.

Such conditions help to explain the enthusiasm of two American companies in particular, the Thanhouser Film Corporation and the Vitagraph Company of America, who produced a remarkable number of Shakespeare films around this period. From 1910 to 1916 Thanhouser produced CYMBELINE, KING LEAR, THE MERCHANT OF VENICE, ROMEO AND JULIET, THE TEMPEST and THE WINTER'S TALE. Similarly, between 1908 and 1912 Vitagraph produced AS YOU LIKE IT, CARDINAL WOLSEY (*Henry VIII*), JULIUS CAESAR, KING LEAR, THE MERCHANT OF VENICE, A MIDSUMMER NIGHT'S DREAM, OTHELLO, RICHARD III, ROMEO AND JULIET and TWELFTH NIGHT. These were generally one- or two-reel films, lasting around fifteen to thirty minutes, as such was the standard length of film, and came to mean drastically compressed plots with familiar quotations sprinkled throughout the intertitles. Such films were sold on their prestige and spectacle, and under their given limitations some are surprisingly effective. The tragedies, reduced to a quick succession of murders and miseries, do tend to absurdity, for example Vitagraph's KING LEAR, but the same company's A MIDSUMMER NIGHT'S DREAM has a lightness and magicality that marks it as something out of the ordinary.

A particularly fine example from this period is, unusually, British. The British fiction film was already falling behind its rivals in ambition and production techniques, but the Clarendon Film Company's THE TEMPEST (1908) is as fine a compression of one of the plays as one could hope to find. The scenes cut between the studio (Prospero's cave) and the countryside, and the overall effect is the same freshness that marks Vitagraph's A MIDSUMMER NIGHT'S DREAM without the unnecessary plot convolutions. The play has been re-imagined to suit the means available. The intertitles from the film indicate how well this was done (an opening title is probably missing from the surviving copy):

Prospero seeks refuge on an island.
The discovery of Caliban.
The fairy spirit Ariel is released from a tree by Prospero.
10 years later. Ariel protects Miranda from Caliban.
The making of 'the Tempest'.
Antonio's son Ferdinand safely landed from the wreck.
Ariel is sent to bring Ferdinand to Miranda.
To humble Prince Ferdinand, Prospero sets him to log shifting.
Antonio's party tricked by Ariel.
Friends once more.
Ariel released.

This is not so much a simplification, rather a discovery of the play's simplicity. The narrative is now chronological; when Ferdinand's punishment is shown, only then is he called Prince, to stress the humbling; the number of named characters is brought to the bare minimum; there are no quotations in the intertitles, or set-pieces scholars of the play might hope to see reproduced (no 'Full fathom five', for instance). The play has been made to work as a ten-minute film. It is not the whole play, of course, but it is a fine film derived from that play.

The desire for literary prestige was also found in France and Italy, resulting in such titles as AMLETO (Italy 1910), RE LEAR (Italy 1910), IL MERCANTE DI VENEZIA (Italy 1910), SHYLOCK (France 1913) and a version of *The Winter's Tale*, UNA TRAGEDIA ALLA CORTE DI SICILIA (Italy 1914), which indicates that the producers were not simply interested in pandering to the masses, but had their art to consider. They had their pockets to consider also, so they emphasised the spectacle, the lasting qualities of the plays, and the great names they sometimes lured in front of the cameras.

Films grew from the single reels of 1910, to two, three and then four or five reels and the arrival of the feature. The opportunity to film a substantial version of a Shakespeare play was now to hand, although the financial risk was greater. In the NFTVA are two contrasting and fascinating versions of *Hamlet*, both featuring a noted actor and given a fairly full, albeit silent, rendition of the play. The British HAMLET of 1913, produced by the Hepworth Manufacturing Company, is a record of Sir Johnston Forbes-Robertson's Drury Lane production of the play, and indeed is little more than that. Overwhelmed by the prestige of having the country's foremost Shakespearean actor act his most celebrated role, the producers abandoned most of the basic common-sense rules of silent film-making. The actors are absurdly allowed to recite their speeches whole, while the intertitles give scarcely adequate indication of sense and motivation. There are some moments of cinematic inventiveness, and the film benefits greatly from location shots at Lulworth Cove and the countryside, and it does preserve a remarkable and subtle interpretation by Forbes-Robertson himself, who was 60 years old and at the end of his career.

How different the Italian HAMLET of 1917. The title role was played by Ruggero Ruggeri, as famous in Italy as Forbes-Robertson was in Britain, but unlike the latter unable to restrain his theatricality for the cameras. Yet this is the superior interpretation. There is still the sense of a stage play as the initial impetus for the production, but virtually every scene has been thought out with the camera in mind. The film-makers have not been afraid to invent new scenes where these best suit the cinematic narrative, and in the impressive cross-cutting between the duel scene and the approach of Fortinbras the film shows the advantages it can have over the stage. This is a version of the play, and a silent version at that, which would have made substantial sense to its audience and served as a reasonably faithful rendition of the play.

A watershed year for Shakespearean cinema was 1916. In that year, the tercentenary of Shakespeare's death, while Britain produced the stage-bound THE MERCHANT OF VENICE with Matheson Lang as Shylock, in America Thanhouser produced an imaginative KING LEAR and MASTER SHAKESPEARE, STROLLING PLAYER (an unusual exposition of the Baconian theory), and there were two major adaptations of *Romeo and Juliet* from Fox and Metro. Most significantly Herbert Beerbohm Tree, whose bold enthusiasm for the cinema needs celebrating, having started the ball rolling in 1899, then seen the storm scene from his production of *The Tempest* filmed by the Charles Urban Trading Company in 1905, and a thirty-minute record made of his *Henry VIII* by Barker Motion Photography in 1911, went to America to film MACBETH, with John Emerson directing and D. W. Griffith producing. This now lost film was apparently an imaginative treatment of the play, and had a largely favourable critical reception in America. But in Britain and among theatrical circles generally his action aroused hilarity. It was all right for Forbes-Robertson to be recorded in literal fashion; it might be expected for Hollywood to make *Romeo and Juliet* with Theda Bara, the original screen vamp, as Juliet; but this was a representative of the true Shakespearean tradition succumbing to Hollywood. In the *Bioscope*, a British film trade paper, a ditty first composed for a New York paper shows the merriment caused by the idea of Shakespeare mingling with the movies:

> *SHAKESPEARE'S SOLILOQUY (As it might have been had he been confronted by the problem that puzzles the modern playwright.)*

> To film or not to film; that is the question;
> Whether 'tis nobler for a man to suffer
> The shrieks and rantings of outrageous actors,
> Than freeze their voices in a moving picture,
> And, by congealing, end them? To screen, to film,
> And by that film to say we end
> The whining Lears, the mewling Romeos,
> And raving Hamlets; 'tis a consummation
> Devoutly to be wished. To screen, to film.
> But in this picture game what Fairbanks flops,
> What Charlie Chaplin walks may be worked in
> Must give us pause. There's the respect
> That puts the puzzled playwright up a tree.
> Or who would bear a melancholy Jacques
> Who piped the Seven Ages in E flat?

A leather lung-ed Brutus, or a Moor
Whose roarings could be heard in Quogue, L. I.?
Or Richard, bleating like a frightened sheep,
When he might silence all the noisy lot
By writing pictures? Who'd these worries bear,
To writhe and cower at his spoken lines
But that the fear of something worse than noise,
Some hideous slapstick-somersaulting Portia,
Or comedy Macbeth, puzzles the will
And makes us rather bear those ills we have
Than fly to others that we know not of?
Thus progress doth make cowards of us all,
And thus our zeal to make our dramas better
Is sicklied o'er with the pale cast of doubt.
And enterprises we were crazy to engage in
In this respect seem hazardous to try.
I'll stick to old style action!⁴

Tree's own comments on the rumpus show a greater understanding of the movies, their popularity and their potential, than that shared by many of his theatrical contemporaries:

> In England we have no conception of the vast influence of the moving picture industry in America, where it has become part of the national life of the people. There is at home a tendency to sneer at the serious work which is undertaken by striving artists such as Mr Griffith – witness the brilliant ridicule by which the film of *Macbeth* was anticipated. I refer, of course, to Sir James Barrie's recent remarkable contribution to Shakespeare's Tercentenary.⁵

Tree is referring to a film parody of Shakespeare written by J. M. Barrie, produced in early 1916 and premiered at a charity show for British troops, before going on wider release, which was made by the British Actors Film Company. The film showed how *Macbeth* might be filmed in both Britain and Hollywood, the latter going in for excessive blood, dancing girls instead of witches, an appearance by 'Charlie Chaplin', and such helpful intertitles as 'If Birnam Wood moves, it's a cinch'. Barrie called the film THE REAL THING AT LAST.⁶

The quest to put Shakespeare on the screen ever since has been a search for 'the real thing at last'. The theatre, epitomised by Shakespeare, and seen as naturally the superior medium, tantalisingly offers something which the cinema instinctively feels that it lacks. Conversely, the cinema, by eliminating the hazards of live performance, and with the added attractions of real locations, lavish budgets and a mass audience, can do more for Shakespeare than the theatre is able to. On television too, invariably Shakespeare has been an event, when the medium rises above itself, where it either emulates the theatre or, by virtue of greater purchasing power, brings together starry casts such as no theatre-goer could hope to see in live performance. And just occasionally artists such as Laurence Olivier, Orson Welles, Grigori Kozintsev, Peter Brook, Trevor Nunn or Derek Jarman have produced Shakespearean films or television programmes that stand out as works of creative inspiration; the real thing at last.

Given the commercial hazards of putting on Shakespeare for a mass public, a remarkable variety of films have been produced in the genre. It may reasonably be argued that such is the infrequency of filmed Shakespeare that it is not a genre at all, too intermittent for strong patterns to emerge. This is so if one considers the few 'straight' versions of the plays that have been filmed for the cinema (leaving television for later consideration); but the phenomenon of Shakespeare on film must include the all-pervasive influence of Shakespeare as cultural icon, the epitome of what any artist might want to achieve. To acquire some of his literary glamour is really very easy. One may allude to Shakespeare in a film's title (NORTH BY NORTHWEST, RICH AND STRANGE, SOMETHING WICKED THIS WAY COMES), one may have characters quoting from the plays to show that they are above the common herd (the *Hamlet* soliloquy quoted by Katharine Hepburn in MORNING GLORY, John Barrymore in PLAYMATES or Victor Mature in MY DARLING CLEMENTINE, three instances among many), one may simply borrow Shakespeare's plots and achieve art that way (JOE MACBETH and MEN OF RESPECT, two attempts to rewrite *Macbeth* as a gangster story). Shakespeare has been present as a symbol throughout the history of film-making, as no other artist or noted figure has been. Filming a straight version of one of the plays is only a part of it.

Given the sheer number of films and television programmes that then fall into this category, too many to discuss in a brief history such as this,[7] what follows is limited in the main to the holdings of the NFTVA, which fortunately provide a very useful overview. Historically, an archive was all the more likely to acquire, or to be offered, a film or television programme if it had the lasting qualities promised by an association with Shakespeare. Like royalty, it was of instant importance, and would endure.

Continuing with the silent era, for the 1920s there are three intriguing German productions, all distancing themselves in some respect from Shakespeare while clearly being representations of the plays. HAMLET (1920) stars the Danish actress Asta Nielsen in the title role and stresses its basis in Saxo Grammaticus's account of the legend, while re-inventing the whole story as that of the Princess Hamlet in disguise; OTHELLO (1922), with Emil Jannings, acknowledges Cinthio, the source material for Shakespeare; DER KAUFMANN VON VENEDIG (1923), with

Werner Krauss, likewise claims that it is based on the sources for *The Merchant of Venice* rather than the play itself. The reasons for such distancing seem obscure, since the films retained both the titles and substantially the plots of the plays, and may be an indirect apology for the absence of dialogue. All stem from a golden period of German film-making and boast the lavish production values and technical mastery which so distinguishes the films of that time.

It has been estimated that 80 per cent of all silent film production is lost, consigned to the rubbish heap when the talkies made the previous thirty years of film production financially worthless. We are lucky that what has survived has, and miracles such as the recent discovery of KING JOHN do occur; but still missing, for example, are Tree's THE TEMPEST, HENRY VIII and MACBETH, British and Colonial's feature-length THE LIFE OF SHAKESPEARE (GB 1914), the 1915 British modernisation of *As You Like It*, LOVE IN A WOOD, Anson Dyer's 1920 series of animated Shakespeare burlesques (of which only OH'PHELIA and a fragment from OTHELLO are known to survive), the experimental German version of *A Midsummer Night's Dream*, EIN SOMMERNACHTSTRAUM (1924), and J. M. Barrie's THE REAL THING AT LAST, which, to go by contemporary descriptions and the published memories of the participants, is a sad loss indeed. Regrettably, the silent Shakespeare film has been found absurd by most commentators on filmed Shakespeare. Jack J. Jorgens, in his otherwise commendable *Shakespeare on Film*, dismisses the period thus:

> First came scores of silent Shakespeare films, one- and two-reelers, struggling to render great poetic drama in dumb show. Mercifully, most of them are lost, for those which survive are for the most part inadequate performances of Shakespeare and pale examples of film art.[8]

Mercifully, many of them are *not* lost, and the NFTVA alone has over twenty examples. Robert Hamilton Ball's exceptional historical survey *Shakespeare on Silent Film* reveals the great riches of this period, but even he can conclude that the silent Shakespeare film was inadequate because it was not 'good Shakespeare'. Certainly, to some eyes such films are a record of quaint manners and no more. But one should judge such films according to their own outlook, viewing the films as texts in their own right. At every stage in the history of film-making, film-makers are restricted, inspired and guided by the contemporary outlook and available technology. French film director René Clair even went so far as to suggest that the silent film was the only medium suitable for filming Shakespeare. Assuming he meant pure visual images replacing poetic ones, then it is an idea worth considering. But no one ever made such a film.[9]

Shakespeare's words were first spoken on film, not by Douglas Fairbanks and Mary Pickford in THE TAMING OF THE SHREW (USA 1929), but by Lewis Casson in

THE MERCHANT OF VENICE (1927), a sound short made in Britain using the De Forest Phonofilm process.[10] This shows the trial scene, with Joyce Lyons as Portia. The director, Widgey R. Newman, was an indefatigable producer of cheap, unambitious fare, who later made the execrable THE IMMORTAL GENTLEMAN (GB 1935), a mini-feature in which Shakespeare, Ben Jonson and Michael Drayton meet at a Southwark Tavern and muse on life, with inept illustrations from Shakespeare's plays.

After Pickford and Fairbanks's brave try, which failed chiefly because its stars were on the wane, there was then a gap before Hollywood took on Shakespeare once more, producing two extravagant all-star features in successive years, Max Reinhardt's A MIDSUMMER NIGHT'S DREAM (1935) for Warners, and Irving Thalberg's ROMEO AND JULIET (1936) for MGM. For both, Shakespeare meant large-scale production. One could not put on modest Shakespeare; it was Art, and Art meant Expense. The former film had its inspiration in Reinhardt's stage pro-duction, with a parade of top stars (James Cagney, Mickey Rooney) there as box-office insurance. Thalberg's dream of *Romeo and Juliet* ('Boy Meets Girl – 1436' as the MGM publicity department put it) stemmed more from a dumb faith in high art. ROMEO AND JULIET is big, expensive, vulgar in every way, yet strangely touched by poetry now and then ('it is frequently saved – by Shakespeare – from becoming a bad film,' observed Graham Greene[11]). A MIDSUMMER NIGHT'S DREAM is much the better film, for its faithfulness to Shakespeare is not really relevant (whereas for ROMEO AND JULIET it became a selling point). It is a mad and often beautiful folly from Hollywood's heyday. It is lovely to look at, which ROMEO AND JULIET seldom is. Both films were hugely expensive, A MIDSUM-MER NIGHT'S DREAM barely making a profit and ROMEO AND JULIET losing heavily. It only goes to prove Orson Welles's observation that film producers are not out to make money; they are out to make certain kinds of movie that they want to be seen making. *Then* they want to make money.

Shakespeare was seen by 30s cinema audiences in less direct ways. Two British comedies, YOU MADE ME LOVE YOU (1933) and SECOND BEST BED (1938), both make use of the plot of *The Taming of the Shrew* for a tale of modern marriage; IT'S LOVE I'M AFTER (USA 1937, not in NFTVA) features Leslie Howard and Bette Davis as a bickering stage couple in a performance of *Romeo and Juliet*; in PEG OF OLD DRURY (GB 1935) Anna Neagle is eighteenth-century actress Peg Woffington, dying in the arms of David Garrick after a performance of *As You Like It*; and in the variety revue ELSTREE CALLING (GB 1930), Donald Calthrop con-tinually interrupts the proceedings and attempts to raise the tone with snatches of *Hamlet* and *Henry V*. He finally appears on a motorcycle as Petruchio, with Anna May Wong as Katharine, in a spoof of the Fairbanks and Pickford THE TAMING OF THE SHREW.

ESSAY ● LUKE McKERNAN

The third major cinema version of a Shakespeare play in the 30s, and staged in a more modest fashion than A MIDSUMMER NIGHT'S DREAM or ROMEO AND JULIET, was Paul Czinner's AS YOU LIKE IT (1936). A British production, it starred Czinner's wife Elisabeth Bergner as a chirpy, acrobatic Rosalind and Laurence Olivier as a rather fine, moody Orlando. Set, like Reinhardt's DREAM, in a studio forest with real animals roaming around, it shows far more confidence in its material, even if the play is soundly bowdlerised and sentimentalised. All three films are enjoyable in a number of ways, but each is really afraid of Shakespeare. Reverence and compromise are the dominating factors. The bolder strokes of the silent era were forgotten – it is as if the producers were starting all over again with the notion of Shakespeare on film, which so far as talking pictures were concerned is indeed what they were doing. But they did not learn to re-invent the cinema, though with alien dialogue and dramatic structure, that was exactly what they had to do.

If 1916 was one watershed year for Shakespearean film-making, when Beerbohm Tree went to Hollywood, 1944 was another, when Laurence Olivier made HENRY V. Shakespeare had been heard and seen intermittently on the screen throughout the Second World War. For the opening of the feature film THE YELLOW CANARY (GB 1943) two air-raid wardens discuss Shakespeare with reference to the London Blitz, one quoting appositely: 'Be not afeard, the isle is full of noises.' In Humphrey Jennings's documentary A DIARY FOR TIMOTHY (GB 1946), scenes of John Gielgud in *Hamlet* are interwoven with a bombing raid, Shakespeare as an integral part of the fabric of a society brought closer together by war. Shakespeare stood for culture and truth in the face of barbarity.

Hence Olivier's first film as a director and what is in truth the first proper Shakespearean film. For with HENRY V there is indeed a re-invention of the cinema. Most previous attempts to tackle Shakespeare on film had seen the producers try to fit him into previously accepted modes of the cinema or theatre. Shakespeare could either be sold as historical epic, drama, romance or whatever, or he was sold as a play on film, a literary or theatrical experience. HENRY V was certainly sold as both of these, but in execution it was something quite new – there was literally no other film like it. Taking the text as the guide, rather than any model of stage performance, Olivier and his collaborators devised a screen spectacle that took its lead from suggestions in that text. The action develops from the first act presented at a re-creation of the Globe Theatre, to stylised sets inspired by *Les Très Riches Heures du Duc de Berry*, to the fully-fledged realism of the Agincourt battle charge. It follows literally the chorus's desire to make 'this cockpit hold the vasty fields of France', the simplest of lessons on the nature of the theatrical and cinematic experience.

HENRY V was the first happy collaboration between theatre and cinema, Olivier

1671-159

Orson Welles (Macbeth) and Edgar Barrier (Banquo) in MACBETH (1948)

the first major actor/producer since Beerbohm Tree to use the cinema of his day
to its fullest advantage. But it was not a 'great play'; it was obvious that they should
throw in battle charges, 'horses printing their proud hoofs i' the receding earth'.
As yet the talkies had not attempted to tackle the major tragedies. Following the
war, and perhaps not coincidentally fitting in with the darker *film noir* phase of the
postwar years, there came two very different interpretations of two of the
tragedies.

Olivier's HAMLET (GB 1948) brought high Shakespeare to the masses as never
before. HENRY V had been a patriotic flourish, but HAMLET was a text meant to
be read and studied. The whole style of the film indicated the thought that had
gone into its expression, and a book of the film was published giving the text of the
play with the cuts marked in discreet parentheses.[12] Olivier described the film as
'an Essay in Hamlet', a consideration of how one might make the play accessible to
the mass audience and yet stay true to its existing status as a work of art. He invited
debate and analysis, and received it. The film treated the postwar audience with
greater intelligence than in its prewar phase, and it was duly popular. Released at a
high time in the fortunes of British cinema, the film won the Academy Award for
best picture. It was the best of British, and the best of British was Shakespeare.

While Olivier was receiving garlands and conducting a careful balancing act
between scholarship and popular appeal, Orson Welles was being execrated for his
version of *Macbeth*. Welles's MACBETH (USA 1948) is a bad film, certainly, but a

bad film made by the single most important figure in Shakespearean cinema; you appreciate what Welles tried to achieve or you do not appreciate the genre at all. Welles, with a background in imaginative theatre to rival Olivier's and a record in imaginative cinema second to none, produced his cut-price tragedy in a ridiculous twenty-three days with a cast most of whom seem completely floored by blank verse, hampered still further by Welles's ill-advised experimenting with the sound-track.[13] But MACBETH was chiefly derided, not so much for its technical short-comings, as for not following the text faithfully. It was ridiculous because it made so bold as to cut and re-order Shakespeare. Olivier had cut out Rosencrantz and Guildenstern, but he had not altered the order of the scenes (beyond a few small transpositions), he had not added a new figure as Welles did with the Holy Father. This was not Shakespeare's *Macbeth* so much as it was Orson Welles's. But that of course was Welles's intention. However, at this early stage, Welles was trying to have it both ways, following his own vision of cinema but still hoping that some of that Shakespeare glamour would rub off. But you cannot, as Welles suggested, make a B-picture 'quickie' out of Shakespeare, with the lack of thought that that implies.[14] Later he would try harder.

As the postwar years brought interpretations of the major tragedies, so allusions to Shakespeare in feature films increased, often taking on a sombre tone as film-makers turned from the pure escapism of the prewar years to a greater sense of their films having something to say. In A DOUBLE LIFE (USA 1947) Ronald Colman is an actor whose playing of Othello spills over into real life as he becomes insanely jealous of his actress wife, the climax being his attempt to strangle her on stage during a performance of the play (this glum theme has also appeared in three British films, the 1921 CARNIVAL, its 1931 remake, and the 1936 MEN ARE NOT GODS). In John Ford's MY DARLING CLEMENTINE (USA 1946), a drunken actor, played by Alan Mowbray, is harassed by the Dalton gang. He tries to recite from the *Hamlet* soliloquy when they order him to perform, but forgets the words. In steps the disillusioned, tubercular Doc Holliday (Victor Mature), who gives a faithful if maudlin recitation before collapsing with a fit of coughing. Holliday is marked out as man on a higher plane to that of his contemporaries, sadder and wiser, and the plot of MY DARLING CLEMENTINE is in part the tragedy of Doc Holliday.

Shakespeare's brushes with the West are full of interest. *King Lear* was transmuted into the tale of a cattle rancher betrayed by his sons in BROKEN LANCE (USA 1954); the themes of jealousy and suspicion in *Othello* are repeated in JUBAL (USA 1956, not in NFTVA); the outlaws riding into a strange ghost town in YELLOW SKY (USA 1948) have wandered into plot parallels with *The Tempest*. Even Hamlet finds himself turned into a gunslinger in the spaghetti Western QUELLA SPORCA STORIA DEL WEST (Italy 1968, not in NFTVA), helpfully retitled JOHNNY HAMLET for its American release. Further shores are explored in FORBIDDEN

PLANET (USA 1956), where *The Tempest* is ingeniously rewritten as science fiction, Prospero now battling with a Caliban-monster created out of his own Id.

In Britain JOE MACBETH (1955) was *Macbeth* in gangster-land; AN HONOURABLE MURDER (1960, not in NFTVA) updated *Julius Caesar* to the boardroom; and THE YOUNG LOVERS (1954) puts the perennial *Romeo and Juliet* theme into a Cold War setting. In France LES AMANTS DE VERONE (1949) translated *Romeo and Juliet* to a modern film set, and Western audiences were startled by Akira Kurosawa's astonishing appropriation of the plot of *Macbeth* into a sixteenth-century Japanese setting in KUMONOSU-JO (1957), known in English as THRONE OF BLOOD.[15]

There is more to Shakespeare than plot, of course, and many film-makers have come unstuck trying to find suitable modern parallels for the movement of Birnam Wood to Dunsinane, for instance. But they stand out as imaginative gestures compared to some of the leaden versions of the plays being produced for the cinema, either condensed versions intended for schools audiences (as in the 1945 *Famous Scenes from Shakespeare* series or the similar 1953 *The World's a Stage* series, examples from both of which are held in the NFTVA), or a misguided exercise such as Renato Castellani's stilted ROMEO AND JULIET (GB/Italy 1954), with sumptuous colour and Italian locations, but wooden leading actors and little sense of poetry. When faced with the real thing, the text, all imagination was lost, or rather too few of the imaginative talents of the cinema were attracted to the idea.

But the 1950s did boast four outstanding 'straight' versions of the plays that run counter to this, from Orson Welles, Joseph Mankiewicz, Sergei Yutkevich and Laurence Olivier. Welles, having had his MACBETH come up against Olivier's HAMLET in 1948, five years later found himself again weighed in the balance, his OTHELLO (Morocco 1952) against Mankiewicz's JULIUS CAESAR (USA 1953). Again, he was found wanting by the general public and most critics. There was an extra irony in that *Julius Caesar* had been one of Welles's many half-planned projects, and he made a show of pique at being beaten to the post in this way, but in truth he had been far too preoccupied over the past four years, hopping from country to country, filming his OTHELLO whenever funds were forthcoming, holding cast, crew and overall conception remarkably together over this period. Indeed, the epic history of the film's production seems as much a part of OTHELLO, or our reading of it, as the film itself, and Micheál MacLiammóir's diary account, *Put Money in Thy Purse*, as essential a part of the work as the note explaining the person from Porlock is to Coleridge's *Kubla Khan*.

OTHELLO is a dazzling visual collage, to which Shakespeare's post-synchronised words can seem strangely distant. In Joseph Mankiewicz's JULIUS CAESAR, by comparison, the word is pre-eminent, and it is a Hollywood studio's (MGM) only fully successful presentation of a Shakespeare play. With its strong performances from Gielgud and Brando, its clarity of language and lack of cinematic artifice, it contrasted strongly with Welles's creation, and remains a favourite of many who generally distrust the cinema's appropriation of Shakespeare. In fact it is no uncinematic exercise at all, propelled along by a newsreel urgency and resolving the problems of staging the later scenes in a way that has eluded many stage productions.

Sergei Yutkevich's OTELLO (Soviet Union 1955) is a conventional reading of the play made distinctive by its rich pictorial values and romantic gestures. Visual motifs of light, air and water abound, and the director rejoices in some striking local scenery. Elaborate camera movement compounds the impression of a director besotted with the idea of visualising Shakespeare's themes. One does not perhaps learn much of the play beyond the expected, but one sees so much.

Laurence Olivier crowned a trio of authoritative interpretations with RICHARD III (GB 1955), a step back from the cinematic flourishes of HENRY V and HAMLET to a more theatrically based presentation, although this rich feast of acting is possibly the most enjoyable and successful of the three. Like HENRY V and HAMLET before it, RICHARD III is something quite new in the cinema, not exactly innovatory, rather the sort of theatrical cinema which other film-makers, less prepared actually to entertain their audiences, had wished for but failed to provide.

There is another way in which RICHARD III and the other Olivier films differ from the common run of Shakespearean cinema, as detected by Raymond Durgnat (no great admirer of the films in themselves):

And yet, when one's irreverence has wreaked its worst upon Olivier's Shakespeare … another interpretation of their hollownesses begins to appear, which may one day vindicate them. Their lack of conviction results, not only from Olivier's acquiescence in the spirit of their age, but from a scepticism which is not quite aware of itself. For what Olivier treats with unconscious criticism is not the film medium, but the plays. The shifting stylisations of *Henry V* oddly prefigure Godard's use of the non-realistic, the non-conviction of life seen through the filter of an art which distorts (the medieval perspectives). The theme Olivier saw in *Hamlet* is a Godardian one – '*Hamlet* is the story of a man who cannot make up his mind' – and its surface conventionality is belied by something in Olivier's screen personality, something hard, stony, resentful, something that rebels, from within, against Hamlet's sensitivity, because it sees through it, as a Commissar or a Castro might have seenn through it. If Richard III confides to the audience, it is because Olivier has gone half way to converting him from villain to hero … Behind all these plays looms the shadowy figure of – The Entertainer.[16]

There is certainly something of this ambiguous quality in Olivier's three films, in his *mise en scène* and in his own central performance. They offer in one sense the optimum performance of the play – the best cast, the finest sets, the limitless space offered by the camera. But in being so they become comments on the plays, on an attitude, not quite questioning but certainly casting an eye on their own cultural respectability. Such a questioning has surfaced surprisingly rarely in filmed Shakespeare, where the film-makers have generally been wholly convinced of the worthiness of their energies. Only in such offbeat works as Celestine Coronado's HAMLET (GB 1976) and Derek Jarman's THE TEMPEST (GB 1979) is a mirror held up to Shakespeare. Olivier is certainly holding up a mirror, perhaps to Shakespeare, perhaps to himself, asking what it is that he is actually doing, the man who could not make up his mind.

The 1950s also introduced television on a wide scale. Shakespeare on the small screen began with the BBC on 5 February 1937, with fifteen minutes of *As You Like It*, produced by Robert Atkins and starring Margaretta Scott, and later that same evening fifteen minutes of *Henry V*, with Henry Oscar as Henry and Yvonne Arnaud as Katharine. The few thousand people able to tune into the BBC television service in the late 30s were treated to numerous such short extracts, including Laurence Olivier in an Old Vic production of *Macbeth* (tx 3 December 1937), gradually growing in length until a fairly full production of *The Tempest* with Peggy Ashcroft as Miranda (tx 5 February 1939). As virtually nothing of television was recorded at this time, one must rely on contemporary reports, and assumptions that such broadcasts were primitive are countered by memories of the broadcasts as 'thrilling' and 'enchanting'. By the standards of their time they no doubt were. (It is also worth noting that Olivier's HENRY V was initially based on Dallas Bower's plans for a prewar BBC production, abandoned on account of the war.)

BBC television closed down for the war, reopening in 1946. It thereafter continued to build on its early experiments and enthusiasm, growing in popularity and influence in the 1950s, and as the only British channel until 1955 could readily enforce the Reithian dictate to 'educate, inform and entertain'. An important part of the BBC's curriculum for the nation was Shakespeare, and by the end of the decade over sixty Shakespeare broadcasts had been made since 1937.[17] Those productions which survive as telerecordings – in the NFTVA there are OTHELLO (1955), THE TEMPEST (1956) and A MIDSUMMER NIGHT'S DREAM (1958) – are unambitious but adequate affairs, studio-bound, reverential towards the text and lacking the fire of live performance or cinematic inventiveness. But the sheer number of productions indicated that filmed Shakespeare was finding its home on television, where the greater range and lower budgets could more easily accommodate such forays into culture.

In the USA, where commercial television was rampant, Shakespeare should have had a hard time making his mark felt, but there was a significant body of his work produced during the 1950s. In the NFTVA are four Shakespeare productions made by and starring Maurice Evans for the Hallmark greetings cards company,[18] whose imaginative, well-targeted sponsorship of 'quality' drama in an era of constant appeals to the lowest common denominator is remarkable. The *Hallmark Hall of Fame* series, which began in 1951 and continues to this day, included regular presentations of Shakespeare. Evans, much like the indefatigable Robert Atkins in Britain, was an ordinary actor and producer given greater exposure by television than his talents perhaps deserved, but the telerecordings of his plays indicate a willingness to experiment and adapt to the peculiarities of the television medium.

Commercial television arrived in Britain in 1955 with the ITV service, introducing American populist techniques and jolting the BBC out of some of its paternalistic, monopolist attitudes. The increasing variety of programmes, particularly with the introduction of a third channel, BBC2, in 1964, gave greater opportunities to schedule the plays, and the 1960s became a rich period for Shakespearean television in Britain. 'Plays', however, is the operative word, as the objective was to transfer onto the small screen works designed for the stage, with the minimum of interference. Cinema, with its imperative of visual appeal, was unable to do this – television could and did. Original plays for television could be approached with greater inventiveness, but the established theatrical canon still retained the sense of curtains drawing and closing again. Perhaps the greatest achievement of televised Shakespeare in the 60s, the *Wars of the Roses* trilogy in 1965, was filmed on an enlarged stage at Stratford, and though not a bald recording from the stalls, being instead focused squarely on the actors, is nevertheless in thrall to the theatre. The acting is marvellous, but the value of the recording is chiefly as a record, not as a creative work.

Meanwhile, in the cinemas the mass audience was drifting away. Films turned from mass appeal values, since they could no longer rely on a regular cinema-going family audience, and increasingly became events in isolation, aimed at a specific corner of the market. Thus in the 60s and 70s, in keeping with the general trend, we get Shakespeare the musical, Shakespeare the horror film, Shakespeare with sex, experimental Shakespeare, Shakespeare the record of a stage production, Shakespeare the political allegorist, animated Shakespeare, Shakespeare in dance and opera, an unfailing means by which to judge the temper of the times.

Central to this time, and to all filmed Shakespeare, is Orson Welles's last completed Shakespeare film, CAMPANADAS A MEDIANOCHE (Spain/Switzerland 1966), known in Britain as CHIMES AT MIDNIGHT and in America as FALSTAFF.[19] There is a curious paradox that while the most successful Shakespeare on television has been based on existing stage productions (ANTONY AND CLEOPATRA in 1974, MACBETH in 1979), the best Shakespeare productions in the cinema have been original conceptions. The exception is CAMPANADAS A MEDIANOCHE, developed out of a failed compression of the history plays, *The Five Kings*, which Welles had been trying to stage for many years, with little success as the conception was clearly cinematic.[20] If Shakespearean cinema can all too often be defined by what it projects itself as rather than what it actually is (the Olivier ambiguity), then Welles's masterpiece is that rarity, the true Shakespearean film. As with his MACBETH and OTHELLO, its technical shortcomings and knack for turning Shakespeare's work into his own property damaged the film on its release and has harmed its reception ever since. It is a difficult film. In essence it is the tragedy of Falstaff, and by Welles's analogy the death of the golden age, the cold *realpolitik* of Hal replacing the Merrie England epitomised by Falstaff. What Welles uncovers here, after the experiments of his earlier films, is a true way to express his love and understanding of Shakespeare. Completely absent are the posture, the desire to improve the audience, the fear of commercial failure, the various disguises to Shakespeare felt necessary by others. It is Shakespeare wholly rewritten by the camera, not simply images as equivalents for passages of text, but a whole new way of getting to the heart of the plays. In fact it is almost the pure cinema of the silent film, with the soundtrack still strangely distant as with OTHELLO yet here more fully developed into another narrative, another text counterpointing the visual one. Welles comments on Shakespeare; Shakespeare comments on Welles.

Welles was not the only artist to appropriate Shakespeare to his own personal vision. The Russian director Grigori Kozintsev made GAMLET (1964) and KOROL LIR (1970), versions of *Hamlet* and *King Lear*, using translations by Boris Pasternak. Both are memorably visualised, the deep thought that went into his interpretations clear from his writings,[21] although in execution his ideas seem comparatively conventional. The theatre director Peter Brook made a notably chilly and apocalyptic KING LEAR (GB/Denmark 1970), Peter Hall a with-it A MIDSUMMER NIGHT'S DREAM (GB 1968), and Roman Polanski a bloody, brutal MACBETH (GB 1971). Franco Zeffirelli successfully popularised Shakespeare with THE TAMING OF THE SHREW (USA/Italy 1966) and ROMEO AND JULIET (GB/Italy 1968), as he was to do later with HAMLET (USA 1990). The biggest disappointment of the decade was OTHELLO (GB 1965), a literal film studio recreation of the National Theatre hit with Laurence Olivier in the title role. Joylessly directed by Stuart Burge, not only is it the negation of cinema, it has subsequently served as a ruthless exposure of the shortcomings in Olivier's acting technique.

There were plot borrowings and allusions to Shakespeare in the cinema as in previous years. *Othello* was translated into a jazz club setting in the endearingly silly ALL NIGHT LONG (GB 1961); *The Tempest* could be detected behind the island idyll of Michael Powell's AGE OF CONSENT (Australia 1969). Allusions tended towards the facetious, Laurence Harvey performing a striptease version of the *Hamlet* soliloquy in THE MAGIC CHRISTIAN (GB 1969), Julie Christie sardonically quoting John of Gaunt's 'royal throne of kings' speech in DARLING (GB 1965), the cheerful schoolboy view of Shakespeare's greatest lines and characters in CARRY ON CLEO (GB 1964). Shakespeare, like the Establishment, needed debunking.

Out on its own is the subtle and wistful SHAKESPEARE WALLAH (India 1965), the story of a troupe of Shakespearean actors touring a post-imperial India and finding that increasingly the brash simplicities of the movies are luring away their audiences. The numerous passages from the plays form apposite comments on the fate of the troupe, and by analogy on modern India and the lessening grip of British cultural influence. At the other end of the cinema spectrum, but no less confident in its allusions and analogies, is THEATRE OF BLOOD (GB 1973), a tasteless but rather splendid romp where Vincent Price plays a ham actor of the old school who takes revenge on the theatre critics by murdering a succession of them in the manner of deaths from Shakespeare's plays. Shakespeare is both the Establishment enemy and the revenger's weapon; and (from *King Lear*) he has the last word too.

Televised Shakespeare came of age in the 1970s with two exceptional programmes, both based on original stage productions but intelligently restaged with the television screen in mind. ANTONY AND CLEOPATRA (1974), based on an acclaimed Trevor Nunn stage production with the Royal Shakespeare Company, uses a minimum of props, yet makes these far more suggestive of scale and theme than a more realistic setting. This effect is heightened by an intense concentration on the actors, revealing the play's interior power rather than its exterior show. MACBETH (1979), similarly derived from a Nunn/RSC production, is another deeply felt interiorisation of the play's impact. The stage and cinema screen offer spectacle in a way that the television screen cannot. Instead Nunn's productions (he was instrumental in their direction for television as well) place the actors as it were in our heads, that private space which is the theatre of the mind. Language and faces are to the fore – pictorial background is all suggestion and shadow.

What Nunn showed was that television was unwise to imitate the cinema, which had the budgets and the scope necessary to place a Shakespeare play in a 'realistic' or visually emphatic framework. Television had to concentrate on the players. It was a half-hearted realism combined with a stubborn refusal to experiment that so restricted the most ambitious cycle of filmed Shakespeare, the *BBC Television Shakespeare* series. Clive James surveyed the scene presented by the BBC's first offering,[22] ROMEO AND JULIET:

> Verona seemed to have been built on a very level ground, like the floor of a television studio. The fact that this artificiality was half accepted and half denied

told you that you were not in Verona at all, but in that semi-abstract, semi-concrete, wholly uninteresting city which is known to students as Messina. [23]

Cedric Messina, founding producer of the series, laid down the rules which determined the series' mundane aesthetics and future financial success. Running between 1978 and 1985, a co-production between the BBC and Time-Life Films of America (where the series was known as *The Shakespeare Plays* and broadcast on PBS), the dominating theme was safety. Safe productions for American sales, safe productions for future educational use on video. And indeed a whole generation of schoolchildren and teachers have benefited greatly from the plain virtues of the recordings. The series was never bad as such, and the best examples – HENRY VIII, MEASURE FOR MEASURE, TWELFTH NIGHT, THE WINTER'S TALE – were outstanding. But the BBC's venture should not be the last of its kind, nor the model for the next.

There was probably more passion and conviction in Granada Television's KING LEAR (GB 1983) than in any of the BBC series. Laurence Olivier played his final Shakespearean role, exploiting his own sad ill-health and evident short-windedness to give a portrayal of a frail and humbled Lear that simply could not have been contemplated on the stage. An extraordinary cast (Leo McKern, John Hurt, Diana Rigg, Robert Lindsay) in an unspectacular but reliable production made for the epitome of the traditional television studio Shakespeare.

Television has also been an excellent vehicle for educational and documentary programmes on Shakespeare. In the NFTVA are two examples from two commendable ITV school series based on *Twelfth Night*, the first from 1959 named after the play, which broke the action up into eight programmes of explanation and performance, before broadcasting a complete production of the play; the second entitled *Preparing a Play*, showing in five programmes the various preparations for a stage production, with scenes from *Twelfth Night* as illustration. Similarly broadcast in the morning, the BBC's three-part HEIL CAESAR (1973), a bold modernisation of *Julius Caesar*'s action and language, was deemed worthy and entertaining enough to be repeated as a single programme for evening broadcast.

Among documentaries, the NFTVA holds many examples from such arts series as *Monitor*, *Tempo*, *The Late Show* and *Omnibus*. London Weekend Television's *South Bank Show* has the popular touch and has often led the field, with analyses of individual plays (its 1989 programme on *Hamlet* showing incidentally how the Olivier and Kozintsev versions provided excellent visual illustration of the play's major themes); but its particular forte is the more personal approach. This is best illustrated by IAN McKELLEN – DIARY OF A YEAR (tx 20 October 1985), where there is a genuine sense of shared experience with the actor as he prepares for the role of Coriolanus; but the approach can tend to the sycophantic, as in the portrait

ESSAY ● LUKE McKERNAN

of Sir Peter Hall and Dustin Hoffman rehearsing *The Merchant of Venice* (tx 24 September 1989). Theatrical awards programmes and entertainment guides such as *Entertainment UK* often contain the only filmed record of some stage productions. And Shakespeare also appears regularly on television in the form of commercials: *Romeo and Juliet* has been used to sell Polo mints and Rolo chocolates, Hamlet was seen juggling Yorick's skull with his feet to promote Carling Black Label lager, and Shakespeare himself appeared in three Whitbread Trophy Bitter commercials in 1978.

Enthusiasm for filmed Shakespeare has not dimmed in recent times, although the *BBC Television Shakespeare* series seems to have quietened activity on British television screens at least. But work in the genre is less naïve than in previous decades. The blinkered, reverential outlook of the 1992 *Shakespeare: The Animated Tales* series of children's films, with its confused mixture of condensed plot, set-piece quotations and lifeless animation, or Christine Edzard's stilted, urban AS YOU LIKE IT (GB 1992, not in NFTVA), has become the exception. There is now Shakespeare with the insider's point of view. Derek Jarman's THE TEMPEST (GB 1979), and to a lesser extent his homage to the sonnets, THE ANGELIC CONVERSATION (GB 1985), rewrites Shakespeare to his own imaginings in the way that Welles indicated. As with Welles, Jarman's cutting and reordering of the text brings key phrases and scenes to the greater attention of a modern audience. The eccentric casting, rich visual style (on a minimal budget), camp humour and joyous conclusion, however, are all Jarman's, and mark the play out for that period of screen time as wholly his own.

Allusions to and appropriations of Shakespeare remain legion. In the animated feature AN AMERICAN TALE (USA 1986) the character Warren T. Rat puts himself above his fellow rodents by frequent quotations from Shakespeare; in SHORT CIRCUIT 2 (USA 1988, not in NFTVA) the robot 'Number Five' plaintively asks his persecutors, 'Hath not a robot eyes?' and proceeds with his own version of Shylock's speech; in DEAD POETS SOCIETY (USA 1989) a schoolboy's rebellion is expressed through his performance in *A Midsummer Night's Dream*; in TRUE IDENTITY (USA 1991) Lenny Henry proves he is no mere comic by getting to play Othello; and in WITHNAIL & I (GB 1986), Hamlet's words to Rosencrantz and Guildenstern ('I have of late (but wherefore I know not) lost all my mirth') form a sardonic, poignant coda to the film.

The parade of distinctive and commendable interpretations continues. Kenneth Branagh's vigorous HENRY V (GB 1988) and his exuberant MUCH ADO ABOUT NOTHING (GB/USA 1993); Franco Zeffirelli's populist HAMLET (USA 1990), boldly casting contemporary screen hero Mel Gibson as Hamlet; Aki Kaurismäki's HAMLET LIIKEMAAILMASSA (Finland 1987, English title HAMLET GOES BUSINESS), eccentrically updating the story of *Hamlet* to the present-day Swedish

ESSAY ● LUKE McKERNAN

Heathcote Williams as Prospero in THE TEMPEST (1979)

rubber-duck industry; the surface complexity and bizarre vision of Peter Greenaway's tribute to *The Tempest*, PROSPERO'S BOOKS (1991). None is perfect, none is dull, all are made for the cinema. The lesson learnt is that the ideal approach to filmed Shakespeare, if there is to be such a thing, lies not in 'correct' staging and textual fidelity, but in an honest, enquiring and intelligent appreciation of the plays. Just what that means in practice is entirely up to the film-maker.

Shakespeare's plays were written for more than the stage. Obviously they were written initially as pieces for the Elizabethan theatre, yet equally they have had a life that has extended far beyond their original staging. Common sense tells us that the poet put more into the plays than was ever apparent when they were first staged, or has been since – they are larger works than mere stage plays. And the unceasing enthusiasm with which film-makers have appropriated, adapted, bowdlerised, interpreted and honoured Shakespeare incontrovertibly proves the plays' adaptability to any medium in the hands of any artist. They are universal property.

Hence Shakespeare's plays were made for the screen, and film-makers have readily adapted them for film and television. Film and television have appropriated not only the works, but their kudos, their plots, their characters, their frames of ref-

ESSAY ● LUKE McKERNAN

erence. A full catalogue, such as the one contained here aims to be, has to acknowledge the *phenomenon* of Shakespeare on film – the whole picture of what Shakespeare has brought to the screen. Faithful versions of the plays, certainly, but also plot borrowings, allusions, parodies, homages, and not just fiction films but documentaries, newsreels, animation, amateur film and commercials. The catalogue records all these.

It also records the key debates that have arisen out of this phenomenon, between stage and screen and between high and popular culture. The question is always present: just what is Shakespeare doing there on the screen? It is a question that filmmakers may have asked themselves, but which has never prevented them from going ahead anyway. They had their reasons, and they followed them. The result has been a rich and hugely entertaining body of work that has approached Shakespeare in a wide variety of ways, yet leaving us with the feeling that any number of fresh interpretations and visions remain to be discovered. There have been follies, certainly, but they have been memorable ones.

A film is not a play. The difference between filmed Shakespeare and staged Shakespeare, the exact definition of which has led scholars down tortuous routes to some opaque conclusions, is possibly very simple. A play is a text which may be performed on a stage, but a film is both text and performance. It has a built-in dialectic. It is not live performance; it is dependent on illusion, movement and light. It must bring its own kind of life to the text of the play. Hence the essential factor in all filmed Shakespeare, authorial intrusion. Those most willing to disorder and re-imagine Shakespeare on the screen have been the most successful, have produced works that are most likely to endure.

Notes

1. Micheál MacLiammóir, *Put Money in Thy Purse: The Diary of the Film of Othello* (London: Methuen, 1952), p. 28; Welles speaking in THE ORSON WELLES STORY (part two, tx 21 May 1982).
2. Further details of this film, its contents and history are given in the catalogue. The film itself, long believed lost, its exact nature unknown, turned up recently in the Nederlands Filmmuseum among a large collection of films produced by the Mutoscope and Biograph Company. The NFTVA has now made its own 35mm copy from the 68mm original.
3. The NFTVA does not hold the original copy of this film, but a short sequence from it was shown as part of a *South Bank Show* programme on *Hamlet* (tx 2 April 1989) which is held by the NFTVA. See also note 10.
4. James A. Montague, *Bioscope*, 1 June 1916, p. 1009. Originally published in the New York *American*.
5. Herbert Beerbohm Tree, 'Not bad for a young country', *The Times*, 8 September 1916, p. 11.

ESSAY ● LUKE McKERNAN

6. Details of THE REAL THING AT LAST may be found in Robert Hamilton Ball, *Shakespeare on Silent Film: A Strange Eventful History* (London: Allen & Unwin, 1968), pp. 223–6, 360–1, and there are also details in the memoirs of some of the participants: Leslie Henson, *My Laugh Story* (London: Hodder and Stoughton, 1938), pp. 288–91, and A. E. Matthews, *Matty* (London: Hutchinson, 1952), pp. 155–8. The film itself is believed lost.

7. For details of the major histories and filmographies of Shakespeare and film, see the Bibliography. No complete filmography of Shakespeare has ever been completed, but Rothwell and Melzer's, though erratic, is the fullest, and that given in Patrick Robertson, *The Guinness Book of Film Facts and Feats* (London: Guinness Superlatives, 1980), pp. 55–7, the most comprehensive list of film versions only (the list is not repeated in later editions).

8. Jack J. Jorgens, *Shakespeare on Film* (Bloomington/London: Indiana University Press, 1977), p. 1.

9. The René Clair comment is reported in Anthony Asquith, 'Shakespeare, Shaw and the Screen', *Cine-Technician*, November–December 1938, p. 123. An interesting case for such a 'pure' film could be made, paradoxically, for the sound films of Russian director Grigori Kozintsev, whose GAMLET (1964) and KOROL LIR (1970) are most assiduous in their precise visual equivalents for Shakespeare's original poetic images. But the effect of showing the sea when referring to 'a sea of troubles' can be rather banal.

10. The first use of sound with a Shakespeare film was actually the 1900 HAMLET with Sarah Bernhardt, mentioned above, which was originally presented with phonographic sound effects. Throughout the silent era there were attempts to exhibit film in varying degrees of synchronisation to sound recordings. The Shakespearean efforts (not in NFTVA and excluding opera) were JULIUS CAESAR (USA 1913, using the Edison Kinetophone system of synchronising film to phonograph) and THE TAMING OF THE SHREW (GB 1915, synchronised to off-stage speakers). Both were records of single scenes. Sound-on-film shorts began to be exhibited in the mid-20s, the De Forest Phonofilm of *The Merchant of Venice* being the first of them to record Shakespeare.

11. Graham Greene, *The Pleasure-Dome* (London: Secker & Warburg, 1972), pp. 109–10. Originally from the *Spectator*, 23 October 1936. Greene reviewed films regularly for the *Spectator* and *Night and Day* in the 30s, and this volume of his collected reviews has some perceptive comments on ROMEO AND JULIET, A MIDSUMMER NIGHT'S DREAM and the British AS YOU LIKE IT (1936).

12. Alan Dent (ed.), *Hamlet: The Film and the Play* (London, World Film Publications, 1948).

13. The soundtrack to Welles's MACBETH was recorded first, then played over a loudspeaker system on the set with the actors lip-synching to the words (there was some live recording of sound as well). The odd effect was compounded by Welles's insistence on Scottish accents, and following adverse reactions the film was re-recorded with American accents and re-released in a shorter version. The NFTVA holds the original 'Scottish' version.

14. MACBETH was made for Republic Studios, purveyors of low-grade B-movies, who were looking to improve the status of their product. Welles always emphasised the

B-movie ambitions of the picture, repeating them in his interview for THE ORSON WELLES STORY (part one, tx 18 May 1982). The film has its enthusiastic supporters, although Claude Beylie's assessment that it is 'one of the most beautiful films ever created' seems excessive. Welles's own comment that it is 'a kind of violently sketched charcoal drawing of a great play' (*Sight and Sound*, January–March 1954, p. 122) is illuminating.

15. Shakespearean films from cultures to which Shakespeare's plays might not seem to be directly addressed are never less than intriguing: examples include (none in NFTVA) from India the 1935 KHOON KA KHOON (a recording of an Urdu *Hamlet* stage production), the 1949 GUNSUNDARI KATHA (an imaginative adaptation of *King Lear*), and the 1957 Hindi AASHA with its strong *Hamlet* plot associations; in Egypt an adaptation of *Romeo and Juliet*, SHUHUDA AL-GHARAM (1945); two Mexican adaptations of *The Taming of the Shrew*, ENAMORADA (1946) and EL CHARRO Y LA DAMA (1949); from Ghana HAMILE (*Hamlet*) (1964); from Hong Kong a version of *The Merchant of Venice*, YI P'ANG JOU (1977, English title POUND OF FLESH); and from Turkey INTIKAM MELEGI (1977), in English ANGEL OF VENGEANCE or FEMALE HAMLET. Kurosawa himself went on to make WARUI YATSU HODO YOKU NEMURU (Japan 1960, English title THE BAD SLEEP WELL), a modernisation of *Hamlet*, and RAN (Japan 1985), which treats *King Lear* much as KUMO-NOSU-JO treats *Macbeth*. Brazil has produced some imaginative interpretations of Shakespeare, and the NFTVA holds a very fine television film ROMEU E JULIETA (1980), a rewriting of the story in a modern Brazilian setting.

16. Raymond Durgnat, *A Mirror for England* (London: Faber & Faber, 1970), pp. 111–12. Jean-Luc Godard did in fact subsequently make a Shakespearean film, KING LEAR (USA 1987, not in NFTVA), which unfortunately was little more than an embarrassment.

17. According to Michael Barry, head of BBC Television Drama, quoted in *Radio Times*, 7 November 1958, p. 7, that week's production of *A Midsummer Night's Dream* was the forty-eighth presentation of a Shakespeare play by the BBC television service. Susan Willis, in *The BBC Shakespeare Plays: Making the Televised Canon* (Chapel Hill/London: University of North Carolina Press, 1991), pp. 322–5, lists sixty-three Shakespeare productions (including single scenes and abbreviated versions) broadcast by the BBC before 1960.

18. These are KING RICHARD II (1954), MACBETH (1954), TWELFTH NIGHT (1956) and THE TAMING OF THE SHREW (1957). The NFTVA also holds the 1970 production HAMLET, which though part of the same series was produced under quite different circumstances. For further details see Tise Vahimagi's essay in this book.

19. As well as his three well-known Shakespeare films, Welles was involved in several other film and television productions relating to Shakespeare. In 1933 a short film was made of a stage production, which he designed, of *Twelfth Night*, with Welles narrating; in 1950 he filmed some scenes from his stage revue *Time Runs*, including the final scene from *3 Henry VI*; in 1953 he was King Lear in a CBS television production directed by Peter Brook; in 1969 he made a film of *The Merchant of Venice* with himself as Shylock (and the role of Portia removed!) – the film was apparently completed but the soundtrack stolen, although a single reel with fully mixed sound has surfaced since; in 1977 he produced an idiosyncratic documentary on one of his earlier films,

FILMING OTHELLO; and at his death in 1985 he was still trying to organise a production of *King Lear* which French television supposedly commissioned, then turned down. Details of Welles's many unfinished or obscure projects are given in Jonathan Rosenbaum's article 'The Invisible Orson Welles', *Sight and Sound*, Summer 1986, pp. 164–71.

20. *The Five Kings* was a long-cherished project of Welles's, developed in the 30s and first staged as a joint Theater Guild/Mercury Theatre production in 1939. The dramatic problems apparent then were still not resolved when a condensed version was performed in Ireland as *Chimes at Midnight* in 1960. For full details of *The Five Kings* and Welles's other theatrical ventures, see Richard France, *The Theatre of Orson Welles* (Lewisburg: Bucknell University Press, 1977).

21. Grigori Kozintsev, *Shakespeare: Time and Conscience* (London: Dennis Dobson, 1967) and Grigori Kozintsev, *King Lear: The Space of Tragedy* (London: Heinemann, 1977). Both publications are English translations of Russian originals.

22. In the USA the first programme shown in the series was JULIUS CAESAR (tx 14 February 1979).

23. Clive James, *The Crystal Bucket* (London: Jonathan Cape, 1981), p. 153. Originally from the *Observer*, 10 December 1978.

Luke McKernan is the author of a newsreel history, *Topical Budget: The Great British News Film* (1992), and regularly programmes films at the National Film Theatre and the Museum of London. He is a cataloguer at the National Film and Television Archive.

A Guide to the Use of the Catalogue

This is a catalogue of the Shakespeare holdings of the National Film and Television Archive (NFTVA). It is arranged play-by-play with further sections on the sonnets and on Shakespeare in general. It includes not only 'straight' versions of the plays but all films and television programmes held by the NFTVA that have a significant bearing on one of the plays; and in the General section all documentaries, newsreels and all fiction films relating to the theme of Shakespeare or to the figure of Shakespeare himself. The play-by-play scheme has been chosen for greatest convenience to the user, but it has led to a number of cross-references where a film (for which also read television programme) relates to more than one of the plays. Where only two or three plays are covered by the single film, then the full filmographic information on the film is repeated under each play. Where a single film covers a large number of the plays (for example, SHAKESPEARE WALLAH), then the full filmographic details will be found in the General section, with simplified entries relating to the individual plays under each of those plays. All such multiple-entries are cross-referenced. The arrangement of the entries is chronological, then alphabetical by title within each year. Television transmission dates and newsreel release dates file after yearly dates and are arranged chronologically within each year. The following is a guide to the individual catalogue sections:

Plays

These are arranged alphabetically by commonest title: hence *Henry V* and *Henry VIII*, but *King John* and *King Lear*. The *Henry IV* and *Henry VI* plays have been simplified to single entries. All the plays in the currently recognised canon are represented in one form or other, with the exception of *The Two Noble Kinsmen*.

Film and programme titles

All titles are the original-language versions, with alternative titles given afterwards. The standard ruling is to use the title as it appears on the screen, but this causes particular problems with Shakespeare as so many producers advertise the film under one title yet use a First Folio page or similar on-screen: for example, Orson Welles's OTHELLO is always known under that title, but the actual on-screen title is THE TRAGEDY OF OTHELLO, THE MOOR OF VENICE. The most striking example is Laurence Olivier's HENRY V, the on-screen title of which is actually THE CHRONICLE HISTORY OF KING HENRY THE FIFT WITH HIS BATELL FOUGHT AT AGINCOURT IN FRANCE. The title HENRY V never appears on-screen, although it does appear in the trailer for the film. The rule we have followed in such cases is to use the title by which the film is most generally referred to. Where a film has no title, this has been supplied by ourselves and is given in parentheses. If a film is part of a series this is given below the country and date.

Country/date

All countries of production are given in full except Great Britain (GB) and the United States of America (USA). For films, dates are copyright or registration dates wherever known (and the date given on the film itself, where this exists); otherwise it is the date of first release in the main country of production. For television programmes, the date is the year of first transmission; the exact transmission date is given in the credits section.

Credits

Wherever possible, information for both credits and cast has been taken from copies of the films themselves. We have listed only the major credits for most productions: director, production company, producer, scriptwriter, photographer and music. Others have been added where it seemed appropriate. The transmission date for television programmes is that in the country of production and is followed by the channel, given in parentheses (for the *BBC Television Shakespeare* series, a GB/USA co-production, transmission dates and channels for both countries are given). Most production companies' names have been given in full. The following abbreviations have been used:

adapt	adapter
anim	animator
arr	arranger
art d	art director
asst	assistant
BBC	British Broadcasting Corporation
C4	Channel 4
chor	choreographer
comp	compiler
cond	conductor
cost	costumes
d	director
des	designer
dial	dialogue
ed	editor
exec p	executive producer
int	interviewer
intro	introduction
ITN	Independent Television News
ITV	Independent Television (Channel 3)
lght	lighting
m	music

nar	narrator
OB	outside broadcast
p	producer
PBS	Public Broadcasting Service
pc	production company
p des	production designer
ph	photography
rel date	release date (newsreels)
rep	reporter
RSC	Royal Shakespeare Company
sc	script
sc ed	script editor
scen	scenario
seq	sequence
spon	sponsor
sup	supervising
tv	television
tx	transmission date

NFTVA holdings

The technical information relates to the materials held in the NFTVA. The NFTVA is first and foremost a preservation organisation, and in the interests of preservation not all of its holdings are immediately accessible; such titles are marked **preservation material** and are not generally available for viewing by private researchers; those marked **viewing copy** are available. The NFTVA has an on-going copying programme, however, so it is always worth enquiring about the status of items listed here as preservation material since there is a chance that they have or will shortly become available. Information has been simplified from the actual technical records for greater clarity. For each record is given the film or tape width, colour or black-and-white, silent or sound, the length in feet for film, and the running time. **Running times for silent films are given at sound speed, 24 frames per second.** This is up to 50 per cent faster than the films were originally intended to run; 'one reel' of film at 24 frames per second runs for approximately ten minutes; originally it could have run for as long as fifteen minutes. On the few occasions where exact lengths of NFTVA films are not known, those lengths given in the British Film Institute's *Monthly Film Bulletin* (latterly *Sight and Sound*) are used. The following abbreviations have been used:

bw	black-and-white
col	colour
col seq	colour sequence
ft	feet
m	metres

mins	minutes
mm	millimetres (i.e. 16, 35, 70)
mu	mute (i.e. sound missing)
NFTVA	National Film and Television Archive
sd	sound (i.e. combined sound and picture)
st	silent

The symbol " is used for inches when measuring videotape (i.e. ½, ¾, 1, 2). If a record is part of a multiple entry for that film, then the technical information is only cited for the main entry, the supplementary entries merely stating that the NFTVA holds the film and has a viewing copy or otherwise. Some brief explanatory notes, usually relating to incomplete films, are given after the technical details; greater details may be given in the Notes section following the description of the film. The language of the intertitles to silent films is given (note: copies of silent films have often only survived in language versions different from that of the country of production).

Cast

Cast members are given first, followed by their role. The order is either that given on-screen or as cited in a standard work of reference (television listings magazines often give cast in order of appearance). Only full versions of the plays have the full cast cited, and even here we have not included every minor spear-carrier. For films less directly related to one of the plays we have only cited a few cast members, normally those that feature in the relevant Shakespeare passage (for example, the four leading characters of the 1968 THE CHARGE OF THE LIGHT BRIGADE are given, plus Donald Wolfit, who appears briefly as Macbeth).

Description

Each entry begins with a short description of the type of film (for example, 'feature film version of the play'). This is followed by a combined plot synopsis and critical assessment. Obviously the plots of 'straight' versions of the plays are omitted, but short descriptions of the plots of unusual versions are given, plus those of feature films containing relevant sequences, and there is a general description of contents for non-fiction films. Where sequences from the plays are featured these are given act and scene number in the form A5S3 (that is, Act 5 Scene 3). For such citations we have referred to the one-volume Pelican text, Alfred Harbage (gen. ed.), *William Shakespeare: The Complete Works* (London: Allen Lane, rev. ed. 1969). The critical assessments have been included to avoid a dry listing of plot summaries and to combine with arguments presented in the accompanying essays. Such opinions remain personal and do not reflect any official NFTVA view of its holdings.

Notes

General information on the films is given, which may include further cast and credit details, additional comment on aspects of the NFTVA's own material, production details and history, plus cross-references to related titles.

References

There is a bibliography of Shakespeare books and journals given at the back of this book, but references to individual titles are cited for the major films and television programmes. Such listings are selective, and do not include references to such standard sources as the *Monthly Film Bulletin*, *Radio Times* or *Variety*. Some of these references are to works cited in the bibliography and are given in abbreviated form. Others are cited in full.

Note

A special feature of the catalogue is sequences from the plays included in feature films. Some of these are well-known, such as Victor Mature's rendition of the *Hamlet* soliloquy (A3S1) in MY DARLING CLEMENTINE, but many are recorded here for the first time. The rule has been to ignore short quotations, but to include substantial references to the plays, particularly where these have some bearing on the overall intentions of the film-makers. There are some variations on this rule; for example, we have tried to include all references to the *Hamlet* soliloquy, no matter how brief. It is, however, impossible to know of every allusion to Shakespeare ever made in a film or television programme. We would welcome further instances from interested readers, bearing in mind that the catalogue is restricted to NFTVA holdings only (hence we are aware of Katharine Hepburn's rendition of the *Hamlet* soliloquy in MORNING GLORY, or the *Romeo and Juliet* sequence in IT'S LOVE I'M AFTER, but the NFTVA does not hold those films). Similarly we would welcome further examples of films using one of Shakespeare's plays as the basis of a plot, again bearing in mind that we are aware of a great many such titles which are, however, not held in the NFTVA.

Ian Richardson (Bertram) and Caroline Hunt (Diana) in ALL'S WELL THAT ENDS WELL (1968)

ALL'S WELL THAT ENDS WELL

ALL'S WELL THAT ENDS WELL

■ **GB • 1968**

■ *Theatre 625*

d	Claude Whatham
pc	BBC
tx	3 June 1968 (BBC2)
p	Ronald Travers
adapt	John Barton
lght	Robert Wright
cost/sets	Timothy O'Brien
des	Susan Spence
m	Derek Oldfield

NFTVA preservation material
2" col sd 120mins

■ **CAST**
Catherine Lacey. . . . . . . *The Countess of Rousillon*
Ian Richardson . . . . *Bertram, her son*
Brewster Mason . . . . *The Lord Lafeu*
Lynn Farleigh . . . . *Helena, the Countess's ward*
Clive Swift . . *Captain Parolles, a follower of Bertram*

Alton Kumalo . . . . *Servant to Bertram*
Sebastian Shaw . . . . *King of France*
William Eedle/Peter Rocca/
  Tom Georgeson . . . . *Gentlemen, attendant upon the King*
Hector Ross . . . . . *Rinaldo, steward to the Countess*
Ian Hogg . . . . *Lavache, a clown*
Colin McCormack . . . . *First suitor*
Matthew Robertson . . . . *Second suitor*
James Vallon. . . . . *Third suitor*
Dallas Adams. . . . . *Fourth suitor*
Daniel Moynihan . . . . *Lord Dumain, the elder*
Philip Hinton . . . . *Lord Dumain, the younger*
David Ashford. . . . . *The Duke of Florence*
David Baile . . . . *Morgan, a soldier*
Elizabeth Spriggs . . . . *Widow*
Natalie Kent . . . . *Mariana, her neighbour*
Caroline Hunt . . . . *Diana, her daughter*
Don Henderson . . . . *Second soldier*

■ **DESCRIPTION** Television presentation of the Royal Shakespeare Company production, adapted and directed for the stage by John Barton. An adequate recording of an imaginative and acclaimed stage production, introducing such obvious points of direction as having close-ups for the soliloquies, but not distinguishing itself particularly in any other way.

ENTERTAINMENT UK

■ **GB • 1992**

pc	Mentorn Films
tx	13 October 1992 (ITV)
p	Claire Hobday/Sue Lloyd
intro	Garry Rice

NFTVA viewing copy
½" col sd 51mins

■ **CAST**
Richard Johnson . . . . *King of France*
Sophie Thompson . . . . *Helena*

■ **DESCRIPTION** Television arts and entertainment magazine. Includes a three-minute item on Sir Peter Hall's production of *All's Well That Ends Well* at the Swan Theatre, Stratford, with short extracts from A2S1 and comments from Richard Johnson and Sophie Thompson.

Richard Johnson and Janet Suzman in ANTONY AND CLEOPATRA (1974)

ANTONY AND CLEOPATRA

CLEOPATRA

■ **France • 1910**

pc   Pathé Frères

NFTVA viewing copy
35mm bw st 819ft 9mins
German titles

■ **CAST**
Madeline Roch. . . . . *Cleopatra*
Stacia Napierkowska. . . . . *Messenger*
Rianza . . . . *Dancer*

■ **DESCRIPTION** Fiction short. Cleopatra at her court; she comes to Mark Antony by boat; watched by Octavius he declares his love for her and they leave on the boat; Antony and Octavius argue in the Roman camp; in Egypt Antony and Cleopatra enjoy the entertainments; Octavius arrives and declares war on Antony; Cleopatra is brought news of Antony's defeat; she is angry and has the messenger poisoned; Antony stabs himself and the Romans enter Cleopatra's palace; she poisons herself with an asp bite; Octavius rushes in to find her dead.

■ **NOTES** Although shorter than the length given for release in the USA (1,170ft), the action portrayed is substantially that given in reviews. The narrative obviously owes something to Shakespeare, but he is not mentioned in reviews or Pathé publicity for the film. Madeline Roch was a noted member of the Comédie Française. Pathé produced a sequel, with the English title CAESAR IN EGYPT (1910), which is held in the NFTVA but has no Shakespearean connection.

■ **REFERENCES** • Ball, *Shakespeare on Silent Film*, pp. 112–14, 330–1.

RAKE'S PROGRESS, The

USA title NOTORIOUS GENTLEMAN, The

■ **GB • 1945**

d   Sidney Gilliat
pc   Individual Pictures
p/sc   Sidney Gilliat/Frank Launder
ph   Wilkie Cooper
m   William Alwyn

NFTVA viewing copy
35mm bw sd 10,892ft 121mins

■ **CAST**
Rex Harrison . . . . *Vivian Kenway*
Lilli Palmer. . . . . *Rikki Krausner*
Margaret Johnston . . . .*Jennifer Calthrop*
Jean Kent . . . . *Jill Duncan*

■ **DESCRIPTION** Feature film. The misadventures of a 1930s playboy, from being sent down from Oxford to his salvation as a war hero. Outstanding comedy-drama with a conscience; in one scene Harrison seduces a friend's girl (Jean Kent) on a punt when she should have been seeing an Oxford University Dramatic Society production of *Antony and Cleopatra*. The lines beginning 'The barge she sat in. . .' (A2S2) are spoken over the scene.

CLEOPATRA

■ **USA • 1963**

d   Joseph L. Mankiewicz

pc	Twentieth Century-Fox Film Corporation/J. L. M./Walwa
p	Walter Wanger
sc	Joseph L. Mankiewicz/Ranald MacDougall/Sidney Buchman
ph	Leon Shamroy
m	Alex North

NFTVA preservation material
35mm col sd 17,241ft 191mins

■ **CAST**

Elizabeth Taylor . . . . *Cleopatra*
Richard Burton . . . . *Mark Antony*
Rex Harrison . . . . *Julius Caesar*
Roddy McDowall . . . . *Octavian*
Richard O'Sullivan . . . . *Ptolemy*
Isabelle Cooley . . . . *Charmian*
Francesca Annis . . . . *Eiras*

■ **DESCRIPTION** Feature film. Cleopatra, queen of Egypt, lures first Julius Caesar and then Mark Antony. After the battle of Actium, Antony and Cleopatra take their own lives and die together in a mausoleum. Notorious, bloated and wildly expensive setting for the Burton-Taylor romance; just occasionally it becomes an interesting film, surprisingly faithful to its sources, which are credited as Plutarch, Suetonius, Appian and *The Life and Times of Cleopatra* by Charles Marie Franzero (London, 1957). Clearly the spirit and action of Shakespeare's *Antony and Cleopatra* hover beneath the surface, but the film strives hard to write its own myths. Doomed to ridicule; the CARRY ON CLEO parody (see below) is infinitely preferable.

■ **NOTES** The original running time was 243mins; in Britain it was released at 226mins (25,312ft) in 35mm and 70mm (one source says 215mins). The NFTVA's 35mm copy derives from Twentieth Century-Fox and is presumably a further reduced re-issue version.

CARRY ON CLEO

■ **GB • 1964**

d	Gerald Thomas
pc	Adder
p	Peter Rogers
sc	Talbot Rothwell

ph	Alan Hume
m	Eric Rogers

NFTVA viewing copy
35mm col sd 8,226ft 91mins

■ **CAST**

Sidney James . . . . *Mark Antony*
Kenneth Williams . . . . *Julius Caesar*
Amanda Barrie . . . . *Cleo*
Kenneth Connor . . . . *Hengist*
Jim Dale . . . . *Horsa*
Joan Sims . . . . *Calpurnia*
Charles Hawtrey . . . . *Seneca*

■ **DESCRIPTION** Feature film. Hengist, an unheroic Ancient Briton and maker of square wheels, is captured by the Romans but inadvertently becomes Julius Caesar's bodyguard. Mark Antony becomes enamoured of Cleopatra, and plans with her to assassinate Caesar in Egypt, but Hengist and his friend Horsa foil the plot. Splendid comic romp, initially a parody of the 1963 CLEOPATRA (see above), but spoofs history in general and British attitudes in particular. Rich in comic character studies and howlingly bad puns, it is probably quite unfunny to all but the British, who worship it. The opening credits state 'Based on an idea by William Shakespeare', so there you are.

■ **NOTES** The 1963 CLEOPATRA began filming at Pinewood in September 1960, but after only a few months shooting and numerous problems the production continued elsewhere. Partly as revenge, partly because the sets had been left behind, this parody was devised. The sets give it production values far above those of the usual *Carry On* films.

SHAKESPEARE WALLAH

■ **India • 1965**

d	James Ivory
pc	Merchant-Ivory Productions

NFTVA viewing copy

■ **CAST**

Geoffrey Kendal . . . . *Enobarbus/Antony*
Laura Liddell . . . . *Cleopatra*

Partap Sharma. *Philo*
Utpal Dutt. . . . . *The Maharajah*

■ **DESCRIPTION** Feature film. The story of a troupe of English actors in India. Includes scenes from a performance of *Antony and Cleopatra* given at a maharajah's palace. The play opens with Enobarbus's description of Cleopatra (A2S2), followed by the start of the opening act proper. Cleopatra also delivers the speech 'Noblest of men, woo't die?' (A4S15). For full details of film see entry in General section.

MORECAMBE AND WISE SHOW, The

■ **GB • 1971**

pc	BBC
tx	3 June 1971 (BBC2)
p	John Ammonds
sc	Eddie Braben

NFTVA preservation material (see note below)
16mm col sd 1,440ft 40mins

■ **CAST**
Glenda Jackson . . . . *Cleopatra*
Eric Morecambe. . . . . *Octavius Caesar*
Ernie Wise . . . . *Mark Antony*

■ **DESCRIPTION** Programme from television comedy series. Includes a sketch, ostensibly written by ever-hopeful playwright Ernie Wise, designed for guest star Glenda Jackson and showing an unlikely showdown between Cleopatra, Caesar and Antony, with some sort of debt to Shakespeare. A liaison between Mark Antony and Cleopatra is interrupted by a Roman guard, who turns out to be none other than Octavius Caesar, 'ruler of the world and certain parts of Birkenhead' (Glenda Jackson was born in Birkenhead). Cleopatra's maid is referred to throughout as Desdemona.

■ **NOTES** The NFTVA has preservation material only for the original programme, but a viewing copy (½" col sd 60mins) made from an off-air recording of a compilation programme THE MORECAMBE AND WISE CHRISTMAS SHOWS (tx 21 December 1991) includes the sketch.

ANTONY AND CLEOPATRA

■ **Spain/Switzerland/GB • 1972**

d/sc	Charlton Heston
pc	Transac/Izaro/Folie Films
p	Peter Snell
ph	Rafael Pacheco
art d	José Alguero/José Maria Alarcón
m	John Scott/Augusto Alegero

NFTVA preservation material
2" col sd 160mins

■ **CAST**
Charlton Heston . . . . *Antony*
Hildegard Neil. . . . . *Cleopatra*
Eric Porter . . . . *Enobarbus*
John Castle . . . . *Octavius*
Fernando Rey. . . . . *Lepidus*
Juan Luis Galiardo . . . . *Alexas*
Jane Lapotaire . . . . *Charmian*
Monica Peterson . . . . *Iras*
Emiliano Redondo. . . . . *Mardian*
Carmen Sevilla. . . . . *Octavia*
Freddie Jones . . . . *Pompey*
Alba . . . . *Schoolmaster*
Peter Arne . . . . *Menas*
Luis Barboo . . . . *Varrius*
Doug Wilmer . . . . *Agrippa*
Fernando Bilbao . . . . *Menecrates*
Warren Clarke. . . . . *Scarus*
Roger Delgado . . . . *Soothsayer*
Julian Glover. . . . . *Proculeius*
Sancho Gracia . . . . *Canidius*
Garrick Hagan . . . . *Eros*
John Hallam. . . . . *Thidias*
Aldo Sambrel . . . . *Ventidius*
Joe Melia . . . . *First Messenger*
Sergio Krumbel . . . . *Second Messenger*
José Manuel Martin . . . . *Guard*
Manolo Otero . . . . *Sentry*
Felipe Solano . . . . *Soldier*

■ **DESCRIPTION** Feature film version of the play. Ponderous, under-produced adaptation, trying too hard to present the play as historical spectacle, too little as credible human drama. It fatally lacks any passion. Strong performances from Eric Porter and from John Castle as a brooding Octavius offer some compensation.

ANTONY AND CLEOPATRA

■ GB • 1974

d	Jon Scoffield
pc	ATV
tx	28 July 1974 (ITV)
des (RSC)	Christopher Morley/Ann Curtis
des (ATV)	Michael Bailey
m	Guy Woolfenden

NFTVA preservation material
2" col sd 162mins

■ CAST

Richard Johnson . . . . *Antony*
Janet Suzman . . . . *Cleopatra*
Rosemary McHale . . . . *Charmian*
Mavis Taylor Blake . . . . *Iras*
Darien Angadi . . . . *Alexas*
Sidney Livingstone . . . . *Mardian*
Geoffrey Hutchings . . . . *Fig seller*
Loftus Burton . . . . *Diomedes*
Lennard Pearce . . . . *Cleopatra's schoolteacher*
Joseph Charles . . . . *Messenger*
Tony Osoba . . . . *Servant*
Patrick Stewart . . . . *Enobarbus*
Constantin de Goguel . . . . *Ventidius*
Morgan Sheppard . . . . *Scarus*
Joe Marcell . . . . *Eros*
Jonathan Holt . . . . *Dercetas*
Christopher Jenkinson . . . . *Silius*
John Bott . . . . *Soothsayer*
Robert Oates . . . . *First watchman*
Arthur Whybrow . . . . *Second watchman*
Michael Radcliffe . . . . *Third watchman*
Corin Redgrave . . . . *Octavius*
Philip Locke . . . . *Agrippa*
Patrick Godfrey . . . . *Maecenas*
Ben Kingsley . . . . *Thidias*
Martin Milman . . . . *Dolbella*
Tim Pigott-Smith . . . . *Proculeius*
Keith Taylor . . . . *Messenger*
Thomas Chesleigh . . . . *Gallus*
Desmond Stokes . . . . *Taurus*
Alan Foss . . . . *Senator*
John Bardon . . . . *Demetrius*
Peter Godfrey . . . . *Sentry*
Malcolm Kaye . . . . *Guard*

■ **DESCRIPTION** Television presentation of the Royal Shakespeare Company's production, directed for the theatre by Trevor Nunn. Richly effective version, probably the first television production to make full use of the possibilities of the medium, making it a model for all that followed. Nunn and Scoffield made the important discovery that it was fatal to try and open out the play in what is meant to be an intimate medium. Instead the focus is all on the actors, with simple but effective props and background. Suggestion rather than realism, richness through intensity, the language pre-eminent.

■ **NOTES** Nunn's production was originally staged by the RSC in 1972.

■ **REFERENCES** ● James, *Clive James on Television* [frequent mentions throughout].

ANTONY AND CLEOPATRA

■ GB/USA • 1981

■ *BBC Television Shakespeare*

d/p	Jonathan Miller
pc	BBC/Time-Life Films
tx (GB)	8 May 1981 (BBC2)
tx (US)	20 April 1981 (PBS)
lght	Dennis Channon
cost	Alun Hughes
des	Colin Lowrey
m	Stephen Oliver

NFTVA preservation material
1" col sd 177mins

■ CAST

John Paul . . . . *Canidius*
Jonathan Adams . . . . *Ventidius*
Jane Lapotaire . . . . *Cleopatra*
Colin Blakely . . . . *Antony*
Darien Angadi . . . . *Alexas*
Janet Key . . . . *Charmian*
Howard Goorney . . . . *Soothsayer*
Cassie McFarlane . . . . *Iras*
Emrys James . . . . *Enobarbus*
Kevin Huckstep/Michael Anthony . . . *Messengers*
Mohammad Shamsi . . . . *Mardian*
Ian Charleson . . . . *Octavius Caesar*
Esmond Knight . . . . *Lepidus*
Harry Waters . . . . *Thyreus*
David Neal . . . . *Proculeius*

Anthony Pedley . . . . *Agrippa*
Geoffrey Collins . . . . *Dolabella*
Donald Sumpter . . . . *Pompeius*
George Innes . . . . *Menas*
Desmond Stokes . . . . *Menecrates*
Lynn Farleigh . . . . *Octavia*
David Kincaid . . . . *Cleopatra's messenger*
Simon Chandler . . . . *Eros*
Pat Connell . . . . *Soldier*
Christopher Ettridge . . . . *Scarus*
George Howe . . . . *Euphronius*
John Eastham . . . . *Servant*
Iain Rattray/Frederick Warner/
  Michael Egan . . . . *Soldiers*
Alec Sabin . . . . *Dercetas*
Jimmy Gardner . . . . *Clown*

■ **DESCRIPTION** Television production. Routine offering from the BBC series, with a carefully cast Antony and Cleopatra, but small-scale in its ambition and with little to excite the imagination or hold one's attention.

■ **REFERENCES** • Richard David, 'Shakespeare in Miniature: The BBC *Antony and Cleopatra*', in Bulman and Coursen, *Shakespeare on Television*, pp. 139–44.

ENTERTAINMENT UK

■ **GB • 1992**

pc	Mentorn Films
tx	8 December 1992 (ITV)
p	Jonathan Challis
intro	Michael Groth

NFTVA viewing copy
½" col sd 51mins

■ **CAST**
Richard Johnson . . . . *Antony*
Clare Higgins . . . . *Cleopatra*

■ **DESCRIPTION** Television arts and entertainment magazine. Includes a three-minute item on Peter Hall's Royal Shakespeare Company's production of *Antony and Cleopatra* at the Royal Shakespeare Theatre, Stratford. Richard Johnson and Clare Higgins talk about the play over brief sequences from A3S11 and A4S12.

Mackenzie Ward (Touchstone), Aubrey Mather (Corin) and Elisabeth Bergner (Rosalind) in AS YOU LIKE IT (1936)

AS YOU LIKE IT

SEVEN AGES, The

■ **USA • 1905**

d	Edwin S. Porter
pc	Edison

NFTVA viewing copy
35mm bw st 205ft
Incomplete – original length c500ft
English titles

■ **DESCRIPTION** Fiction short. A depiction of the seven ages of Man, in eight tableaux, the four in the NFTVA's incomplete copy being The Judge, Lovers, The Soldier and Second Childhood. In each tableau a couple are seen embracing, followed by a close-up of them kissing. The producers were clearly more interested in the kissing than any allusions to Shakespeare.

■ **NOTES** The complete set of tableaux, each with its own title, were Infancy, Playmates, Schoolmates, Lovers, The Soldier, The Judge, Second Childhood and What Age? (showing an old maid alone with her cat). The film was probably inspired by a series of lantern slides entitled *Shakespeare's Seven Ages*, produced by the Kleine Optical Company.

■ **REFERENCES** • *Cinema 1900/1906: Filmography* (Brussels: FIAF, 1982), pp. 244–5.

YELLOW WEEK AT STANWAY, The

■ GB • 1923

d/p/sc   J. M. Barrie

NFTVA viewing copy
35mm bw st 2,483ft 28mins
English titles

■ **CAST**
Nicholas Llewellyn-Davies . . . . *Himself*

■ **DESCRIPTION** Amateur film. Whimsical record of a house party held by the author J. M. Barrie at Stanway in Gloucestershire, written and 'directed' by Barrie and featuring a semi-dramatised dream sequence in which Nicholas Llewellyn-Davies (Barrie's adopted son) is rejected by all the female house guests in turn. The intertitles refer to the Forest of Arden and (in verse and in imitation of the verses in *As You Like It* A3S2) make it clear that he is seeking 'his Rosalind'.

■ **NOTES** Barrie held regular summer parties at Stanway, home of Lord Wemyss. Nicholas (Nico) Llewellyn-Davies, here aged 18, was one of the models for the 'Lost Boys' of *Peter Pan*. Barrie appears in the film, as do Cynthia Asquith and others of his circle. Barrie also made a script contribution to the 1936 AS YOU LIKE IT (see below).

BEAUTY AND BRIGHTNESS NO. 4

■ GB • c1925

d/pc   Harry B. Parkinson

NFTVA preservation copy
35mm bw st 490ft 5mins
English titles

■ **DESCRIPTION** Interest film showing scenes of London life. Includes the view of St Paul's Cathedral from the site of the old Globe Theatre, followed by scenes from a performance of *As You Like It* played on a brewer's dray at the Old George Inn, Southwark.

IMMORTAL GENTLEMAN, The

■ GB • 1935

d   Widgey R. Newman
pc   Bernard Smith

NFTVA viewing copy

■ **CAST**
Basil Gill . . . . *William Shakespeare*
Dennis Hoey . . . . *Soldier*
Anne Bolt . . . . *Jane*

■ **DESCRIPTION** Feature film. Shakespeare and his friends meet in a Southwark tavern and their reminiscences give rise to sequences from Shakespeare's plays. Shakespeare himself gives a rendition of the 'Seven Ages of Man' speech (A2S7), the lines being illustrated by people in the tavern. Later a soldier and his cousin Jane sing 'It was a Lover, and his Lass' (A5S3). For full details of film see entry in General section.

PEG OF OLD DRURY

■ GB • 1935

d/p   Herbert Wilcox
pc   British and Dominions Film
       Corporation
sc   Miles Malleson
ph   F. A. Young/L. P. Williams

NFTVA preservation material
35mm bw sd 6,750ft 75mins

■ **CAST**
Anna Neagle . . . . *Peg Woffington*
Cedric Hardwicke . . . . *David Garrick*
Margaretta Scott . . . . *Kitty Clive*
Jack Hawkins . . . . *Michael O'Taffe*

■ **DESCRIPTION** Feature film. The life of eighteenth-century actress Peg Woffington, based on the play *Masks and Faces* by Charles Reade and Tom Taylor. Dublin-born Peg comes to London and becomes a celebrated actress under David Garrick's guidance, but she suffers from a weak heart and dies at Drury Lane following a performance of *As You Like It*. A satisfactory period piece, whose appeal is tied to one's taste for Anna Neagle; in the 1930s she was very popular, and the film did very well. There are also short scenes from *The Merchant of Venice*, *Richard III* and Jonson's *The Alchemist*.

■ **NOTES** The real Peg Woffington (c1714–1760) did collapse on stage while playing *As You Like It*, but lived on for a few years after that. The NFTVA holds a 1917 film production, MASKS AND FACES, based on the play with Irene Vanbrugh as Peg, but this does not feature the *As You Like It* episode.

AS YOU LIKE IT

■ **GB • 1936**

d/p	Paul Czinner
pc	Inter-Allied Film Producers
sc	R. J. Cullen ['treatment suggested by J. M. Barrie']
dial sup	Leon Quartermaine
ph	Hal Rosson
ed	David Lean
sets	Lazare Meerson
cost	John Armstrong/Joe Strassner
m	William Walton

NFTVA preservation material
16mm bw sd 3,419ft 95mins

■ **CAST**
Henry Ainley . . . . *Exiled Duke*
Felix Aylmer . . . . *Duke Frederick*
Stuart Robertson . . . . *Amiens*
Leon Quartermaine . . . . *Jacques*
Austin Trevor . . . . *Le Beau*
Lionel Braham . . . . *Charles*
John Laurie . . . . *Oliver*
Laurence Olivier . . . . *Orlando*
J. Fisher White . . . . *Adam*
Mackenzie Ward . . . . *Touchstone*
Aubrey Mather . . . . *Corin*
Richard Ainley . . . . *Sylvius*
Peter Bull . . . . *William*
Elisabeth Bergner . . . . *Rosalind*
Sophie Stewart . . . . *Celia*
Joan White . . . . *Phebe*
Dorice Fordred . . . . *Audrey*

■ **DESCRIPTION** Feature film version of the play. A charming if somewhat bowdlerised presentation, set in an elaborate stage forest with real animals. There are some dreary stage performances from the older hands, notably Leon Quartermaine's ponderous delivery of the 'Seven Ages' (A2S7) speech, but Elisabeth Bergner's sprightly Rosalind and Olivier's petulant Orlando more than make up for this. Czinner could direct cinematically yet chose not to, but this is a happy and enjoyable production, perhaps the model of what any school production might hope to achieve.

■ **REFERENCES** • Graham Greene, *The Pleasure-Dome* (London: Secker & Warburg, 1972), pp. 98–100. • Manvell, *Shakespeare and the Film*, pp. 30–4.

JOHN GIELGUD

■ **USA • 1963**

■ *Playback*

pc	CBS
intro	Goddard Lieberson

NFTVA preservation material
16mm bw sd c 150ft 4mins

■ **DESCRIPTION** Promotional film. John Gielgud reads the 'Seven Ages of Man' speech from *As You Like It* (A2S7).

■ **NOTES** *Playback* was a series of short promotional films produced by CBS for US television, promoting Columbia Records artists. Gielgud's one man show, 'Ages of Man', a portrait of Shakespeare's world and works devised by George

Rylands, was put on first at the Edinburgh Festival in 1957 and went on to become a huge success, notably in the United States. The recording and promotional film were produced to coincide with the 1963 Broadway production. In 1966 the complete show (not in NFTVA) was broadcast in two parts on US television (23/30 January), and subsequently in Britain (2/9 October).

AS YOU LIKE IT

■ **GB/USA • 1978**

■ *BBC Television Shakespeare*

d	Basil Coleman
pc	BBC/Time-Life Films
tx (GB)	17 December 1978 (BBC2)
tx (US)	28 February 1979 (PBS)
p	Cedric Messina
sc ed	Alan Shallcross
cost	Robin Fraser-Pye
des	Don Taylor
m	Geoffrey Burgon

NFTVA preservation material
1" col sd 150mins

■ **CAST**

Chris Sullivan	*Dennis*
Clive Francis	*Oliver*
Brian Stirner	*Orlando*
Arthur Hewlett	*Adam*
Dave Prowse	*Charles*
Angharad Rees	*Celia*
Helen Mirren	*Rosalind*
James Bolam	*Touchstone*
John Quentin	*Le Beau*
Richard Easton	*Duke Frederick*
Peter Tullo/Mike Lewin	*Palace lords*
Tony Church	*Banished Duke*
Tom McDonnell	*Amiens*
Carl Forgione/Max Harvey	*Forest lords*
David Lloyd Meredith	*Corin*
Maynard Williams	*Silvius*
Richard Pasco	*Jacques*
London Pro Musica	*Musicians*
Marilyn Le Conte	*Audrey*
Timothy Bateson	*Sir Oliver Martext*

Victoria Plucknett	*Phebe*
Jeffrey Holland	*William*
Paul Phoenix/Barry Holden	*Pages*
John Moulder-Brown	*Hymen*
Paul Bentall	*Jacques de Boys*

■ **DESCRIPTION** Television production of the play. Third production in the *BBC Television Shakespeare* series, charmingly played and satisfactorily cast, but seriously compromised by choosing to film in a real wood. It thereby loses much of its conviction, as the characters are all too obviously actors making their way through the greenery, although the change from the usual nondescript BBC sets is refreshing. Pedestrian direction likewise dulls the appeal to the imagination.

■ **NOTES** Filming took place outside Glamis Castle, Scotland, best known for its *Macbeth* associations.

■ **REFERENCES** • J. C. Bulman, '*As You Like It* and the Perils of Pastoral' in Bulman and Coursen, *Shakespeare on Television*, pp. 174–9.

CAUGHT IN THE ACT

■ **GB • 1988**

d/p	Mary Gwatkin
pc	Reconnaissance Films/MV Films
tx	26 December 1988 (C4)

NFTVA viewing copy

■ **CAST**

Kenneth Branagh	*Touchstone*

■ **DESCRIPTION** Television documentary on the work of Kenneth Branagh's Renaissance Theatre Company, in particular its three touring productions of *As You Like It*, *Hamlet* and *Much Ado About Nothing*. Geraldine McEwan talks about the experience of directing *As You Like It* and the numerous challenges it presented. There are several scenes from the play in rehearsal and performance, including Branagh delivering 'Ay, now I am in Arden' (A2S4). For full details of programme see entry in General section.

Martha Raye singing 'The Greeks Have a Word for it' in THE BOYS FROM SYRACUSE (1940)

COMEDY OF ERRORS

BOYS FROM SYRACUSE, The

■ **USA • 1940**

d	A. Edward Sutherland
pc	Universal Pictures
p	Jules Levey
sc	Leonard Spigelgass/Charles Grayson
ph	Joe Valentine
art d	Jack Otterson

NFTVA preservation material
35mm bw sd 6,017ft 67mins

■ **CAST**

Allan Jones. . . . . *Antipholus of Ephesus/*
Antipholus of Syracuse
Joe Penner . . *Dromio of Ephesus/Dromio of Syracuse*
Martha Raye . . . . *Luce*
Rosemary Lane . . . . *Phyllis*
Charles Butterworth . . . . *Duke of Ephesus*
Irene Hervey. . . . . *Adriana*
Alan Mowbray. . . . . *Angelo*
Eric Blore. *Pinch*
Samuel S. Hinds . . . . *Aegon*

■ **DESCRIPTION** Feature film version of the Broadway musical by George Abbott, Richard Rogers and Lorenz Hart, itself a free adaptation of *The Comedy of Errors*. Cheerful, fast-paced and satisfactory musical employing Shakespeare's plot, the Ephesus background and resolutely twentieth-century language and manners. The film producers added anachronistic gags such as taxi chariots with meters, cigar-smoking and stone newspapers. Those who knew the stage version felt that it had been done a disservice. The screenwriting credit states 'After a play by Shakespeare … long, long after!'

■ **NOTES** First produced as a musical on Broadway in 1938. The original length of the film was 74mins.

COMEDY OF ERRORS, The

■ **GB • 1964**

■ *Festival*

d	Peter Duguid
pc	BBC
tx	1 January 1964 (BBC)
p (RSC)	Clifford Williams
p (BBC)	Peter Luke
cost	Anthony Powell
des	John Wyckham/Clifford Williams
m	Peter Wishart

NFTVA preservation material
¾" bw sd 81mins

■ **CAST**

Donald Sinden . . . . *Solinus, Duke of Ephesus*
John Welsh . . . . . . *Aegeon, a merchant of Syracuse*
Ian Richardson . . . . *Antipholus of Ephesus*
Alec McCowen . . . . *Antipholus of Syracuse*
Clifford Rose . . . . *Dromio of Ephesus*
Barry MacGregor. . . . . *Dromio of Syracuse*
Michael Murray . . . . *Balthazar, a merchant*
Ken Wynne . . . . *Angelo, a goldsmith*
Philip Brack. . . . . *First merchant*
John Hussey . . . . *Second merchant*
Derek Smith . . . *Pinch, a schoolmaster and conjurer*
John Corvin . . . . *An officer*
Ronald Falk . . . . *A messenger*
Martin Jenkins. . . . . *A gaoler*
Madoline Thomas . . . *Aemilia, an abbess at Ephesus*

Diana Rigg . . . . *Adriana*
Janet Suzman . . . . *Luciana, her sister*
Caroline Maud . . . . *Luce, servant to Adriana*
Susan Engel . . . . *A courtezan*

■ **DESCRIPTION** Television presentation of the Royal Shakespeare Company production of the play, broadcast as part of the quatercentenary celebrations. A literal recording of a moderately with-it production, not televisual in any great sense but engrossing as filmed theatre and for a fine cast.

■ **NOTES** The play was broadcast while still running at the Aldwych Theatre.

COMEDY OF ERRORS, The

■ **GB • 1978**

d	Philip Casson
pc	ATV
tx	18 April 1978 (ITV)
p	Peter Roden
chor	Gillian Lynne
des (ATV)	Norman Smith
des (RSC)	John Napier
lyrics	Trevor Nunn
m	Guy Woolfenden

NFTVA viewing copy
½"col sd 130mins

■ **CAST**
Brian Coburn . . . . *Solinus*
Griffith Jones . . . . *Aegeon*
Roger Rees . . . . *Antipholus of Syracuse*
Mike Gwilym . . . . *Antipholus of Ephesus*
Michael Williams . . . . *Dromio of Syracuse*
Nickolas Grace . . . . *Dromio of Ephesus*
Judi Dench . . . . *Adriana*
Francesca Annis . . . . *Luciana*
Paul Brooke . . . . *Angelo*
Norman Tyrrell . . . . *Balthazar*
Barbara Shelley . . . . *Courtezan*
Robin Ellis . . . . *Dr Pinch*
Marie Kean . . . . *Aemelia*
Richard Griffiths . . . . *Officer*
Jacob Witkin . . . . *Merchant at The Porpentine*
Keith Taylor . . . *Merchant to whom Angelo is in debt*
Susan Dury . . . . *Luce*

Meg Davies . . . . *Nell*
Tim Brierley . . . . *Waiter at The Tiger*
Paul Whitworth/
    Peter Woodward . . . . . *Waiters at The Porpentine*
Marjorie Bland/Bobbie Brown/
    Pippa Guard . . . . *Girls at The Porpentine*

■ **DESCRIPTION** Television presentation of the Royal Shakespeare Company's production, directed for the stage and 'conceived for television' by Trevor Nunn. Exuberant version of a popular modern-dress stage production, which takes plenty of liberties with the text, and adds plenty of slapstick, some wonderful dance routines by Gillian Lynne and some less wonderful songs with lyrics by Trevor Nunn. Still a recording of a stage production, and valuable in that respect alone, it is colourful, energetic and very 1970s.

■ **NOTES** First produced at Stratford in 1976; recorded for television at the Royal Shakespeare Theatre in Stratford over a week.

COMEDY OF ERRORS, The

■ **GB/USA • 1983**

■ *BBC Television Shakespeare*

d	James Cellan Jones
pc	BBC/Time-Life Films
tx (GB)	24 December 1983 (BBC2)
tx (US)	20 February 1984 (PBS)
p	Shaun Sutton
lght	Dave Sydenham
cost	June Hudson
des	Don Homfray
m	Richard Holmes

NFTVA preservation material
1" col sd 110mins

■ **CAST**
Cyril Cusack . . . . *Aegeon*
Charles Gray . . . . *Solinus, Duke of Ephesus*
Bunny Reed . . . . *Jailer*
Nicolas Chagrin . . . . *Master of the Mime*
Marsha Fitzalan . . . . *Luce*
Michael Kitchen . . . . *Antipholus of Syracuse/*
                                    Antipholus of Ephesus
Roger Daltrey . . . . *Dromio of Syracuse/*
                                    Dromio of Ephesus

Noel Johnson . . . . *First merchant*
Suzanne Bertish . . . . *Adriana*
Joanne Pearce . . . . *Luciana*
Sam Dastor . . . . *Angelo*
David Kelly . . . . *Balthazar*
Alfred Hoffman . . . . *Second merchant*
Frank Williams . . . . *Officer*
Ingrid Pitt . . . . *Courtezan*
Geoffrey Rose . . . . *Pinch*
Wendy Hiller . . . . *Aemelia*
Peter Mackriel . . . . *Messenger*

■ **DESCRIPTION** Television production. A rather serious interpretation, the director having decided that it was 'full of dark, strange imaginings'. Whether this is really so or not, as a comedy it is not much fun, the casting of pop singer Roger Daltrey as the two Dromios being a severe handicap. A *commedia dell'arte* mime troupe appear throughout and the costumes were influenced by the *commedia dell'arte* tradition.

■ **REFERENCES** • Willis, *The BBC Shakespeare Plays*, pp. 260–91. • Robert E. Wood, 'Cooling the Comedy: Television as a Medium for Shakespeare's *Comedy of Errors*', *Literature/Film Quarterly*, 14, 4 (1986), pp. 195–202 [reprinted in Bulman and Coursen, *Shakespeare on Television*, pp. 200–7].

Alan Howard in CORIOLANUS (1984)

CORIOLANUS

CORIOLANO, EROE SENZA PATRIA

English title THUNDER OF BATTLE

■ Italy/France 1963

d	Giorgio Ferroni
pc	Dorica Film/Explorer Film 58/ Comptoir Français du Film
p	Diego Alchimede
sc	Remigio Del Grosso
ph	Augusto Tiezzi
m	Carlo Rustichelli

NFTVA viewing copy
35mm col sd 7,920ft 88mins

■ **CAST**
Gordon Scott . . . . *Caius Martius Coriolanus*
Lilla Brignone . . . . *Volumnia*
Philippe Hersent . . . . *Cominius*
Angela Minervini . . . . *Livia*
Alberto Lupo . . . . *Sicinius*
Rosalba Neri . . . . *Virgilia*
Aldo Bufi Landi . . . . *Marcus*

■ **DESCRIPTION** Feature film based on the life of the Roman commander Coriolanus, 'inspired' (so the credits state) by Plutarch's *Lives* and Shakespeare's *Coriolanus*. In practice a routine Ancient Rome historical spectacle, flatly presented and produced.

NOTE The original running time was 101mins; the NFTVA holds the dubbed British release version.

NATIONAL YOUTH THEATRE

■ **GB • 1966**

d	John Bloom/John Crome
pc	Melstrum Films
nar	Michael Croft
m	Peter Shade

NFTVA preservation material
16mm bw sd 1,968ft 27mins

■ **DESCRIPTION** Documentary on the work of the National Youth Theatre, giving the story of the company and showing them in rehearsal and in performance in London with a production of *Coriolanus*.

CORIOLANUS

■ **GB/USA • 1984**

■ *BBC Television Shakespeare*

d	Elijah Moshinsky
pc	BBC/Time-Life Films
tx (GB)	21 April 1984 (BBC2)
tx (US)	26 March 1984 (PBS)
p	Shaun Sutton
sc ed	David Snodin
lght	John Summers
cost	Michael Burdle
des	Dick Coles
m	Stephen Oliver

NFTVA viewing copy
½" col sd 145mins

■ **CAST**

Paul Jesson . . . . *First citizen*
Ray Roberts. . . . . *Second citizen*
Leon Lissek . . . . *Third citizen*
John Rumney . . . . *Fourth citizen*
Russell Kilmister. . . . . *Fifth citizen*
Joss Ackland . . . . *Menenius*
Alan Howard . . . . *Caius Marcius (later Coriolanus)*
Patrick Godfrey . . . . *Cominius*
John Rowe . . . . *First Roman senator*
Peter Sands . . . . *Titus Lartius*
John Burgess . . . . *Sicinius*
Anthony Pedley . . . . *Brutus*
Mike Gwilym . . . . *Aufidius*
Valentine Dyall . . . . *Adrian*
Brian Poyser . . . . *First Volscian senator*
Reginald Jessup. . . . . *Second Volscian senator*
Irene Worth. . . . . *Volumnia*
Joanna McCallum . . . . *Virgilia*
Patsy Smart . . . . *Gentlewoman*
Heather Canning . . . . *Valeria*
Jay Ruparelia . . . . *Roman soldier*
Damien Franklin . . . . *Young Marcius*

Nicholas Amer . . . . *Aedile*
Teddy Kempner . . . . *Nicanor*
Stephen Finlay . . . . *Citizen of Antium*

■ **DESCRIPTION** Television production of the play. A much shortened version of the play which cuts down the large-scale political issues to focus attention on the domestic scenes. Visually static, the vigour and complexity of the piece deriving from Howard's ironic, venomous and intensely physical performance in the central role. Howard successfully creates for television the controlled passion and total command of rhetoric that he demonstrated in his stage performance for the Royal Shakespeare Company in 1977. He is well supported by Mike Gwilym's violent and sinister Aufidius.

CORIOLANUS

■ **GB • 1984**

■ *Shakespeare in Perspective*

d	Sally Kirkwood
pc	BBC
tx	21 April 1984 (BBC2)
p	Victor Poole

NFTVA viewing copy
½" col sd 25mins

■ **DESCRIPTION** Talk given by General Sir John Hackett to accompany the screening of CORIOLANUS above, analysing Coriolanus' soldierly qualities and failings.

■ **NOTES** The NFTVA holds two examples from the *Shakespeare in Perspective* series, short talks accompanying each of the plays in the *BBC Television Shakespeare* series, details of which are given under the other example, for *Richard II* (1978, qv).

(IAN McKELLEN – DIARY OF A YEAR)

■ **GB • 1985**

■ *South Bank Show*

d/p	Kim Evans
pc	London Weekend Television
tx	20 October 1985 (ITV)
ed/pres	Melvyn Bragg

NFTVA viewing copy
½" col sd 54mins

■ **CAST**
Ian McKellen . . . . *Coriolanus*
Greg Hicks . . . . *Aufidius*

■ **DESCRIPTION** Television arts documentary. When Ian McKellen joined the National Theatre in 1984, he was asked by the *South Bank Show* to keep a diary (audiotape) of his experiences as an actor over the next twelve months. Beginning June 1984, the programme shows McKellen in rehearsal for Sir Peter Hall's production of *Coriolanus* (readings and rehearsals from A1S8 and A4S5). McKellen comments on his view of the role, including his finding inspiration for the character in tennis player John McEnroe. There are numerous backstage scenes during performances and brief glimpses of the play itself (A1S4, A1S9), giving nevertheless a good impression of the staging of the battle scenes. McKellen is seen receiving the London Standard Award for best actor for his role in *Coriolanus*. The *South Bank Show* at its best, with an articulate subject and a vivid impression of the work of an actor and the scale of the National Theatre's operations.

SHAKESPEARE; OR, WHAT YOU WILL

■ **GB • 1992**

■ *Dark Horses/Without Walls*

pc	Wall to Wall Television
tx	13 October 1992 (C4)

NFTVA viewing copy

■ **DESCRIPTION** Television documentary on Shakespeare and homosexuality. Includes a reading of Aufidius's speech beginning 'O Marcius, Marcius!' (A4S5). For full details of programme see entry in General section.

A beheaded Arthur Lowe in THEATRE OF BLOOD (1973)

CYMBELINE

THEATRE OF BLOOD

■ **GB • 1973**

d	Douglas Hickox
pc	Cineman

NFTVA preservation material

■ **CAST**
Vincent Price . . . . *Edward Lionheart*
Arthur Lowe . . . . *Horace Sprout*
Joan Hickson . . . . *Mrs Sprout*

■ **DESCRIPTION** Feature film. An actor (Vincent Price) murders his critics in the manner of deaths from Shakespeare's plays. In a parody of the beheading of Cloten, Horace Sprout's head is sawn off in his sleep. For full details of film see entry in General section.

(SIR PETER HALL DIRECTS SHAKESPEARE'S LAST PLAYS)

■ **GB • 1988**

■ *South Bank Show*

d/p	Chris Hunt
pc	London Weekend Television
tx	24 April 1988 (ITV)
ed/pres	Melvyn Bragg

NFTVA viewing copy
½" col sd 55mins

■ **CAST**
Tim Pigott-Smith . . . . *Iachimo*
Sarah Miles . . . . *Imogen*
Peter Woodward . . . . *Posthumus*

■ **DESCRIPTION** Television arts documentary. Engrossing account of Sir Peter Hall's final productions as director of the National Theatre, *Cymbeline*, *The Winter's Tale* and *The Tempest*, using the same group of actors throughout and showing preparations from first read-through to final dress rehearsal. From *Cymbeline*, rehearsals for scenes A1S7, A2S2 and A2S4 are shown in some detail, with comments from actors and director.

■ **NOTES** Sarah Miles left the production after these rehearsals were filmed and was replaced at very short notice by Geraldine James. For further details of programme see entries under *The Winter's Tale* and *The Tempest*.

David Meyer (Hamlet) and Helen Mirren (Gertrude) in HAMLET (1976)

HAMLET

AMLETO

■ **Italy • 1910**

d	Mario Caserini
pc	Cines

NFTVA viewing copy
35mm bw st 556ft 6mins [incomplete]
German titles

■ **CAST**
Amleto Novelli . . . . *Hamlet*
Fernanda Negri Pouget . . . . *Ophelia*

■ **DESCRIPTION** Abbreviated version of the play. [Section 1–119ft see note below] Hamlet, standing by a waterfall, learns that his father's ghost has been seen. The ghost appears to him. Hamlet has the players re-enact the murder scene before Claudius and Gertrude. The eavesdropping Polonius is run through by Hamlet's sword. Ophelia goes mad and wanders down to a river. Hamlet talks to the gravedigger, meditates upon Yorick's skull and confronts Laertes, Claudius separating them.

■ **NOTES** The Italian production company Cines produced versions of *Hamlet* in 1908 and 1910. The first 119ft of the NFTVA copy consist of fragments of several scenes: Hamlet courting Ophelia, Hamlet greeting the players, Ophelia's mad scene, and Hamlet feigning madness while reading a book. The film is also incomplete. The original Italian release was around 1,000ft. Ball gives Dante Capelli as Hamlet.

■ **REFERENCES** • Ball, *Shakespeare on Silent Film*, pp. 107, 328–9. • Kliman, *Hamlet*, pp. 228–36 [Kliman is unsure whether she is describing the 1908 or 1910 version: it is the 1910].

HAMLET

■ **GB • 1913**

d	E. Hay Plumb
pc	Hepworth Manufacturing Company

p	Cecil Hepworth
sets	Hawes Craven

NFTVA viewing copy
35mm bw st 5,344ft 59mins [see note below]
English titles

■ **CAST**

Johnston Forbes-Robertson	*Hamlet*
Walter Ringham	*Claudius*
S. A. Cookson	*Horatio*
J. H. Barnes	*Polonius*
Alexander Scott-Gatty	*Laertes*
Percy Rhodes	*Ghost of Hamlet's father*
Grendon Bentley	*Fortinbras*
Montague Rutherford	*Rosencrantz*
E. A. Ross	*Guildenstern*
George Hayes	*Osric*
A. Roberts [Robert Atkins]	*Marcellus*
G. Richards [Richard Andean]	*Bernardo*
E. Ericson [Eric Adeney]	*Francisco*
Eric Adeney	*Reynaldo*
Robert Atkins	*First Player*
Richard Andean	*Second Player*
J. H. Ryley	*First Gravedigger*
S. T. Pearce	*Second Gravedigger*
R. Montague [Montague Rutherford]	*Priest*
Adeline Bourne	*Gertrude*
Olive Richardson	*Player Queen*
Gertrude Elliott	*Ophelia*

■ **DESCRIPTION** Feature film. A record of Sir Johnston-Forbes Robertson and the Drury Lane Company's production of the play. The action is substantially that of the play, with some reduced Shakespearean intertitles. Statically presented, but with some welcome beach and woodland locations used, the film's chief purpose is to preserve a performance and a production, and makes few concessions to those ignorant of the play (virtually no mention is made of Hamlet's father's murder or Gertrude's re-marriage). But Forbes-Robertson's subtle, active, individual performance makes it clear why he was considered the greatest Hamlet of his time. Forbes-Robertson was 60 years old when he made the film.

■ **NOTES** Filmed at Hepworth's Walton-on-Thames studios and on location at Lulworth Cove, Dorset. Some scenes were shot in the grounds of Hartbourne Manor, home of Maxine Elliott, Forbes-Robertson's sister-in-law. The NFTVA holds three viewing copies, 4,846ft

(35mm), 1,924ft (16mm) and 5,344ft (35mm). The original copy received by the NFTVA (5,344ft) was partially out of order and contained some repeated scenes. The short version corrects these features. The length given on release was 5,800ft.

■ **REFERENCES** • Ball, *Shakespeare on Silent Film*, pp. 188–99, 349–51. • *Hamlet: The Story of the Play Concisely Told* (Cinema Books No. 1) (London, 1913) [The 'book of the film']. • Kliman, *Hamlet*, pp. 247–74.

WHEN HUNGRY HAMLET FLED

■ **USA • 1915**

pc	Thanhouser Film Corporation

NFTVA viewing copy
35mm bw st 809ft 9mins [incomplete]
English titles

■ **CAST**

Harry Benham	*Jealous young man*
Claude Cooper	*Director*

■ **DESCRIPTION** Comedy short. An experienced actor directs a melodrama for an amateur troupe. A jealous young man sabotages the set, causing much hilarity to the audience.

■ **NOTES** Only the first reel is held by the NFTVA; the missing second reel may have contained some reference to *Hamlet* other than that suggested by the title.

AMLETO

■ **Italy • 1917**

d/sc	Eleuterio Rodolfi
pc	Rodolfi-Film
sc	Carlo Chiaves
ph	Luigi Fiorio
art d	Antonio Rovescalli
cost	Caramba

NFTVA preservation material
35mm bw st 4,441ft 50mins
French titles

■ **CAST**

Ruggero Ruggeri . . . . *Hamlet*
Elena Markowska . . . . *Ophelia*
Mercedes Brignone . . . . *Gertrude*
Armand Pouget . . . . *Ghost*
Gerardo Peña . . . . *Laertes*
Martelli . . . . *Claudius*
Enrico Gemelli

■ **DESCRIPTION** Feature film. A largely complete rendition of the action of the play, featuring the noted Italian actor Ruggero Ruggeri as Hamlet. Ruggeri's performance certainly focuses one's attention, but is too expressive. What most distinguishes the film is its direction and occasional glosses on Shakespeare. Rodolfi finds an intriguing halfway style between film and theatre, eschewing a more conventional cutting scheme. Key thoughts are shown in close-up, there are thoughtful compositions throughout, and the final duel scene is impressively complex. Among the striking additions are Yorick's living face superimposed on his skull, Fortinbras' marching army intercut with the final scene, and Hamlet sitting on the throne to die and being handed his crown and sceptre ('borrowed' from the 1913 Forbes-Robertson version but much improved here). The death of Ophelia is inspired by Millais' painting of the same.

■ **NOTES** There are some short sequences missing and some nitrate damage to the picture in places. Length on release 2,270m (7,448ft).

■ **REFERENCES** • Ball, *Shakespeare on Silent Film*, pp. 254–62, 368.

OH'PHELIA

■ **GB • 1919**

d/anim/sc   Anson Dyer
pc   Hepworth Picture Plays
p   Cecil Hepworth

NFTVA preservation material
16mm bw st 371ft 10mins
English titles

■ **DESCRIPTION** Animated cartoon burlesque of *Hamlet*. 'Amlet, the Gloomy Dane, drives Ophelia dotty by offering her vegetables instead of flowers, then cutting off her hair ('to bob or not to bob'). Laertes (bearing a close resemblance to cowboy star William S. Hart) complains to the King of 'Amlet's behaviour, and Ophelia pelts the court with vegetables. 'Amlet, filled with remorse, joins the Boy Scouts. Ophelia falls into the river, and 'Amlet is able to apply first-aid on account of his Boy Scout manual. They embrace. Somewhat primitively executed, but engagingly done, this and a fragment from his OTHELLO are all that survive from Anson Dyer's series of animated Shakespeare burlesques. From these two films, and Dyer's other delightful extant work, the loss is great indeed.

■ **NOTES** Anson Dyer produced animated films from the First World War to the 1950s. The other titles in this particular series (1919–20) were the above film's companion-piece, 'AMLET (Horatio 'played' by Horatio Bottomley), THE MERCHANT OF VENICE (set in Wardour Street), OTHELLO (qv, fragment held in NFTVA), ROMEO AND JULIET (featuring Charlie Chaplin and Mary Pickford) and THE TAMING OF THE SHREW (possibly not released).

■ **REFERENCES** • Ball, *Shakespeare on Silent Film*, pp. 264–5. • Denis Gifford, *British Animated Films, 1895–1985: A Filmography* (Jefferson/London: McFarland & Company, 1987), pp. 59–62.

HAMLET

English title **HAMLET: THE DRAMA OF VENGEANCE**

■ **Germany • 1920**

d   Svend Gade/Heinz Schall
pc   Art-Film
sc   Erwin Gepard
ph   Curt Courant/Axel Graatkjaer
cost   Hugo Baruch/L. Verch

NFTVA viewing copy
35mm bw st 6,610ft 73mins
English flash titles

■ **CAST**

Asta Nielsen . . . . *Hamlet*
Eduard von Winterstein . . . . *Claudius*
Anton de Verdier . . . . *Laertes*
Lilly Jacobsson . . . . *Ophelia*
Paul Conradi . . . . *Ghost*
Mathilde Brandt . . . . *Queen Gertrude*
Heinz Stieda . . . . *Horatio*
Hans Junkermann . . . . *Polonius*
Fritz Achterberg . . . . *Fortinbras*

■ **DESCRIPTION** Feature film based not so much on Shakespeare as on the original Danish legend, with the added twist of a Princess Hamlet, who is obliged to masquerade as a prince. While the King of Denmark is seriously ill his wife gives birth to a daughter, telling the court that a son has been born to safeguard the crown. The King recovers and the baby is brought up as a boy. Hamlet grows up and at college encounters Horatio, Laertes and Fortinbras. Hamlet's uncle Claudius and the Queen plot to kill the King. Hamlet returns to find her father dead and the Queen and Claudius married. A voice within tells her to revenge the death and she feigns madness the better to observe Claudius. Ophelia is taken to meet Hamlet, but Hamlet falls in love with Horatio, who is himself in love with Ophelia. Hamlet feigns a love for Ophelia to thwart Horatio. Hamlet instructs a group of players to re-enact her father's murder to the court. Hamlet fails to kill a praying Claudius but kills Ophelia's father Polonius. Claudius sends Hamlet to Norway with secret instructions for her to be killed, which she discovers. In Norway she is greeted by Fortinbras. Ophelia drowns. The Norwegian army approaches Denmark. Hamlet starts a fire at Elsinore and kills her father. The Queen and Laertes plan Hamlet's death. During a fencing match between Hamlet and Laertes, the Queen inadvertently drinks poison and dies, Hamlet is struck by a poisoned rapier and as she dies Horatio learns of her secret and her love for him. Generally held to be one of the finest silent interpretations of Shakespeare, even if the plot is at some variance with him, chiefly on account of Asta Nielsen's mesmerising, intense performance.

■ **NOTES** Original German release length 2,367m (7,764ft). Ball gives a detailed account of the film with reference to its various sources.

■ **REFERENCES** • Ball, *Shakespeare on Silent Film*, pp. 272–8, 375–6.

ALTE GESETZ, Das

Alternative title **BARUCH**
English title **ANCIENT LAW, The**

■ **Germany • 1923**

d	E. A. Dupont
pc	Comedia-Film
sc	Paul Reno
ph	Theodor Sparkuhl
sets	Alfred Junge / Curt Kahle

NFTVA viewing copy
35mm bw st 7,550ft 84mins
Swedish titles

■ **CAST**

Avram Morewski . . . . *The Rabbi*
Ernst Deutsch . . . . *Baruch, his son*
Henny Porten . . . . . . *Archduchess Elisabeth Theresa*
Robert Garrison . . . . *Ruben Pick*
Margarete Schlegel . . . . *Esther*

■ **DESCRIPTION** Feature film. In nineteenth-century Austria a young Jew leaves the ghetto to become an actor, eventually becoming famous and reconciled with his disapproving Rabbi father. Ernst Deutsch, as the Jew Baruch, moves from a humble production of *Romeo and Juliet* (qv) to become a celebrated actor. He acts the role of Hamlet (opening and closing of play shown), this being intercut with scenes of his father conducting the Yom Kippur ceremonies.

■ **NOTES** The actual title on this Swedish release version is EN JUDE.

OLD BILL 'THROUGH THE AGES'

■ **GB • 1924**

d	Thomas Bentley
pc	Ideal Films

NFTVA viewing copy

■ **DESCRIPTION** Feature film comedy based on the First World War characters created by Bruce

Bairnsfather. Old Bill goes back in time to various stages in British history, including a meeting with William Shakespeare, whom he takes to Queen Elizabeth's court, where Shakespeare delivers the 'To be or not to be' soliloquy (A3S1) amongst other readings. For full details of film see entry in General section.

ELSTREE CALLING

■ **GB • 1930**

d	Adrian Brunel
pc	British International Pictures

NFTVA viewing copy

■ **DESCRIPTION** Feature film of variety acts in revue, hosted by Tommy Handley and featuring many celebrated British artistes of the day. Interspersed throughout the film is a running sketch featuring Donald Calthrop as someone determined to put on Shakespeare. This includes his delivery of the 'To be or not to be' soliloquy (A3S1) while performing a number of magic tricks. For full details of the film see the entry under *The Taming of the Shrew*.

IMMORTAL GENTLEMAN, The

■ **GB • 1935**

d	Widgey R. Newman
pc	Bernard Smith

NFTVA viewing copy

■ **CAST**
Terence de Marney . . . . *Hamlet*
Rosalinde Fuller . . . . *Ophelia*

■ **DESCRIPTION** Feature film. Shakespeare and his friends meet in a Southwark tavern and their reminiscences give rise to sequences from Shakespeare's plays. The sight of a melancholy man in a tavern inspires first a reading of the 'To be or not to be' soliloquy (A3S1) over various images from the play, then later Hamlet advising Ophelia to enter a nunnery. For full details of the film see entry in General section.

ARIZONIAN, The

■ **USA • 1935**

d	Charles Vidor
pc	RKO
p	Cliff Reid
sc	Dudley Nichols
ph	Harold Wenstrom
m	Roy Webbs

NFTVA viewing copy
35mm bw sd 6,808ft 76mins

■ **CAST**
Richard Dix . . . . *Clay Tallant*
Margot Grahame . . . . *Kitty Rivers*
Preston Foster . . . . *Tex Randolph*
Willie Best

■ **DESCRIPTION** Feature film Western. Marshall Tallant protects Silver City from outlaws. The films opens with a variety show in a saloon bar which features the 'Ghost Scene from *Hamlet*' (A1S4) with black comedian Willie Best playing a timorous ghost and an unnamed Hamlet. Members of the audience fire their guns to frighten Best.

SOUTH RIDING

■ **GB • 1937**

d/p	Victor Saville
pc	London Film Productions
sc	Ian Dalrymple
ph	Harry Stradling
m	Richard Addinsell

NFTVA viewing copy
35mm bw sd 7,625ft 85mins

■ **CAST**
Ralph Richardson . . . . *Robert Carne*
Ann Todd . . . . *Madge Carne*
Edna Best . . . . *Sarah Burton*
John Clements . . . . *Astell*
Joan Ellum . . . . *Lydia Holly*

■ **DESCRIPTION** Feature film. Sensitive drama portraying the tensions behind local government in Yorkshire and the clash between Tories and socialists, from the novel by Winifred Holtby.

HAMLET

Joan Ellum plays a working-class girl of scholastic promise. Her particular situation is emphasised when she quotes 'the slings and arrows of outrageous fortune' while doing the washing-up.

PLAYMATES

■ USA • 1941

d   David Butler
pc   RKO

NFTVA preservation material

■ **DESCRIPTION** Feature film. The Kay Kyser swing band teams up with John Barrymore to put on updated Shakespeare. Barrymore delivers the inevitable ponderous rendition of the *Hamlet* soliloquy (A3S1). Full details of the film's allusions to Shakespeare are given in its entry in the General section.

TO BE OR NOT TO BE

■ USA • 1942

d/p   Ernst Lubitsch
pc   Romaine Film Productions
sc   Edwin Justus Mayer
ph   Rudolph Maté
m   Miklos Rosza

NFTVA preservation material
35mm bw sd 8,897ft 99mins

■ **CAST**
Jack Benny . . . . *Joseph Tura*
Carole Lombard . . . . *Maria Tura*
Robert Stack . . . . *Lieut Stanislav Sobinski*
Sig Rumann . . . . *Colonel Ehrhardt*
Olaf Hytten. . . . . *Polonius*

■ **DESCRIPTION** Feature film. Comedy-drama set during the German occupation of Warsaw during World War Two, featuring the tribulations of a troupe of Polish players, headed by the vain Joseph Tura. Benny, playing Tura, is seen on stage several times as Hamlet, where his attempts to deliver more than the opening words of the soliloquy (A3S1) are invariably interrupted by someone from the audience getting up to leave. The words 'to be or not to be' are also misinterpreted by the Nazis as a secret coded message. Controversial at the time for its combination of black humour and sensitive subject matter (most notoriously the Nazi comment on Tura's performance as Hamlet, 'What he did to Shakespeare, we are now doing to Poland'), the film is now accepted as a comic masterpiece and as a noble statement in the defence of human values.

■ **NOTES** There are also references to *The Merchant of Venice* in the film, for which see the entry under that play. The film was remade in 1983 by Mel Brooks (see below).

IN WHICH WE LIVE; BEING THE STORY OF A SUIT TOLD BY ITSELF

■ GB • 1943

d/sc   Richard Massingham
pc   Public Relationship Films
spon   Ministry of Information/Board of Trade
p   Lewis Grant Wallace
ph   Alex Strasser
m   H. J. Roeber

NFTVA viewing copy
35mm bw sd 1,151ft 13mins

■ **CAST**
John Carol . . . . *Husband*
Rosalyn Boulter . . . . *Wife*
Richard Massingham . . . . *Man in pub*
Russell Waters . . . . *Best man/Man in pub*

■ **DESCRIPTION** Propaganda short. Government information film on how to get maximum service from a man's suit, narrated by one such suit in the form of an autobiography. When the suit is being cut up to make clothes for the children it murmurs words from the *Hamlet* soliloquy, 'To die, to sleep . . .' (A3S1).

DIARY FOR TIMOTHY, A

■ GB • 1946

d   Humphrey Jennings

pc	Crown Film Unit
p	Basil Wright
sc	E. M. Forster
nar	Michael Redgrave
ph	Fred Gamage
ed	Alan Orbiston
m	Richard Addinsell

NFTVA viewing copy
35mm bw sd 3,481ft 39mins

■ **CAST**

John Gielgud	Hamlet
George Woodbridge	Gravedigger
Francis Lister	Horatio

■ **DESCRIPTION** Documentary. A film 'diary' of the first six months in the life of a baby born 3 September 1944, showing events and the pattern of daily life in Britain during this period of the war. Outstanding, 'poetic' portrait composed of the sights, sounds, hopes and fears of the British people. In a key sequence, London's Haymarket theatre is shown advertising a performance of *Hamlet*; John Gielgud is seen on stage performing the graveside scene (A5S1); a uniformed reservist in a canteen discusses the trajectory of the V2 bombs; Gielgud speaks the 'Alas, poor Yorick' lines; there is an explosion near the canteen; Gielgud continues the scene; the reservist and others are seen digging in the rubble for survivors.

■ **NOTES** Filmed between Autumn 1944 and April 1945, but not released until 1946. The Theatre Royal, Haymarket production of *Hamlet* was part of Gielgud's repertory season at the theatre for 1944–45.

■ **REFERENCES** • Anthony W. Hodgkinson and Rodney E. Sheratsky, *Humphrey Jennings: More Than a Maker of Films* (Hanover and London: University Press of New England, 1982), pp. 155–61 [detailed description of the film].

MY DARLING CLEMENTINE

■ **USA • 1946**

d	John Ford
pc	Twentieth Century-Fox Film Corporation

p	Samuel G. Engel
sc	Samuel G. Engel/Winston Miller
ph	Joseph P. MacDonald
m	Cyril J. Mockridge/David Buttolph

NFTVA viewing copy
35mm bw sd 8,646ft 96mins

■ **CAST**

Henry Fonda	Wyatt Earp
Linda Darnell	Chihuahua
Victor Mature	Doc Holliday
Walter Brennan	Old Man Clanton
Cathy Downs	Clementine
Alan Mowbray	Granville Thorndyke

■ **DESCRIPTION** Feature film Western. The story of marshal Wyatt Earp's fight against the Clanton gang at Tombstone, climaxing in the gunfight at the OK Corral. Alan Mowbray plays a drunken actor who is forced to recite in a saloon for the Clanton gang. When he forgets his words from the *Hamlet* soliloquy (A3S1), Victor Mature playing the tubercular Doc Holliday takes his place and completes the soliloquy in somewhat maudlin fashion, ending in a fit of coughing. Given that the fatalistic Holliday is meant to be a tragic figure, the choice is appropriate.

HAMLET

■ **GB • 1948**

d/p	Laurence Olivier
pc	Two Cities
sc	Alan Dent
ph	Desmond Dickinson
des/cost	Roger Furse
art d	Carmen Dillon
m	William Walton

NFTVA viewing copy
35mm bw sd 13,827ft 153mins

■ **CAST**

Laurence Olivier	Hamlet
Eileen Herlie	Queen Gertrude
Basil Sydney	King Claudius
Jean Simmons	Ophelia
Norman Wooland	Horatio
Felix Aylmer	Polonius
Terence Morgan	Laertes

Stanley Holloway . . . . *Gravedigger*
John Laurie . . . . *Francisco*
Esmond Knight . . . . *Bernardo*
Anthony Quayle . . . . *Marcellus*
Niall McGinnis . . . . *Captain*
Harcourt Williams . . . . *Chief Player*
Peter Cushing . . . . *Osric*
Russell Thorndike . . . . *Priest*
Patrick Troughton . . . . *Player King*
Tony Tarver . . . . *Player Queen*

■ **DESCRIPTION** Feature film adaptation of the play. The most famous of all Shakespearean films and the only one to win an Oscar for best film. The opening, where Olivier pronounces that this is simply 'the tragedy of a man who could not make up his mind', instantly sets up a debate between cinema entertainment and faithfulness to the text. The many excisions (as detailed in Alan Dent's published script, noted below), particularly the removal of Rosencrantz and Guildenstern, offended the purists, yet Olivier's literary and theatrical credentials have likewise deterred the cineastes. In truth, though it is a little cold in manner and there is a certain amount of superfluous meandering camera movement, it is nevertheless a dazzling piece of cinema, its compositions, deep focus photography and sheer cinematic verve a marvel to have come from someone still so deeply rooted in the theatrical tradition.

■ **NOTES** Winner at the 1949 Academy Awards for best picture, best actor (Laurence Olivier), best photography, art direction and costumes.

■ **REFERENCES** • Brenda Cross (ed.), *The Film Hamlet: A Record of its Production* (London: The Saturn Press, 1948). • Davies, *Filming Shakespeare's Plays*, pp. 40–64. • Alan Dent (ed.), *Hamlet: The Film and the Play* (London: World Film Publications, 1948). • Manvell, *Shakespeare and the Film*, pp. 40–7.

PARIS 1900

■ **France • 1948**

d/sc   Nicole Védrès
pc   Panthéon
p   Pierre Braunberger
ed   Myriam
m   Guy Bernard

NFTVA viewing copy
French version 35mm bw sd 7,368ft 82mins
English version 35mm bw sd 4,544ft 50mins

■ **DESCRIPTION** Compilation from contemporary film and photographic sources of Parisian life 1900–1914. Includes brief film sequence of the French actor Mounet-Sully in the graveyard scene from *Hamlet* (A5S1).

■ **NOTES** The NFTVA holds both the French and shortened English version; the Mounet-Sully sequence appears in both, preceded by the actor in a scene from *Oedipus Rex*. The date of the material, which came from the Cinémathèque Française, is not known. The French version also contains sequences from *Julius Caesar* and *The Merchant of Venice* (qv).

■ **REFERENCES** • Ball, *Shakespeare on Silent Film*, pp. 108, 329.

ROYALTY HONOURS 'HAMLET' PREMIERE

■ **GB • 1948**

■ *British Movietone News Vol 20 No 988*

pc   British Movietone News
rel date   10 May 1948

NFTVA preservation material
35mm bw sd 115ft 1min

■ **DESCRIPTION** Newsreel item. Royal guests and cabinet ministers arriving for the film première of Laurence Olivier's HAMLET. After the performance members of the cast are presented to the Queen.

■ **NOTES** The item is followed by one on Olivier delivering a speech in Canberra on ANZAC day on the theme that Britain is not finished.

GREAT MOMENTS FROM HAMLET

■ **GB • 1950**

pc   J. Arthur Rank [released by
            Castle Films]

pres   Laurence Olivier

NFTVA preservation material
35mm bw sd 830ft 9mins

■ **CAST**
Laurence Olivier. . . . . *Hamlet*
Jean Simmons . . . . *Ophelia*
Terence Morgan . . . . *Laertes*
Felix Aylmer . . . . *Polonius*

■ **DESCRIPTION** Three extracts from the 1948
HAMLET (A1S2, A1S3, A3S1), compiled for
8mm release via Castle Films. The NFTVA holds
the 35mm original.

KING OF DENMARK SEES HAMLET

■ **GB • 1950**

■ *Television Newsreel 256*

pc   BBC
tx   15 June 1950 (BBC)

NFTVA preservation material
35mm bw sd 190ft 2mins

■ **CAST**
Michael Redgrave . . . . *Hamlet*

■ **DESCRIPTION** Television news item. King
Frederick and Queen Ingrid of Denmark see the
Old Vic production of *Hamlet* at Elsinore, with
Michael Redgrave.

IN BLACK AND WHITE

■ **GB • 1951**

d/sc   John Rowdon
pc   Worldwide Pictures
p   Hindle Edgar
sc   Ronald Anscombe

NFTVA preservation material
35mm bw mu 1,732ft 19mins

■ **DESCRIPTION** Documentary. 'An evocation of
the tradition of British printing.' Includes quotations from a number of Shakespeare's plays, and a

schoolboy giving a hesitant rendition of the 'To be
or not to be' soliloquy (A3S1).

HANCOCK'S 43 MINUTES

■ **GB • 1957**

pc   BBC
tx   23 December 1957 (BBC)
p   Duncan Wood
sc   Ray Galton / Alan Simpson

NFTVA viewing copy
¾" bw sd 43mins

■ **DESCRIPTION** Television comedy Christmas
special. For the finale there is a comic production
of *The Three Musketeers*, with Tony Hancock and
Sid James as musketeers, and guest star John
Gregson as D'Artagnan who makes his entrance
by delivering the 'To be or not to be' soliloquy
(A3S1).

■ **NOTES** Also billed as 'The East Cheam
Repertory Company: Christmas Special', an
extension of Tony Hancock's usual comedy series,
Hancock's Half Hour.

DANGER WITHIN

USA title   BREAKOUT

■ **GB • 1958**

d   Don Chaffey
pc   Colin Lesslie Productions
p   Colin Lesslie
sc   Bryan Forbes
ph   Arthur Grant
m   Francis Chagrin

NFTVA preservation material
35mm bw sd 10,150ft 113mins

■ **CAST**
Richard Todd . . . . *Lt Col David Baird, M.C.*
Bernard Lee. . . . . *Lt Col Huxley*
Michael Wilding. . . . . . . *Major Charles Marquand*
Richard Attenborough. . . *Captain 'Bunter' Phillips*
Dennis Price . . . . *Captain Rupert Callender*

■ **DESCRIPTION** Feature film. A group of British officers in an Italian prisoner-of-war camp are planning to escape by tunnel, but realise that one of their number is a traitor. A more than efficient mixture of standard British war heroics with a mystery element. It is decided that the escape will take place under the cover of the camp performance of *Hamlet*, with Dennis Price in the title role. The play is seen in rehearsal and production during the escape. There is no plot parallel with the play, unless one counts the inclusion of the gravedigger's scene.

PURE HELL OF ST TRINIAN'S, The

■ **GB • 1960**

d	Frank Launder
pc	Vale Film Productions
p	Sidney Gilliat/Frank Launder
sc	Sidney Gilliat/Frank Launder/
	Val Valentine
ph	Gerald Gibbs
m	Malcolm Arnold

NFTVA preservation material
35mm bw sd 8,460ft 94mins

■ **CAST**

Cecil Parker . . . . *Professor Canford*
Joyce Grenfell. . . . . *Sgt Ruby Gates*
George Cole. . . . . *Flash Harry*

■ **DESCRIPTION** Feature film comedy about an unruly girls' school, based on the drawings by Ronald Searle. Short sequence during a 'culture festival' at the school where one of the pupils performs a striptease while reciting the 'To be or not to be' soliloquy (A3S1).

■ **NOTES** Another *Hamlet* striptease occurs in THE MAGIC CHRISTIAN (1969), for which see below. Other films in the St Trinian's series are THE BELLES OF ST TRINIAN'S (1954), BLUE MURDER AT ST TRINIAN'S (1957), THE GREAT ST TRINIAN'S TRAIN ROBBERY (1966) and THE WILDCATS OF ST TRINIAN'S (1980).

HAMLET AT ELSINORE [EXTRACTS]

■ **Denmark/GB 1963**

d	Philip Saville
pc	Danmarks Radio/BBC
tx (GB)	19 April 1964 (BBC)
p	Peter Luke
lght	Robert Wright
cost	Olive Harris

NFTVA preservation material
16mm bw sd 495ft 14mins
Original running time 170mins

■ **CAST**

Christopher Plummer . . . . *Hamlet*
Robert Shaw. . . . . *Claudius*
Michael Caine . . . . *Horatio*
Alec Clunes. . . . . *Polonius*

■ **DESCRIPTION** Extracts from original 1963 footage subsequently used in the television broadcast of the play. Includes Hamlet's meeting with the Ghost (A1S5) and the 'To be or not to be' soliloquy (A3S1).

■ **NOTE** Filmed at Kronborg Castle, Elsinore, in Denmark. Others in a remarkable cast were Donald Sutherland as Polonius, Lindsay Kemp as the Player Queen and Steven Berkoff as Lucianus. Intended as the BBC's main contribution to the Shakespeare quatercentenary celebrations. The first television play to be filmed entirely with outside-broadcast cameras working on location.

■ **REFERENCES** • Kliman, *Hamlet*, pp. 154–67.

GAMLET

English title **HAMLET**

■ **Soviet Union • 1964**

d/sc	Grigori Kozintsev [script based on translation by Boris Pasternak]
pc	Lenfilm
ph	I. Gritsyus
ed	E. Makhankova
art d	E. Ene/G. Kropachev
m	Dmitri Shostakovich

NFTVA viewing copy
35mm bw sd 13,368ft 149 mins
English subtitles

■ **CAST**

Innokenti Smoktunovsky . . . . *Hamlet*
Michail Nazwanov. . . . . *Claudius*
Elza Radzin-Szolkonis . . . . *Queen Gertrude*
Yuri Tolubeyev. . . . . *Polonius*
Anastasia Vertinskaya . . . . *Ophelia*
V. Erenberg . . . . *Horatio*
S. Oleksenko . . . . *Laertes*
V. Medvedev . . . . *Guildenstern*
I. Dmitriev. . . . . *Rosencrantz*
A. Krevald . . . . *Fortinbras*
V. Kolpakor. . . . . *Gravedigger*
A. Chekaerskii . . . . *First Actor*
R. Aren . . . . *Second Actor*
Y. Berkun . . . . *Third Actor*
A. Lauter. . . . . *Priest*

■ **DESCRIPTION** Feature film version of the play, with heavily cut text based on Pasternak translation (inevitably simplified for the English subtitles on this print), with a strong emphasis on visual action and flair. A brooding and impressive visualisation, but a sometimes rather pedestrian interpretation of the actual text.

■ **NOTES** Kozintsev subsequently made KOROL LIR (1970, not in NFTVA), a film of *King Lear* in a similar thoughtful and expressive vein. His two books on Shakespeare and film, that cited below on HAMLET and *King Lear: The Space of Tragedy* on KOROL LIR, are fascinating accounts of the director's deeply considered views on his work.

■ **REFERENCES** • Jorgens, *Shakespeare on Film*, pp. 218–34, 300–4. • Grigori Kozintsev, *Shakespeare: Time and Conscience* (London: Dennis Dobson, 1967). • Manvell, *Shakespeare and the Film*, pp. 77–85.

HAMLET

■ **USA • 1964**

d	Bill Colleran
pc	Electronovision Theatrofilm
p	William Sargent Jnr/
	Alfred W. Crown/John Heyman
lght	Jean Rosenthal/Jim Kilgore
art d/des	Ben Edwards

NFTVA viewing copy
35mm bw sd 17,196ft 191 mins

■ **CAST**

Richard Burton. . . . . *Hamlet*
Hume Cronyn . . . . *Polonius*
Alfred Drake . . . . *Claudius*
Eileen Herlie . . . . *Gertrude*
William Redfield . . . . *Guildenstern*
George Rose . . . . *1st Gravedigger*
George Voskovec. . . . . *Player King*
Philip Coolidge . . . . *Voltimand*
John Cullum. . . . . *Laertes*
Michael Ebert. . . . . *Francisco*
Dillon Evans . . . . *Osric/Reynaldo*
Clement Fowler . . . . *Rosencrantz*
Geoff Garland. . . . . *Lucianus*
Barnard Hughes. . . . . *Marcellus/Priest*
Linda Marsh . . . . *Ophelia*
Robert Milli. . . . . *Horatio*
Frederick Young. . . . . *Barnardo*
Hugh Alexander. . . . . . *Cornelius/2nd Gravedigger/ English Ambassador*
John Gielgud . . . . *Ghost*
John Hetherington . . . . *Player Prologue*
Christopher Culkin . . . . *Player Queen*
Richard Sterne. . . . . *A Gentleman*
Alex Giannini . . . . *A Messenger*

■ **DESCRIPTION** Feature film version of the play, filmed in the Electronovision process by using fifteen cameras covering two performances of the play at the Lunt-Fontanne Theatre in New York. Although visually and aurally not of normal cinema standard, the chief aim of the project was to create an approximation of the John Gielgud theatrical production. In this it is reasonably successful, with spare sets and modern dress, no music, a powerful performance by Burton, and a noteworthy performance as Polonius in Hume Cronyn. Eileen Herlie also played Gertrude in the 1948 Olivier version. There is an intermission break in Reel 5.

■ **NOTES** Filmed over two performances 30 June/1 July 1964 and subsequently relayed to American audiences in cinemas across the country, offering a kind of live theatre experience for cinema audiences who might not otherwise get to the theatre. Given limited release in America as a feature film in September 1964; first shown in Britain at the Shakespeare Film Festival in 1972.

PRINCE MAKER, The

■ **GB • 1964**

■ *Tempo*

pc	ABC Television
tx	13 September 1964 (ITV)
p	Reginald Collin
sc	Derek Prouse
pres	David Mahlowe

NFTVA viewing copy
½" bw sd 21mins

■ **CAST**

John Stride	Hamlet
Pamela Brown	Gertrude
Giorgio Albertazzi	Hamlet
Anna Proclemer	Gertrude

■ **DESCRIPTION** Television arts documentary. Prior to the opening of Franco Zeffirelli's Italian production of *Hamlet* at the National Theatre in London, Zeffirelli is shown directing the scene between Hamlet and his mother (A3S4) with John Stride and Pamela Brown, intercut with the same scene in Zeffirelli's Italian production, filmed in Italy. A well-observed, too brief piece of filming; the Italian scenes having some entertaining differences of opinion over interpretation. The Italian film is conventional.

■ **NOTES** The programme is substantially a repeat of *Tempo*'s A WIND OF CHANGE: THE ART OF FRANCO ZEFFIRELLI (tx 12 April 1964), re-broadcast to coincide with the production appearing at the Old Vic. The British scenes were re-created for the studio; the Italian scenes appear to be extracts from a full-length film. Zeffirelli later made the feature film HAMLET (1990, not in NFTVA) with Mel Gibson as Hamlet.

■ **REFERENCES** • Angus Wilson, *Tempo: The Impact of Television on the Arts* (London: Studio Vista, 1964), pp. 39–40.

SHAKESPEARE WALLAH

■ **India • 1965**

d	James Ivory
pc	Merchant-Ivory Productions

NFTVA viewing copy

■ **CAST**

Felicity Kendal	Ophelia
Laura Liddell	Gertrude
J. D. Tytler	Polonius
Partap Sharma	Laertes
Pincho Kapoor	Claudius

■ **DESCRIPTION** Feature film. The story of a troupe of English actors in India. Includes scenes from a performance of *Hamlet*. The closet scene (A3S4) is mostly seen from the wings or through audience reactions (the actor playing Hamlet is not identified); Ophelia singing (A4S5) is played to camera. For full details of the film see entry in General section.

HAMLET

■ **GB • 1969**

d	Tony Richardson
pc	Woodfall Film Productions
p	Neil Hartley
ph	Gerry Fisher
art d	Jocelyn Herbert
m	Patrick Gowers

NFTVA viewing copy
35mm col sd 10,569ft 117 mins

■ **CAST**

Nicol Williamson	Hamlet
Anthony Hopkins	Claudius
Judy Parfitt	Gertrude
Mark Dignam	Polonius
Marianne Faithfull	Ophelia
Michael Pennington	Laertes
Gordon Jackson	Horatio
Ben Aris	Rosencrantz
Clive Graham	Guildenstern
Peter Gale	Osric
John Carney	Marcellus / Player King
John Trenaman	Barnardo / Player / 2nd Sailor
Robin Chadwick	Francisco / Courtier / Player
Richard Everett	Player / Queen / Courtier
Roger Livesey	Lucianus / Gravedigger
John Railton	1st Sailor / Courtier
Roger Lloyd-Pack	Reynaldo / Courtier
Michael Elphick	Captain / Courtier
Bill Jarvis	Courtier
Ian Collier	Priest / Courtier

Jennifer Tudor . . . . *Court Lady*
Anjelica Huston . . . . *Court Lady*
Mark Griffith . . . . *Messenger / Courtier*

■ **DESCRIPTION** Feature film version of the play, based on Richardson and Williamson's production at the Round House, London, and shot on the stage there. Notable for its extensive use of close-ups and Williamson's brooding performance, a model for the times. A successful blend of the theatrical and cinematic experience from a director well-versed in both worlds.

■ **REFERENCES**
• Kliman, *Hamlet*, pp. 167–79. • Glen Litton, 'Diseased Beauty in Tony Richardson's *Hamlet*', *Literature / Film Quarterly*, Spring 1976, pp. 108–22. • Michael Mullin, 'Tony Richardson's *Hamlet*: Script and Screen', *Literature / Film Quarterly*, Spring 1976, pp. 123–33.

MAGIC CHRISTIAN, The

■ **GB • 1969**

d	Joseph McGrath
pc	Grand Films
p	Denis O'Dell
sc	Joseph McGrath / Terry Southern / Peter Sellers / Graham Chapman / John Cleese
ph	Geoffrey Unsworth
m	Ken Thorne

NFTVA preservation material
35mm col sd 8,550ft 95mins

■ **CAST**
Peter Sellers . . . . *Sir Guy Grand*
Ringo Starr . . . . *Youngman Grand*
Laurence Harvey. . . . . *Hamlet*

■ **DESCRIPTION** Feature film. Satirical comedy, based on the novel by Terry Southern, on the theme that people will do anything for money. Features Laurence Harvey as a famous Shakespearean, who after he has been paid to do so by Peter Sellers, recites the *Hamlet* soliloquy (A3S1) while performing a striptease.

■ **NOTES** For a similar striptease-with-Shakespeare, see THE PURE HELL OF ST TRINIAN'S (1960) above.

PROTEST AND COMMUNICATION

■ **GB • 1969**

■ *Civilisation*

d	Peter Montagnon
pc	BBC
tx	30 March 1969 (BBC2)
p	Michael Gill / Peter Montagnon
ph	A. A. Englander
pres	Kenneth Clark

NFTVA preservation material
16mm col sd 1,800ft 50mins

■ **CAST**
Ian Richardson . . . . *Hamlet*
Patrick Stewart. . . . . *Horatio*
Ronald Lacey . . . . *Gravedigger*
William Devlin . . . . *King Lear*
Eric Porter. . . . . *Voice of Macbeth*

■ **DESCRIPTION** Television documentary in celebrated series tracing the history and progress of Western civilisation. Exploring the theme of protest and communication, Kenneth Clark discusses the Reformation; the Germany of Dürer and Luther, Erasmus, the France of Montaigne and the England of Shakespeare. Illustrating the last are short speeches from *King Lear* and *Macbeth*, and an open-air performance of the graveside scene from *Hamlet* (A5S1).

HAMLET

■ **GB/USA 1970**

■ *Hallmark Hall of Fame*

d	Peter Wood
pc	Chamberlain-LeMaire in association with ATV / Universal Television
tx (US)	17 November 1970 (NBC)
tx (GB)	8 August 1971 (ITV)
p	George LeMaire
adapt	John Barton
des	Peter Roden
m	John Addison

NFTVA viewing copy
½" col sd 115mins

■ **CAST**

Richard Chamberlain. . . . . *Hamlet*
Michael Redgrave . . . . *Polonius*
Margaret Leighton. . . . . *Gertrude*
Richard Johnson . . . . *Claudius*
John Gielgud . . . . *The Ghost*
Ciaran Madden . . . . *Ophelia*
Nigel Stock . . . . *The First Player*
Norman Rossington . . . . *The Gravedigger*
Alan Bennett. *Osric*
Martin Shaw . . . . *Horatio*
Nicholas Jones. . . . . *Laertes*
James Laurenson . . . . *Rosencrantz*
Desmond MacNamara. . . . . *Guildenstern*
Godfrey James . . . . *Marcellus*
Philip Brack. . . . . *Barnardo*
Robert Oates . . . . *Francisco*
Robert Coleby. . . . . *Fortinbras*
Donald Layne-Smith . . . . *Priest*
Helen Bourne/David Belcher/Alan Adams/
Stephen Williams/Donald Barclay . . . . . . *Players*

■ **DESCRIPTION** Television production of the play, adapted by John Barton, first broadcast in the USA in 1970 and in Britain in 1971. Very much a romantic conception of the play, in its Regency costumes, rich settings and the casting of 'Dr Kildare' in the leading role. A simple interpretation, but put over with clarity and handsomely designed. The location shooting is less successful, with some poor post-synching. Martin Shaw is a personable Horatio, and Richard Chamberlain tries hard.

■ **NOTES** Filmed over six months with much location shooting in England; Hamlet's castle is Raby Castle in Durham. The production was nominated for thirteen Emmys and won five (for scenery, lighting, sound, costumes and Margaret Leighton). Chamberlain decided to make the film after a successful performance as Hamlet with Birmingham Rep., forming a production company with George LeMaire to do so. The first *Hallmark Hall of Fame* Shakespeare production in 1953 was also of *Hamlet* (not in NFTVA).

■ **REFERENCES** • Kliman, *Hamlet*, pp. 180–7.

EVERYTHING YOU ALWAYS WANTED TO KNOW ABOUT SEX, BUT WERE AFRAID TO ASK

■ **USA • 1972**

d/sc	Woody Allen
pc	United Artists
p	Charles H. Joffe
ph	David M. Walsh
m	Mundell Lowe

NFTVA preservation material
35mm col sd 7,830ft 87mins

■ **CAST**

Woody Allen . . . . *The Fool*
Anthony Quayle. . . . . *The King*
Lynn Redgrave . . . . *The Queen*

■ **DESCRIPTION** Feature film comedy comprising seven sketches inspired by questions raised in the book of the same title by Dr David Reuben. In the first sketch, 'Do Aphrodisiacs Work?', Woody Allen plays a court jester. He recites a parody of the soliloquy (A3S1), 'T.B. not T.B.'.

THEATRE OF BLOOD

■ **GB • 1973**

d	Douglas Hickox
pc	Cineman

NFTVA preservation material

■ **CAST**

Vincent Price . . . . *Edward Lionheart*

■ **DESCRIPTION** Feature film. An actor (Vincent Price) murders his critics in the manner of deaths from Shakespeare's plays. In a flashback sequence, Lionheart confronts the critics who have denied him the Critics Circle award for best actor, then goes out onto a balcony and recites the *Hamlet* soliloquy (A3S1) before jumping into the Thames. He survives. For full details of the film see entry in General section.

HAMLET

■ **GB • 1976**

d/p/sc	Celestino Coronado
pc	Royal College of Art
ed	Richard Melling

ph   Robina Rose/Dick Perrin/
        Andy Humphries/R. Anthony
cost   Mircea Marosin
sets   Celestine Coronado/Anthony Meyer
        et al
m   Carlos Miranda

NFTVA viewing copy
16mm col sd 2,378ft 66mins

■ **CAST**
Anthony Meyer and
   David Meyer . . . . *Hamlet/Hamlet's Father*
Helen Mirren . . . . *Gertrude/Ophelia*
Quentin Crisp . . . . *Polonius*
Barry Stanton . . . . *Claudius*
Vladek Sheybal . . *1st Player/Player Queen/Lucianus*
Valentine Moon
Sally Bentley-Leek
Marina Saura
Inno Sorcy
Jonathan O'Hara
Henry-Jean
Kazimir Janus

■ **DESCRIPTION** Feature film adaptation of the
play. An abbreviated version of the play with the
overall intention of presenting Hamlet as a split
personality, most clearly by casting two actors
(twins) to play him. Despite the inevitable short-
comings of a minuscule budget and one week's
shooting schedule, this is a most thought-provok-
ing production, paradoxically drawing emphasis
on the verse by accentuating the visual effect, 'an
examination of modes of representation and of
plastic/dramatic imagery' (Tim Pulleine, *Monthly
Film Bulletin*). But not a film for those unac-
quainted with the play.

■ **NOTES** Shot on video and transferred to
16mm.

MEPHISTO

■ **Hungary • 1981**

d   István Szabó
pc   Mafilm/Manfred Durniok
        Productions
p sup   Lajos Óvári
sc   Péter Dobai/István Szabó
ph   Lajos Koltai
m   Zdenko Tamássy

NFTVA preservation material
35mm col sd 12,960ft 144mins
English subtitles

■ **CAST**
Klaus Maria Brandauer . . . . *Henrik Höfgen*
Ildikó Bánsági . . . . *Nicoletta von Niebuhr*
Krystyna Janda . . . . *Barbara Bruckner*

■ **DESCRIPTION** Feature film, based on the novel
by Klaus Mann. The career of an ambitious actor
in 1920s and 30s Germany and his compromises
during the Nazi regime. The film concludes with
the preparations for his triumphant 'Nazi' production of *Hamlet*, but he is taken away and
humiliated at the Berlin Olympic Games.

HAMLET

■ **GB • 1983**

■ *Shakespeare Lives*

d   Mary McMurray
pc   Quintet Films
tx   16 March 1983 (C4)
p   Victor Glynn/Mike Ockrent

NFTVA preservation material
1" col sd c60mins

■ **CAST**
Clive Arrindell
Suzanne Bertish
Michael Bryant
Joss Buckley
John Darrell
John Labanowski
Dinsdale Landen
Bill Wallis

■ **DESCRIPTION** Television theatre workshop.
Michael Bogdanov leads a group of National
Theatre actors through scenes from *Hamlet*; a discussion is held with a studio audience on the
play's themes and relevance – is it about the
Oedipal conflict, or does it have something to say
about modern power-politics? One of an excellent series combining provocative analysis from
Bogdanov, fascinating insights into the work in
progress and lively contributions from members
of the audience.

■ **NOTES** Other plays covered in this series are *Measure for Measure, Richard III, The Taming of the Shrew, The Tempest* and *Timon of Athens* (qqv).

ENGLISHMAN ABROAD, An

■ **GB • 1983**

d	John Schlesinger
pc	BBC
tx	29 November 1983 (BBC1)
p	Innes Lloyd
sc	Alan Bennett
ph	Nat Crosby
m	George Fenton

NFTVA viewing copy
½" col sd 62mins

■ **CAST**
Alan Bates . . . . *Guy Burgess*
Coral Browne. . . . . *Herself/Gertrude*
Charles Gray . . . . *Claudius*
Mark Wing-Davey. . . . . *Hamlet*
Harold Innocent . . . . *Rosencrantz*
Vernon Dobtcheff. . . . . *Guildenstern*

■ **DESCRIPTION** Television drama. Much-praised recreation of the meeting between actress Coral Browne and British spy and defector Guy Burgess, in Moscow in 1958. The initial meeting takes place at a theatre, where Browne (who plays herself) is appearing as Gertrude in a Royal Shakespeare Company performance of *Hamlet*. Includes two sequences from the play in performance: the introduction of Rosencrantz and Guildenstern (A2S2) and Hamlet after the death of Polonius and the entrance of the King and Queen (A3S4/A4S1). If there are parallels intended between Hamlet and Guy Burgess they are not made clear.

■ **NOTES** NFTVA viewing copy recorded off-air 17 August 1992 as part of BBC2's Alan Bennett retrospective.

TO BE OR NOT TO BE

■ **USA • 1983**

d	Alan Johnson
pc	Brooksfilms

p	Mel Brooks
sc	Thomas Meehan/Ronny Graham
ph	Gerald Hirschfeld
m	John Morris

NFTVA preservation material
35mm col sd 9,657ft 107mins

■ **CAST**
Mel Brooks . . . . *Frederick Bronski*
Anne Bancroft. . . . . *Anna Bronski*
Tim Matheson. . . . . *Andre Sobinski*
Charles Durning . . . . *Colonel Erhardt*

■ **DESCRIPTION** Feature film. Competent but unnecessary remake of the 1942 Lubitsch film (see above). Mel Brooks is seen in similar fashion to Jack Benny as Hamlet.

WITHNAIL & I

■ **GB • 1986**

d/sc	Bruce Robinson
pc	HandMade Films
p	Paul Heller
ph	Peter Hannan
m	David Dundas/Rick Wentworth

NFTVA viewing copy
35mm col sd 9,659ft 107mins

■ **CAST**
Richard E. Grant . . . . *Withnail*
Paul McGann . . . . *&I [Marwood]*
Richard Griffiths . . . . *Monty*

■ **DESCRIPTION** Feature film. Excellent, unusual comedy-drama about two unemployed actors taking a holiday in the Lake District in 1969. Richard Griffiths, as Withnail's lecherous uncle, quotes variously from *Hamlet*, and the films ends memorably with Richard E. Grant, standing in the rain in Regent's Park having just said goodbye to McGann, turning to the camera and delivering the speech 'I have of late (but wherefore I know not) lost all my mirth' (A2S2). The closing line, 'no, nor woman neither' is emphatically repeated.

■ **NOTES** The story is a semi-autobiographical account of writer-director Bruce Robinson's own experiences. Among his acting credits is Benvolio in Zeffirelli's ROMEO AND JULIET (1968, qv).

OTHER PEOPLE'S DREAMS

■ GB • 1986

■ *The Inner Eye*

d/p	Andrew Snell
pc	Artifax Productions
tx	5 May 1986 (C4)
m	Stephen Oliver
pres	Nicholas Humphrey

NFTVA viewing copy
½" col sd 52mins

■ **CAST**
Simon Callow . . . . *Hamlet*
Geraldine James . . . . *Gertrude*

■ **DESCRIPTION** Television documentary. Programme in series on human consciousness. Psychologist Nicholas Humphrey discusses why we care about fictional characters, using as illustration a performance from *Hamlet* (A3S4). During the five-minute sequence Humphrey comments on his involvement in the action from the audience.

■ **NOTES** The *Hamlet* sequence is preceded by scenes in the Haymarket Theatre, and was apparently filmed there, but there was no such production at the Haymarket, the play being staged specially for the programme.

OPHELIA BY JOHN EVERETT MILLAIS

■ GB • 1988

■ *Masterworks*

d/p	Reiner Moritz
pc	RM Arts
tx	11 January 1988 (C4)
sc/nar	Edwin Mullins

NFTVA viewing copy
½" col sd 10mins

■ **DESCRIPTION** Television documentary. Edwin Mullins discusses John Everett Millais' painting 'Ophelia' in the Tate Gallery in London.

CAUGHT IN THE ACT

■ GB • 1988

d/p	Mary Gwatkin
pc	Reconnaissance Films/MV Films
tx	26 December 1988 (C4)

NFTVA viewing copy

■ **CAST**
Kenneth Branagh . . . . *Hamlet*
Sophie Thompson . . . . *Ophelia*
David Parfitt . . . . *Rosencrantz*
Jay Villiers . . . . *Laertes*

■ **DESCRIPTION** Television documentary on the work of Kenneth Branagh's Renaissance Theatre Company, in particular its three touring productions of *As You Like It*, *Hamlet* and *Much Ado About Nothing*. *Hamlet* is shown in rehearsal and production at Elsinore, Denmark, in the presence of the King and Queen of Denmark. Derek Jacobi comments on his approach to directing the play, and there are numerous extracts from rehearsal and performance, including the 'To be or not to be' soliloquy (A3S1), Hamlet's speech to the players (A3S2), Hamlet talking with Rosencrantz (A3S2), 'The play's the thing' (A2S2), Laertes' reaction to Ophelia's madness (A4S5) and the final scene. For full details of the programme see entry in General section.

NIGHT OF COMIC RELIEF 2, A

■ GB • 1989

pc	BBC
tx	10 March 1989 (BBC2)
hosts	Lenny Henry/Griff Rhys Jones/ Jonathan Ross

NFTVA viewing copy
½"col sd 377mins

■ **CAST**
Jonathan Pryce . . . . *Hamlet*
Harry Enfield . . . . *Hamlet's Dead Dad*

■ **DESCRIPTION** Television charity variety revue. An evening of comedy acts, classic comedy shows and reports on charitable causes benefiting from the programme, in Africa and Britain. Includes

Jonathan Pryce and comedian Harry Enfield in his 'Stavros' guise, with a four-minute item entitled 'Hamlet by the Stavros Shakespearian Players', based on A1S4/5 where Hamlet meets his father's ghost.

■ **NOTES** The programme also includes a brief excerpt from a celebrated version of the balcony scene in *Romeo and Juliet* with comedian Lenny Henry as Romeo and boxer Frank Bruno as Juliet, from the original Comic Relief stage show (tx 24 April 1986, not in NFTVA). The first A NIGHT OF COMIC RELIEF was broadcast in 1988 and features a spoof on *Macbeth* (qv).

(HAMLET)

■ **GB • 1989**

■ *South Bank Show*

d/p	Chris Hunt
pc	An Iambic Production for LWT
tx	2 April 1989 (ITV)
ed/pres	Melvyn Bragg

NFTVA viewing copy
½" col sd 52mins

■ **DESCRIPTION** Television arts documentary. Documentary on *Hamlet* and its many different interpretations and performances, roughly following the narrative line of the play. The impetus was the three 1989 productions of the play directed by Richard Eyre (National Theatre), Yuri Lyubimov (touring production) and Ron Daniels (RSC), all of whom are interviewed, along with John Barton, Michael Pennington (who gives readings), Mark Rylance (the RSC Hamlet), and archive interviews with Tyrone Guthrie (1960) and Orson Welles (1963). An entertaining introduction to the play in the *South Bank Show*'s better manner, it is illustrated with numerous clips from film and television versions, of which those not otherwise held by the NFTVA are a brief glimpse of Sarah Bernhardt from 1900 (credited as 1899 on screen), John Barrymore's colour screen test from 1933, Charles Marowitz's *Collage Hamlet* (1969), Jonathan Pryce possessed by his father's ghost (Royal Court, 1980), Derek Jacobi from the BBC series (1980) and Rylance in rehearsal (A4S3).

■ **NOTES** Sarah Bernhardt made a film of the duelling scene from *Hamlet* in 1900 (with Pierre Magnier as Laertes). Ball gives a detailed account of how it was accompanied by phonograph sound effects at the Paris Exposition of 1900. The short clip shows Hamlet's falling body being caught by Horatio. In 1933 John Barrymore made a colour test for an unrealised film version of *Hamlet*, performing the 'O, what a rogue and peasant slave am I!' soliloquy (A2S2) and the ghost scene (A1S5, shown here). The Jonathan Pryce scenes are from an earlier edition of the *South Bank Show* (tx 1 June 1980, not in NFTVA).

■ **REFERENCES** ● Ball, *Shakespeare on Silent Film*, pp. 23–8, 304–5 [on Bernhardt].

MIDSUMMER NIGHT'S MYSTERY, A

■ **GB • 1989**

■ *First Tuesday*

d/p	Kevin Sim
pc	Yorkshire Television
tx	4 July 1989 (ITV)

NFTVA viewing copy
½" col sd 51mins

■ **CAST**
Nicholas Gecks . . . . *Hamlet*
Patrick O'Connell . . . . *Polonius*

■ **DESCRIPTION** Television documentary on the claims for Edward de Vere, Earl of Oxford to be the true author of Shakespeare's works. The arguments for and against are intercut with speeches from *Hamlet* delivered mostly by Nicholas Gecks in Hedingham Castle. For full details of the programme see entry in General section.

GREAT EXPECTATIONS: CHAPTER FOUR

■ **GB/USA 1989**

d	Kevin Connor
pc	Disney Channel/HTV/Primetime/ Tesauro Television

tx (USA) 30 July 1989 (Disney Channel)
tx (GB) 11 August 1991 (ITV)
p Greg Smith
sc John Goldsmith

NFTVA viewing copy
½"col sd 48mins

■ **CAST**
Anthony Hopkins . . . . *Magwitch*
Jean Simmons . . . . *Miss Havisham*
Ray McAnally . . . . *Mr Jaggers*
Anthony Calf . . . . *Pip*
Kim Thomson . . . . *Estella*
John Quentin . . . . *Mr Wopsle / Hamlet*

■ **DESCRIPTION** Fourth episode in television mini-series, based on the novel by Charles Dickens. Features a performance from a badly acted *Hamlet*, with Mr Wopsle in the title role giving the 'To be or not to be' soliloquy (A3S1).

■ **NOTES** The NFTVA copy is an off-air recording of the British transmission.

LATE SHOW, The

■ **GB** • **1989**

d Rena Butterwick
item d Samira Osman
pc BBC
tx 14 September 1989 (BBC2)
ed Michael Jackson
rep Michael Goldfarb

NFTVA viewing copy
½" col sd 43mins [item 16mins]

■ **CAST**
Daniel Webb . . . . *Hamlet*
Veronica Smart . . . . *Ophelia*
Richard Durden . . . . *Polonius*
Andrew Jarvis . . . . *Claudius*

■ **DESCRIPTION** Television arts magazine. Includes item on Russian theatre director Yuri Lyubimov's British production of *Hamlet*, in rehearsal at the Leicester Haymarket Theatre. Lyubimov directs through a translator, assistant director Michael Wasserman, who explains how he has to tone down Lyubimov's instructions for English consumption. The actors reflect on the experience and the change from British theatrical practices. Shows the distinctive staging, including the use of a huge curtain.

LATE SHOW, The

■ **GB** • **1989**

d Janet Fraser Crook
item d Renee Knight
pc BBC
tx 22 November 1989 (BBC2)
ed Michael Jackson

NFTVA viewing copy
½" col sd 38mins [item 9mins]

■ **DESCRIPTION** Television arts magazine. Includes item on Michael Bogdanov's role as artistic director of the Deutsches Schauspielhaus in Hamburg, featuring extracts from his production of *Hamlet*: the 'To be or not to be' soliloquy (A3S1), and Hamlet's fight with Laertes (A5S1).

HYSTERIA 2

■ **GB** • **1989**

d David Croft
pc Tiger Television
tx 1 December 1989 (C4)
p Trevor Hopkins
event d Stephen Fry

NFTVA viewing copy
½" col sd 108mins

■ **CAST**
Hugh Laurie . . . . *William Shakespeare*
Rowan Atkinson

■ **DESCRIPTION** Television charity variety revue. Comedy and music acts performing on World AIDS Day. Includes a sketch with Rowan Atkinson and Hugh Laurie (as Shakespeare) discussing the need for cuts in *Hamlet* and the 'To be or not to be' soliloquy (A3S1).

■ **NOTES** The first HYSTERIA programme was broadcast in 1987.

HAMLET

VOICE OVER QUEEN, The

■ **USA • 1990**

d/sc	Alyse Rosenberg
pc	Alyse & Her Big Ideas
p	Paula Schaap
ph	Claudia Raschke
m	Lesley Barber

NFTVA viewing copy
½" col sd 12mins

■ **CAST**
Joan La Barbara. . . . . *Naomi Strutski*

■ **DESCRIPTION** Fiction short. Odd, stylised drama about an actress expert in making noises to match household appliances in television commercials. Seeking something better, she fails an audition to play Hamlet but gives a recitation of the 'To be or not to be' soliloquy (A3S1) to a room full of household appliances which applaud her afterwards.

■ **NOTES** The NFTVA's copy is an off-air recording from British television, 20 July 1992 (C4).

JFK

■ **USA • 1991**

d	Oliver Stone
pc	Warner Bros.
p	A. Kitman Ho/Oliver Stone
sc	Oliver Stone/Zachary Sklar
ph	Robert Richardson
m	John Williams

NFTVA preservation material
35mm col sd 16,974ft

■ **CAST**
Kevin Costner . . . . *Jim Garrison*
Gary Oldman. . . . . *Lee Harvey Oswald*
Tommy Lee Jones . . . . *Clay Shaw*
Sissy Spacek. . . . . *Liz Garrison*

■ **DESCRIPTION** Feature film. District Attorney Jim Garrison uncovers the conspiracy behind the assassination of President John Kennedy. A hysterical and unbalanced fusillade of political paranoia, with some intriguing and apparently intentional *Hamlet* parallels. At one point Garrison pronounces, 'We have all become Hamlets in our country, children of a slain father-leader whose killers still possess the throne. The ghost of John Kennedy confronts us with the secret murder at the heart of the American dream.' Stone apparently originally intended to have the ghost of Kennedy appear to Garrison.

■ **REFERENCES** • Alexander Cockburn, 'John and Oliver's Bogus Adventure', *Sight and Sound*, February 1992, pp. 22–4.

BEST OF TOMMY COOPER, The

■ **GB • 1991**

pc	Thames Television
tx	23 July 1991 (ITV)
exec p	John Fisher

NFTVA viewing copy
½" col sd 24mins

■ **DESCRIPTION** Television comedy compilation. Highlights from the career of comedian and failed magician Tommy Cooper, including his attempt at the 'To be or not to be' soliloquy (A3S1) (original transmission date not known).

PACKET OF 3

■ **GB • 1991**

d	John Stroud
pc	Jon Blair Film Company
tx	20 September 1991 (C4)

NFTVA viewing copy

■ **DESCRIPTION** Television comedy series. Individual programme arranged around the theme of Shakespeare, with spoof performances including the duel scene from *Hamlet* performed by two accordionists playing 'Duelling Banjos'. The Reduced Shakespeare Company perform a 47 second version of *Hamlet* followed by one of 3 seconds. For further details of their contribution and full details of the programme see entry in General section.

■ **NOTES** The Reduced Shakespeare Company

repeat the same versions of *Hamlet* in the children's programme WHAT'S UP DOC? (tx 12 September 1992, see General section).

SPITTING IMAGE

■ **GB • 1992**

d	Steve Bendelack / Andy De Emmony
pc	Spitting Image Productions
tx	3 May 1992 (ITV)
p	Bill Dare

NFTVA viewing copy
½" col sd 24mins

■ **DESCRIPTION** Television satirical puppet show. Includes two brief sketches, one where film director Michael Winner tries to direct television presenter Jim Bowen as Hamlet, the other where the producers of a new production of *Hamlet* vainly test a number of actresses for the part of Ophelia. A dog named Fifi Redgrave turns up and gets the part instantly.

TECTONIC PLATES

■ **GB • 1992**

d/adapt	Peter Mettler
pc	Hauer Rawlence Productions
tx	2 January 1993 (C4)
p	Debra Hauer / Niv Fichman

NFTVA viewing copy
½" col sd 95mins

■ **CAST**
Marie Gignac . . . . *Madeleine*
Robert Lepage. . . . . *Jacques/Jennifer*
Celine Bonnier . . . . *Constance*

■ **DESCRIPTION** Television adaptation of Robert Lepage's experimental stage drama. The movements of the earth's crust are used as a metaphor for the conflicts and interactions between people on different continents. Crossing from continent to continent Madeleine, a French-Canadian painter, encounters various 'spirits', including Jim Morrison, Frédéric Chopin, Oprah Winfrey and Shakespeare's Ophelia.

■ **NOTES** Robert Lepage's dark and muddy interpretation of *A Midsummer Night's Dream* was presented at the National Theatre in 1992.

HAMLET

■ **GB • 1993**

d	Roger Jenkins
RSC credits:	
d	Adrian Noble
des	Bob Crowley
lght	Alan Burrett
m	Guy Woolfenden

NFTVA preservation material
½" col sd 255mins

■ **CAST**
Anthony Douse . . . . *Barnardo/Priest*
David Birrell . . . . *Francisco/Lucianus*
Tim Hudson. . . . . *Marcellus/Player*
Rob Edwards . . . . *Horatio*
Clifford Rose . . . . *Ghost of Hamlet's father*
John Shrapnel . . . . *Claudius*
Jane Lapotaire. . . . . *Gertrude*
Kenneth Branagh. . . . . *Hamlet*
Richard Clothier . . . . *Cornelius*
Peter Bygott . . . . *Voltemand*
David Bradley . . . . *Polonius*
Richard Bonneville . . . . *Laertes*
Joanne Pearce . . . . *Ophelia*
Ian Hughes . . . . *Reynaldo/Fortinbras*
Michael Gould . . . . *Rosencrantz*
Angus Wright . . . . *Guildenstern*
Jonathan Newth. . . . . *Player King*
Sian Radinger . . . . *Player Queen*
Howard Crossley . . . . . *Player/Second Gravedigger*
Kenn Sabberton . . . . *Player/Norwegian Captain/Messenger*
Virginia Denham . . . . *Player/Gentlewoman*
Richard Moore . . . . *First Gravedigger*
Guy Henry . . . . *Osric*
Nick Simons . . . . *English Ambassador*

■ **DESCRIPTION** Video recording of the Royal Shakespeare Company production of *Hamlet* at the Barbican Theatre, London. The second of the first two National Video Archive of Stage Performance recordings (along with RICHARD III from 1992, qv), intended not as commercial entertainment but as a simple record and an invaluable tool for future researchers. The production itself, which first opened at the Barbican in December 1992, was a rare performance of a very full version of the text.

■ **NOTES** Recorded on 9 March 1993. Filmed with three video cameras, one (fixed) giving a view of the full stage in long shot, the other two (controlled) giving closer shots of the players as seen from left and right. The intention is to create a video record of the stage performance without editorial interference, and the recordings are to be viewed simultaneously on three adjacent monitors, allowing the researcher to select the desired image. Viewing copies are held at the Theatre Museum, Covent Garden, with the master tapes held by the NFTVA. For further details see the entry for the National Video Archive of Stage Performance in the Archives and Libraries section.

■ **REFERENCES** • *Viewfinder*, February 1993, no. 17, pp. 11–13 [on the plans for the Archive].

HENRY IV

CAMPANADAS A MEDIANOCHE

GB title CHIMES AT MIDNIGHT
USA title FALSTAFF

■ **Spain/Switzerland 1966**

d/sc	Orson Welles
pc	Internacional Films/Alpine
p	Emiliano Piedra/Angel Escolano
ph	Edmond Richard
art d	José Antonio de la Guerra/ Mariano Erdorza
m	Angelo Francesco Lavagnio
nar	Ralph Richardson

NFTVA preservation material
35mm bw sd 10,350ft 115mins

■ **CAST**

Orson Welles	*Sir John Falstaff*
Keith Baxter	*Prince Hal*
John Gielgud	*King Henry IV*

Orson Welles (Falstaff) and Jeanne Moreau (Doll Tearsheet) in CAMPANADAS A MEDIANOCHE (1966)

Margaret Rutherford	*Mistress Quickly*
Jeanne Moreau	*Doll Tearsheet*
Norman Rodway	*Henry Percy*
Marina Vlady	*Kate Percy*
Alan Webb	*Justice Shallow*
Tony Beckley	*Poins*
Fernando Rey	*Worcester*
Walter Chiari	*Silence*
Michael Aldridge	*Pistol*
Beatrice Welles	*Falstaff's page*
Andrew Faulds	*Westmoreland*
José Nieto	*Northumberland*
Jeremy Rowe	*Prince John*
Paddy Bedford	*Bardolph*

■ **DESCRIPTION** Feature film. The story of Sir John Falstaff, his friendship with Prince Hal and his rejection by Hal when the latter becomes King Henry V, adapted from Shakespeare's *Richard II*, *1 Henry IV*, *2 Henry IV*, *Henry V* and *The Merry Wives of Windsor*. Not the most immediately approachable of Shakespearean films, but probably the most outstanding, certainly the one with the most sense of collaboration between film-maker and playwright. There are problems with the soundtrack, which seems bewilderingly separated from the images, but even this gradually takes on a hypnotic, natural quality. Welles plays Falstaff as a tragic figure, 'almost entirely a good man' and in focusing the plays together has created a genuine film tragedy, a reduction that would not work on stage yet takes its lead from the cinematic indications offered by the structure and language of the plays.

■ **NOTES** The film developed out of Welles's 'Five Kings' project, an ill-fated attempt to stage a condensed version of the Bolingbroke/Falstaff plays (for further details see footnote 20 to opening essay and Richard France below). The narration is taken from Holinshed's *Chronicles*. The film was made in Spain, mostly in locations around Barcelona. The NFTVA holds the English version; the Spanish version ran for 119 mins. 'It is funnier in the English version than in Spanish' (Welles).

■ **REFERENCES** • Juan Cobos and Miguel Rubio, 'Welles and Falstaff', *Sight and Sound*, Autumn 1966, pp. 158–63. • Davies, *Filming Shakespeare's Plays*, pp. 119–42. • Richard France, *The Theatre of Orson Welles* (Lewisburg: Bucknell University Press, 1977), pp. 155–70. • Robert Hapgood, 'Chimes at Midnight from Stage to Screen: the Art of Adaptation', *Shakespeare Survey* 39, 1987, pp. 39–52. • Jorgens, *Shakespeare on Film*, pp. 106–21, 268–72. • Bridget Gellert Lyons (ed.), *Chimes at Midnight* (New Brunswick/London: Rutgers University Press, 1988). • Manvell, *Shakespeare and the Film*, pp. 64–70.

HENRY IV PART TWO

■ **GB/USA 1979**

■ *BBC Television Shakespeare*

d	David Giles
pc	BBC/Time-Life Films
tx (GB)	16 December 1979 (BBC2)
tx (US)	9 April 1980 (PBS)
p	Cedric Messina
sc ed	Alan Shallcross
lght	Dennis Channon
des	Don Homfray
cost	Odette Barrow

NFTVA preservation material
16mm col sd 5,343ft 148mins

■ **CAST**

Jon Finch	*King Henry IV*
David Gwillim	*Henry, Prince of Wales*
Rob Edwards	*Prince John of Lancaster*
Martin Neil	*Prince Humphrey of Gloucester*
Roger Davenport	*Thomas, Duke of Clarence*
Bruce Purchase	*Earl of Northumberland*
David Neal	*Scroop, Archbishop of York*
Michael Miller	*Lord Mowbray*
Richard Bebb	*Lord Hastings*
John Humphry	*Lord Bardolph*
Salvin Stewart	*Sir John Colville*
David Strong	*Travers*
Carol Oatley	*Morton*
Rod Beacham	*Earl of Warwick*
David Buck	*Earl of Westmoreland*
Brian Poyser	*Gower*
Ralph Michael	*Lord Chief Justice*
Tim Brown	*Servant to Lord Chief Justice*
Anthony Quayle	*Sir John Falstaff*
Jack Galloway	*Poins*
Gordon Gostelow	*Bardolph*
Bryan Pringle	*Pistol*
Steven Beard	*Peto*
John Fowler	*Page to Sir John Falstaff*
Colin Dunn	*Messenger*
Robert Eddison	*Justice Robert Shallow*
Leslie French	*Justice Silence*
Raymond Platt	*Davy, servant to Shallow*
Frederick Proud	*Fang, Sheriff's officer*
Julian Battersby	*Ralph Mouldy*
Roy Herrick	*Simon Shadow*
Alan Collins	*Thomas Wart*
John Tordoff	*Francis Feeble*
Roger Elliott	*Peter Bullcalf*
Jenny Laird	*Lady Northumberland*
Michele Dotrice	*Lady Percy, Hotspur's widow*
Brenda Bruce	*Hostess Quickly*
Frances Cuka	*Doll Tearsheet*

■ **DESCRIPTION** Television production of the play. The BBC series showed *1 Henry IV* (not in NFTVA), *2 Henry IV* and *Henry V* in succession with the same cast throughout, as they subsequently did for the *Henry VI* trilogy and *Richard III* (not in NFTVA). As with most of the BBC series, the production was routine but the performances at the very least professional, and in Anthony Quayle's case subtle and richly memorable.

■ **REFERENCES** • Pilkington, *Screening Shakespeare*, pp. 64–86 [discussing the two *Henry IV* plays]. • *Radio Times*, 15–21 December 1979, pp. 92–101 [article on all three Henry plays]

Laurence Olivier in HENRY V (1944)

HENRY V

ELSTREE CALLING

■ **GB • 1930**

d   Adrian Brunel
pc   British International Pictures

NFTVA viewing copy

■ **DESCRIPTION** Feature film of variety acts in revue, hosted by Tommy Handley and featuring many celebrated British performers of the day. Interspersed throughout the film is a running sketch featuring Donald Calthrop as someone determined to put on Shakespeare. This includes him delivering a patriotic rendition of the 'Once more unto the breach, dear friends' speech (A3S1) in front of a huge Union Jack while performing a number of magic tricks. For full details of the film see the entry under *The Taming of the Shrew*.

ROYAL CAVALCADE

■ **GB • 1935**

d   Herbert Brenon/Norman Lee/
        Walter Summers/Will Kellino

sup d   Thomas Bentley
pc   British International Pictures
p   Frank Mills/Roy Goddard/
        Jack Martin/Donald Wilson/
        B. Horne/John Sloan
sc   Val Gielgud/Holt Marvell/
        Marjorie Deans
ph   Jack Cox/H. Wheddon/
        Bryan Langley/L. Rowson/
        P. Grindrod
m   Walter Collins

NFTVA viewing copy
35mm bw sd 9,224ft 103mins

■ **CAST**
Marie Lohr . . . . *Mother*
Hermione Baddeley . . . . *Barmaid*
Frank Vosper . . . . *Captain Scott*
Alice Lloyd . . . . *Marie Lloyd*
Matheson Lang . . . . *Henry V*

■ **DESCRIPTION** Compilation of actuality film, fiction film extracts and reconstructions, showing events and aspects of British life during the 25 years of King George V's reign. Amongst a huge cast, including such people as Lady Astor and Florrie Forde appearing as themselves, Matheson Lang appears briefly as Henry V and delivers the Agincourt speech (A4S3).

■ **NOTES** The film was the British film industry's contribution to the Silver Jubilee celebrations of King George V.

JACK OF ALL TRADES

■ **GB • 1936**

d   Jack Hulbert/Robert Stevenson
pc   Gainsborough Pictures
sc   J. O. C. Orton
ph   Charles Van Enger
m   M. Sigler/A. Goodhart/A. Hoffman

NFTVA viewing copy
35mm bw sd 6,836ft 76 mins

■ **CAST**
Jack Hulbert . . . . *Jack Warrender*
Gina Malo . . . . *Frances Wilson*
Robertson Hare . . . . *Fitch*

■ **DESCRIPTION** Musical comedy. Naïve, happy satire featuring the irrepressible Jack Hulbert as a penniless young man who bluffs his way into big business. To stir spirits at a board meeting to discuss his proposal for a shoe factory, he delivers an abbreviated version of the 'Once more unto the breach, dear friends' speech from *Henry V* (A3S1), with the desired results.

HENRY V

■ **GB • 1944**

d	Laurence Olivier ['in close association with the editor Reginald Beck']
pc	Two Cities
assoc p	Dallas Bower
p	Laurence Olivier
text ed	Alan Dent
ph	Robert Krasker
art d	Paul Sheriff
cost	Roger Furse
m	William Walton

NFTVA viewing copy
35mm col sd 12,332ft 137mins

■ **CAST**

Laurence Olivier . . . . . . *King Henry V of England*
Robert Newton . . . . *Ancient Pistol*
Leslie Banks . . . . *Chorus*
Renée Asherson . . . . *Princess Katherine*
Esmond Knight . . . . *Fluellen*
Leo Genn . . . . *Constable of France*
Felix Aylmer . . . . *Archbishop of Canterbury*
Ralph Truman . . . . . . *Mountjoy, the French Herald*
Nicholas Hannen . . . . *Duke of Exeter*
Harcourt Williams . . . . . *King Charles VI of France*
Robert Helpmann . . . . *Bishop of Ely*
Ivy St Helier . . . . *Alice, lady-in-waiting*
Freda Jackson . . . . *Mistress Quickly*
Ernest Thesiger . . . . *Duke of Berri, the French Ambassador*
Jimmy Hanley . . . *Williams, soldier in English camp*
Max Adrian . . . . *The Dauphin*
John Laurie . . . . . . *Jamy, Captain in English Army*
Valentine Dyall . . . . *Duke of Burgundy*
George Robey . . . . *Sir John Falstaff*
Francis Lister . . . . *Duke of Orleans*
Niall MacGinnis . . . . *MacMorris, Captain in English Army*
Russell Thorndike . . . . *Duke of Bourbon*

Roy Emmerton . . . . *Lieutenant Bardolph*
Michael Shepley . . *Gower, Captain in English Army*
Griffith Jones . . . . *Earl of Salisbury*
Morland Graham . . . . *Sir Thomas Erpingham*
Arthur Hambling . . . *Bates, soldier in English camp*
Brian Nissen . . . . . . *Court, soldier in English camp*
Frederick Cooper . . . . *Corporal Nym*
Gerald Case . . . . *Earl of Westmoreland*
Michael Warre . . . . *Duke of Gloucester*
Janet Burnell . . . . *Queen Isabel of France*
Frank Tickle . . . . *Governor of Harfleur*
George Cole . . . . *Boy*
Jonathan Field . . . . *French messenger*
Ernest Hare . . . . *A priest*
Vernon Greeves . . . . *English herald*

■ **DESCRIPTION** Feature film version of the play. A Technicolor spectacular, Olivier's first attempt at directing Shakespeare for the screen is remarkable for its confident and imaginative use of the resources of the cinema. Beginning with the play being performed at the Globe, the film opens out to stylised sets, then by degrees to realistic battlefields. Olivier's touch is not always so sure – given that so much was cut elsewhere, the opening act is absurdly prolonged – but it was the mixture of conviction with ability that made this the first true marriage of Shakespearean drama and the cinema. Intended as wartime propaganda: the most significant cuts are all those scenes criticising Henry's conduct.

■ **NOTES** The actual title that appears on the film (on a playbill) is THE CHRONICLE HISTORY OF KING HENRY THE FIFT WITH HIS BATELL FOUGHT AT AGINCOURT IN FRANCE. The title HENRY V does not appear on the film. The French cavalry charge was filmed at Enniskerry, Ireland.

■ **REFERENCES** • Davies, *Filming Shakespeare's Plays*, pp. 26–39. • Harry M. Geduld, *Filmguide to Henry V* (Bloomington/London: Indiana University Press, 1973). • C. Clayton Hutton, *The Making of Henry V* (London, 1945).

HENRY V [TRAILER]

■ **GB • 1944**

NFTVA viewing copy
35mm col mu 230ft 2 mins

■ **DESCRIPTION** Trailer for the above. Laurence Olivier is seen seated at Denham Studios in 1944. He reads a letter from him to Filippo Del Giudice telling him of the completion of the film. There follows a letter from Del Giudice to Eagle-Lion, the distributors, an extract from the film (the Agincourt charge), title and credits, and a final advertisement for the Carlton Theatre, Haymarket, with prices.

■ **NOTES** The soundtrack for the NFTVA copy is missing. Unlike the main feature, this does have the title HENRY V on-screen. Del Giudice was managing director of Two Cities Films, and was also largely responsible for the setting up of Olivier's HAMLET (1948).

CAMPANADAS A MEDIANOCHE

■ **Spain/Switzerland 1966**

d	Orson Welles
pc	Internacional Films/Alpine

NFTVA preservation material

■ **DESCRIPTION** Feature film. The life of Shakespeare's Sir John Falstaff, with material taken from the plays *Richard II*, *1 Henry IV*, *2 Henry IV*, *Henry V* and *The Merry Wives of Windsor*. For full details see entry under *Henry IV*.

HENRY V

■ **GB/USA 1979**

■ *BBC Television Shakespeare*

d	David Giles
pc	BBC/Time-Life Films
tx (GB)	23 December 1979 (BBC2)
tx (US)	23 April 1980 (PBS)
p	Cedric Messina
sc ed	Alan Shallcross
lght	Dennis Channon
des	Don Homfray
cost	Odette Barrow

NFTVA viewing copy
½" col sd 170mins

■ **CAST**

David Gwillim	The King
Alec McCowen	Chorus
Jocelyne Boisseau	Katherine
Martin Smith	Duke of Gloucester
Rob Edwards	Duke of Bedford
Roger Davenport	Duke of Clarence
Clifford Parrish	Duke of Exeter
Derek Hollis	Duke of York
Robert Ashby	Earl of Salisbury
David Buck	Earl of Westmoreland
Rob Beacham	Earl of Warwick
Trevor Baxter	Archbishop of Canterbury
John Abineri	Bishop of Ely
William Whymper	Earl of Cambridge
Ian Price	Lord Scroop
David Rowlands	Sir Thomas Grey
George Howe	Sir Thomas Erpingham
Brian Poyser	Gower
Tim Wylton	Fluellen
Paddy Ward	MacMorris
Michael McKevitt	Jamy
Ronald Forfar	Bates
Joe Ritchie	Court
David Pinner	Williams
Jeffrey Holland	Nym
Gordon Gostelow	Bardolph
Bryan Pringle	Pistol
John Fowler	Boy
Simon Broad	Herald
Thorley Walters	Charles VI, King of France
Keith Drinkel	Lewis, the Dauphin
Robert Harris	Duke of Burgundy
John Saunders	Duke of Orleans
John Bryans	Duke of Bourbon
Julian Glover	The Constable of France
Carl Forgione	Rambures
Alan Brown	Governor of Harfleur
Garrick Hagon	Mountjoy, a French herald
Pamela Ruddock	Isabel, Queen of France
Anna Quayle	Alice, a lady attending Katherine
Brenda Bruce	Hostess
Graham Pountney	French soldier
Ronald Chenery	Messenger

■ **DESCRIPTION** Television production of the play. The same cast are carried over from *1 Henry IV* and *2 Henry IV* (qv), and there is a little more fire here than in the play's predecessors. It is perhaps most successful in not being like the Olivier film at all.

■ **REFERENCES** • Pilkington, *Screening Shakespeare*, pp. 87–99.

LITTLE TOUCH OF HARRY: THE MAKING OF HENRY V, A

■ **GB • 1989**

d	Mary Gwatkin
pc	Mindseye Films
p	Ron Fisher/David Parfitt
sc	Iain Johnstone
nar	Judi Dench
m	Pat Doyle

NFTVA viewing copy
½" col sd 30mins

■ **DESCRIPTION** Promotional documentary on the making of Kenneth Branagh's HENRY V (1989, not in NFTVA). Shows the film in production, extracts from the finished film, interviews with actors and crew (including Derek Jacobi, Paul Scofield and Emma Thompson), and in particular focusing on actor/director Kenneth Branagh, stopping just short of hagiography.

■ **NOTES** First television broadcast 29 December 1989 (C4).

ROYAL GALA: SYMPHONY FOR THE SPIRE

■ **GB • 1991**

d	Mike Mansfield
pc	TVS/Mike Mansfield Television
tx	8 September 1991 (ITV)
p	Hilary Stewart

NFTVA viewing copy
½" col sd 89mins

■ **DESCRIPTION** Charity concert devised by Prince Charles in aid of the Salisbury Cathedral spire appeal, including Placido Domingo, Jessye Norman, Ofra Harnoy, Charlton Heston, Phil Collins, and Kenneth Branagh giving readings from *Henry V*. He speaks the opening Chorus, 'Once more unto the breach' (A3S1) and the St Crispin's Day speech (A4S3); the English Chamber Orchestra play music from Patrick Doyle's score to Branagh's HENRY V feature; Branagh then reads from A4S7, finishing with Henry's final words in A4S8, after which comes the 'Non Nobis Domine' from Doyle's score.

■ **NOTES** The event was held in the grounds of Salisbury Cathedral in the presence of the Prince and Princess of Wales. The Prince of Wales, patron of the appeal, introduces the programme which was broadcast the following night.

David Warner as Henry VI in the HENRY VI episode from *The Wars of the Roses* (1965)

HENRY VI

WARWICK PAGEANT

■ **GB • 1906**

pc	Charles Urban Trading Company

NFTVA preservation material
35mm bw st 1,526ft 17mins
English titles

■ **DESCRIPTION** A record of the Warwick pageant, held in Warwick Castle grounds 2–9 July 1906, showing incidents in the history of the town of Warwick from AD 40 to 1572. Includes scenes from a performance of Christopher Marlowe's *Edward II* and from Shakespeare's *3 Henry VI*, showing Warwick and Queen Margaret at the court of King Louis in France (A3S3), and Warwick seizing Edward on his return to England (A4S3).

■ **NOTES** The fashion for pageants began in 1905 with the pageant devised by Louis N. Parker for Sherborne. His second pageant, held at Warwick, celebrated 'the thousandth anniversary of the conquest of Mercia by Queen Ethelfelda'. It was divided into 11 episodes depicting various stages in the history of Warwick: the first featured Cymbeline, amongst others, the sixth was based on Marlowe, the seventh on Shakespeare. The tenth episode includes a scene where the boy William Shakespeare meets Queen Elizabeth. Scenes from all the episodes are featured in the film. A later example of the vogue for pageants is GLASTONBURY PAST AND PRESENT (1922, see under General section).

■ **REFERENCES** • Louis N. Parker, *Several of My Lives* (London: Chapman and Hall, 1928), pp. 277–300. • Louis N. Parker, *The Warwick Pageant* (Warwick, 1906) [text of pageant].

RICHARD III

■ **GB • 1911**

pc   Co-operative Cinematograph Company

NFTVA viewing copy

■ **DESCRIPTION** Record of F. R. Benson's production of *Richard III*. The opening two scenes, showing the Battle of Tewkesbury and the murder of King Henry VI are from *3 Henry VI* and were included in the original production at Stratford. See entry under *Richard III* for complete details of the film.

VOICE THAT THRILLED THE WORLD, The

■ **USA • 1943**

d	Jean Negulesco
pc	Warner Bros.
sc	James Bloodworth
ph	Sidney Hickox
nar	Art Gilmore

NFTVA preservation material
35mm bw sd 1,487ft 17mins

■ **CAST**
John Barrymore . . . . . *Richard, Duke of Gloucester*

■ **DESCRIPTION** Documentary short. A history of sound films, with the emphasis on Warner Bros. productions, including John Barrymore delivering a speech in the grand style as Richard, Duke of Gloucester, credited as being *Richard III* but actually from *3 Henry VI* (A3S2).

■ **NOTES** The Barrymore sequence was originally filmed in two-strip Technicolor for the variety feature SHOW OF SHOWS (USA 1929). The NFTVA also holds a shortened version of SHOW OF SHOWS which excludes the Barrymore sequence.

RICHARD III

■ **GB • 1955**

d	Laurence Olivier
pc	London Films

NFTVA viewing copy

■ **DESCRIPTION** Feature film version of the play. Includes the coronation of Edward IV from *3 Henry VI* (A5S7), with Cedric Hardwicke as Edward. For full details of the film see entry under *Richard III*.

HENRY VI

■ **GB • 1965**

■ *The Wars of the Roses*

d (RSC)	Peter Hall/John Barton
d (BBC)	Robin Midgley/Michael Hayes
pc	BBC
tx	8 April 1965 (BBC1)
p	Michael Barry
adapt	John Barton
lght	Robert Wright
cost/sets	John Bury
m	Guy Woolfenden

NFTVA viewing copy
¾" bw sd 165mins

■ **CAST**

John Normington . . . . *Bedford / Simpcox*
Paul Hardwick . . . . *Gloucester*
Donald Burton . . . . *Exeter*
Nicholas Selby . . . . *Winchester*
David Waller . . . . *Captain to Talbot*
Donald Sinden . . . . *Plantagenet*
William Squire . . . . *Suffolk*
Philip Brack . . . . *Somerset*
Brewster Mason . . . . *Warwick*
Rhys McConnochie . . . . *Vernon /
Messenger to Gloucester*
Peter Forbes-Robertson. . . . *Lawyer / French soldier*
Stephen Hancock . . . . *Bassett*
Charles Thomas . . . . *Mortimer*
Ted Valentine . . . . *Lieutenant of the Tower*
Clive Morton . . . . *Lord Talbot*
Peter Gale. . . . . *John Talbot*
David Rowlands . . . . . *English soldier / A townsman*
David Warner . . . . *King Henry VI*
James Laurenson . . . . *Messenger to the Council*
Anthony Boden . . . . *Messenger to York*
Colette O'Neil . . . . *Eleanor*
Charles Kay . . . . *Sir John Hume / The Dauphin*
Gareth Morgan . . . . *Bolingbroke / Orleans*
Madoline Thomas. . . . . *Margery Jourdain*
Sheila Grant. . . . . *Simpcox's wife*
William Dysart. . . . . *First murderer*
Gavin Morrison . . . . *Second murderer*
Stanley Lebor . . . . *First citizen*
Roger Jones . . . . *Second citizen*
David Hargreaves. . . . . *Third citizen*
Donald Layne-Smith. . . . . *Reignier*
Peter Geddis . . . . *Alençon*
Hugh Sullivan . . . . *Burgundy*
Janet Suzman . . . . *Joan la Pucelle*
Peggy Ashcroft . . . . *Margaret*
Murray Brown . . . . *French messenger*
John Hales . . . . *Papal legate*

■ **DESCRIPTION** First of three-part adaptation by
John Barton of the three *Henry VI* plays and
Richard III, originally staged in 1963 as *The Wars of
the Roses* by the Royal Shakespeare Company. A
key stage in the history of televised Shakespeare
was the BBC's primetime broadcast of a specially
recorded performance of the RSC's celebrated
Wars of the Roses trilogy of plays. The intention
was to give a sense of the impact of the stage
production televisually, rather than a plain record
of the plays in performance. In this, and for its
time, the result is very successful, the emphasis
being laid on close-ups rather than scenery. A
notable preservation of a famous production

and a significant advance in the televising of
Shakespeare.

■ **NOTES** Filming was done following the 1964
run of the plays at Stratford, and took place in the
theatre over eight weeks. The stage was extended
specially to accommodate the expanded battle
scenes. The programme ends with Margaret
lamenting Suffolk's death (*2 Henry VI*, A4S4). The
trilogy continued with EDWARD IV (see below)
and RICHARD III (see under *Richard III*).

■ **REFERENCES** • Alice V. Griffin, 'Shakespeare
Through the Camera's Eye: IV', *Shakespeare
Quarterly*, 17 (Autumn 1966) [reprinted in
Bulman and Coursen, *Shakespeare on Television*, pp.
242–3].

EDWARD IV

■ **GB • 1965**

■ *The Wars of the Roses*

d (RSC)	Peter Hall / John Barton
d (BBC)	Michael Hayes / Robin Midgley
pc	BBC
tx	15 April 1965 (BBC1)
p	Michael Barry
adapt	John Barton
lght	Robert Wright
cost / sets	John Bury
m	Guy Woolfenden

NFTVA viewing copy
¾" bw sd 175mins

■ **CAST**

David Warner . . . . *King Henry VI*
Peggy Ashcroft . . . . *Margaret*
Alan Tucker . . . . *Prince Edward*
Donald Burton . . . . *Exeter*
Donald Layne-Smith . . . . *Lord Say*
John Corvin . . . . *Lord Clifford*
John Normington. . . . . *Young Clifford*
Jeffrey Dench . . . . *Sir Humphrey Stafford /
Second keeper*
Philip Brack . . . . *Somerset*
Maurice Jones . . . . *Oxford*
Peter Geddis . . . . . *A son that has killed his father /
Alençon*
David Waller. . . . . . *A father that has killed his son*
Lee Menzies . . . . *Richmond*

Andrew Lodge . . . . *Messenger to the Council*
Gavin Morrison . . . . *First Lancastrian soldier*
William Dysart . . . . *Second Lancastrian soldier*
Guy Gordon . . . . *Lancastrian messenger*
Brewster Mason . . . . *Warwick*
Donald Sinden . . . . *York*
Roy Dotrice . . . . *King Edward IV / Jack Cade*
Charles Kay . . . . *Clarence*
Ian Holm . . . . *Gloucester*
Fergus McClelland . . . . *Rutland*
Madoline Thomas . . . . *Duchess of York*
Anthony Boden . . . . *Messenger*
David Hargreaves . . . . *Norfolk*
Susan Engel . . . . *Lady Elizabeth Grey*
Hugh Sullivan . . . . *Hastings / Burgundy*
Derek Waring . . . . *Rivers*
William Squire . . . . *Buckingham*
Marshall Jones . . . . *First Watch / Smith*
Roger Jones . . . . *Second Watch*
David Rowlands . . . . *Third Watch*
Ted Valentine . . . . . . *Dick / Lieutenant of the Tower*
Tim Wylton . . . . *Michael / First keeper*
Stephen Hancock . . . . *Clerk of Chatham*
Malcolm Webster . . . . *Alexander Iden*
John Hussey . . . . *Lewis XI*
Colette O'Neil . . . . *The Lady Bona*

■ **DESCRIPTION** Second of three-part adaptation by John Barton of the three *Henry VI* plays and *Richard III*, originally staged in 1963 as *The Wars of the Roses* by the Royal Shakespeare Company. Continuation (see above) through to the end of *3 Henry VI*, introducing a unforgettable performance by Ian Holm as Gloucester.

■ **NOTES** The entry for the third part of *The Wars of the Roses* is given under *Richard III*.

THEATRE OF BLOOD

■ **GB • 1973**

d   Douglas Hickox
pc   Cineman

NFTVA preservation material

■ **CAST**
Vincent Price . . . . *Edward Lionheart*
Coral Browne . . . . *Miss Chloe Moon*

■ **DESCRIPTION** Feature film. An actor (Vincent Price) murders his critics in the manner of deaths

from Shakespeare's plays. Disguised as a hairdresser, Lionheart lures Chloe Moon into his salon and electrocutes her in a chair, her burning echoing that of Joan La Pucelle (Joan of Arc) from *1 Henry VI*. For full details of the film see entry in General section.

Clara Kimball Young (Anne Boleyn) and Tefft Johnson (Henry VIII) in CARDINAL WOLSEY (1912)

HENRY VIII

CARDINAL WOLSEY

■ **USA • 1912**

d   J. Stuart Blackton / Lawrence Trimble
pc   Vitagraph Company of America
sc   Hal Reid

NFTVA viewing copy
35mm bw st 873ft 10mins
English titles

■ **CAST**
Tefft Johnson . . . . *Henry VIII*
Clara Kimball Young . . . . *Anne Boleyn*
Julia Swayne Gordon . . . . *Catherine of Aragon*
Hal Reid . . . . *Cardinal Wolsey*
Logan Paul . . . . *Archbishop of Canterbury*
Robert Gaillard . . . . *King's secretary*
Harold Wilson . . . . *King's friend*
George Ober . . . . *Bishop of Essex*

■ **DESCRIPTION** Fiction short. The historic disagreement between Henry VIII and Cardinal Thomas Wolsey concerning the king's divorce from Catherine of Aragon. Unusual Vitagraph Shakespeare, with cramped sets, a sour Wolsey, but a jolly performance by Johnson that anticipates Charles Laughton's interpretation. The debt to Shakespeare is revealed in one intertitle bearing the lines: 'Had I but served my God with half the zeal/I served my King, he would not in mine age/Have left me naked to mine enemies' (A3S2). The quotation does not really follow on from the depicted action, and the connection with *Henry VIII* is only incidental.

■ **NOTES** Ball indicates gaps in the action (the length on release was 997ft) and identifies these apparently missing scenes.

■ **REFERENCES** • Ball, *Shakespeare on Silent Film*, pp. 136–9, 338.

HENRY VIII

■ **GB/USA 1979**

■ *BBC Television Shakespeare*

d	Kevin Billington
pc	BBC/Time-Life Films
tx (GB)	25 February 1979 (BBC2)
tx (US)	25 April 1979 (PBS)
p	Cedric Messina
sc ed	Alan Shallcross
lght	Hugh Cartwright
des	Don Taylor
cost	Alun Hughes
m	James Tyler

NFTVA viewing copy
½" col sd 145mins

■ **CAST**
Tony Church . . . . *Prologue*
John Stride . . . . *Henry VIII*
Julian Glover . . . . *Duke of Buckingham*
Jeremy Kemp . . . . *Duke of Norfolk*
David Rintoul . . . . *Lord Abergavenny*
Timothy West . . . . *Cardinal Wolsey*
John Rowe . . . . *Cromwell*
Lewis Fiander . . . . *Duke of Suffolk*
Alan Leith . . . . *Sergeant-at-arms*
Claire Bloom . . . . *Katharine of Aragon*

John Bailey . . . . *Griffith, gentleman-usher*
David Troughton . . . . *Surveyor*
John Nettleton . . . . *Lord Chamberlain*
Charles Lloyd Pack . . . . *Lord Sandys*
Nigel Lambert . . . . *Sir Thomas Lovell*
Barbara Kellermann . . . . *Anne Bullen*
Adam Bareham . . . . *Sir Henry Guildford*
Jeffrey Daunton . . . . *Servant*
John Cater . . . . *First gentleman*
Roger Lloyd Pack . . . . *Second gentleman*
Jack McKenzie . . . . *Sir Nicholas Vaux*
Michael Poole . . . . *Cardinal Campeius*
Peter Vaughan . . . . . *Gardiner, Bishop of Winchester*
Sylvia Coleridge . . . . *Old lady, Anne Bullen's best friend*
Michael Gaunt . . . . *Crier*
Ronald Pickup . . *Cranmer, Archbishop of Canterbury*
David Dodimead . . . . *Bishop of Lincoln*
Emma Kirkby . . . . *Singer*
Sally Home . . . . *Patience*
Oliver Cotton . . . . *Earl of Surrey*
Michael Walker . . . . *Messenger*
John Rhys-Davies . . . . . *Capucius, Ambassador from Emperor Charles V*
Timothy Barker . . . . *Page to Gardiner*
Brian Osborne . *Door-keeper of the Council Chamber*
John Rogan . . . . *Dr Butts*
Jack May . . . . *Lord Chancellor*

■ **DESCRIPTION** Television production of the play. An unexpectedly fine interpretation from early on in the BBC series, engrossing and intelligent, and benefiting greatly from the unobtrusive use of stately home backgrounds. From a rich cast Claire Bloom's poignant Queen Katharine is particularly notable. The chance to see such unfamiliar works performed, and to find them so entertaining, was one of the chief pleasures of the series.

■ **NOTES** Filmed on location in Kent at Hever Castle, Leeds Castle and Penshurst Place.

JULIUS CAESAR

JULIUS CAESAR

■ **USA • 1908**

d	William V. Ranous
pc	Vitagraph Company of America

Kenneth Williams as Julius Caesar in CARRY ON CLEO (1964)

sup	J. Stuart Blackton
sc	Liebler

NFTVA viewing copy
35mm bw st 836ft 9mins
German titles

■ **CAST**

William V. Ranous	*Cassius*
Charles Kent [?]	*Julius Caesar*
Florence Lawrence [?]	*Calpurnia*
Earle Williams [?]	*Brutus*
William Shea	*First Citizen*

■ **DESCRIPTION** Abbreviated version of the play. At the Capitol Julius Caesar leaves with Mark Antony while Cassius is seen plotting with another man. In the arena Antony offers a crown to Caesar three times. Cassius persuades Brutus to join the conspiracy and they meet in Brutus' garden. Calpurnia tells Caesar of her dream and tries to persuade him not to go to the Capitol. A soothsayer has prepared a letter warning Caesar to beware Brutus and stay away from Cassius and Casca, but Caesar does not take it. The conspirators murder Caesar and Brutus addresses the people. Mark Antony brings out the body of Caesar and addresses the people. At an army camp Brutus and Cassius argue and then resolve their differences. The ghost of Caesar visits Brutus in a dream. The conspirators lead their armies into battle. Cassius makes his servant kill him and Brutus falls on his sword. Antony has Brutus' corpse burnt on a pyre. A cut-price epic from Vitagraph, interesting for its use of low camera angles for the speeches to the crowd and the battle scenes.

■ **NOTES** Identification of the actors is difficult; Julius Caesar himself is very heavily made-up.

■ **REFERENCES** • Ball, *Shakespeare on Silent Film*, pp. 48–50, 312. • William Uricchio and Roberta E. Pearson, *Reframing Culture: The Case of the Vitagraph Quality Films* (Princeton: Princeton University Press, 1993).

GIULIO CESARE

English titles JULIUS CAESAR; BRUTUS

■ **Italy • 1909**

d	Giovanni Pastrone
pc	Itala
p	Louis Albert

NFTVA viewing copy
35mm bw st 644ft 7mins
Incomplete – original length 875ft
English titles

■ **DESCRIPTION** Abbreviated version of the play. Caesar returns in triumph to Rome. Caesar informs Mark Antony of his tyrannical ambitions, Brutus overhears and remonstrates with him. Mark Antony is awarded a triumph by the Senate. Brutus and the other conspirators are overheard by a spy. Calpurnia dreams of Caesar's murder, then learns of the plotting from the spy. Caesar refuses to listen to her and attends the Senate. Caesar is murdered. Mark Antony rouses the people against the conspirators and they flee Rome. Brutus, waiting at Philippi, sees Caesar's ghost. The battle rages. Brutus is defeated and kills himself. A rather poorly staged effort, little imagination having gone into its presentation.

■ **REFERENCES** • Ball, *Shakespeare on Silent Film*, pp. 98–101, 327.

BRUTO

English title BRUTUS

■ **Italy • 1911**

d   Enrico Guazzoni
pc   Cines

NFTVA preservation material
35mm st bw 1,028ft 11mins
English titles

■ **DESCRIPTION** Fiction short based on *Julius Caesar*. Roughly the major action of the play from the death of Caesar to the death of Brutus. A well-organised and impressive interpretation, with strong emphasis on the visual aspects of the story and a taste for spectacle that would have gone better with a longer film.

■ **NOTES** The description given by Ball (pp. 333–4) is of a 340ft print now held by the NFTVA. A substantially complete print has been acquired subsequently. Guazzoni remade the story for Cines in 1914 for the feature-length CAJUS JULIUS CAESAR (see below).

■ **REFERENCES** • Ball, *Shakespeare on Silent Film*, pp. 116–20, 333–4.

CAJUS JULIUS CAESAR

English title JULIUS CAESAR

■ **Italy • 1914**

d   Enrico Guazzoni
pc   Cines
story Raffaele Giovanoli
ph   Antonio Cufaro

NFTVA viewing copy
35mm bw st 7,035ft 78mins
German titles

■ **CAST**
Amleto Novelli . . . . *Julius Caesar*
Gianna Terribili-Gonzales
Lia Orlandini
Irene Mattalia
Ruffo Geri
Augusto Mastripietri

Ignazio Lupi
Bruto Castellani
Carlo Duse
Signor Ricci

■ **DESCRIPTION** Feature film. The story of Julius Caesar with borrowings from Shakespeare rather than a version of his play, this is a production in the Italian spectacle tradition. The plot covers much of Julius Caesar's life, and only in the final reel and Caesar's death are there parallels with Shakespeare, which appear deliberate (English-language prints used quotations from Shakespeare for these scenes).

■ **REFERENCES** • Ball, *Shakespeare on Silent Film*, pp. 208–10, 354.

PLAYMATES

■ **USA • 1941**

d   David Butler
pc   RKO

NFTVA preservation material

■ **DESCRIPTION** Feature film. Kay Kyser and his swing band team up with John Barrymore to put on updated Shakespeare. Contains a short sequence spoofing *Julius Caesar*. For full details of the film see entry in General section.

JULIUS CAESAR

■ **GB • 1945**

■ *Famous Scenes from Shakespeare*

d   Henry Cass
pc   Theatrecraft
spon British Council
p   Sydney Box
des   Compton Bennett
m   Ben Frankel

NFTVA viewing copy
35mm bw sd 1,737ft 19mins

■ **CAST**
Felix Aylmer . . . . *Brutus*
Leo Genn . . . . *Mark Antony*

John Slater/Emrys Jones/Frederick Cooper/
Ben Williams/Grace Allardyce/Arthur
Hambling/Sydney Monckton . . . . *The Mob*

■ **DESCRIPTION** A scene from *Julius Caesar*;
Brutus and Mark Antony in the Forum following
Caesar's murder (A3S2). Quite striking sets, but
clumsily directed and not too convincingly
played. Designed for educational use.

■ **NOTES** The other title produced in the *Famous
Scenes from Shakespeare* series was MACBETH
(1945, qv).

PARIS 1900

■ **France • 1948**

d   Nicole Védrès
pc   Panthéon

NFTVA viewing copy

■ **DESCRIPTION** Compilation film covering Paris
1900–14. Features a brief sequence of the actor
Firmin Gémier posing in the role of Julius
Caesar, in the longer French version of the film
only. For full details of the film see entry under
Hamlet.

JULIUS CAESAR

■ **GB • 1953**

■ *The World's a Stage*

d   Charles Deane
pc   Emile Katzka Productions
ph   A. T. Dinsdale
nar   Ronald Harwood

NFTVA preservation material
35mm bw sd 1,140ft 13mins

■ **CAST**
Young Vic Theatre Company

■ **DESCRIPTION** Drama short. The tent scene
from *Julius Caesar* (A4S3). Apparently originally
made for television, this is one title in a series of
which the *Monthly Film Bulletin* said that they
'must be as bewildering to those who are not

familiar with the plays as they are distressing to
those who are'.

■ **NOTES** Other titles in *The World's a Stage* series
were OTHELLO (also held by the NFTVA), THE
WINTER'S TALE, TWELFTH NIGHT and
MACBETH.

JULIUS CAESAR

■ **USA • 1953**

d/adapt   Joseph L. Mankiewicz
pc   MGM
p   John Houseman
ph   Joseph Ruttenberg
art d   Cedric Gibbons/Edward Carfagno
sets   Edwin B. Willis/Hugh Hunt
m   Miklos Rozsa

NFTVA preservation material
35mm bw sd 10,821ft 120mins

■ **CAST**
Marlon Brando . . . . *Mark Antony*
James Mason . . . . *Brutus*
John Gielgud . . . . *Cassius*
Louis Calhern . . . . *Julius Caesar*
Edmond O'Brien . . . . *Casca*
Greer Garson . . . . *Calpurnia*
Deborah Kerr. . . . . *Portia*
George Macready . . . . *Marullus*
Michael Pate. . . . . *Flavius*
Alan Napier. *Cicero*
John Hoyt . . . . *Decius Brutus*
Tom Powers . . . . *Metellus Cimber*
William Cottrell. . . . . *Cinna*
Jack Raine . . . . *Trebonius*
Douglas Watson . . . . *Octavius Caesar*
Rhys Williams . . . . *Lucilius*
Richard Hale . . . . *Soothsayer*
Ian Wolfe . . . . *Ligarius*
Lumsden Hare . . . . *Publius*
Morgan Farley . . . . *Artemidorus*
Victor Perry . . . . *Popilius Lena*
Douglas Dumbrille . . . . *Lepidus*
Michael Ansara . . . . *Pindarus*
Dayton Lummis . . . . *Messala*
John Lupton . . . . *Varro*
Preston Hanson . . . . *Claudius*
John Parrish. . . . . *Titinius*
Joe Waring. *Clitus*

Stephen Roberts . . . . *Dardanius*
Thomas Browne Henry . . . . *Volumnius*
Edward Purdon . . . . *Strato*
John Doucette . . . . *Carpenter*
Chester Stratton . . . . *Servant to Caesar*
Bill Phipps . . . . *Servant to Antony*
Michael Tolan . . . . *Officer to Octavius*

■ **DESCRIPTION** Feature film version of the play. One of the most wholly successful Shakespearean films, presented with intelligence, wit and good sense from a director particularly suited to letting the words speak for themselves. But it must be chiefly valued for two exceptional performances: Brando's revelatory, impassioned Antony and Gielgud's aloof, bitter Cassius. James Mason's Brutus is weak by comparison.

■ **REFERENCES** • Robert Harding (ed.), *Julius Caesar and the Life of William Shakespeare* (London: Gawthone Press, 1953) [intended for school use]. • Jorgens, *Shakespeare on Film*, pp. 92–105, 265–8. • Manvell, *Shakespeare and the Film*, pp. 86–91.

CARRY ON CLEO

■ **GB • 1964**

d   Gerald Thomas
pc   Adder

NFTVA viewing copy

■ **DESCRIPTION** Feature film comedy. A spoof of the 1963 CLEOPATRA, with several comic allusions to *Julius Caesar*, in particular the line 'Friends, Romans, countrymen'. For full details of the film see entry under *Antony and Cleopatra*.

JULIUS CAESAR

■ **GB • 1970**

d   Stuart Burge
pc   Commonwealth United
p   Peter Snell
adapt   Robert Furnival
ph   Ken Higgins
p des   Julia Trevelyan Oman

art d   Maurice Pelling
m   Michael Lewis

NFTVA preservation material
16mm col sd 4,133ft 114mins

■ **CAST**

Charlton Heston . . . . *Mark Antony*
Jason Robards . . . . *Brutus*
John Gielgud . . . . *Julius Caesar*
Richard Johnson . . . . *Cassius*
Robert Vaughn . . . . *Casca*
Richard Chamberlain . . . . *Octavius Caesar*
Diana Rigg . . . . *Portia*
Jill Bennett . . . . *Calpurnia*
Christopher Lee . . . . *Artemidorus*
Alan Browning . . . . *Marullus*
Norman Bowler . . . . *Titinius*
Andrew Crawford . . . . *Volumnius*
David Dodimead . . . . *Lepidus*
Peter Eyre . . . . *Cinna the Poet*
Edwin Finn . . . . *Publius*
Derek Godfrey . . . . *Decius Brutus*
Michael Gough . . . . *Metellus Cimber*
Paul Hardwick . . . . *Messala*
Laurence Harrington . . . . *Carpenter*
Thomas Heathcote . . . . *Flavius*
Ewan Hooper . . . . *Strato*
Robert Keegan . . . . *Lucilius*
Preston Lockwood . . . . *Trebonius*
John Moffatt . . . . *Popilus Lena*
André Morell . . . . *Cicero*
David Neal . . . . *Cinna the Conspirator*
Steven Pacey . . . . *Lucius*
Ron Pember . . . . *Cobbler*
John Tate . . . . *Clitus*
Damien Thomas . . . . *Pindarus*
Ken Hutchinson . . . . *First Plebian*
Michael Keating . . . . *Second Plebian*
Derek Hardwicke . . . . *Third Plebian*
Michael Wynne . . . . *Fourth Plebian*
David Leland . . . . *Fifth Plebian*
Ronald McGill . . . . *Servant to Caesar*
Linbert Spencer . . . . *Second Servant to Caesar*
Trevor Adams . . . . *Third Servant to Caesar*
Robin Chadwick . . . . *Servant to Octavius*
Christopher Cazenove . . . . *Servant to Antony*
Roy Stewart . . . . *Slave to Lepidus*
Liz Geghardt . . . . *Maid to Calpurnia*

■ **DESCRIPTION** Feature film version of the play, the epitome of the pedestrian. In some kind of limbo between theatre and cinema, the performances are uniformly lifeless.

■ **REFERENCES** • Manvell, *Shakespeare and the Film*, pp. 91–5 [a more generous assessment].

JULIUS CAESAR [TRAILER]

■ **GB** • **1970**

NFTVA viewing copy
35mm col sd 322ft 3mins

■ **DESCRIPTION** Trailer for the above.

HEIL CAESAR

Part One: MURDER OF A PRESIDENT
Part Two: DEFEAT

■ **GB** • **1973**

pc	BBC
tx	19 November 1973 (BBC1) [part one]
	26 November 1973 (BBC1) [part two]
p	Ronald Smedley
sc	John Bowen
des	Humphrey Jaeger

NFTVA preservation material
2" col sd 2x30mins [part three missing]

■ **CAST** (for all three episodes)
Anthony Bate . . . . *Brutus*
John Stride . . . . *Mark Antony*
Frank Middlemass. . . . . *Messala*
Geoffrey Bayldon . . . . *Lepidus*
Peter Howell . . . . *Caesar*
David Allister . . . . *Cassius*
Angela Thorne . . . . *Portia*
Alan Rowe. . . . . *Trebonius*
John Baker. *Cicero*
William Simons . . . . *Casca*
John Sterland . . . . *Publius*
Dorothy Primrose . . . . *Fortune-teller*
Angela Crow. . . . . *Calpurnia*
Jeffry Wickham . . . . *Metellus*
Arthur Blake . . . . *Decius*
Erik Chitty . . . . *Caius Ligarius*
Peter Settelen . . . . *Octavius*
Andrew Bradford . . . . *Captain*
Gareth Armstrong . . . . *Sergeant*

Anthony Smee . . . . *ADC to Messala*
John Salthouse. . . . . *Radio operator*
Clive Jacobs . . . . *Newscaster*
Valerie Colgan . . . . *Secretary*
Frank Tadeusz. . . . . *Stickman*
Andrew Kyriakides . . . . *Croupier*
John Barton . . . . *Croupier*

■ **DESCRIPTION** Television production for schools, adapting *Julius Caesar* to a modern political setting, with modern dialogue to match from John Bowen. Shakespeare's language is gone, but this is an intelligent, persuasive and well acted exposition of Shakespeare's themes; ideally suited to its original school audience, sufficiently impressive as drama to be repeated for evening broadcast.

■ **NOTES** HEIL CAESAR was originally broadcast in three episodes, the first of which, THE CONSPIRATORS (tx 12 November 1973) is not held by the NFTVA. It was then shown as a single play on BBC 2 (tx 21 October 1974). The programme won the 'Flame of Knowledge' Award of the Society of Film and Television Arts in 1974 as well as the Tokyo Prize. The text was published by the BBC and then subsequently rewritten, published and performed as a play for the theatre.

THEATRE OF BLOOD

■ **GB** • **1973**

d	Douglas Hickox
pc	Cineman

NFTVA preservation material

■ **CAST**
Vincent Price . . . . *Edward Lionheart*
Michael Hordern . . . . *George Maxwell*
Renée Asherson . . . . *Mrs Maxwell*

■ **DESCRIPTION** Feature film. An actor (Vincent Price) murders his critics in the manner of deaths from Shakespeare's plays. On the Ides of March, George Maxwell ignores the warnings of his wife and goes to evict some tramps from a derelict building. The tramps turn on him and like Caesar he is stabbed to death. For full details of the film see entry in General section.

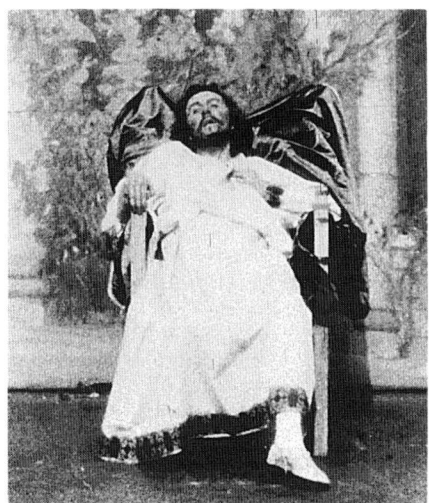

Herbert Beerbohm Tree in KING JOHN (1899)

KING JOHN

KING JOHN

■ **GB • 1899**

d/ph	William Kennedy-Laurie Dickson
pc	British Mutoscope and Biograph Company
des	Walter Pfeffer Dando

NFTVA viewing copy
35mm bw st 84ft + 5ft 1min [incomplete]

■ **CAST IN SURVIVING FILM**
The Orchard of Swinstead Abbey (first scene):
Herbert Beerbohm Tree . . . . *King John*
Dora Senior . . . . *Prince Henry*
F. M. Paget . . . . *Robert Bigot*
James Fisher . . . . *Earl of Pembroke*

■ **CAST IN MISSING SCENES**
The Battlefield Near Angiers:
Herbert Beerbohm Tree . . . . *King John*
Franklyn McLeay . . . . *Hubert de Burgh*
Arthur Sefton . . . . *Arthur*
The French King's Tent:
Gerald Lawrence . . . . *Lewis, the Dauphin*

Julia Neilson . . . . *Constance*
William Mollison . . . . *Philip, King of France*
Louis Calvert . . . . *Cardinal Pandulph*
The Orchard of Swinstead Abbey (second scene):
Herbert Beerbohm Tree . . . . *King John*
Dora Senior . . . . *Prince Henry*
F. M. Paget . . . . *Robert Bigot*
James Fisher . . . . *Earl of Pembroke*
S. A. Cookson . . . . *Earl of Salisbury*
Lewis Waller [?] . . . . *Philip Faulconbridge*

■ **DESCRIPTION** A recreation of part of A5S7 from the Beerbohm Tree production of *King John*. The action in the NFTVA print in detail is as follows: Tree seated in chair wearing white robe, man in period battledress and woman in dark tunic to left of him, man in battledress to right (these three stare briefly at camera before falling into their roles), Tree sits up, clutches chest, flops back in chair (speaking on-and-off all the while), retainers look concerned, Tree shakes head back and forth, reaches hand out, woman steps nearer (other men remain at edges of frame throughout), woman takes his hand but he turns away from her, clutches chest again, eyes stare, sits up, clutches stomach, lies back, she kneels, she takes his hand but he pulls it away and wipes at it with his other hand, clutches chest with one hand. A further brief fragment continues the action with Tree rising out of his chair and the others moving towards him. The whole action of the film takes place in a single shot.

■ **NOTES** This is the first ever Shakespearean film, long thought lost, its nature previously the subject of much speculation. It derives from the Her Majesty's Theatre production of *King John*, which opened on 20 September 1899, with Herbert Beerbohm Tree, actor-manager of the theatre, in the title role. The film, however, is not an exact reproduction of a scene from the production, nor does it show the Magna Carta scene, as several writers have suggested (following the lead set by Robert Hamilton Ball). It was filmed at the Biograph company's open air studio on the Thames embankment, using a simple backdrop, and shows the final scene of the play; the exact sequence appears to be King John's speech from 'Ay, marry, now my soul hath elbow-room' to 'On unreprievable-condemned blood'. Working from the original theatre programme, the cast in the film are Tree as King John, Dora Senior as Prince Henry, and, judging from clues given by the costumes, F. M. Paget as Bigot and James

Fisher as Pembroke.

Frame stills reproduced in *The Sketch,* 27 September 1899, p. 413, along with copyright records for these photographs, make it clear that there were four scenes: 'The Battlefield Near Angiers', 'The French King's Tent', and two separate scenes set in 'The Orchard of Swinstead Abbey', showing first the death of King John and then the crowning of Prince Henry. (Tree's version of the play was actually divided into three acts, and each setting came from one of these acts). The surviving film is therefore from the third scene only. Other accounts suggest that the complete film was four minutes long, which agrees with the photographic evidence (see note on contents below). It was filmed in early September 1899 and premiered at the Palace Theatre, London and various other theatres in Britain, Europe and America which showed the films produced by the Biograph company on the same night as the play's premiere, that is, 20 September 1899. It was filmed in 68mm using the Biograph camera, the 'widescreen' effect of which caused amazement at the time, with its greatly enlarged picture size and high picture quality (the NFTVA copy has been copied onto 35mm stock). It was also made available as a set of Mutoscope cards, to be viewed through a 'What the Butler Saw' machine. As a record of a performance it tells us little, beyond showing that Tree's histrionics would not be to modern taste, but as the cornerstone of the phenomenon of Shakespeare on film, it is a fascinating, richly rewarding artefact.

■ **NOTE ON CONTENTS** Although there is clear contemporary photographic evidence that the original film comprised four separate scenes, records of the film's exhibition suggest that in some cases the death scene only was screened. Programmes for the Palace Theatre call the film A SCENE – 'KING JOHN', NOW PLAYING AT HER MAJESTY'S THEATRE, and in a 1902 catalogue of the American Mutoscope and Biograph Company the film is advertised as BEERBOHM TREE, THE GREAT ENGLISH ACTOR, with the description: 'With leading members of his company in the death scene of "King John". Taken with all the scenery and effects of the original production.' The latter statement is false, but both these records would seem to indicate just the one scene. It is also likely that the Mutoscope version showed just the one scene. Such evidence may also explain the survival of this particular scene.

■ **NOTE ON CREDITS** Copyright records of photographs from both stage production and film credit W. K-L. Dickson (leading figure of the British Mutoscope and Biograph Company) and Walter Pfeffer Dando (formerly stage manager of the Palace Theatre, but by this time a Biograph employee) as the 'authors' of the work. Dando is known to have taken stage photographs at the Palace on other occasions, but here it is likely that he was concerned with the props to the film, with Dickson controlling the filming.

■ **REFERENCES** • Ball, *Shakespeare on Silent Film*, pp. 21–3, 303–4. • John Barnes, *Filming the Boer War* (London: Bishopsgate Press, 1992), pp. 143–4, 189. • B. A. Kachur, 'The First Shakespeare Film: A Reconsideration and Reconstruction of Tree's *King John*', *Theatre Survey* 32, May 1991, pp. 43–63 [written before discovery of the film]. • Luke McKernan, 'Beerbohm Tree's *King John* Rediscovered: The First Shakespeare Film, September 1899', *Shakespeare Bulletin* (Winter 1993), pp. 35–6. • Luke McKernan, 'Further News on Beerbohm Tree's *King John*', *Shakespeare Bulletin* (Spring 1993), pp. 49–50.

HOME GUARD

■ **GB • 1941**

d	Donald Taylor/Ivan Moffat
pc	Strand Film Company
spon	Ministry of Information
p	Donald Taylor
ph	George Noble

NFTVA preservation material
35mm bw sd 745ft 8mins

■ **CAST**
Bernard Miles

■ **DESCRIPTION** Propaganda documentary short. In a Hertfordshire pub Bernard Miles chats to his friends about his week at the local Home Guard training school. As part of this he gives a quotation from *King John*, reading from a battered exercise book.

LIFE AND DEATH OF KING JOHN, The

■ **GB/USA 1984**

■ *BBC Television Shakespeare*

d	David Giles
pc	BBC/Time-Life Films
tx (GB)	24 November 1984 (BBC2)
tx (US)	11 January 1985 (PBS)
p	Shaun Sutton
lght	Howard King
cost	Juanita Waterson
des	Chris Pemsel
m	Colin Sell

NFTVA viewing copy
½" col sd 155mins

■ **CAST**

Leonard Rossiter	King John
William Whymper	Chatillon
Mary Morris	Queen Elinor
Robert Brown	Earl of Pembroke
John Castle	Earl of Salisbury
John Flint	Lord Bigot
John Thaw	Hubert de Burgh
George Costigan	Philip, the Bastard
Edward Hibbert	Robert Faulconbridge
Phyllida Law	Lady Faulconbridge
Mike Lewin	James Gurney
Charles Kay	King Philip of France
Jonathan Coy	Lewis, the Dauphin
Luc Owen	Arthur
Gorden Kaye	Lymoges
Claire Bloom	Constance
John Moreno	Count Melun
Ian Barritt	French herald
Janet Maw	Blanch
Carl Oatley	English herald
Clifford Parrish	French citizen
Richard Wordsworth	Cardinal Panulph
Ian Brimble	First executioner
Ronald Chenery	English messenger
Alan Collins	Peter of Pomfret
Tim Brown	French messenger
Rusty Livingstone	Prince Henry

■ **DESCRIPTION** Television production of the play, with an unlooked-for lugubriousness in that Leonard Rossiter died shortly after recording the programme. A clever stroke of casting, Rossiter's versatile performance makes King John both menacing and pathetic, but cannot lift a routine production.

Laurence Olivier (Lear) and John Hurt (Fool) in KING LEAR (1983)

KING LEAR

KING LEAR

■ **USA • 1909**

d	William V. Ranous [?]
pc	Vitagraph Company of America
sup	J. Stuart Blackton
sc	Eugene Mullin

NFTVA viewing copy
35mm bw st 868ft 10mins
German titles

■ **CAST**

William V. Ranous	King Lear
William Humphrey [?]	Fool
Florence Auer [?]	Goneril
Julia Arthur [?]	Regan
Mary Fuller [?]	Cordelia

■ **DESCRIPTION** Abbreviated version of the play. Ill-advised attempt by Vitagraph to cram as much of the plot as possible into ten minutes; far wiser to have dropped the Edgar subplot as Film d'Arte Italiana did the following year (see below). Shot wholly in the studio, with the storm interestingly suggested by actual scratchings on the film itself. The rapid changes of scene cannot have made much sense to the contemporary audience, but the film has a certain wild vigour that harks back to nineteenth-century melodramatic conventions. The blinding of Gloucester takes place backstage.

■ **NOTES** Identification of the actors is uncertain, and reference sources are contradictory. The film was copyrighted under the title SHAKE-SPEARE'S TRAGEDY, KING LEAR.

■ **REFERENCES** • Ball, *Shakespeare on Silent Film*, pp. 51–2, 313.

RE LEAR

English title KING LEAR

■ **Italy • 1910**

d   Gerolamo Lo Savio
pc   Film d'Arte Italiana

NFTVA viewing copy
35mm bw st 966ft 11mins
English titles

■ **CAST**
Ermete Novelli . . . . *King Lear*
Francesca Bertini . . . . *Cordelia*
Giannina Chiantoni

■ **DESCRIPTION** Abbreviated version of the play, showing most of the key incidents but leaving out the Edgar subplot. Unlike the 1909 Vitagraph version of the play (see above) here the plot seems adequately simplified for its intended audience, with judicious use of intertitles. It is filmed in a variety of locations, mostly open air, with some care taken over composition, although there is nothing to suggest a storm. The result is a well-presented tale of love and cruelty, most affecting where the intertitles tell us that Lear regains his reason, swiftly followed by the death of Cordelia and Lear's ultimate madness.

■ **NOTES** There were two RE LEARs produced in Italy in 1910; the other (not in the NFTVA) was directed by Giuseppe De Liguoro and produced by Milano Films.

■ **REFERENCES** Ball, *Shakespeare on Silent Film*, pp. 120–2, 334.

HOUSE OF STRANGERS

■ **USA • 1949**

d   Joseph L. Mankiewicz
pc   Twentieth Century-Fox Film
         Corporation
p   Sol C. Siegel
sc   Philip Yordan
ph   Milton Krasner
m   Daniele Amfitheatrof

NFTVA viewing copy
35mm bw sd 9,201ft 102mins

■ **CAST**
Richard Conte . . . . *Max Monetti*
Edward G. Robinson . . . . *Gino Monetti*
Susan Hayward . . . . *Irene Bennett*
Luther Adler . . . . *Joe Monetti*
Paul Valentine . . . . *Pietro Monetti*
Efrem Zimbalist Jnr . . . . *Tony Monetti*

■ **DESCRIPTION** Feature film, based on the novel *I'll Never Go There Any More* by Jerome Weidman. A tyrannical Italian-American banker (Robinson) finds that three of his sons turn against him when he is prosecuted by the state for illegal financial practices. He is defended in court by a fourth son (Conte), a maverick lawyer who tries to bribe a jury member and is betrayed to the police by one of his brothers. Coming out of prison, with the father dead, he swears revenge on his brothers, but changes his mind and merely turns his back on them. Frequently referred to as an adaptation of *King Lear*, this is rather more apparent in its Western remake BROKEN LANCE (see below).

BROKEN LANCE

■ **USA • 1954**

d   Edward Dmytryk
pc   Twentieth Century-Fox Film
         Corporation
p   Sol C. Siegel
sc   Richard Murphy
ph   Joe MacDonald
m   Leigh Harline

NFTVA viewing copy
35mm col sd 8,586ft 95mins

■ **CAST**

Spencer Tracy . . . . *Matt Deveraux*
Robert Wagner . . . . *Joe Deveraux*
Jean Peters . . . . *Barbara*
Richard Widmark . . . . *Ben Deveraux*
Earl Holliman . . . . *Denny Deveraux*
Hugh O'Brian . . . . *Mike Deveraux*

■ **DESCRIPTION** Feature film, from a story by Philip Yordan (scriptwriter of HOUSE OF STRANGERS), about a cattle baron (Tracy) who tyrannises his three eldest sons. The father leads a raid on a copper mine and is put on trial; his youngest son Joe, half-brother to the others, saves him by going to jail in his place. When he is released his father is dead, the land having been divided up between the three brothers who refused to bail out Joe and subsequently sold the land. Joe swears revenge, is persuaded against it by his mother, but Ben pursues him anyway. Ben is shot dead and the vendetta is over. The love Joe is seen to bear for his unlovable father gives the film a closer relationship to *King Lear* than HOUSE OF STRANGERS, which it otherwise closely resembles.

SHAKESPEARE AT HARROW

■ **GB • 1957**

NFTVA preservation material
16mm bw sd 448ft 12mins

■ **DESCRIPTION** Amateur film showing scenes from *King Lear* performed in the Speech Room at Harrow School in 1956, under the supervision of Ronald Watkins.

NEW KING LEAR, A

■ **GB • 1971**

■ *Review*

seq d	Alan Yentob
pc	BBC
tx	1 October 1971 (BBC2)
p	Tony Staveacre/Peter Adam/ Barrie Gavin
ed	Colin Nears

NFTVA preservation material
16mm col sd 538ft 15mins

■ **CAST**

Harry Andrews. . . . . *Lear*

■ **DESCRIPTION** Item from television arts magazine. Interview with playwright Edward Bond on his new play *Lear*, with extracts from the play directed by Alan Yentob, with Harry Andrews in the title role.

■ **NOTES** For another view of Shakespeare from Bond, see the 1990 broadcast of his play *Bingo: Scenes of Money and Death* in the General section.

THEATRE OF BLOOD

■ **GB • 1973**

d	Douglas Hickox
pc	Cineman

NFTVA preservation material

■ **CAST**

Vincent Price . . . . *Edward Lionheart*
Diana Rigg . . . . *Edwina Lionheart*
Ian Hendry . . . . *Peregrine Devlin*

■ **DESCRIPTION** Feature film about an actor (Vincent Price) who murders his critics in the manner of deaths from Shakespeare's plays. Peregrine Devlin, Lionheart's final victim, is taken to a theatre and strapped to a chair. Two red-hot knives slowly slide down runners towards his eyes, an allusion to the blinding of Gloucester. The police arrive, Lionheart's daughter is killed in the melée, and in his final role Lionheart delivers Lear's words over the dead Cordelia before falling into the burning theatre. Devlin is saved in the nick of time. For full details of the film see entry in General section.

KING LEAR

■ **GB • 1975**

■ *Play of the Month*

d	Jonathan Miller
pc	BBC
tx	23 March 1975 (BBC1)
p	Cedric Messina
des	Vic Symonds

NFTVA viewing copy
¾" col sd 121mins

■ **CAST**

Michael Hordern	King Lear
Frank Middlemass	Fool
Angela Down	Cordelia
Sarah Badel	Goneril
Penelope Wilton	Regan
Ronald Pickup	Edgar
Michael Jayston	Edmund
Anthony Nicholls	Earl of Gloucester
Ewan Hooper	Earl of Kent
Benjamin Whitrow	Duke of Albany
John Shrapnel	Duke of Cornwall

■ **DESCRIPTION** Television production. Excellent televisual adaptation of the play, with Michael Hordern, more commonly cast in light roles, proving a compelling, brooding and convincing Lear. Pacing, lighting and overall conception are admirable. Miller tried for the same effect in 1982 with Hordern and Middlemass again but failed.

■ **NOTES** Jonathan Miller first directed Hordern and Middlemass in *King Lear* in 1969 at Nottingham Playhouse; he subsequently directed the same pair for the *BBC Television Shakespeare* production of the play in 1982 (see below).

■ **REFERENCES** • Miller, *Subsequent Performances*, pp. 128–46.

KING LEAR

■ **GB • 1976**

d	Steven Rumbelow
pc	British Film Institute Production Board
ed	Mick Audsley/Michael Zimbrich
ph	Peter Harvey
m	David Kitson/Gengiz Saner

NFTVA preservation material
16mm bw sd 1,625ft 45mins

■ **CAST**
Chris Auvache
Gengiz Saner
Monia Buferd
Helena Paul

■ **DESCRIPTION** Shortened version of the play, based on the Triple Action Theatre Group's 1973 stage production. Filmed entirely on location and at night, the only lighting being torches carried by the actors. The film focuses on 'key moments' from the play, highlighting the dilemmas faced by Lear and Gloucester.

KING LEAR

■ **GB/USA 1982**

■ *BBC Television Shakespeare*

d	Jonathan Miller
pc	BBC/Time-Life Films
tx (GB)	19 September 1982 (BBC2)
tx (US)	18 October 1982 (PBS)
p	Shaun Sutton
sc ed	David Snodin
lght	John Treays
cost	Raymond Hughes
des	Colin Lowrey

NFTVA preservation material
1" col sd 180mins

■ **CAST**

John Shrapnel	Earl of Kent
Norman Rodway	Earl of Gloucester
Michael Kitchen	Edmund
Michael Hordern	King Lear
Gillian Barge	Goneril
Brenda Blethyn	Cordelia
Penelope Wilton	Regan
John Bird	Duke of Albany
Julian Curry	Duke of Cornwall
David Weston	Duke of Burgundy
Harry Waters	King of France
Anton Lesser	Edgar
John Grillo	Oswald
Iain Armstrong	First gentleman
Frank Middlemass	Fool
Ken Stott	Curan
Stuart Blake	First servant
Tony Sympson	Second servant
Peter Walmsley	Third servant
George Howe	Doctor
John Dallimore	Second gentleman
Tim Brown	Captain
Adam Kurakin	Herald
Fraser Wilson	Third gentleman
Richard Albrecht	Officer

■ **DESCRIPTION** Television production of the play. Most of what went right for Miller in 1975 (see above) goes wrong here, despite a fuller text and a starry cast. The choice of Hordern, which previously seemed so inspired, now seems ill advised, a lessening of the tragedy. There is strangely little interaction between the characters, and some bold casting strokes (notably John Bird) simply fail. Anton Lesser brings some much needed passion, but the overall effect is deadly.

■ **REFERENCES** • Miller, *Subsequent Performances*, pp. 128–46.

DRESSER, The

■ **GB • 1983**

d/p	Peter Yates
pc	Goldcrest/World Film Services
sc	Ronald Harwood
ph	Kelvin Pike
p des	Stephen Grimes
art d	Colin Grimes
m	James Horner

NFTVA preservation material
35mm col sd 10,657ft 118mins

■ **CAST**

Albert Finney	'Sir'
Tom Courtenay	Norman
Edward Fox	Oxenby
Zena Walker	'Her Ladyship'
Eileen Atkins	Madge
Michael Gough	Frank Carrington
Cathryn Harrison	Irene

■ **DESCRIPTION** Feature film, adapted by Ronald Harwood from his own play. An ageing actor, known only as 'Sir', heads his repertory company as it tours England during the Second World War. His dresser Norman attends to his every need and tries to see that the rambling, absent-minded 'Sir' is fit to go on stage. Forgetting that he is about to go on stage as King Lear, 'Sir' blacks up for *Othello*, and complains about the heavy Cordelia he has to carry. He flirts with Irene, a young member of the cast who idolises him, but it is only to test her weight. Due on stage, 'Sir' becomes completely immobile, but once pushed on stage by Norman he revives and gives a great performance. Later he dies peacefully in the dressing room. Largely a play on film, and not a great play at that. There are sequences from *King Lear* shown during the film – the opening and closing scenes, shown mostly from the wings, the storm scene's sound effects heard only. Moreover, the structure of the play echoes that of the performance of *King Lear*, with appropriate echoes in 'Sir's' own life. Finney is playing an over-the-top character and may be excused his outlandish performance, but fails to move us with the death of Cordelia. He also quotes *Macbeth* from his hospital bed ('Macbeth shall sleep no more . . . ') and is seen in performance as Othello (the death scene).

■ **NOTES** Ronald Harwood based the play on his own experiences with the Wolfit company.

KING LEAR

■ **GB • 1983**

d	Michael Elliott
pc	Granada Television
tx	3 April 1983 (C4)
cost	Tanya Moiseiwitsch
des	Roy Stonehouse
m	Gordon Crosse

NFTVA viewing copy
½" col sd 159mins

■ **CAST**

Colin Blakely	Kent
Leo McKern	Gloucester
Robert Lindsay	Edmund
Laurence Olivier	King Lear
Dorothy Tutin	Goneril
Anna Calder-Marshall	Cordelia
Diana Rigg	Regan
Robert Lang	Albany
Jeremy Kemp	Cornwall
Brian Cox	Burgundy
Edward Petherbridge	King of France
David Threlfall	Edgar
Geoffrey Bateman	Oswald
John Cording	Lear's knight
John Hurt	Fool
Benny Young	Cornwall's servant
Esmond Knight	Old man
Ian Ruskin	Edmund's officer
Paul Curran	Doctor
Ronald Forfar	First officer
Harry Walker	Second officer

■ **DESCRIPTION** Television production of the play. A version of almost overwhelming pathos, with a frail Olivier ending his Shakespearean career with an outstanding, pitiful King Lear. Staged in the television studio with pseudo-Stonehenge settings, it is one of the few outstanding British television productions of a Shakespeare play not to be based on a prior stage original. A wonderfully rich cast could have drowned the play, but each is perfect for their part. Olivier's swan song, and perhaps his finest screen performance in one of the plays.

■ **NOTES** The NFTVA off-air recording is of a repeat broadcast on 21 May 1987 (C4).

(KING LEAR)

■ **GB • 1987**

■ *South Bank Show*

d/p	Chris Hunt
pc	London Weekend Television
tx	11 January 1987 (ITV)
lght	Laurie Bild
cost	Linda Mattock
des	Gordon Melhuish
ed/pres	Melvyn Bragg

NFTVA viewing copy
½" col sd 52mins

■ **CAST FOR NATIONAL THEATRE REHEARSAL**
Anthony Hopkins. . . . . *King Lear*
Suzanne Bertish . . . . *Regan*
Michael Bryant . . . . *Gloucester*
Ken Drury. . . . . *Duke of Albany*
Miranda Foster . . . . *Cordelia*
Philip Locke. . . . . *Earl of Kent*
Bill Nighy . . . . *Edgar*

■ **CAST FOR NAHUM TATE VERSION**
Graham Crowden . . . . *King Lear*
Clive Swift . . . . *Gloucester*
Angela Down . . . . *Cordelia*
Peter Eyre . . . . *Edgar*
John Shrapnel
John Grillo

■ **DESCRIPTION** Television arts documentary. Programme on the staging of *King Lear*, based around a rehearsal in the National Theatre of David Hare's production. David Hare, Jonathan Miller, Anthony Hopkins, Peter Brook and Eric Fried all offer comment on the various approaches to the play, and as well as the rehearsal scenes there are extracts from the Peter Brook film (GB 1970, not in NFTVA), Jonathan Miller's two television productions (GB 1975 and 1982, qqv), Akira Kurosawa's RAN (Japan 1985, not in NFTVA) and Grigori Kozintsev's's KOROL LIR (Soviet Union 1970, not in NFTVA). The programme roughly follows the action of the play, as with Chris Hunt's later *South Bank Show* programme on *Hamlet* (tx 2 April 1989, qv). Most interestingly, there is a staging of the final scene from Nahum Tate's 1681 re-writing of the play, directed by Jonathan Miller, where Goneril and Regan have poisoned one another, Edgar marries Cordelia, and all ends happily.

■ **NOTES** David Hare's production of *King Lear*, with Anthony Hopkins in the title role, opened at the Olivier Theatre in December 1986.

KING LEAR II

■ **GB • 1993**

■ *Nightingales*

d	Tony Dow
pc	Alomo Productions
tx	3 February 1993 (C4)
p	Rosie Bunting
sc	Paul Makin

NFTVA viewing copy
½" col sd 25mins

■ **CAST**
James Ellis . . . . *Sarge*
Robert Lindsay . . . . *Carter*
David Threlfall . . . . *Bell*
Ian Sears . . . . *Eric*

■ **DESCRIPTION** Television comedy series about night security staff. A direct copy of an idea from an earlier programme in the series, TAKEAWAY (qv), which alluded to *Richard III*, but now with copious references to *King Lear*. Carter and Bell decide to be rid of Sarge. They first indulge in lunatic behaviour to convince him of his old age and madness, then organise a birthday party where they give him a throne, crown and sceptre, but Eric (a new recruit), Sarge's proposed successor, is fooled into giving him a Zimmer frame. Sarge spurns Eric with Lear's words to Cordelia (A1S1), then renounces his authority. Carter and Bell take over, panic, ask Eric for help, Eric turns into a werewolf, and Sarge cleans up the blood. There are numerous quotations and references to Shakespeare throughout.

Maureen Lipman in LOVE'S LABOUR'S LOST (1985)

LOVE'S LABOUR'S LOST

TWA CORBIES/SPRING AND WINTER

■ GB • 1951

■ *Poet and Painter no. 1*

d/p	John Halas
pc	Halas & Batchelor
spon	British Film Institute
painter	Mervyn Peake
singer	Peter Pears
m	Matyas Seiber

NFTVA preservation material
35mm bw sd 776ft 8mins

■ **DESCRIPTION** One of a series of films produced by animators John Halas and Joy Batchelor for the Festival of Britain in 1951, where a number of poems were illustrated by specially commissioned still drawings or paintings. *Twa Corbies*, the anonymous Scottish poem, is read by John Laurie and illustrated by Michael Rothenstein; it is accompanied by Shakespeare's songs *Spring* and *Winter* from the end of *Love's Labour's Lost*, illustrated by Mervyn Peake and sung by Peter Pears.

LOVE'S LABOUR'S LOST

■ **GB/USA 1985**

■ *BBC Television Shakespeare*

d	Elijah Moshinsky
pc	BBC/Time-Life Films
tx (GB)	5 January 1985 (BBC2)
tx (US)	31 May 1985 (PBS)
p	Shaun Sutton
lght	John Summers
cost	Colin Lavers
des	Barbara Gosnold
m	Stephen Oliver

NFTVA viewing copy
½" col sd 120mins

■ **CAST**

Jonathan Kent	*King*
Christopher Blake	*Longaville*
Geoffrey Burridge	*Dumain*
Mike Gwilym	*Berowne*
David Warner	*Don Armado*
John Kane	*Moth*
Paul Jesson	*Costard*
Frank Williams	*Dull*
Paddy Navin	*Jaquenetta*
Clifford Rose	*Boyet*
Maureen Lipman	*Princess of France*
Katy Behean	*Maria*
Petra Markham	*Katharine*
Jenny Agutter	*Rosaline*
Jay Ruparella	*Adrian*
John Burgess	*Sir Nathaniel*
John Wells	*Holofernes*
Valentine Dyall	*Marcade*
Linda Kitchen	*Spring*
Susanna Ross	*Winter*

■ **DESCRIPTION** Television production of the play. A fine example of the BBC series' ability to make the most of the lesser-known plays. Set convincingly in the eighteenth century, beautifully lit, and staged in a stylised fashion that successfully puts into practice Jonathan Miller's idea of adopting painting styles for the production design. The keynote is clarity, the mood lightly melancholic, and the performances are perfectly judged. David Warner is particularly happy as Don Armado.

Paul Douglas as Joe and Ruth Roman as Lily in JOE MACBETH (1955)

MACBETH

B. B. C. THE VOICE OF BRITAIN

■ **GB • 1935**

d	Stuart Legg
pc	GPO Film Unit
p	John Grierson/Stuart Legg
ph	George Noble/J. D. Davidson

NFTVA viewing copy
35mm bw sd 5,477ft 61mins

■ **DESCRIPTION** Documentary. Celebrated impressionistic survey of the work of the BBC. Includes scenes of a rehearsal for a radio broadcast of *Macbeth*, featuring the three witches, one of whom is played by documentary film-maker Humphrey Jennings.

VILLAGE SQUIRE, The

■ **GB • 1935**

d	Reginald Denham
pc	British and Dominions Film Corporation/Paramount British
p	Anthony Havelock-Allan
sc	Sherard Powell

NFTVA preservation material
35mm bw sd 6,800ft 76mins

■ **CAST**
David Horne . . . . *Squire Hollis*
Leslie Perrins . . . . *Richard Venables*
Moira Lynd . . . . *Mary Hollis*
Vivien Leigh . . . . *Rose Venables*

■ **DESCRIPTION** Feature film, adapted from a play by Arthur Jarvis Black. Mild village comedy about the local squire who insists on putting on an unwanted production of *Macbeth*. A visiting film star halts the play's progress and falls in love with the squire's daughter.

MARCH OF TIME 3RD YEAR NO. 1 [British edition]

■ **USA • 1937**

item d	Jimmy Shute
pc	Time Inc
p	Louis de Rochemont

NFTVA viewing copy
35mm bw sd 2,089ft 23mins [nitrate]

■ **DESCRIPTION** News cinemagazine. Comprises three items: CHILD LABOUR; UNCLE SAM, IMPRESARIO and D. O. R. A. The second item covers the Works Progress Administration's (WPA) programme of theatrical entertainments, including a very brief (two shots) sequence from the touring production of the WPA Negro Theatre Project's *Macbeth*, as directed by Orson Welles. Macbeth cries 'Lay on, Macduff' (A5S8), they exchange gun-fire, take up swords, and a large crowd of people run on stage whooping.

■ **NOTES** The NFTVA holds the British editions of the *March of Time* series. The above item was originally released in the USA as AN UNCLE SAM PRODUCTION, along with two different items, as MARCH OF TIME VOL. 3 ISSUE 4 (1936). Welles's 1936 'Voodoo *Macbeth*', with its all-black cast, was a considerable success at the Lafayette Theatre, Harlem, transferring to the Adelphi Theatre, Manhattan, before going on an equally successful tour. The sequence featured here is apparently of the touring production, so Macbeth is not played by Jack Carter, who had left the play after its initial run. Macduff may be Maurice Ellis.

■ **REFERENCES** • Richard France, *The Theatre of Orson Welles* (Lewisburg: Bucknell University Press, 1977), pp. 54–73.

MACBETH

■ **GB • 1945**

■ *Famous Scenes from Shakespeare*

d	Henry Cass
pc	Theatrecraft
p	Sydney Box
des	Compton Bennett
m	Ben Frankel

NFTVA viewing copy
35mm bw sd 1,456ft 16mins

■ **CAST**
Wilfrid Lawson . . . . *Macbeth*
Cathleen Nesbitt. . . . . *Lady Macbeth*
Felix Aylmer . . . . *Doctor*
Catherine Lacey . . . . *Gentlewoman*

■ **DESCRIPTION** Excerpt intended for schools audience, adequately if unexcitingly performed, showing the murder of Duncan (A2S2) and the sleepwalking scene (A5S1).

■ **NOTES** The NFTVA also holds JULIUS CAE-SAR (1945), the other title in the series.

MACBETH

■ **USA • 1946**

d	Thomas A. Blair
pc	Willow Productions
p/adapt/ des/ed/ph	David Bradley
cost des	Charlton Heston

NFTVA viewing copy
16mm bw sd 2,533ft 70mins

■ **CAST**
David Bradley . . . . *Macbeth*
Jain Wilimovsky . . . . *Lady Macbeth*
William Bartholomay . . . . *Macduff*
Virginia Nelson. . . . . *Lady Macduff*
Louis Northrop . . . . *Duncan*
William Sweeney . . . . *Doctor/Porter*
J. Royal Mills . . . . *Malcolm*
J. Norton Dunn . . . . *Seyton*
Ann Thompson/Irene Elster/
    Alexander Winter . . . . *Three witches*

■ **DESCRIPTION** Amateur production of the play. A low-budget but tolerably imaginative version made at Northwestern University, Chicago, using local settings and student talent, including a young Charlton Heston as the costume designer. The limitation imposed by a $5,000 budget merely led the film-makers to greater inventiveness, but the performances are quite weak.

■ **NOTES** David Bradley subsequently directed a similar film of *Julius Caesar* in 1950 (not in NFTVA) before becoming a professional film-maker.

MACBETH

■ **USA • 1948**

d/p/adapt	Orson Welles
pc	Mercury Productions for Republic Pictures
ph	John L. Russell
art d	Fred Ritter
cost	Orson Welles/Fred Ritter/ Adele Palmer
m	Jacques Ibert

NFTVA viewing copy
35mm bw sd 9,633ft 107mins

■ CAST

Orson Welles	Macbeth
Jeanette Nolan	Lady Macbeth
Dan O'Herlihy	Macduff
Edgar Barrier	Banquo
Roddy McDowall	Malcolm
Erskine Sandford	Duncan
Alan Napier	A holy father
John Dierkes	Ross
Keene Curtis	Lennox
Peggy Webber	Lady Macduff / Witch
Lionel Braham	Siward
Archie Heugly	Young Siward
Christopher Welles	Macduff child
Brainerd Duffield	First murderer / Witch
William Aland	Second murderer
Robert Alan	Third murderer
George Chirello	Seyton
Gus Schilling	Porter
Jerry Farber	Fleance
Lurene Tuttle	Gentlewoman / Witch
Charles Lederer	Witch
Morgan Farley	Doctor

■ DESCRIPTION Feature film adaptation of the play. Welles's rough-hewn, B-movie production has much that is great in it, but equally much that is foolish. A dazzling mid-credit sequence with the witches' cauldron and a voodoo doll of Macbeth builds up hopes which are dashed the moment the actors open their mouths. All, Welles included, seem to have little awareness of what they are saying, and are impeded in any case by Welles's desire for Scottish accents. The takes are far too long, the very opposite of what Welles would do with OTHELLO, and it is only when they stop speaking that one notices Welles's astonishing visual virtuosity. What good there is in the film is there in spite of Shakespeare.

■ NOTES The NFTVA's copy is at the original release length. According to Brady (see below), the film Welles originally delivered was cut by nearly half an hour down to 107 minutes for release in 1948. Following adverse reactions, particularly to the Scottish accents, Welles largely re-recorded the soundtrack, the film being cut to 89 minutes and re-released in 1951. It is in this form that the film was most widely reviewed and is referred to in most reference sources.

■ REFERENCES ● Claude Beylie, 'Macbeth, or the Magical Depths', *Études Cinématographiques*, 24–25 (1963), pp. 86–9 [translation in Eckert, *Focus on Shakespearean Films*, pp. 72–5]. ● Frank Brady, *Citizen Welles* (New York: Charles Scribner's Sons, 1989), pp. 404–16. ● Davies, *Filming Shakespeare's Plays*, pp. 83–99. ● Manvell, *Shakespeare and the Film*, pp. 55–61. ● Henry Raynor, 'Shakespeare Filmed', *Sight and Sound*, July–September 1952, pp. 10–15.

MACBETH [TRAILER]

■ USA ● 1948

NFTVA preservation material
35mm bw sd 198ft 2mins

■ DESCRIPTION Trailer to the above.

BAD AND THE BEAUTIFUL, The

■ USA ● 1952

d	Vincente Minnelli
pc	MGM
p	John Houseman
sc	Charles Schnee
ph	Robert Surtees
m	David Raskin

NFTVA viewing copy
35mm bw sd 10,558ft 117mins

■ CAST

Kirk Douglas	Jonathan Shields
Lana Turner	Georgia Lorrison

■ DESCRIPTION Feature film. Stylish Hollywood look at Hollywood, where a director, star and writer all look back on their unhappy associations with producer Jonathan Shields. In the story headed by Lana Turner she plays an alcoholic star haunted by memories of her equally alcoholic father. In one sequence she listens to a recording of her father giving the 'Tomorrow and tomorrow…' speech (A5S5).

LAXDALE HALL

USA title SCOTCH ON THE ROCKS

■ GB • 1952

d   John Eldridge
pc   Group 3
exec p   John Grierson
sc   John Eldridge/Alfred Shaughnessy
ph   Arthur Grant
m   Frank Spencer

NFTVA preservation material
35mm bw sd 6,924ft 77mins

■ CAST
Ronald Squire . . . . *General Matheson*
Kathleen Ryan . . . . *Catriona Matheson*
Raymond Huntley . . . . *Samuel Pettigrew MP*
Sebastian Shaw . . . . *Hugh Marvell MP*
Fulton Mackay . . . . *Andrew Flett*

■ **DESCRIPTION** Feature film comedy, based on the novel by Eric Linklater. A group of car owners in the remote Hebridean village of Laxdale refuse to pay their road fund licences until they have been given a proper road. A parliamentary delegation arrives, and among the entertainments put on for them is an open-air production of *Macbeth* staged during a storm. Various incidents ensue until the villagers get their road. Tame comedy on an overworked theme.

MACBETH

■ USA • 1954

■ *Hallmark Hall of Fame*

d   George Schaefer/Hudson Faussett
pc   NBC
tx   28 November 1954 (NBC)
p   Hudson Faussett
des   Otis Riggs
cost   Noel Taylor
m   Lehman Engel

NFTVA preservation material
16mm bw sd 4,291ft 119mins

■ CAST
Maurice Evans . . . . *Macbeth*
Staats Cotsworth . . . . *Banquo*
Judith Anderson . . . . *Lady Macbeth*
House Jameson . . . . *King Duncan*
Richard Waring . . . . *Macduff*
Peter Fernandez . . . . *Donalbain*
Roger Hamilton . . . . *Malcolm*
John Reese . . . . *Fleance*
Margot Stevenson . . . . *Lady Macduff*

■ **DESCRIPTION** Television production of the play. Third of the *Hallmark* Shakespeares to be produced, and the first to be broadcast in colour for the handful of American homes then able to receive colour pictures. Of itself, despite some interesting directorial gestures in a confined setting, a rather mundane interpretation with only Judith Anderson able to rise to the occasion.

■ **NOTES** The NFTVA holds a black and white kinescope (i.e. telerecording) of the live transmission, which includes some commercials for Hallmark greetings cards. In 1960 a second *Hallmark* MACBETH was produced (not in NFTVA) with Evans and Anderson again in the leads, which received a theatrical release before its television broadcast. Again the play defeated what few talents the film-makers possessed. See Clayton Hutton, *Macbeth: The Making of the Film* (London: Max Parrish, 1960).

FESTIVAL IN EDINBURGH

■ GB • 1955

d   Douglas Clarke
pc   Associated British-Pathé
p   Howard Thomas
ph   Jo Jago
nar   Alastair Sim

NFTVA viewing copy
35mm bw sd 1,270ft 14mins

■ **DESCRIPTION** Promotional film for the Edinburgh festival, showing highlights from 1954 Festival, including a short scene from the Old Vic production of *Macbeth*.

JOE MACBETH

■ **GB • 1955**

d	Ken Hughes
pc	Film Locations
p	M. J. Frankovich
sc	Philip Yordan
ph	Basil Emmott
m	Trevor Duncan

NFTVA preservation material
35mm bw sd 8,107ft 90mins

■ **CAST**

Paul Douglas . . . . *Joe Macbeth*
Ruth Roman . . . . *Lily*
Bonar Colleano . . . . *Lennie*
Gregoire Aslan . . . . *Duca*
Sidney James . . . . *Banky*
Nicholas Stuart . . . . *Duffy*
Robert Arden . . . . *Ross*
Minerva Pious . . . . *Rosie*
Harry Green . . . . *Dutch*
Kay Callard . . . . *Ruth*
Walter Crisham . . . . *Angus*
George Margo . . . . *Assassin*

■ **DESCRIPTION** Feature film presenting the
Macbeth plot as a modern gangster story. Joe
Macbeth is number two in the underworld to
'kingpin' Duca. Goaded on by his wife Lily, who
wants Joe to become the 'kingpin', and half-
believing the words of Rosie, a fortune teller, Joe
invites Duca to his lakeside house and knifes him
while he is swimming. Joe is now head of the
underworld. His friend Banky is loyal to him, but
Banky's son Lennie is resentful, and Joe hires gun-
men to dispose of Lennie. By mistake, Banky is
murdered instead. Banky's ghost appears to Joe at
a party, and Joe feels that he is losing control over
his gang. Another plan is bungled when Lennie's
wife and baby are killed during a kidnap attempt.
Joe barricades himself in. Joe accidentally kills
Lily, then is gunned down by Lennie. A not
entirely unsuccessful experiment, suffering from
having to keep to unnecessary (if sometimes inge-
nious) parallels, but put over with style and
boasting a memorably lugubrious performance
from Paul Douglas.

■ **NOTES** Scriptwriter Philip Yordan wrote the
script for HOUSE OF STRANGERS (1949) and
the story of BROKEN LANCE (1954), both *King
Lear* derivatives (qv). A number of Yordan's stories and scripts appear to take their lead from
classical drama.

KUMONOSU-JO

English title THRONE OF BLOOD

■ **Japan • 1957**

d	Akira Kurosawa
pc	Toho
assoc p	Akira Kurosawa/Sojiro Motoki
sc	Hideo Oguni/Shinobu Hashimoto/
	Ryuzo Kikushima/Akira Kurosawa
ph	Asaichi Nakai
art d	Yoshiro Murai
m	Masaru Sato

NFTVA viewing copy
35mm bw sd 9,844ft 109mins

■ **CAST**

Toshiro Mifune . . . . *Taketoki Washizu*
Isuzu Yamada . . . . *Asaji, his wife*
Takashi Shimura . . . . *Noriyasu Odagura*
Minoru Chiaki . . . . *Yoshiaki Miki*
Akira Kubo . . . . *Yoshiteru, his son*
Takamaru Sasaki . . . . *Kuniharu Tsuzuki*
Yoichi Tachikawa . . . . *Kunimaru, his son*
Chieko Naniwa . . . . *Weird Woman*

■ **DESCRIPTION** Feature film. A translation of
the plot of *Macbeth* to medieval Japan. Washizu
and Miki are two Samurai owing allegiance to
Tsuzuki, lord of Cobweb Castle. Having defeated
the forces of Inui, they encounter an old woman
in a forest who tells Washizu that he will gain
control of the North Mansion, then of Cobweb
Castle, but that Miki's son will succeed him.
Washizu soon learns that the first part of the
prophecy has come true. His wife Asaji persuades
him to have Tsuzuki murdered. Washizu becomes
lord of Cobweb Castle but announces that Miki's
son will succeeed him. Asaji informs him that she
is pregnant and demands that he murder both
Miki and his son Yoshiteru. Miki is murdered, but
Yoshiteru escapes to the forces of Inui. Washizu
consults the old woman again, and she assures
him that he will be safe until Cobweb Forest is

seen to move. Inui's army cut down the trees as camouflage as they approach Cobweb Castle. Washizu is shot to death by the arrows of his own men. One of the most dazzling and accomplished of Shakespearean films, 'a transmutation, a distillation of the *Macbeth* theme, not an adaptation' (Manvell).

■ **NOTES** The title translates as *Cobweb Castle*. Kurosawa made two other Shakespearean derivatives (neither in NFTVA): WARUI YATSU HODO YOKU NEMURU (1960, English title THE BAD SLEEP WELL), updating the *Hamlet* story to a modern Japanese business setting; and RAN (1985), a similar exercise to KUMONOSU-JO, translating *King Lear* to a setting in medieval Japan.

■ **REFERENCES** ● J. Blumenthal, 'Macbeth into Throne of Blood', *Sight and Sound*, Autumn 1965, pp. 190–5. ● Collick, *Shakespeare, Cinema and Society*, pp. 174–81. ● John Gerlach, 'Shakespeare, Kurosawa, and *Macbeth*: A Response to J. Blumenthal', *Literature/Film Quarterly*, Fall 1973, pp. 352–9. ● Manvell, *Shakespeare and the Film*, pp. 101–13.

ANNE SHELTON SHOW, The

■ **GB ● 1959**

d	Bill Hitchcock
pc	A Jack Hylton Production for Associated-Rediffusion
tx	23 February 1959 (ITV)
sc	Dick Vosburgh/Brad Ashton
sets	Robert Freemantle
m	Billy Ternent and his Orchestra

NFTVA viewing copy
35mm bw sd 2,375ft 26mins

■ **CAST**
Anne Shelton . . . . *Lady Macbeth*
Dick Bentley . . . . *Matt Macbeth*
Dick Emery

■ **DESCRIPTION** Television variety programme. The second half of the programme contains a sketch entitled 'The Life and Legend of Matt Macbeth', by Wild Will Shakespeare, presenting *Macbeth* as a musical Western. Dick Bentley is Matt Macbeth, dressed in full cowboy gear, Anne

Shelton plays Lady Macbeth dressed as Annie Oakley, and the three witches are American Indians. Macbeth kills Dick Emery's character (not named) and his son to become Marshal. Songs are sung to such tunes as 'Row, Row, Row' and 'Ragtime Cowboy Joe'.

■ **NOTES** Scriptwriter Dick Vosburgh had previously devised (with Jack Bentley) a version of *Macbeth* on roller skates for the Associated-Rediffusion variety programme HERE WE GO (tx 17 November 1955, not in NFTVA, alas).

BANQUO'S CHAIR

■ **USA ● 1959**

■ *Alfred Hitchcock Presents*

d	Alfred Hitchcock
pc	Shamley Productions
tx	3 May 1959 (CBS)
p	Alfred Hitchcock/Joan Harrison
sc	Francis Cockrell

NFTVA preservation material
16mm bw sd 873ft 55mins

■ **CAST**
Reginald Gardiner
John Williams
Kenneth Haigh
Max Adrian

■ **DESCRIPTION** Television play. A murderer is found out by the ghost of his victim appearing at the dinner table (the real ghost appears before an actress supposed to be playing the part can turn up).

■ **NOTES**
One of the few titles in the *Alfred Hitchcock Presents* series to be directed by Hitchcock himself.

DAME EDITH SITWELL

■ **GB ● 1959**

pc	BBC
tx	16 September 1959 (BBC)
pres	Elwyn Jones

NFTVA preservation material
16mm bw sd 574ft 36mins

■ **DESCRIPTION** Television programme. Dame Edith Sitwell repeats a recital of poems she gave at the Edinburgh Festival, 1959. Among the recitations are the song 'Take, O! take those lips away' from *Measure for Measure* and the sleepwalking scene from *Macbeth* (A5S1).

NO, MY DARLING DAUGHTER

■ **GB • 1961**

d	Ralph Thomas
pc	Five Star Films
p	Betty E. Box
sc	Frank Harvey
ph	Ernest Steward
m	Norrie Paramor

NFTVA preservation material
35mm bw sd 8,671ft 96mins

■ **CAST**
Juliet Mills . . . . *Tansy*
Rad Fulton . . . . *Cornelius*

■ **DESCRIPTION** Feature film. Feeble comedy about a British tomboy and her American boyfriend. Includes a scene where Mills demonstrates the effect of St Paul's Cathedral's Whispering Gallery to Fulton by quoting the 'Out, damned spot!' lines (A5S1).

DEADLY AFFAIR, The

■ **GB • 1966**

d/p	Sidney Lumet
pc	Sidney Lumet Productions
sc	Paul Dehn
ph	Freddie Young
m	Quincy Jones

NFTVA viewing copy
35mm col sd 9,603ft 107mins

■ **CAST**
James Mason . . . . *Charles Mason*
Simone Signoret . . . . *Elsa Fennan*
Maximilian Schell . . . . *Dieter Frey*

Harry Andrews . . . . *Inspector Mendel*

■ **DESCRIPTION** Feature film, based on the novel *Call for the Dead* by John Le Carré, about spies in London. Includes a noted scene of the Royal Shakespeare Company's production of Marlowe's *Edward II* (the murder of Edward parallels that of Signoret), but also features a short scene from a production of *Macbeth* in rehearsal at a theatre: the witches' 'Double, double, toil and trouble' (A4S1).

(WILLIAM SHAKESPEARE/ MARTHA GRAHAM)

■ **GB • 1967**

■ *This Week – The Arts*

d	John Phillips
pc	Rediffusion
tx	7 April 1967 (ITV)
pres	David Robinson

NFTVA viewing copy
35mm bw sd 1,636ft 18mins

■ **CAST**
Bob Grant . . . . *MacBird*
Toni Palmer . . . . *Lady MacBird*

■ **DESCRIPTION** Television arts documentary. Scenes from Barbara Garson's satirical play *MacBird*: MacBird (a skit on Lyndon B. Johnson) learns from a fruit machine that he is to be Vice President to John Kennedy, and then President in his own right. He and his wife discuss the situation, she declaring that the Vice President never gets to be President. David Robinson then talks of the difficulties he feels Shakespeare presents for modern audiences and reviews two contemporary Shakespeare film releases, Zeffirelli's THE TAMING OF THE SHREW (1966) and Welles's CAMPANADAS A MEDIANOCHE (1966), with extracts from the latter.

■ **NOTES** The *MacBird* scenes come from Joan Littlewood's production at the Theatre Royal, Stratford. The play, originally produced in New York, was a satirical portrait of American politics, finding in *Macbeth* parallels for Johnson, Kennedy and Adlai Stevenson. The second half of the programme is on choreographer Martha Graham.

There are several sequences missing from the Shakespeare section, including a probable introduction by Bryan Magee, an explanation of the *MacBird* production, and an extract from the Zeffirelli film.

CHARGE OF THE LIGHT BRIGADE, The

■ **GB • 1968**

d	Tony Richardson
pc	Woodfall Film Productions
p	Neil Hartley
sc	Charles Wood
ph	David Watkin
m	John Addison

NFTVA preservation material
35mm col sd 12,690ft 141mins

■ **CAST**

Trevor Howard . . . . *Lord Cardigan*
Vanessa Redgrave . . . . *Clarissa Codrington*
John Gielgud . . . . *Lord Raglan*
David Hemmings. . . . . *Captain Nolan*
Donald Wolfit . . . . *'Macbeth'*

■ **DESCRIPTION** Feature film. A colourfully presented history of the catastrophic charge of the Light Brigade during the Crimean War, 1854. Includes a scene from *Macbeth* at a London theatre, where Macbeth meets the witches for the second time (A4S1).

MACBETH

■ **GB • 1970**

■ *Play of the Month*

d	John Gorrie
pc	BBC
tx	20 September 1970 (BBC1)
p	Cedric Messina
des	Natasha Knoll
cost	John Bloomfield
m	Christopher Whelen

NFTVA viewing copy
¼" col sd 135mins

■ **CAST**

Daphne Heard/Sylvia Coleridge/
  Hilary Mason. . . . . *Witches*
Michael Goodliffe. . . . . *Duncan*
John Alderton . . . . *Malcolm*
Robin Browne . . . . *Donalbain*
Michael Beint . . . . *Sergeant*
Donald Douglas. . . . . *Lennox*
Alan Rowe. . . . . *Ross*
Eric Porter . . . . *Macbeth*
John Thaw . . . . *Banquo*
Geoffrey Palmer . . . . *Menteith*
Colin Fisher. . . . . *Caithness*
Janet Suzman . . . . *Lady Macbeth*
John Kelland . . . . *Messenger*
Malcolm McFee . . . . *Fleance*
David Spenser . . . . *Seyton*
Wolfe Morris . . . . *Porter*
John Woodvine . . . . *Macduff*
George Merritt. . . . . *Old man*
Leon Eagles/Tony Caunter . . . . *Murderers*
Ray Davis . . . . *Servant*
Rupert Tillyard/Christopher Guard . . *Apparitions*
Rowena Cooper . . . . *Lady Macduff*
Nicholas Dashwood. . . . . *Son to Macduff*
John Bailey . . . . *Doctor*
Rosamond Burne. . . . . *Gentlewoman*
Paul Greenhalgh . . . . *Servant*
Norman Tyrrell. . . . . *Siward*
David Sadgrove . . . . *Young Siward*

■ **DESCRIPTION** Television production. Uninspired studio-bound dry-run for Gorrie and Messina's work for the *BBC Television Shakespeare* series, hoping to lure a primetime audience with Eric Porter, star of the recently hugely popular *Forsyte Saga*. Janet Suzman consistently holds one's attention, the rest are just passing through.

MACBETH

■ **GB • 1971**

d	Roman Polanski
pc	Playboy Productions/Caliban Films
exec p	Hugh Hefner
p	Andrew Braunsberg
adapt	Roman Polanski/Kenneth Tynan
ph	Gilbert Taylor
p des	Wilfrid Shingleton
art d	Fred Carter
cost	Anthony Mendelson
m	The Third Ear Band

NFTVA preservation material
35mm col sd 12,639ft 140mins

■ **CAST**

Jon Finch . . . . *Macbeth*
Francesca Annis . . . . *Lady Macbeth*
Martin Shaw. . . . . *Banquo*
Nicholas Selby . . . . *Duncan*
John Stride. *Ross*
Stephan Chase. . . . . *Malcolm*
Paul Shelley . . . . *Donalbain*
Terence Bayler. . . . . *Macduff*
Andrew Laurence . . . . *Lennox*
Frank Wylie . . . . *Menteith*
Bernard Archard. . . . . *Angus*
Bruce Purchess. . . . . *Caithness*
Keith Chegwin . . . . *Fleance*
Noel Davis . . . . *Seyton*
Noelle Rimmington. . . . . *Young witch*
Maisie MacFarquhar . . . . *Blind witch*
Elsie Taylor . . . . *First witch*
Vic Abbott. . . . . *Cawdor*
Bill Drysdale . . . . *King's groom 1*
Roy Jones. . . . . *King's groom 2*
Patricia Mason. . . . . *Gentlewoman*
Ian Hogg . . . . *First minor Thane*
Geoffrey Reed . . . . *Second minor Thane*
Nigel Ashton . . . . *Third minor Thane*
Mark Dignam. . . . . *Macduff's son*
Diane Fletcher . . . . *Lady Macduff*
Richard Pearson. . . . . *Doctor*
Sydney Bromley . . . . *Porter*
William Hobbs . . . . *Young Seyward*
Alf Joint . . . . *Old Seyward*
Michael Balfour . . . . *First murderer*
Andrew McCulloch . . . . *Second murderer*
Howard Lang. . . . . *First old soldier*
David Ellison. . . . . *Second old soldier*
Terence Mountain . . . . *Soldier*
Paul Hennen . . . . *Boy apprentice*

■ **DESCRIPTION** Feature film version of the play. Admirably fresh and imaginative reading of the play, which has been adapted for the screen with intelligent understanding of both play and film medium. The two leads are not of the strongest, and Finch is rather less than a tragic figure, more 'a delinquent who has never been given a plausible reason to restrain his desires' (Philip Strick, *Monthly Film Bulletin*). A determinedly realistic interpretation, which Polanski directs with clarity and insight. There is much blood.

■ **NOTES** Filmed on location in Wales.

■ **REFERENCES** • Normand Berlin, '*Macbeth*: Polanski and Shakespeare', *Literature/Film Quarterly*, Fall 1973, pp. 291–8. • Roger Manvell, *Theater and Film* (London: Associated University Presses, 1979), pp. 151–64.

VERDI'S MACBETH

■ **GB • 1972**

tv d	David Heather
pc	Southern Television
tx	27 December 1972 (ITV)
p	Michael Hadjimischev
tv p	Humphrey Burton
lght	Hedley Varsey
des	Emanuele Luzzati
subtitles	Spike Hughes

NFTVA preservation material
1" col sd c200mins

■ **CAST**

Kostas Paskalis. . . . . *Macbeth*
James Morris . . . . *Banquo*
Josephine Barstow. . . . . *Lady Macbeth*
Rae Woodland . . . . *Gentlewoman*
Keith Erwen . . . . *Macduff*
Ian Caley . . . . *Malcolm*
Brian Donlan. . . . . *Doctor*
Ian Caddy . . . . *Servant*
John Tomlinson . . . . *Murderer/First apparition*
Angela Whittingham . . . . *Bloody child*
Linda Esther Gray . . . . *Third apparition*
Geoffrey Gilbertson . . . . *Duncan*
Tom Redman . . . . *Fleance*

■ **DESCRIPTION** Television presentation of the 1972 Glyndebourne production of Verdi's opera *Macbeth*, recorded at Glyndebourne, with music played by the London Philharmonic Orchestra, conducted by John Pritchard. A full-blooded and imaginative production wholly successful in its transference to the screen.

■ **NOTES** The programme caused some controversy at the time on account of the Independent Broadcasting Authority's insistence (through Humphrey Burton's influence) that the ITV companies should balance their light Christmas fare with a primetime broadcast of a 'quality' programme, namely this recording of Verdi's *Macbeth*. Fears (as expressed in the *TV Times* letters page) that Christmas would be spoiled were allayed when the opera was broadcast on 27 December.

BENTINE

■ **GB • 1975**

d	Leon Thau
pc	Thames Television
tx	22 September 1975 (ITV)
p	David Clark
sc	Michael Bentine/John Ennis
des	Colin Andrews

NFTVA preservation material
2" col sd 45mins

■ **DESCRIPTION** Television comedy programme starring the eccentric Michael Bentine. Includes a 'flowing version of Shakespeare's *Macbeth* guaranteed to make the Bard turn in his tomb' (*TV Times*).

MACBETH

■ **GB • 1979**

tv d	Philip Casson
pc	Thames Television
tx	4 January 1979 (ITV)
p	Trevor Nunn
tv des	Mike Hall

NFTVA viewing copy
¾" col sd 120mins

■ **CAST**
Ian McKellen. . . . . *Macbeth*
Judi Dench . . . . *Lady Macbeth*
John Bowen . . . . *Lennox*
Marie Kean . . . . *First witch*
Judith Harte . . . . *Second witch/Gentlewoman*
Susan Drury . . . . *Third witch/Lady Macduff*
Greg Hicks. . . . . *Donalbain/Seyton*
David Howey. . . . . *Sergeant/First murderer/Doctor*
Griffith Jones. . . . . *Duncan*
Ian McDiarmid . . . . *Ross/Porter*
Bob Peck . . . . *Macduff*
Duncan Preston . . . . *Angus*

Roger Rees. *Malcolm*
Zak Taylor . . . . *Fleance/Messenger*
Stephen Warner . . . . *Young Macduff*
John Woodvine. . . . . *Banquo*

■ **DESCRIPTION** Television presentation of Trevor Nunn's Royal Shakespeare Company production. A great production in the theatre, and as reimagined here an astonishingly powerful piece of television as well, brilliantly, sparingly designed and lit, with two leading performances probably unmatched in the history of the play. Psychological, not pictorial realism was the intention: sensual, brutal, deeply felt, it could convince anyone that Shakespeare was made for the screen.

■ **NOTES** The production was originally staged by the Royal Shakespeare Company in 1976 at The Other Place, Stratford.

■ **REFERENCES** • Michael Mullin, 'Stage and Screen: The Trevor Nunn *Macbeth*', *Shakespeare Quarterly*, 38 (Autumn 1987), pp. 350–9 [reprinted in Bulman and Coursen, *Shakespeare on Television*, pp. 107–15].

SHAKESPEARE'S MOUNTED FOOT

■ **GB • 1979**

d/ed	Bert Eeles
pc	A Breck/Campbell Production
spon	Scottish Arts Council
p	Douglas Eadie/Mick Campbell
sc	Douglas Eadie ['additional material by William Shakespeare and Henry Stamper']
ph	Mick Campbell
m	Owen Hand

NFTVA preservation material
16mm col sd 1,600ft 44mins

■ **CAST**
Alex Norton . . . . *Mr Melford*
James Copeland . . . . *Mr Montani*
Russell Hunter . . . . *Mr Mowther*
Vari Sylvester . . . . *Leading lady*
Sandy Neilson . . . . *Macbeth*

■ **DESCRIPTION** Fiction short. Amiable comedy about a turn-of-the-century theatrical troupe in the barnstorming tradition touring the North Country and the Scottish Borders, and based on contemporary accounts of such troupes. Includes an appropriate sequence from the troupe's version of *Macbeth*.

MACBETH A TRAGEDY

■ **GB • 1983**

d   Anne Rees-Mogg

NFTVA preservation material
16mm sd col c125ft 4mins

■ **DESCRIPTION** Art film comparing a text from *The Oxford Companion to English Literature* with the 'Tomorrow and tomorrow' speech from *Macbeth* (A5S5).

NIGHT OF COMIC RELIEF, A

■ **GB • 1988**

pc   BBC
tx   5 February 1988 (BBC1)
hosts   Lenny Henry/Griff Rhys Jones/
           Jonathan Ross

NFTVA viewing copy
½" col sd 388mins

■ **CAST**
Martin Jarvis . . . . *Mr Macbeth*
Penelope Wilton . . . . *Mrs Macbeth*
Derek Nimmo . . . . *The Vicar*

■ **DESCRIPTION** Television charity variety revue. An evening of comedy acts, classic comedy shows and reports on charitable causes benefiting from the programme, in Africa and Britain. Includes a two-minute spoof version of *Macbeth* played as a television sit-com. In their living room Mrs Macbeth tells her unsure husband that he must kill the King ('Oh, it's always tomorrow and tomorrow and tomorrow with you, Macbeth'). He does so; meanwhile the vicar calls round for tea.

■ **NOTES** A *Hamlet* spoof is featured in the following year's A NIGHT OF COMIC RELIEF 2 (qv).

MIDSUMMER NIGHT'S MYSTERY, A

■ **GB • 1989**

■ *First Tuesday*

d/p   Kevin Sim
pc   Yorkshire Television
tx   4 July 1989 (ITV)

NFTVA viewing copy
½" col sd 51mins

■ **CAST**
Patrick O'Connell . . . . *Macbeth*

■ **DESCRIPTION** Television documentary on the claims for Edward de Vere, Earl of Oxford to be the true author of Shakespeare's works. Includes a reading of the 'To-morrow, and to-morrow, and to-morrow' speech (A5S5). For full details of the programme see entry in General section.

PACKET OF 3

■ **GB • 1991**

d   John Stroud
pc   Jon Blair Film Company
tx   20 September 1991 (C4)

NFTVA viewing copy

■ **DESCRIPTION** Television comedy series. Includes a brief version of the play performed by the Reduced Shakespeare Company in heavy Scottish accents. For full details of the programme see entry in General section.

ENTERTAINMENT UK

■ **GB • 1993**

pc   Mentorn Films
tx   18 March 1993 (ITV)

p John Needham/Jonathan Challis
pres Toyah Willcox

NFTVA viewing copy
½" col sd 51mins

■ **CAST**
Rory Edwards . . . . *Macbeth*
Kathryn Hunter . . . . *Lady Macbeth*

■ **DESCRIPTION** Television arts and entertainment magazine. Includes short item on a production of *Macbeth* at the Haymarket Theatre, Leicester, interviewing actors Rory Edwards and Kathryn Hunter, plus director Julia Bardsley, and illustrated with three brief scenes from the production (A3S2).

■ **NOTES**
The programme also includes a similar item on a production of *Othello* in Birmingham (qv).

Kate Nelligan as Isabella in MEASURE FOR MEASURE (1983)

MEASURE FOR MEASURE

DAME EDITH SITWELL

■ **GB • 1959**

pc BBC

tx 16 September 1959 (BBC)
pres Elwyn Jones

NFTVA preservation material
16mm bw sd 574ft 36mins

■ **DESCRIPTION** Television programme. Dame Edith Sitwell repeats a recital of poems she gave at the Edinburgh Festival, 1959. Among the recitations are the song 'Take, O! take those lips away' from *Measure for Measure* (A4S1) and the sleepwalking scene from *Macbeth*.

FAREWELL TO THE VIC

■ **GB • 1963**

d/p David Jones
pc BBC
tx 15 June 1963 (BBC)
OB d Mary Evans
intro Michael Flanders

NFTVA preservation material
16mm bw sd 2,346ft 65mins

■ **DESCRIPTION** Television documentary. An extraordinary line-up of theatre folk tell the story of the Old Vic theatre company: Robert Atkins, Michael Benthall, John Blatchley, Richard Burton, Michael Elliott, Edith Evans, John Gielgud, Alec Guinness, Tyrone Guthrie, John Neville, Laurence Olivier, Michael Redgrave, Ralph Richardson, Tommy Steele, Sybil Thorndike and Ninette de Valois. There is also live coverage of the closing moments of the final performance of *Measure for Measure*.

■ **NOTES** The programme was broadcast on the last night itself and was produced by the BBC's *Monitor* arts series team.

MONTY PYTHON'S FLYING CIRCUS

■ **GB • 1970**

pc BBC
tx 24 November 1970 (BBC1)
p Ian MacNaughton
sc/cast Graham Chapman/John Cleese/

Terry Gilliam/Eric Idle/
Michael Palin/Terry Jones
des   Richard Hunt

NFTVA viewing copy
½" col sd 30mins

■ **DESCRIPTION** Television comedy series. Features a short extract from the first underwater production of *Measure for Measure* (filmed above the waves, sequence featured indistinct).

■ **NOTES** The NFTVA copy was recorded off-air 21 December 1990. Other *Monty Python* tributes to Shakespeare held by the NFTVA, and perhaps too brief for individual entries, are *Julius Caesar* performed with an Aldis lamp (tx 22 September 1970) and a meeting between Beethoven and Shakespeare, who offers the former advice on composing his Fifth Symphony (tx 17 November 1970). A complete episode from the series, entitled HAMLET (tx 21 November 1974) and following some of the action and characters of the play (Terry Jones plays Hamlet) is not held by the NFTVA.

MEASURE FOR MEASURE

■ **GB/USA** • **1979**

■ *BBC Television Shakespeare*

d   Desmond Davis
pc   BBC/Time-Life Films
tx **(GB)** 18 February 1979 (BBC2)
tx **(US)** 11 April 1979 (PBS)
p   Cedric Messina
sc ed   Alan Shallcross
cost   Odette Barrow
m   James Tyler/London Early Music Group

NFTVA viewing copy
½" col sd 150mins

■ **CAST**
Kenneth Colley . . . . *Vincentio, the Duke*
Kate Nelligan . . . . *Isabella*
Tim Pigott-Smith . . . . *Angelo, the Deputy*
Christopher Strauli . . . *Claudio, a young gentleman*
John McEnery . . . . *Lucio, a fantastic*
Jacqueline Pearce . . . *Mariana, betrothed to Angelo*

Frank Middlemass . . . . *Pompey*
Alun Armstrong . . . . *Provost*
Adrienne Corri . . . . *Mistress Overdone, a bawd*
Ellis Jones . . . . *Elbow, a simple constable*
John Clegg . . . . *Froth, a foolish gentleman*
William Sleigh . . . . *Barnardine, a dissolute prisoner*
Neil McCarthy . . . . *Abhorson, an executioner*
Yolande Palfrey . . . . *Juliet, beloved of Claudio*
Eileen Page . . . . *Francisca, a nun*
Kevin Stoney . . . . *Escalus, an ancient lord*
Godfrey Jackman . . . . *Friar Thomas*
Alan Tucker . . . . *First gentleman*
John Abbott . . . . *Second gentleman*
David Browning . . . . *A justice*
Geoffrey Cousins . . . . *Servant*
David King Lassman . . . . *Pageboy*
Tony Friel . . . . *First gaoler*
Harry Jones . . . . *Second gaoler*
John Sarbutt . . . . *First arresting officer*
Nicholas Tudor . . . . *Second arresting officer*

■ **DESCRIPTION** Television production of the play. A better-than-usual offering from the BBC series, an intense, claustrophobic interpretation, designed and lit for the screen with care. Fine leading performances helped to make a difficult play palatable to the general audience.

■ **REFERENCES** • H. R. Coursen, 'Why *Measure for Measure?*', *Literature/Film Quarterly*, 12 (1984), pp. 65–9 [reprinted in Bulman and Coursen, *Shakespeare on Television*, pp. 179–84].

MEASURE FOR MEASURE

■ **GB** • **1983**

■ *Shakespeare Lives*

d   Mary McMurray
pc   Quintet Films
tx   2 March 1984 (C4) [part one]
        9 March 1984 (C4) [part two]
p   Victor Glynn/Mike Ockrent

NFTVA preservation material
1" col sd c30+30mins

■ **CAST**
Suzanne Bertish . . . . *Isabella*
Clive Arrindell

Michael Bryant
Joss Buckley
Dinsdale Landen
Bill Wallis

■ **DESCRIPTION** Television theatre workshop,
broadcast in two parts. National Theatre director
Michael Bogdanov guides a group of National
Theatre players through aspects of *Measure for
Measure* in front of a studio audience. Bogdanov
asks whether the play is a dated piece about a
woman's dilemma over her virtue, or whether it
is more properly about 'a sinister chain of pro-
curement'. One of a lively, informal workshop
series, with Bogdanov fielding questions from the
audience, putting the actors through their paces,
and revelling in argument.

■ **NOTES** Other plays covered in this series are
Hamlet, *Richard III*, *The Taming of the Shrew* and
Timon of Athens (qqv).

ENTERTAINMENT UK

■ **GB • 1993**

pc	Mentorn Films
tx	1 April 1993 (ITV)
p	Jonathan Challis/John Needham
rep	Hilary Fennell

NFTVA viewing copy
½" col sd 51mins

■ **DESCRIPTION** Television arts and entertainment magazine. Includes a three-minute item on
the Gallowglass Theatre Company's production of
Measure for Measure, on tour in Ireland. Includes
extracts from A2S4 and A2S1, the latter illustrating the striking use of masks.

MERCHANT OF VENICE

MERCANTE DI VENEZIA, il

English title MERCHANT OF VENICE, The

■ **Italy • 1910**

d	Gerolamo Lo Savio
pc	Film d'Arte Italiana

Werner Krauss in DER KAUFMANN VON
VENEDIG (1923)

NFTVA viewing copy
35mm col st 568ft 6mins
Incomplete – original length 890ft
English titles

■ **CAST**

Ermete Novelli	*Shylock*
Francesca Bertini	*Portia*
Ferruccio Garavaglia	
Olga Giannini Novelli	

■ **DESCRIPTION** Abbreviated version of the play,
showing most of the key stages of the action, but
omitting the caskets and the business with Portia's
ring. The NFTVA's incomplete print ends with
Shylock appealing to the court after Portia has
warned him not to spill 'one drop of Christian
blood' (A4S1). The missing scene showed
Shylock's punishment by the court.

■ **NOTES** Sources differ over the date of this
film, but Aldo Bernadini's *Archivio del Cinema
Italiano: Volume 1 – Il Cinema Muto* (1991) gives
1910. The NFTVA's copy is stencil-coloured,
these colour effects being reproduced on the
safety dupe viewing copy. Includes scenes filmed
in Venice.

■ **REFERENCES ●** Ball, *Shakespeare on Silent Film*,
pp. 122–5, 334–5.

SHYLOCK

■ **France • 1913**

d	Henri Desfontaines
pc	Eclipse
p	Clément Maurice
sc	Louis Mercanton

NFTVA viewing copy
35mm bw st 1,970ft 22mins
English titles

■ **CAST**

Harry Baur	Shylock
Romauld Joubé	Antonio
Jean Hervé	Bassanio
Pepa Bonafé	Portia

■ **DESCRIPTION** Abbreviated version of the play, leaving out the Jessica plot and some minor incidents. Studio-bound and unimaginative interpretation, all involved being too much in thrall to the stage. It is of most value for Harry Baur's vivid, if somewhat primitive, portrayal of Shylock. A detailed description of the NFTVA print, with intertitles, is given in Ball.

■ **NOTES** The NFTVA has previously catalogued this film as being directed by Clément Maurice, which appears to be wrong. The French production company Eclipse produced a number of other Shakespeare films: HAMLET (1910), FALSTAFF (1911) and LA MÉGÈRE APPRIVOISÉE (1911, *The Taming of the Shrew*). None of these is held in the NFTVA. All were directed by Henri Desfontaines.

■ **REFERENCES** • Ball, *Shakespeare on Silent Film*, pp. 177–83, 348.

MERCHANT OF VENICE, The

■ **GB • 1916**

d/p	Walter West
pc	Broadwest Film Company

NFTVA preservation material
35mm bw st 1,849ft 20mins
Incomplete – original length 6,000ft
English titles

■ **CAST**

Matheson Lang	Shylock
Hutin Britton	Portia
J. R. Tozer	Bassanio
Kathleen Hazel Jones	Jessica
George Skillan	Antonio
Ernest Caselli	Lorenzo
Terence O'Brien	Tubal
John Daly	Prince of Morocco
Marguerite Westlake	Nerissa
George Morgan	Launcelot Gobbo

■ **DESCRIPTION** Reels two and three only of a five-reel feature film, a literal transcription to the screen of a St James's Theatre production. Although of some value as a record of a reasonably sound stage production, moderately performed, the stage settings and total deference to the theatre make this a dated effort by 1916, and a very dull one now. Its chief virtue is Lang's Shylock, invested with genuine humanity (the whole of the 'hath not a Jew eyes' speech is given in the intertitles). The surviving footage in the NFTVA shows the action from Antonio first agreeing with Shylock to his bond (A1S3) to Portia saying 'Is your name Shylock?' in court (A4S1). A detailed description of the footage, with intertitles, is given by Ball.

■ **NOTES** Hutin Britton was Matheson Lang's wife and theatrical partner. George Morgan does not appear in the NFTVA footage. According to a review in the *Cinema News and Property Gazette* (reproduced by Ball) George Skillan was made up to look like Shakespeare.

■ **REFERENCES** • Ball, *Shakespeare on Silent Film*, pp. 245–52, 366–7.

KAUFMANN VON VENEDIG, Der

Alternative title **SHYLOCK, DER JUDE VON VENEDIG**
GB title **JEW OF MESTRI, The**

■ **Germany • 1923**

d/p/adapt	Peter Paul Felner
pc	Peter Paul Felner Produktion
ph	Axel Graatkjaer/Rudolf Maté
sets	Hermann Warm

NFTVA viewing copy
35mm bw st 6,436ft 71mins [tinted nitrate]
35mm bw st 5,363ft 60mins
English titles

■ **CAST (Character names in parentheses from English version)**

Werner Krauss . . . . Shylock (Mordecai, the Jew of Mestri)
Henny Porten . . . . Portia (Beatrice, the Lady of Belmonte)
Carl Ebert . . . . Antonio (Benito)
Harry Liedtke . . . . Bassanio (Giannetto)
Max Schreck . . . . Doge of Venice
Ferdinand von Alten . . . . Prince of Arragon
Cläre Rommer . . . . Nerissa
Albert Steinrück . . . . Tubal
Max Grünberg . . . . Graziano
Gustav May . . . . Salario
Heinz-Rolf Münz . . . . Lorenzo
Emil Helfer . . . . Marco
Frida Richard . . . . Shylock's wife
Lia Eibenschütz . . . . Rachela
Friedrich Lobe . . . . Elias, Tubal's son
Hans Brausewetter. . . . . Launcelot Gobbo
Jacob Tiedtke. . . . . Beppo
Carl Geppert . . . . Reppo
Willi Allen. . . . . Ali, Portia's page

■ **DESCRIPTION** Feature film, supposedly based as much on Shakespeare's sources for The Merchant of Venice as his play (for details see note below), but in practice part Felner's invention and part Shakespeare's. Mordecai, the Jew of Mestri, has betrothed his daughter Rachela to the son of Elias, but she is secretly in love with Lorenzo, a Christian. Giannetto has his debts paid off for him by Benito. Mordecai sends his wife to Giannetto and Benito to recover his money for the wedding expenses; they laugh at her, she curses them, has a seizure and dies. Giannetto introduces Benito to Beatrice, Lady of Belmonte, and they are attracted to one another. Benito's ships are overdue and he is obliged to borrow from Mordecai. Seeking revenge for his wife's death, Mordecai makes the bond for the loan a pound of Benito's flesh. Rachela and Lorenzo elope, and Mordecai collapses when he learns that she has gone. Benito's ships have all foundered. Elias tells Mordecai that Rachela has become a Christian and then commits suicide. Benito is arrested for being in debt. Rachela comes to plead with her father but he does not listen. On the day of the trial Beatrice disguises

herself as a lawyer. Mordecai refuses all offers, insisting on his pound of flesh. Beatrice points out that he must take no blood with his pound of flesh, and Benito is released. After testing Giannetto's love over a ring, then revealing her disguise, Beatrice and he are married, and Lorenzo and Rachela too. Mordecai is left desolate. The early scenes with Giannetto and Beatrice are Felner's invention and are the weakest, Henny Porten's winsome manner soon becoming tedious, but the court scene is impressively staged and overall the story has been properly thought out as film narrative. The English intertitles (and accompanying action) for the NFTVA's print are given in Ball.

■ **NOTES** There is much confusion over the correct cast for this film. The NFTVA's print is a shortened English version released by Stoll Pictures as THE JEW OF MESTRI in 1926, and English sources differ with German on some parts and players. German sources have been followed as much as possible. These also state that the film was based on the works of Giovanni Fiorentino, Masuccio (both Shakespeare's sources) and Pietro Arentino. For the English version Stoll seem to have emphasised the pre-Shakespearean sources, but the original German cast names may have been closer to Shakespeare. Co-cinematographer Rudolf (later Rudolph) Maté became a noted Hollywood cameraman and director. Original German length 2,806m (9,206ft).

■ **REFERENCES** ● Ball, Shakespeare on Silent Film, pp. 286–97, 377–8.

MERCHANT OF VENICE, The

■ **GB • 1927**

d   Widgey R. Newman
pc   De Forest Phonofilms

NFTVA preservation material
35mm bw sd 934ft 10mins

■ **CAST**
Lewis Casson . . . . Shylock
Joyce Lyons . . . . Portia
Christine Murray . . . . Nerissa

■ **DESCRIPTION** Early sound short filmed using the De Forest sound-on-film process. The trial scene from *The Merchant of Venice* (A4S1).

■ **NOTES** Lee De Forest pioneered a system of photographing sound on film which is the basis of all sound film today, and his company De Forest Phonofilms made a large number of sound shorts exploiting the process in Britain and America in the mid to late 20s. This film would appear to be the first talking Shakespeare film, although there is ROMEO E GIULIETTA (c1927, qv), an extract from Gounod's opera, also produced by De Forest Phonofilms.

IMMORTAL GENTLEMAN, The

■ **GB • 1935**

d   Widgey R. Newman
pc   Bernard Smith

NFTVA viewing copy

■ **CAST**
Leo Genn . . . . *Merchant / Shylock*

■ **DESCRIPTION** Feature film. Shakespeare and his friends meet in a Southwark tavern and their reminiscences give rise to sequences from Shakespeare's plays. Includes Leo Genn as a merchant in their tavern who turns into Shylock speaking 'Let him look to his bond ' (A3S1). For full details of the film see entry in General section.

CALLING THE TUNE

■ **GB • 1936**

d   Reginald Denham
pc   Phoenix
p   Hugh Perceval
sc   Basil Mason
ph   Franz Weihmayer

NFTVA viewing copy
35mm bw sd 6,511ft 72mins

■ **CAST**
Adele Dixon . . . . *Julia Harboard*
Sally Gray . . . . *Margaret Gordon*

Donald Wolfit . . . . *Dick Finlay*
Clifford Evans . . . . *Peter Mallory*
Cedric Hardwicke . . . . *Himself*

■ **DESCRIPTION** Feature film. Sprightly, wholly fictitious acount of the rise of the gramophone industry, featuring various recording artists in performance dotted throughout the plot. Cedric Hardwicke gives a deadly recitation of the speech 'How Sweet the Moonlight' (A5S1) with accompanying string quartet.

TEDDY BERGMAN'S INTERNATIONAL BROADCAST

■ **USA • 1936**

d   Milton Schwarzwald
pc   Mentone
ph   Frank Zucker
m   Joseph Gertenson

NFTVA viewing copy
35mm bw sd 1,854ft 21mins

■ **DESCRIPTION** Variety short hosted by comedian Teddy Bergman. Features a scene from *The Merchant of Venice*, where Shylock replies to Antonio's request for a loan (A1S3). First played straight, Billy Reyes then challenges Bergman to repeat the speech in a variety of accents, which he does: Dutch, 'blackface', Irish, Scottish, Cockney, Swedish, a farmer, Russian and Italian. Bizarre, but adroit and very funny.

■ **NOTES** Teddy Bergman, a noted radio star of the 30s, later changed his name to Alan Reed and acted under that name for many years, eventually ending up as the voice of Fred Flintstone on television. The film also features Rita Rio, the Hernandez Brothers, Adrienne, and the 16 Sophisticates.

TO BE OR NOT TO BE

■ **USA • 1942**

d   Ernst Lubitsch
pc   Romaine Film Productions

Teddy Bergman . . . . *Shylock*
Billy Reyes . . . . *Antonio*

■ **DESCRIPTION** Feature film. Comedy-drama about a troupe of Polish actors in wartime Warsaw. The lines ' . . if you prick us, do we not bleed?' (A3S1) are used throughout as a comment on the situation of the Jews. For full details of the film see entry under *Hamlet*.

GREEN FOR DANGER

■ **GB • 1946**

d	Sidney Gilliat
pc	Individual Pictures
p	Frank Launder/Sidney Gilliat
sc	Sidney Gilliat/Claud Gurney
ph	Wilkie Cooper
m	William Alwyn

NFTVA viewing copy
35mm bw sd 8,199ft 91mins

■ **CAST**
Alastair Sim . . . . *Inspector Cockrill*
Sally Gray . . . . *Nurse Freddi Linley*
Trevor Howard . . . . *Dr Barnes*
Rosamund John . . . . *Nurse Sanson*
Leo Genn . . . . *Dr Eden*

■ **DESCRIPTION** Feature film. Splendid comedy-thriller set in a wartime hospital, with Sim memorable as Christianna Brand's fallible detective. In one short scene Leo Genn recites, and Sim completes, 'In such a night as this . . .' (A5S1).

PARIS 1900

■ **France • 1948**

d	Nicole Védrès
pc	Panthéon

NFTVA viewing copy

■ **DESCRIPTION** Compilation film covering Paris 1900–14. Features a brief sequence showing actor Firmin Gémier posing as Shylock, in the longer French version only. For full details of the film see entry under *Hamlet*.

BEFORE YOUR VERY EYES

■ **GB • 1956**

d	Kenneth Carter
pc	A Jack Hylton Production for Associated-Rediffusion
tx	23 March 1956 (ITV)
sets	Frank Gillman
m	Steve Race

NFTVA preservation material
35mm bw sd 2,408ft 27mins

■ **DESCRIPTION** Television comedy programme, hosted by Arthur Askey. Includes a running gag where Askey tries to prove that he is a serious actor by quoting from 'The quality of mercy . . .' speech (A4S1) but is continually interrupted. Also features Jerry Desmonde and Sabrina.

THEATRE OF BLOOD

■ **GB • 1973**

d	Douglas Hickox
pc	Cineman

NFTVA preservation material

■ **CAST**
Vincent Price . . . . *Edward Lionheart*
Harry Andrews . . . . *Trevor Dickman*
Diana Rigg . . . . *Edwina Lionheart*

■ **DESCRIPTION** Feature film. An actor (Vincent Price) murders his critics in the manner of deaths from Shakespeare's plays. Trevor Dickman is tricked into taking part in a production of *The Merchant of Venice*, with Lionheart as Shylock and his daughter as Portia. The dialogue follows the trial scene (A4S1) until Shylock takes his pound of flesh, which he does unhindered. For full details of the film see entry in General section.

NEWS AT TEN

■ **GB 1989**

pc	ITN
tx	14 April 1989 (ITV)
rep	Penny Marshall

MERCHANT OF VENICE

NFTVA viewing copy
½" col sd 3mins [item length]

■ **DESCRIPTION** News item. Report on Dustin Hoffman in rehearsal with the Peter Hall Company in *The Merchant of Venice*. Hoffman, Hall and the company read through the play, Geraldine James reads from 'The quality of mercy' speech (A4S1), and Hoffman comments on Hall's advice about verse-speaking and his awe of British stage actors.

(DUSTIN HOFFMAN AND PETER HALL)

■ **GB • 1989**

■ *South Bank Show*

d/p	Tony Know
pc	LWT
tx	24 September 1989 (ITV)
ed/pres	Melvyn Bragg

NFTVA viewing copy
½" col sd 55mins

■ **CAST**
Dustin Hoffman . . . . *Shylock*
Geraldine James . . . . *Portia*
Abigail McKern . . . . *Nerissa*
Francesca Buller . . . . *Jessica*
Peter Hugo Daly . . . . *Launcelot Gobbo*
Michael Siberry . . . . *Gratiano*
Basil Henson . . . . *The Duke*
Leigh Lawson . . . . *Antonio*
Nathaniel Parker . . . . *Bassanio*

■ **DESCRIPTION** Television arts documentary. Sir Peter Hall rehearses with Dustin Hoffman for the Peter Hall Company's London stage production of *The Merchant of Venice*, filmed over one complete day's rehearsal. The scenes covered are A1S3, A2S5 and A4S1, mostly Hoffman's contribution each time. Both Hoffman and Hall give their comments on the role of Shylock, with particular emphasis on anti-Semitism. A tolerably interesting but rather bland and self-congratulatory exercise.

■ **NOTES** Broadcast the day after the final performance at the Phoenix Theatre, London.

Geraint Evans (Falstaff) and Oralia Dominguez (Mistress Quickly) in FALSTAFF (1960)

MERRY WIVES OF WINDSOR

AMOURS DE LA REINE ELISABETH, Les

Other titles **QUEEN ELIZABETH; QUEEN BESS (HER LOVE STORY); REINE ELISABETH, La; ELISABETH, REINE D'ANGLETERRE**

■ **France • 1912**

d	Louis Mercanton/Henri Desfontaines
pc	Histrionic Film
art d	Théâtre Sarah Bernhardt, Paris

NFTVA viewing copy
35mm bw (tinted) st 3,138ft 35mins
German and German/English intertitles

■ **CAST**
Sarah Bernhardt . . . . *Queen Elizabeth*
Lou Tellegen . . . . . . *Robert Devereux, Earl of Essex*
Mlle Romain . . . . *Countess of Nottingham*
M. Chameroy . . . . *Lord Bacon*

■ **DESCRIPTION** Film drama, based on a play by Emile Moreau, telling the love story of Queen

Elizabeth I and the Earl of Essex. A considerable bore now, the sheer prestige and wonder of seeing Bernhardt on the screen made this film a huge success, notably in America where it made distributor Adolph Zukor's fortune (he went on to form Paramount Pictures). The film opens with a performance of *The Merry Wives of Windsor* (the Falstaff-basket scene is shown, A3S3) put on to celebrate victory over the Armada. After the performance the Queen congratulates William Shakespeare (actor not known).

■ **NOTES** The NFTVA's viewing copy was constructed from two different sources, hence the change in intertitles. Bernhardt first appeared on film in 1900 as Hamlet, a short sequence from which is given in the 1989 *South Bank Show* (HAMLET) (qv).

C. E. M. A.

■ **GB • 1942**

pc	Strand Films
spon	Ministry of Information
p	Alexander Shaw
sc	Charles de Lautour/
	Alan Osbiston/Peter Scott/
	Dylan Thomas/Desmond Dickinson
pres	R. A. Butler

NFTVA viewing copy
35mm bw sd 1,564ft 17mins [nitrate]

■ **DESCRIPTION** Promotional documentary on the activities of the Council for the Encouragement of Music and the Arts. Earnest propaganda for the arts in wartime, which includes a production of *The Merry Wives of Windsor* by the Old Vic Company, in rehearsal and in production at a provincial theatre.

MERRY WIVES OF WINDSOR (ACT 2)

■ **GB • 1955**

d	Glen Byam Shaw
pc	BBC
tx	2 October 1955 (BBC)
tv presentation	Stephen Harrison/
	Barrie Edgar

sets/cost	Motley
intro	Alan Dent
m	Leslie Bridgewater

NFTVA preservation material
35mm bw sd 5,641ft 63mins

■ **CAST**

Michael Denison	*Dr Caius*
John Southworth	*Rugby, his servant*
Patrick Wymark	*Host of the Garter Inn*
Edward Atienza	*Justice Shallow*
Geoffrey Bayldon	*Slender*
Ralph Michael	*Master Page*
William Devlin	*Sir Hugh Evans*
Geoffrey Sasse	*Simple, Slender's servant*
Angela Baddeley	*Mistress Page*
John Rogers	*Robin, Falstaff's page*
Keith Michell	*Master Ford*
Joyce Redman	*Mistress Ford*
Rex Robinson	*Their servant, John*
Alan Haywood	*Their servant, Robert*
Anthony Quayle	*Sir John Falstaff*
Jill Dixon	*Anne Page*
Trader Faulkner	*Fenton*
Rosalind Atkinson	*Mistress Quickly*
Robert Hunter	*Bardolph*
Philip Thomas	*William Page*

■ **DESCRIPTION** Telerecording of a live television broadcast of Part Two of the Stratford production of *The Merry Wives of Windsor*. The play as shown here opens at A3S1. A valuable record of Anthony Quayle's celebrated Falstaff, and the first television broadcast from Stratford. The performance took place in front of a specially invited audience.

■ **NOTES** The programme was preceded by a production of Shaw's *The Dark Lady of the Sonnets*, also in the NFTVA (see General section).

FALSTAFF

■ **GB • 1960**

d	Peter Ebert
pc	BBC
tx	15 September 1960 (BBC)
tv presentation	Peter Ebert/Noble Wilson
stage p	Carl Ebert
des	Osbert Lancaster

NFTVA preservation material
35mm bw sd 1,656ft 18mins

■ **CAST**

Hugues Cuenod . . . . . *Dr Caius, a French physician*
Geraint Evans . . . . *Sir John Falstaff*
Mario Carlin . . . . . . *Bardolph, follower of Falstaff*
Marco Stefanoni . . . . . . *Pistol, follower of Falstaff*
Anna Maria Rota . . . . *Mrs Page (Meg)*
Ilva Ligabue . . . . *Mrs Ford (Alice)*
Oralia Dominguez . . . . *Mistress Quickly*
Mariella Adani . . . . *Anne Ford (Nanetta)*
Juan Oncina . . . . *Fenton, a young gentleman*
Sesto Bruscantini . . . . *Ford, a wealthy*
townsman of Windsor
Harold Williams . . . . *The Innkeeper*

■ **DESCRIPTION** Telerecording excerpt of a live
television production of Verdi's *Falstaff* at
Glyndebourne Opera House, before an invited
audience, preserving a famous Falstaff by Geraint
Evans. The complete programme ran 65mins.

CAMPANADAS A MEDIANOCHE

■ **Spain/Switzerland • 1966**

d   Orson Welles
pc   Internacional Films/Alpine

NFTVA preservation material

■ **DESCRIPTION** Feature film. The life of
Shakespeare's Sir John Falstaff, with material
taken from the plays *Richard II*, *1 Henry IV*, *2
Henry IV*, *Henry V* and *The Merry Wives of Windsor*.
For full details see entry under *Henry IV*.

FALSTAFF

■ **GB • 1978**

pc   Southern Television
tx   29 April 1978 (ITV)
tv p   Dave Heather
stage des/p   Jean-Pierre Ponnelle

NFTVA viewing copy
½" col sd 130mins

■ **CAST**

John Fryatt . . . . *Dr Caius (a French physician)*

Donald Gramm . . . . *Sir John Falstaff*
Bernard Dickerson . . . *Bardolph, follower of Falstaff*
Ugo Trama . . . . *Pistol, follower of Falstaff*
Reni Penkova . . . . *Mrs Page (Meg)*
Kay Griffel . . . . *Mrs Ford (Alice)*
Elizabeth Gale . . . . *Anne Ford (Nanetta)*
Max René Cosotti . . . . *Fenton (a young gentleman)*
Benjamin Luxon . . *Ford (a young wealthy townsman)*

■ **DESCRIPTION** Televised performance of the
Glyndebourne Festival production of Verdi's
opera with the London Philharmonic Orchestra
conducted by John Pritchard.

Victor Jory as Oberon in A MIDSUMMER
NIGHT'S DREAM (1935)

MIDSUMMER NIGHT'S DREAM

MIDSUMMER NIGHT'S DREAM, A

■ **USA • 1909**

d   J. Stuart Blackton/Charles Kent
pc   Vitagraph Company of America

NFTVA viewing copy
35mm bw st 667ft 8mins
Incomplete – original length 993ft
English titles

■ **CAST**

William V. Ranous. . . . . *Bottom*
Maurice Costello. . . . . *Lysander*
Walter Ackerman . . . . *Demetrius*
Julia Swayne Gordon . . . . *Helena*
Rose Tapley . . . . *Hermia*
Gladys Hulette. . . . . *Puck*
Charles Chapman . . . . *Quince*
Helene Costello/Dolores Costello . . . . . . *Fairies*

■ **DESCRIPTION** Abbreviated version of the play. The action closely follows the original with the exception of a fresh character, the fairy Penelope (actress not identified). It is she who quarrels with Titania and who instructs Puck to bewitch Titania. Although suffering a little from Vitagraph's tendency to squeeze in too much of the plot into too short a time, the woodland location filming and a number of engaging performances make this probably their most successful Shakespearean adaptation.

■ **NOTES** The NFTVA's copy is incomplete, ending with the tradesmen commencing their play before Theseus.

■ **REFERENCES** ● Ball, *Shakespeare on Silent Film*, pp. 52–6, 313–14.

FELIX MENDELSSOHN

■ **USA ● 1925**

■ *Famous Music Masters*

d/pc/sc	James A. Fitzpatrick
ph	Bert Dawley
chor	Madame Serova

NFTVA viewing copy
35mm bw st 546ft 6mins
Incomplete – preservation copy complete at 1,030ft
English titles

■ **DESCRIPTION** Dramatic short, showing how Mendelssohn came to compose his wedding march (from his *A Midsummer Night's Dream* music). The composer Mendelssohn sees a young couple playing and is impressed by the boy's violin playing. He invites them to supper. The girl dreams of fairies. Mendelssohn offers to send the boy to the Leipzig conservatory, sending the girl

as well when he learns that they wish to marry first. He will write the couple's wedding march. The wedding procession.

■ **NOTES** The film is of course silent but would have been accompanied by Mendelssohn's music.

MISTER CINDERS

■ **GB ● 1934**

d	Friedrich Zelnik
pc	British International Pictures
p	Walter C. Mycroft
sc	Clifford Grey/Frank Miller/ Jack Davies/Kenneth Western/ George Western [The Western Brothers]
ph	Otto Kanturek
m	Vivian Ellis

NFTVA viewing copy
35mm bw sd 6,450ft 72mins

■ **CAST**

Clifford Mollison . . . . *Jim*
Zelma O'Neil . . . . *Jill Kemp*
Renée Houston . . . . *Mrs Phipps*
The Western Brothers . . *Lumley and Guy Lancaster*
Finlay Currie . . . . *Henry Kemp*

■ **DESCRIPTION** Feature film based on the play by Clifford Grey, Frank Miller and Greatrex Newman, with songs by Vivian Ellis. Delightful musical-comedy about a male Cinderella who wins the heart of an American heiress. Features a village production of *A Midsummer Night's Dream* in rehearsal and in chaotic performance (Hermia ends up wearing the ass's ears).

MIDSUMMER NIGHT'S DREAM, A

■ **USA ● 1935**

d	Max Reinhardt/William Dieterle
pc	Warner Bros.
p	Max Reinhardt
sc	Charles Kenyon/Mary McCall
ph	Hal Mohr
m	Felix Mendelssohn
md	Leo F. Forbstein/Erich Korngold

NFTVA viewing copy
35mm bw sd 10,495ft 117 mins

■ CAST

James Cagney . . . . *Bottom*
Dick Powell . . . . *Lysander*
Olivia de Haviland [sic] . . . . *Hermia*
Ross Alexander . . . . *Demetrius*
Jean Muir . . . . *Helena*
Anita Louise . . . . *Titania*
Victor Jory . . . . *Oberon*
Mickey Rooney . . . . *Puck*
Joe E. Brown . . . . *Flute*
Hugh Herbert . . . . *Snout*
Frank McHugh . . . . *Quince*
Grant Mitchell . . . . *Egeus*
Nini Theilade . . . . *Prima Ballerina Fairy*
Ian Hunter . . . . *Theseus*
Verree Teasdale . . *Hippolyta, Queen of the Amazons*
Dewey Robinson . . . . *Snug*
Hobart Cavanaugh . . . . *Philostrate*
Otis Harlan . . . . *Starveling*
Arthur Treacher . . . . *Ninny's Tomb*
Katherine Frey . . . . *Pease-Blossom*
Helen Westcott . . . . *Cobweb*
Fred Sale . . . . *Moth*
Billy Barty . . . . *Mustard Seed*
Kenneth Anger . . . . *The Changeling*

■ DESCRIPTION Feature film version of the Max Reinhardt stage production. Visually stunning Hollywood folly, which seems more of an illustration to the Mendelssohn music than a presentation of the play as such. A starry cast play as best they know how, but only Jory and Rooney get the full measure of their parts.

■ NOTES Original release length 132mins.

■ REFERENCES • Graham Greene, *The Pleasure-Dome* (London: Secker & Warburg, 1972), pp. 28–9. • Jorgens, *Shakespeare on Film*, pp. 36–50, 252–5.

MATTER OF LIFE AND DEATH, A

USA title STAIRWAY TO HEAVEN

■ GB • 1946

d/p/sc   Michael Powell/Emeric Pressburger
pc   The Archers

ph   Jack Cardiff
p des   Alfred Junge
m   Allan Gray

NFTVA viewing copy
35mm bw/col sd 9,346ft 103mins

■ CAST

David Niven . . . . *Peter Carter*
Kim Hunter . . . . *June*
Roger Livesey . . . . *Doctor Reeves*
Robert Coote . . . . *Bob*
Marius Goring . . . . *Conductor 71*
Raymond Massey . . . . *Abraham Farlan*
Robert Atkins . . . . *The Vicar*

■ DESCRIPTION Feature film. Heaven and Earth battle for the possession of crashed RAF pilot Peter Carter. Outstanding fantasy film ostensibly produced with the intention of improving Anglo-American relations after the war. A key sequence features a rehearsal of an amateur production of *A Midsummer Night's Dream*, the Pyramus and Thisbe scene (A3S1). Two lovers trying to communicate and being held back by an imaginary wall echoes one of the film's major themes.

■ NOTES The vicar organising the production of the play is Robert Atkins, a noted Shakespearean actor who also appears in HAMLET (1913) and THE TEMPEST (1956).

MUSIC BOX, The

■ GB • 1957

d   Douglas Hurn
pc   A Jack Hylton Production for
       Associated-Rediffusion
tx   1 February 1957 (ITV)
sets   Kenneth Carey
m   Billy Ternent and his Orchestra

NFTVA viewing copy
35mm bw sd 2,337ft 26mins

■ CAST

Bud Flanagan . . . . *Pyramus*
Teddy Knox . . . . *Peter Quince*
Jimmy Nervo . . . . *Lion*
Charlie Naughton . . . . *Thisbe*
Jimmy Gold . . . . *Moonshine*
'Monsewer' Eddie Gray . . . . *Wall*

■ **DESCRIPTION** Television musical variety show. An extraordinary thing for a 50s variety show, but the second half of the programme is wholly devoted to a performance of the Pyramus and Thisbe play from *A Midsummer Night's Dream* (A5S1) performed by the Crazy Gang. Minus only the interruptions from the wedding guests, it is a straight reading and an enormously funny one as well, beautifully spoken and with some splendid comic business throughout. The casting, especially Flanagan, is quite perfect. A delight.

■ **NOTES** Felix Mendelssohn's music is used. The Crazy Gang, one of Britain's most celebrated comic teams, at the end of their careers were revitalised by Jack Hylton, who featured them throughout the 1950s in a series of shows at London's Victoria Palace, with regular appearances on Hylton television shows. At the time of this programme they were appearing in the show *These Foolish Kings*, part of which was the *Dream* sketch featured here. Original member Chesney Allen had retired by this time, replaced by Eddie Gray. Other acts featured are Rosalina Neri, Bryan Johnson and Les Joyeux Rossignols.

MIDSUMMER NIGHT'S DREAM, A

■ **GB • 1958**

■ *Sunday-Night Theatre*

d/p	Rudolph Cartier
pc	BBC
tx	9 November 1958 (BBC)
adapt	Eric Crozier
chor	Alfred Rodrigues
des	Clifford Hatts
m	Felix Mendelssohn (arr Leslie Bridgewater)

NFTVA viewing copy
16mm bw sd 3,697ft 103mins

■ **CAST**
John Westbrook . . . . *Theseus*
Margaret Whiting . . . . *Hippolyta*
John Longden . . . . *Egeus*
Christine Finn . . . . *Hermia*
Vivienne Drummond . . . . *Helena*
Eric Lander . . . . *Demetrius*
David Oxley . . . . *Lysander*

Geoffrey Bayldon . . . . *Philostrate*
Miles Malleson . . . . *Quince*
Paul Rogers . . . . *Bottom*
Ronald Fraser . . . . *Flute*
Peter Sallis . . . . *Snug*
John Warner . . . . *Snout*
Michael Bates . . . . *Starveling*
John Justin . . . . *Oberon*
Natasha Parry . . . . *Titania*
Gillian Lynne . . . . *Puck*
Jennifer Daniel . . . . *First Fairy*
Jane Shore . . . . *Peaseblossom*
Gaynie MacSweenie . . . . *Mustardseed*
Vernie Ruthven . . . . *Cobweb*
Hazel Merry . . . . *Moth*

■ **DESCRIPTION** Television production. A worthy, traditional interpretation, with a mobile camera to prevent staginess but still a little slow-paced and lacking in inspiration. The ballet sequences are well-choreographed and blend satisfactorily with the action, the verse is well-spoken and there are strong performances from John Justin as Oberon, an athletic Gillian Lynne as Puck, and an appealing Snug from Peter Sallis. The ass's head is disappointing. Miles Malleson also plays Peter Quince in the 1964 version (see below). A little more humour and magic would have been welcome.

THREE SEASONS

■ **GB • 1958**

pc	Associated-British Pathé
spon	British Travel Association
exec p	Terry Ashwood
m	Robert Irving

NFTVA preservation material
16mm col sd 1,113ft 31mins

■ **CAST**
Frankie Howerd . . . . *Bottom*
Joyce Redman . . . . *Titania*
Paul Daneman . . . . *Quince*

■ **DESCRIPTION** Travelogue. English life in Autumn, Winter and Spring. Includes sequences from the Old Vic production of *A Midsummer Night's Dream* with comedian Frankie Howerd as Bottom at the play rehearsal and Titania falling in love with him as an ass (A3S1).

MIDSUMMER NIGHT'S DREAM, A

■ GB • 1964

d	Joan Kemp-Welch
pc	Rediffusion
tx	24 June 1964 (ITV)
des	Michael Yates
chor	Juan Corelli
m	Felix Mendelssohn

NFTVA viewing copy
16mm bw sd 3,959ft 110mins

■ CAST

Benny Hill . . . . Bottom
Jill Bennett. . . . . Helena
Maureen Beck . . . . Hermia
John Fraser. Lysander
Clifford Elkin . . . . Demetrius
Patrick Allen . . . . Theseus
Anna Massey . . . . Titania
Peter Wyngarde . . . . Oberon
Tony Tanner. . . . . Puck
Miles Malleson . . . . Quince
Alfie Bass . . . . Flute
Bernard Bresslaw . . . . Snout
Bill Shine . . . . Starveling
Kay Frazer . . . . Fairy
Eira Heath . . . . Hippolyta
Cyril Luckham . . . . Egeus
Tony Bateman. . . . . Philostrate

■ DESCRIPTION Television production of the play. Long held to be one of the most successful television versions and highly popular in its day (largely on account of comedian Benny Hill's performance as Bottom). Entertaining and rewarding still, chiefly for the performances of Massey, Bennett and Beck. Hill largely repeats his television persona, which is entertaining enough in itself, but one might have hoped for more.

DREAM, The

■ GB • 1967

d/p	Margaret Dale
pc	BBC
tx	26 March 1967 (BBC1)
chor	Frederick Ashton

sets	Henry Bardon
cost	David Walker
tv des	Darrol Blake
m	Felix Mendelssohn (arr John Lanchbery)

NFTVA viewing copy
½" bw sd 44mins

■ CAST

Antoinette Sibley . . . . Titania
Anthony Dowell . . . . Oberon
Keith Martin . . . . Puck
Alexander Grant . . . . Bottom
Derek Rencher . . . . Lysander
Jane Robinson . . . . Hermia
David Drew . . . . Demetrius
Carole Needham . . . . Helena
Ann Howard . . . . Peaseblossom
Carole Hill. . . . . Cobweb
Ann Jenner. . . . . Moth
Jennifer Penney. . . . . Mustardseed
John Gray . . . . Changeling
Artists of the Royal Ballet . . . . Fairies

■ DESCRIPTION Ballet. Television adaptation of the Royal Ballet's production of Frederick Ashton's ballet The Dream. Plainly but adequately presented in the television studio, with the principal dancers from the original 1964 stage production.

■ NOTES Director Margaret Dale specialised in such faithful transcriptions of ballets for the BBC in the 1950s and 60s. The programme in the Dance Master Class series below (tx 9 April 1988) reunites Ashton with Dowell and Sibley in a rehearsal of the pas de deux from The Dream. The production also appears below with Dowell as Oberon.

DREAM, The

■ GB • 1978

■ Dance Month

tv presentation	John Vernon/Colin Nears
pc	BBC
tx	7 May 1978 (BBC2)
intro	Robin Ray
chor	Frederick Ashton

sets	Henry Bardon
cost	David Walker
m	Felix Mendelssohn
	(arr John Lanchbery)

NFTVA viewing copy
½" col sd 53mins

■ **CAST**

Merle Park . . . . *Titania*
Anthony Dowell . . . . *Oberon*
Wayne Sleep . . . . *Puck*
Gary Grant . . . . *Bottom*
Vergie Derman . . . . *Hermia*
Rosalind Eyre . . . . *Helena*
Derek Rencher . . . . *Lysander*
David Drew . . . . *Demetrius*

■ **DESCRIPTION** Ballet. Television broadcast from the Royal Opera House, Covent Garden, of the Royal Ballet's production of Frederick Ashton's *The Dream*. A basic recording with cameras firmly in the stalls.

■ **NOTES** For an earlier version of the same production see above. The NFTVA copy of the full programme runs for 106mins and includes an interval interview with Ashton and a performance of his ballet *A Month in the Country*, based on Turgenev.

GREGORY'S GIRL

■ **GB • 1980**

d/sc	Bill Forsyth
pc	Lake Film Productions
p	Davina Belling/Clive Parsons
ph	Michael Coulter
m	Colin Tully

NFTVA preservation material
¾" col sd 91mins

■ **CAST**

Gordon John Sinclair . . . . *Gregory*
Dee Hepburn . . . . *Dorothy*
Clare Grogan . . . . *Susan*
Robert Buchanan . . . . *Andy*

■ **DESCRIPTION** Feature film. An awkward Scottish schoolboy eventually finds love. Charming, observant comedy set in a Scottish

new town. Includes a scene in a classroom where character Andy reads aloud from Puck's speech ending '. . . and straightway loved an ass' (A3S2), appropriate to the theme of the film.

MIDSUMMER NIGHT'S DREAM, A

■ **GB/USA 1981**

■ *BBC Television Shakespeare*

d	Elijah Moshinsky
pc	BBC/Time-Life Films
tx (GB)	13 December 1981 (BBC2)
tx (US)	19 April 1982 (PBS)
p	Jonathan Miller
des	David Myerscough-Jones
m	Stephen Oliver

NFTVA viewing copy
½" col sd 120mins

■ **CAST**

Pippa Guard . . . . *Hermia*
Nicky Henson . . . . *Demetrius*
Robert Lindsay . . . . *Lysander*
Cherith Mellor . . . . *Helena*
Phil Daniels . . . . *Puck*
Helen Mirren . . . . *Titania*
Peter McEnery . . . . *Oberon*
Estelle Kohler . . . . *Hippolyta*
Nigel Davenport . . . . *Theseus*
Hugh Quarshie . . . . *Philostrate*
Geoffrey Lumsden . . . . *Egeus*
Brian Glover . . . . *Bottom*
Geoffrey Palmer . . . . *Quince*
John Fowler . . . . *Flute*
Don Estelle . . . . *Starveling*
Nat Jackley . . . . *Snout*
Ray Mort . . . . *Snug*
Bruce Savage . . . . *Peaseblossom*
Massimo Mezzofanti . . . . *Cobweb*
Dominic Martelli . . . . *Moth*
Timothy Gross . . . . *Mustardseed*
Tania Bennett/Alexandra Segal/Louise Mason/
Lee MacDonald . . . . *Fairies*

■ **DESCRIPTION** Television production of the play. A rather grim interpretation, with a punkish Puck, gloomy lighting and composition, and not much of a spirit of fun. Much use is made of a studio pond, and as with other titles in the BBC series which came under Jonathan Miller's regime there is a strong painterly influence on the design. But what has Rembrandt to do with Shakespeare, except to be his near contemporary? There seems also to be the influence of Derek Jarman's idiosyncratic THE TEMPEST (GB 1979, qv), which sits uneasily with the traditional BBC house style.

MIDSUMMER NIGHT'S SEX COMEDY, A

■ **USA • 1982**

d/sc	Woody Allen
pc	Orion Pictures
p	Robert Greenhut
ph	Gordon Willis
m	Felix Mendelssohn

NFTVA preservation material
35mm col sd 7,877ft 88mins

■ **CAST**

Woody Allen . . . . *Andrew Hobbs*
Mia Farrow . . . . *Ariel Weymouth*
José Ferrer . . . . *Professor Leopold Sturgis*
Julie Hagerty . . . . *Dulcy Ford*
Tony Roberts . . . . *Dr Maxwell Jordan*
Mary Steenburgen . . . . *Adrian Hobbs*

■ **DESCRIPTION** Feature film. A group of friends meet at a country house at the turn of the century. The magical sequences and the pairs of lovers connect the film with Shakespeare, but a stronger influence is Ingmar Bergman, particularly his SOMMARNATTENS LEENDE (Sweden 1955, English title SMILES OF A SUMMER NIGHT, held in NFTVA).

■ **NOTES** Woody Allen's 1983 feature film ZELIG, also in the NFTVA, contains a fleeting reference to *A Midsummer Night's Dream*, where Leonard Zelig's father takes part in a production as Puck.

MIDSUMMER NIGHT'S DREAM, A

■ **GB • 1985**

d	Dave Heather
pc	TVS
tx	26 May 1985 (C4)
p	Peter Hall
des	John Bury
cond	Bernard Haitink

NFTVA viewing copy
½" col sd 96mins

■ **CAST**

James Bowman . . . . *Oberon*
Ileana Cotrubas . . . . *Tytania*
Damien Nash . . . . *Puck*
Ryland Davies . . . . *Lysander*
Dale Duesing . . . . *Demetrius*
Felicity Lott . . . . *Helena*
Cynthia Buchan . . . . *Hermia*
Curt Appelgren . . . . *Bottom*

■ **DESCRIPTION** Television presentation of Peter Hall's Glyndebourne production of Benjamin Britten's opera, based on Shakespeare's play. Broadcast in the 'Opera on Four' slot.

MIDSUMMER NIGHT'S DREAM, A

■ **Netherlands/GB/ West Germany • 1986**

d/anim	Tissa David
pc	NOS/Channel Four/ZDF
tx (GB)	25 September 1987 (C4)
p	Jet Willers
sc	Tissa David/Richard Fehsl/ Kalman Kozelka/ Ida Kozelka-Mocsary
m	Felix Mendelssohn

NFTVA viewing copy
½" col sd 38mins

■ **DESCRIPTION** Television programme. A performance of Mendelssohn's *A Midsummer Night's Dream*, by the Rotterdam Philharmonic Orchestra, conductor David Zinman, is interrupted and interwoven by animated characters from Shakespeare's play. A complex, rather peculiar exercise, but appealing enough and ingeniously done.

DREAM, The

■ **GB • 1988**

■ *Dance Master Class*

pc	BBC
tx	9 April 1988 (BBC2)
p	Bob Lockyer
ph	Maurice Abel/Ian Gibb

NFTVA viewing copy
½" col sd 44mins

■ **CAST**
Antoinette Sibley . . . . *Titania*
Anthony Dowell . . . . *Oberon*
Karen Paisey. . . . . *Titania*
Phillip Broomhead. . . . . *Oberon*

■ **DESCRIPTION** Ballet. In the De Valois rehearsal rooms at the Royal Opera House, Sir Frederick Ashton rehearses Antoinette Sibley and Anthony Dowell in the *pas de deux* from his ballet *The Dream*, based on Shakespeare and Mendelssohn. Anthony Dowell is also seen directing two younger members of the Royal Ballet, Karen Paisey and Phillip Broomhead, in the same scene.

■ **NOTES** For complete performances of *The Dream*, see 1967 and 1978 above. Dowell and Sibley were the leads in the original 1964 production and were brought back together for a revival in 1988.

DEAD POETS SOCIETY

■ **USA • 1989**

d	Peter Weir
pc	Touchstone Pictures
p	Steven Haft/Paul Juner Witt/ Tony Thomas
sc	Tom Schulman
ph	John Seale
m	Maurice Jarre

NFTVA preservation material
35mm col sd 11,572ft 129mins

■ **CAST**
Robin Williams . . . . *John Keating*
Robert Sean Leonard . . . . *Neil Perry/Puck*
Ethan Hawke . . . . *Todd Anderson*

■ **DESCRIPTION** Feature film. In 1950s America an unconventional schoolteacher has an inspirational effect on his pupils, one of whom (Neil Perry) is seen as Puck in a production of *A Midsummer Night's Dream* (extracts from A2S1, A2S3 and A5S2). His stern father forbids an acting career and Neil shoots himself.

(PETER BROOK)

■ **GB • 1989**

■ *South Bank Show Special*

d	David Thomas
pc	London Weekend Television
tx	3 December 1989 (ITV)
p	David Thomas
ed/pres	Melvyn Bragg

NFTVA viewing copy
½" col sd 79mins

■ **DESCRIPTION** Television arts documentary. Melvyn Bragg interviews theatre director Peter Brook, covering the whole of his career, with special reference to his production of *The Mahabharata*, but also including rare extracts from the celebrated 1970 Royal Shakespeare Company production of *A Midsummer Night's Dream* and Brook's thoughts on that production.

MUCH ADO ABOUT NOTHING

GONE TO EARTH
USA title WILD HEART, The

■ **GB • 1950**

d/sc	Michael Powell/Emeric Pressburger
pc	London Films
p	David O. Selznick
ph	Christopher Challis
m	Brian Easdale

Kenneth Branagh in CAUGHT IN THE ACT (1988)

NFTVA viewing copy
35mm col sd 9,981ft 111mins

■ **CAST**
Jennifer Jones . . . . Hazel Woodus
David Farrar . . . . Jack Reddin
Cyril Cusack . . . . Edward Marston

■ **DESCRIPTION** Feature film based on Mary Webb's novel of a wild girl of Shropshire. Richly photographed and staged, but if anything dafter than the novel in its attempt to invest the story with greater meaning. In one scene Jones sings 'Sigh no more, ladies' (A2S3).

QUESTIONING CITY, The

■ **GB • 1959**

d	Eric Fullilove
pc	Associated British Pathé
spon	British Travel Association
nar	Michael Redgrave

NFTVA viewing copy
35mm col sd 1,919ft 21mins

■ **DESCRIPTION** Travelogue of Cambridge. Among various scenes of students at Cambridge University, a group of students are seen in costume rehearsing A2S1 of *Much Ado About Nothing*.

MUCH ADO ABOUT NOTHING

■ **GB/USA 1984**

■ *BBC Television Shakespeare*

d	Stuart Burge
pc	BBC/Time-Life Films
tx (GB)	22 December 1984 (BBC2)
tx (US)	30 October 1984 (PBS)
p	Shaun Sutton
lght	Derek Slee
cost	June Hudson
des	Jan Spoczynski
m	Simon Rogers

NFTVA preservation material
1" col sd 150mins

■ **CAST**
Lee Montague . . . . Leonato
Tim Faulkner. . . . . Messenger
Cherie Lunghi . . . . Beatrice
Katharine Levy . . . . Hero
Jon Finch . . . . Don Pedro
Robert Lindsay . . . . Benedick
Robert Reynolds . . . . Claudio
Gordon Whiting. . . . . Antonio
Vernon Dobtcheff. . . . . Don John
Robert Gwilym . . . . Conrade
Tony Rohr . . . . Borachio
Pamela Moiseiwitsch . . . . Margaret
Ishia Bennison . . . . Ursula
Oz Clarke . . . . Balthasar
Ben Losh . . . . Boy
Michael Elphick . . . . Dogberry
Clive Dunn . . . . Verges
Gorden Kaye . . . . First watch
Perry Benson . . . . Second watch
Graham Crowden. . . . . Friar Francis
John Kidd . . . . Sexton

■ **DESCRIPTION** Television production. Yet another title in the BBC series which, in searching for the dark undertones, entirely missed the main point of the play – to entertain. An intriguing cast boasts some fine comic talent, most of whom seem strangely uninspired.

CAUGHT IN THE ACT

■ **GB • 1988**

d/p   Mary Gwatkin
pc   Reconnaissance Films/MV Films
tx   26 December 1988 (C4)

NFTVA viewing copy

■ **CAST**

Kenneth Branagh . . . . *Benedick*
Samantha Bond . . . . *Beatrice*
Tam Hoskyns . . . . *Hero*
Dearbhla Molloy . . . . *Ursula*
James Larkin . . . . *Claudio*
David Lloyd Meredith . . . . *Dogberry*
Richard Easton . . . . *Leonato*

■ **DESCRIPTION** Television documentary on the work of Kenneth Branagh's Renaissance Theatre Company, in particular its three touring productions of *As You Like It*, *Hamlet* and *Much Ado About Nothing*. Judi Dench discusses the experience of directing *Much Ado About Nothing*, and various scenes from the play in rehearsal and production are shown, including Hero talking with Ursula (A3S1), Benedick and Claudio (A1S1) and Dogberry and Leonato (A3S5). For full details see entry in General section.

ONE, TWO, BUCKLE MY SHOE

■ **GB • 1992**

■ *Agatha Christie's Poirot*

d   Ross Devenish
pc   London Weekend Television
tx   19 January 1992 (ITV)
p   Brian Eastman
sc   Clive Exton

NFTVA viewing copy
½" col sd 103mins

■ **CAST**

David Suchet . . . . *Hercule Poirot*
Joanna Phillips-Lane . . . . *Gerda/Beatrice*

■ **DESCRIPTION** Television adaptation of the Agatha Christie whodunnit, in which Poirot investigates the murder of his dentist. One of the suspects is an actress and in a flashback scene she is shown as part of a touring rep company in India, who are seen in a production of *Much Ado About Nothing* (A5S4). Lines from the play are also heard over the final exposition.

Anson Dyer's animated OTHELLO (1920)

OTHELLO

OTHELLO

■ **GB • 1920**

d/anim/sc   Anson Dyer
pc   Hepworth Picture Plays
p   Cecil Hepworth

NFTVA viewing copy
35mm bw st 200ft 2mins
Incomplete – original length 850ft
English titles

■ **DESCRIPTION** Animated cartoon burlesque of *Othello*. The NFTVA holds a fragment, the entire film being reviewed thus: 'The Moor of Venice becomes a seaside Nigger Minstrel whilst Desdemona (known as Mona for short) is the lovely daughter of the local bathing machine proprietor. After many humorous adventures in which the main parts of the famous tragedy are ingeniously if irreverently introduced, Othello smothers Desdemona with burnt cork and kisses' (*Bioscope*, 29 July 1920, quoted in Gifford below). The NFTVA print shows Othello blacking up, Mona at work at the seaside, Othello showing her a handkerchief, and the final kisses. The cut-out animation style is primitive but still charming.

■ **NOTES** The NFTVA holds one other (complete) title from the series of animated Shakespeare burlesques produced by Dyer. For further details of the series see the entry for OH'PHELIA (GB 1919) under *Hamlet*.

■ **REFERENCES** • Denis Gifford, *British Animated Films, 1895–1985: A Filmography* (Jefferson/ London: McFarland & Company, 1987), p. 61.

CARNIVAL

■ GB • 1921

d	Harley Knoles
pc	Alliance Film Corporation
sc	Adrian Johnson/Rosina Henley
ph	Philip Hatkin

NFTVA viewing copy
35mm bw st 4,835ft 54mins
English titles

■ **CAST**

Matheson Lang	. . . . *Silvio Steno*
Hilda Bayley	. . . . *Simonetta, his wife*
Ivor Novello	. . . . *Count Andrea Scipione*
Maria de Bernaldo	. . . . *Ottavia*
Clifford Grey	. . . . *Lelio*
Victor McLaglen	. . . . *Baron*
Florence Hunter	. . . . *Nino*

■ **DESCRIPTION** Feature film, from the play by H. C. Hardinge and Matheson Lang ('adapted from the Italian'). Simonetta, the neglected wife of the great Italian Shakespearean actor Silvio Steno, amuses herself with his best friend Scipione, while Steno is engrossed with his forthcoming production of *Othello*. Steno becomes increasingly suspicious of his wife, and she enjoys herself with Scipione at the Venice carnival. During the production of *Othello* Steno becomes so maddened with jealousy that he nearly strangles his wife, who is playing Desdemona. Recovering, she explains that she repulsed Scipione's amorous advances, and they are reconciled. First in too long a line of jealous actors playing Othello (see the 1931 CARNIVAL, MEN ARE NOT GODS and A DOUBLE LIFE below), this is a slow trudge through the obvious that does not even make the most of its Venice settings. The film features several scenes from *Othello*, including the dramatic finale.

■ **NOTES** The play, starring Lang and Bayley, had been a success at the New Theatre in 1920, and Lang's name and a comparatively lavish production (by British standards) made the film a reasonable hit. Partly filmed in Venice. Matheson Lang remade the film in 1931 (see below).

OTHELLO

English title MOOR, The

■ Germany • 1922

d	Dmitri Buchowetski
pc	Wörner-Film
adapt	Dmitri Buchowetski/Carl Hagen
ph	Karl Hasselmann/Friedrich Paulmann
art d	Fritz Kraencke/Karl Machus

NFTVA viewing copy
16mm bw st 2,341ft 65mins [see note]
English titles

■ **CAST**

Emil Jannings	. . . . *Othello*
Ica von Lenkeffy	. . . . *Desdemona*
Werner Krauss	. . . . *Iago*
Theodor Loos	. . . . *Cassio*
Friedrich Kühne	. . . . *Brabantio*
Ferdinand von Alten	. . . . *Roderigo*
Lya de Putti	. . . . *Emilia*
Magnus Stifter	. . . . *Montano*
Ludwig Rex	

■ **DESCRIPTION** Feature film, based on both Cinthio's original tale (acknowledged in German sources) and Shakespeare's play. Buchowetzki was a journeyman among the great German directors of his time, and this is a disappointing effort, with echoes of Reinhardt and Expressionism but little idea of how to present the material as cinema. The starry cast still think themselves on the stage, but Krauss's near-manic Iago is memorable. The plot is given in considerable detail by Ball.

■ **NOTES** The NFTVA's copy is the American version, produced by Ben Blumenthal (who part-financed the picture) and David P. Howells, and edited by Don Bartlett. The original German release length was 2,662m (8,731ft, 35mm).

■ **REFERENCES** • Ball, *Shakespeare on Silent Film*, pp. 279–84, 376–7.

MME ALDA SINGING 'AVE MARIA' BY VERDI

■ **USA • 1930**

pc   Vitaphone Corporation

NFTVA preservation material
16mm bw sd c300ft 8mins

■ **DESCRIPTION** Musical short. Frances Alda sings the 'Ave Maria' from Verdi's opera *Otello*.

CARNIVAL

USA title VENETIAN NIGHTS

■ **GB • 1931**

d/p Herbert Wilcox
pc   British and Dominions
sc   Donald Macardle
ph   F. A. Young/Jack Parker

NFTVA preservation material
35mm bw sd 7,192ft 80mins

■ **CAST**
Matheson Lang . . . . *Silvio Steno*
Joseph Schildkraut . . . . *Count Andreas Scipio*
Dorothy [Chili] Bouchier . . . . . . *Simonetta Steno*
Lilian Braithwaite . . . . *Italia*
Kay Hammond . . . . *Helen*
Brian Buchel . . . . *Lelio*
Dickie Edwards . . . . *Nino*
Brember Wills . . . . *Stage manager*

■ **DESCRIPTION** Feature film. A remake of the 1921 success, also starring Matheson Lang (see above), about a great Italian actor, like Othello, becoming irrationally jealous of his wife. This version boasts considerably better photography, but is otherwise very ponderous and plain. Nor did they go to Venice this time.

OTELLO

■ **Portugal • c1932**

NFTVA preservation material
35mm bw sd 728ft 8mins

■ **CAST**
Lelane Rivera [?] . . . . *Desdemona*

■ **DESCRIPTION** Opera. An opera singer (believed to be Lelane Rivera) sings one aria from Verdi's *Otello*. No production information has been traced for this film.

MEN ARE NOT GODS

■ **GB • 1936**

d   Walter Reisch
pc   London Film Productions
exec p Alexander Korda
sc   Walter Reisch/G. B. Stern/
       Iris Wright
ph   Charles Rosher
sets Vincent Korda
m   based on themes from Samuel
       Coleridge-Taylor's *Othello* suite

NFTVA viewing copy
35mm bw sd 7,429ft 83mins

■ **CAST**
Miriam Hopkins . . . . *Ann*
Gertrude Lawrence . . . . *Barbara*
Sebastian Shaw . . . . *Edmond Davey*
Rex Harrison . . . . *Tommy*
A. E. Matthews . . . . *Skeates*
Val Gielgud . . . . *The Producer*
Laura Smithson . . . . *Katherine*
Laurence Grossmith . . . . *Stanley*

■ **DESCRIPTION** Feature film. Ann, secretary to a theatrical reviewer Skeates, is persuaded to alter his review of a production of *Othello*, starring Edmond Davey, by Davey's wife Barbara. The production is a success. Ann is sacked, then falls in love with Davey and he with her. He determines to murder Barbara on stage during a performance of *Othello*, leaving him free to marry Ann. He proceeds to carry out his plan, but Ann's screams from the audience halt him and the Daveys are eventually reunited. Competently made but ridiculouly plotted, the film descends from amiable light comedy to absurd emotionalism. The scenes from *Othello* are effectively staged and well spoken by Shaw, but Lawrence could never convince as Desdemona. Rex Harrison offers a fine comic cameo as an obituary writer.

■ **NOTES** Val Gielgud, the elder brother of John, was well known at this time as a BBC radio producer.

EAST OF PICCADILLY
USA title STRANGLER, The

■ **GB • 1940**

d	Harold Huth
pc	Associated British Picture Corporation
p	Walter C. Mycroft
sc	J. Lee Thompson/Lesley Storm
ph	Claude Friese-Greene

NFTVA viewing copy
35mm bw sd 7,110ft 79mins

■ **CAST**
Judy Campbell . . . . *Penny Sutton*
Sebastian Shaw . . . . *Tamsie Green*
George Hayes . . . . *Mark Struberg*

■ **DESCRIPTION** Feature film. Stilted whodunnit set in London's Soho, where a crime reporter and a writer of detective thrillers capture a silk stocking murderer. Features an over-the-top cameo from George Hayes as an insane actor who keeps effigies of theatre critics (including James Agate) in his room, dresses up as Othello and, quoting variously from the play (mostly A5S2), threatens the crime reporter (Campbell) who has been tied up in a chair by other hands.

VOLUNTEER, The

■ **GB • 1943**

d/p/sc	Michael Powell/Emeric Pressburger
pc	The Archers
spon	Ministry of Information
ph	Fred Ford
des	Alfred Junge
m	Allan Gray

NFTVA viewing copy
35mm bw sd 3,964ft 44mins

■ **CAST**
Ralph Richardson . . . . *Himself*
Pat McGrath . . . . *Fred Davy*

■ **DESCRIPTION** Propaganda mini-feature film. Fred is a clumsy but willing dresser to a famous actor, played by Ralph Richardson, who makes himself up to play Othello. The news of the invasion of Poland comes in, and (in full Othello costume) Richardson talks to Fred, who is trying to decide which service to volunteer for. They both join the Fleet Air Arm, Fred as an engineer, Richardson as a pilot. Fred is wounded in action and awarded the DSM. A warm and human tribute, its *Othello* passages are incidental.

■ **NOTES** In the film Fred visits Denham Studios, and among the people he meets are Anna Neagle and Laurence Olivier.

OTHELLO

■ **GB • 1946**

d/adapt	David MacKane
pc	Marylebone
p	Henry Halstead
ph	Stanley Clinton

NFTVA preservation material
35mm bw sd 4,036ft 45mins

■ **CAST**
John Slater . . . . *Othello*
Luanne Shaw . . . . *Desdemona*
Sebastian Cabot . . . . *Iago*
Sheila Raynor . . . . *Emilia*

■ **DESCRIPTION** Condensed version of Shakespeare's play, presumably aimed at schoolteachers, pleased to see the cinema adopt culture, and their hapless pupils. It is, in fact, a more than adequate précis of the play, hampered by a third division cast, although John Slater is convincingly miserable. There is, of course, no attempt to use any cinematic device to illuminate the action.

■ **NOTES** David MacKane and Marylebone apparently planned a series of abbreviated versions of Shakespeare, which never materialised.

■ **REFERENCES** • David MacKane, 'Forty-Five Minutes of "Othello"', *Cine-Technician*, September–October 1946, pp. 129–30.

DOUBLE LIFE, A

■ **USA • 1947**

d	George Cukor
pc	Kanin/Universal-International
p	Michael Kanin
sc	Ruth Gordon/Garson Kanin
ph	Milton Krasner
m	Miklos Rozsa
advisor to Othello	
sequences	Walter Hampden

NFTVA viewing copy
35mm bw sd 9,396ft 105mins

■ **CAST**
Ronald Colman. . . . . *Anthony John*
Signe Hasso. . . . . *Brita*
Edmond O'Brien . . . . *Bill Friend*
Shelley Winters . . . . *Pat Kroll*
Ray Collins . . . . *Victor Donlan*

■ **CAST OF OTHELLO**
Guy Gates Post
David Bond
Leslie Denison
Virginia Patton
Thayer Roberts
Fay Kanin
Arthur Gould-Porter
Frederic Warlock
Boyd Irwin
Percival Vivian

■ **DESCRIPTION** Feature film. A serious case of this-is-Shakespeare-so-it-must-be-Art. Anthony John is a great but unbalanced classical actor. Outwardly gentlemanly, he is taken over by any role that he plays, and playing Othello becomes insanely jealous. In just such a manic fit he strangles Pat Kroll, a waitress. Bill Friend, a publicity agent, ties the unsolved murder to the production of *Othello*. A furious John attacks Friend. Friend sets up John with a Kroll-lookalike, and the police decide from his reaction that he must be the murderer. They decide to arrest him after the performance of *Othello*. On stage, knowing that he has been found out, John is gradually taken over by the role and nearly strangles Desdemona (also his former wife). He pulls back just in time, stabs himself, and dies in the wings. Whether Colman's rich performance is one of the greatest

or one of the worst ever recorded on film seems a matter of taste. Overall a silly but suspenseful melodrama that would convince far more if the scenes from *Othello* itself were not so poorly staged.

■ **NOTES** Colman won the Academy Award for best actor. Some way down the cast, as 'Girl in wig shop' is Betsy Blair, one of several actresses who almost became Desdemona in Orson Welles's OTHELLO (1952, see below). She also appears as Emily in the *Othello* derivative ALL NIGHT LONG (1961, see below).

UPLIFT AT THE LOCAL

■ **GB • 1947**

■ *British Movietone News Vol 18 No 927A*

rel date   13 March 1947

NFTVA preservation material
35mm bw sd 101ft 1min

■ **DESCRIPTION** Newsreel item. An amateur theatrical company, 'The Taverners', perform the final scene from *Othello* at a pub in Carshalton.

RETURN TO GLENNASCAUL

■ **Ireland • 1951**

d/sc	Hilton Edwards
pc	Dublin Gate Theatre
p	Hilton Edwards/Micheál MacLiammóir
ph	Georg Fleischmann
nar	Orson Welles
m	Hans Gunther Stumpf

NFTVA viewing copy
35mm bw sd 2,106ft 23mins

■ **CAST**
Orson Welles. . . . . *Himself*
Michael Laurence . . . . *Sean Merriman*
Sheila Richards . . . . *Mrs Campbell*
Helena Hughes . . . . *Lucy Campbell*

■ **DESCRIPTION** Fiction short. Orson Welles, taking a break from filming OTHELLO, gives a lift to a man who tells him of his encounter on the same road with two women who turned out to be ghosts. A somewhat wooden if not unpleasing effort, with poor post-synching. The film opens with Welles, seen in silhouette, on a film set, speaking as Othello of how he wooed Desdemona (A1S3). As narrator he states that he is interrupting the production of one film to take part in another. He wears his Othello beard during the film.

■ **NOTES** The film was produced during a gap in the OTHELLO schedule. There is a notice in the 'studio' (no part of OTHELLO was filmed in Ireland) for Mercury Productions (Welles's production company).

OTHELLO

■ **Morocco • 1952**

d/adapt/p	Orson Welles
pc	Films Marceau/Mercury Productions/Mogador Films
ph	Anchise Brizzi/G. R. Aldo/George Fanto/Obadan Troini/Alberto Fusi
art d	Alexandre Trauner
cost	Maria de Matteis
ed	Jean Sacha/John Shepridge/Renzo Lucidi/William Morton
m	Francesco Lavagnino/Alberto Barberis

NFTVA viewing copy
35mm bw sd 8,157ft 91mins

■ **CAST**

Orson Welles	Othello
Micheál MacLiammóir	Iago
Suzanne Cloutier	Desdemona
Robert Coote	Roderigo
Michael Lawrence	Cassio
Hilton Edwards	Brabantio
Fay Compton	Emilia
Nicholas Bruce	Lodovico
Jean Davis	Montano
Doris Dowling	Bianca
Joseph Cotten	Senator
Joan Fontaine	Page boy

■ **DESCRIPTION** Feature film adaptation of the play. From its Eisenstein-inspired opening, showing Othello and Desdemona's funeral procession and a caged Iago suspended in the air, through a succession of dazzlingly (and often bewilderingly) staged scenes, building up to a truly tragic dénouement, this is a brilliant Shakespearean film. The story of its piecemeal production over three years, as Welles struggled to find the finance and keep cast and crew together, has been memorably documented by Micheál MacLiammóir. Certainly it is a difficult film, beautiful images whisked away on account of a far too rapid editing scheme, and with a quite dreadful dubbed vocal track, but it is a text most rewarding when studied in detail. Shakespeare's words have been pruned to bear most fruit, and of the performances MacLiammóir is the quintessence of Iago; Welles is imposing if little else; Cloutier's much-derided performance deserves a kinder reception, if only for the shocking slap in the face delivered to her; Fay Compton belongs too much to the stage.

■ **NOTES** The chief locations employed were the fortress at Mogador (Morocco), Venice, Viterbo and the Scalera Studios, Rome. Other scenes were filmed at Safi and Mazagan in Morocco, and Tuscany, Perugia and Torcello in Italy. Filming began May 1949 and ended late 1951. It was premiered at the Cannes Film Festival on 10 May 1952, where it won the Grand Prix, was released in the United States in June 1955 and in Britain in February 1956. The actual title on the film is THE TRAGEDY OF OTHELLO, THE MOOR OF VENICE. In 1992 a 'restored and enhanced' version was released, with a re-recorded soundtrack. Welles also made a meditative documentary record of his experiences, FILMING OTHELLO (USA 1977, not in NFTVA).

■ **REFERENCES** • André Bazin, *Cahiers du Cinéma*, 13 (June 1952), pp. 18–19 [translation in Eckert, *Focus on Shakespearean Films*, pp. 77–8]. • Eric Bentley, *What is Theatre?* (London: Methuen, 1969) [a revealing attack on Welles] • Davies, *Filming Shakespeare's Plays*, pp. 100–18. • David Impastato, 'Orson Welles' *Othello* and the Welles-Smith Restoration: Definitive Version?', *Shakespeare Bulletin* (Fall 1992), pp. 38–41. • Jorgens, *Shakespeare on Film*, pp. 175–90, 290–4. • Micheál MacLiammóir, *Put Money in thy Purse: The Diary of the Film of Othello* (London: Methuen, 1952).

OTHELLO

■ **GB • 1953**

■ *The World's a Stage*

d/p	Charles Deane
pc	Emil Katzka Productions
ph	A. T. Dinsdale
nar	Ronald Harwood

NFTVA preservation material
35mm bw sd 1,250ft 14mins

■ **CAST**
Young Vic Theatre Company

■ **DESCRIPTION** Drama short. The handkerchief scene from *Othello* (A3S3), one of a series of films of little merit featuring the Young Vic Theatre Company, details of which are given in the entry for JULIUS CAESAR from the same series.

OTELLO

English title OTHELLO

■ **Soviet Union • 1955**

d/sc	Sergei Yutkevich
pc	Mosfilm
ph	Evgeny Andrikanis
sets/cost	A. Vaisfeld/V. Dorrer/
	M. Kariakin/O. Krochinina
m	Aram Khachaturian

NFTVA preservation material
35mm col sd 9,572ft 106mins

■ **CAST**
Sergei Bondarchuk . . . . *Othello*
Irina Skobtseva . . . . *Desdemona*
Andrei Popov . . . . *Iago*
Vladimir Soshalsky . . . . *Cassio*
E. Vesnik . . . . *Roderigo*
A. Maximova. . . . . *Emilia*
E. Teterin . . . . *Brabantio*
M. Troyanovsky . . . . *The Doge*
A. Kelberer . . . . *Montano*
P. Brilling . . . . *Lodovico*

■ **DESCRIPTION** Feature film adaptation of the play. Sometimes imaginative, sometimes stolid interpretation, taking every opportunity to get out of the studio; in common with a number of non-English Shakespearean films the film-makers are less in thrall to the word, far more prepared to represent Shakespeare with the image. If he does not quite find the ease and depth of expression that characterises Kozintsev's films, Yutkevich certainly likes to move the camera, and there are rich performances to match.

■ **NOTES** An English dubbed version printed in Technicolor was made available in Britain, with Howard Marion Crawford supplying the voice of Othello and Kathleen Byron of Desdemona. The NFTVA holds the original Sovcolor version.

■ **REFERENCES** • Manvell, *Shakespeare and the Film*, pp. 72–7.

OTHELLO

■ **GB • 1955**

d	Tony Richardson
pc	BBC
tx	15 December 1955 (BBC)
des	Reece Pemberton
m	Leonard Chase/Tony Richardson

NFTVA viewing copy
¼" bw sd 230mins

■ **CAST**
James Maxwell . . . . *Roderigo, a Venetian gentleman*
Paul Rogers . . . . *Iago, Othello's ancient*
Edmund Willard . . . . *Brabantio, a Senator*
Gordon Heath . . . . *Othello, a noble Moor*
Robert Hardy . . . . *Cassio, his Lieutenant*
Peter Welch . . . . *First officer*
George Skillan. . . . . *Duke of Venice*
Frank Royde . . . . *First senator*
Jefferson Clifford . . . . *Second senator*
Stephen Dartnell . . . . *Sailor*
Kim Grant . . . . *Messenger*
Nigel Davenport . . . *Lodovico, kinsman to Brabantio*
Rosemary Harris . . . . *Desdemona, daughter to*
Brabantio and wife to Othello
Patrick Wymark . . . . *Montano, Othello's predecessor*
in the Government of Cyprus
Kevin Miles . . . . *First gentleman*
Patrick Horgan . . . . *Second gentleman*
Joby Blanshard . . . . *Third gentleman*
Christopher Fettes . . . . *Messenger*

Daphne Anderson . . . . *Emilia, wife to Iago*
George A. Cooper . . . . *Herald*
Billie Whitelaw . . . . *Bianca, mistress to Cassio*
Milton Rosmer . . . . *Gratiano, brother to Brabantio*

■ **DESCRIPTION** Television production of the play. At last, a black Othello (see all the above). An intelligent if not too remarkable televisualisation of the play - soliloquies spoken to camera, a sensible mix of open staging and the more intimate – its chief virtue is Heath's modest, elegant, soft-spoken interpretation, a world away from ranting madness and dripping black paint.

■ **NOTES** The original production was part-live, with recorded 'Venice' sequences because two sets could not be accommodated in the studio. The videotape held by the NFTVA is of a telerecording of the actual broadcast. Gordon Heath, an American, came to Britain in 1947 and was cast by Kenneth Tynan to play Othello in his 1950 Arts Council production.

■ **REFERENCES** • Elwyn Jones, 'Bringing "Othello" to Television', *Radio Times*, 11–17 December 1955, p. 5.

MONITOR

■ **GB • 1959**

pc	BBC
tx	12 April 1959 (BBC)
p	Peter Newington
ed/pres	Huw Weldon

NFTVA viewing copy
¾" bw sd 11mins

■ **DESCRIPTION** Item from television arts series. Alfred Alvarez interviews Paul Robeson, then appearing as Othello at Stratford. Robeson recalls his playing of the role in the past and puts strong emphasis on the racial theme. *Othello* shows a black man in a white society, and Othello is not merely 'jealous' but is motivated by the insults to his race – to Robeson, it is 'a play essentially of honour'.

■ **NOTES** Tony Richardson's production of *Othello* opened at Stratford on 7 April 1959 with Paul Robeson in the title role, Mary Ure as Desdemona and Sam Wanamaker as Iago.

OTHELLO

■ **GB • 1959**

d/p	Rudolph Cartier
pc	BBC
tx	1 October 1959 (BBC)
trans	Eric Crozier
chor	Margaret Dale
des	Clifford Hatts

NFTVA preservation material
35mm bw sd 11,258ft 125mins

■ **CAST**
Charles Holland . . . . *Othello, the Moor, Admiral of the Venetian Fleet*
Ronald Lewis . . . . *Iago, his Ancient*
John Ford . . . . *Cassio, Captain*
John Kentish . . . . . *Roderigo, a Venetian gentleman*
Forbes Robinson . . . . . *Lodovico, Ambassador of the Republic of Venice*
James Atkins . . . . *Montano, Othello's predecessor as Governor of Cyprus*
George MacPherson . . . . *A herald*
Heidi Krall . . . . *Desdemona, Othello's wife*
Barbara Howitt . . . . *Emilia, Iago's wife*

■ **DESCRIPTION** Opera. Television studio production of Verdi's *Otello*, with the Royal Philharmonic Orchestra, conducted by Bryan Balkwill, and the Glyndebourne Festival Chorus. A largely uncut version, with black American tenor Charles Holland in the title role.

■ **NOTES** The NFTVA holds a telerecording made of the original broadcast.

ALL NIGHT LONG

■ **GB • 1961**

d/p	Basil Dearden/Michael Relph
pc	Bob Roberts Productions
sc	Nel King/Peter Achilles
ph	Ted Scaife
m	Philip Green

NFTVA viewing copy
16mm bw sd 3,286ft 91mins

■ **CAST**
Patrick McGoohan . . . . *Johnny Cousin*

Marti Stevens . . . . *Delia Lane*
Betsy Blair . . . . *Emily*
Keith Michell . . . . *Cass Michaels*
Richard Attenborough . . . . *Rod Hamilton*
Paul Harris . . . . *Aurelius Rex*
Bernard Braden . . . . *Berger*
Maria Velasco . . . . *Benny*
Harry Towb . . . . *Phales*

■ **APPEARING AS THEMSELVES**
Dave Brubeck, Johnny Dankworth, Charles Mingus, Tubby Hayes, Keith Christie, Ray Dempsey, Allan Ganley, Bert Courtley, Barry Morgan, Kenny Napper, Colin Purbrook, Johnny Scott, Geoffrey Holder.

■ **DESCRIPTION** Feature film updating the story of *Othello* to a jazz club setting. Aurelius Rex is a famous black jazzman with a white wife, former singer Delia. He throws a jazz party, one of the guests being drummer Johnny Cousin who wants Delia as a singer in his new band. Delia refuses, and Johnny starts to employ lies and insinuations to try to break up her marriage. He edits a taped conversation to make it sound as if Delia is having an affair with Rex's manager, Cass. Having heard the tape, Rex becomes so furious that he nearly strangles Delia, but Johnny's schemes are revealed and Rex and Delia are reunited. A real oddity, mixing Shakespeare with a parade of real-life jazz stars and some embarrassing attempts at hip talk from the stars. One of a number of British movies of the period nervously dipping their toes into the teenage/pop phenomenon, ALL NIGHT LONG should be viewed in the spirit of fun with which it was played.

■ **NOTES** Patrick McGoohan subsequently directed CATCH MY SOUL (USA 1973, not in NFTVA), a feature film version of the 'rock opera' based on *Othello*.

OTHELLO

■ **GB • 1965**

d	Stuart Burge
pc	British Home Entertainment
p	Anthony Havelock-Allan/ John Brabourne
ph	Geoffrey Unsworth
art d	William Kellner
sets	Jocelyn Herbert
m	Richard Hampton

NFTVA preservation material
70mm col sd 18,675ft 166mins

■ **CAST**
Laurence Olivier . . . . *Othello*
Maggie Smith . . . . *Desdemona*
Frank Finlay . . . . *Iago*
Joyce Redman . . . . *Emilia*
Derek Jacobi . . . . *Cassio*
Robert Lang . . . . *Roderigo*
Kenneth Mackintosh . . . . *Lodovico*
Anthony Nicholls . . . . *Brabantio*
Sheila Reid . . . . *Bianca*
Michael Turner . . . . *Gratiano*
Edward Hardwicke . . . . *Montano*
Harry Lomax . . . . *Duke of Venice*
Roy Holder . . . . *Clown*
David Hargreaves/Malcolm Terris . *Senate officers*
Terence Knapp . . . . *Duke's officer*
Keith Marsh . . . . *Senator*
Tom Kempinski . . . . *Sailor*
Nicholas Edmett . . . . *Messenger*
William Hobbs/Trevor Martin . . . *Cypriot officers*

■ **DESCRIPTION** Feature film version of John Dexter's National Theatre stage production. A fairly literal recording of a famous stage production and central performance, filmed in the most basic manner in the studio. Inevitably a disappointment after Olivier's own imaginative and cinematic HENRY V, HAMLET and RICHARD III, this is best accepted as a useful record. Not that it is a wholly faithful record: having the camera come in close alters the tenor of some performances (particularly a dulled Maggie Smith), notoriously accentuating Olivier's mannerisms, the overall effect being that of a rather bad-tempered member of *The Black and White Minstrel Show*. Frank Finlay's impressive Iago is more restrained.

■ **NOTES** The stage production was produced by John Dexter at the National Theatre for the Shakespeare quatercentary celebrations in 1964. In the 1992 television programme LAURENCE OLIVIER, in the *J'Accuse* series (see General section), the film is repeatedly referred to as evidence of Olivier's supposedly poor acting.

■ **REFERENCES** • James E. Fisher, 'Olivier and the Realistic *Othello*', *Literature/Film Quarterly*, Fall 1973, pp. 321–31. • Jorgens, *Shakespeare on Film*, pp. 191–206, 294–6.

SHAKESPEARE WALLAH

■ **India • 1965**

d   James Ivory
pc   Merchant-Ivory Productions

NFTVA viewing copy

■ **CAST**

Geoffrey Kendal . . . . *Othello*
Felicity Kendal . . . . *Desdemona*
Madhur Jaffrey . . . . *Manjula*

■ **DESCRIPTION** Feature film about a troupe of English actors in India. Includes a performance of the final scene from *Othello* (A5S2), during which Manjula, a famous Indian film star, causes considerable interruption when she joins the audience. For full details of the film see entry in General section.

THEATRE OF BLOOD

■ **GB • 1973**

d   Douglas Hickox
pc   Cineman

NFTVA preservation material

■ **CAST**

Vincent Price . . . . *Edward Lionheart*
Jack Hawkins . . . . *Solomon Psaltery*
Diana Dors . . . . *Mrs Psaltery*

■ **DESCRIPTION** Feature film. An actor (Vincent Price) murders his critics in the manner of deaths from Shakespeare's plays. In the film's least convincing sequence, Solomon Psaltery believes that his wife is having an affair with her 'doctor' (Lionheart in disguise) and smothers her in a fit of jealous rage. An old man, he will die in prison. For full details of the film see entry in General section.

OTHELLO

■ **GB/USA • 1981**

■ *BBC Television Shakespeare*

d/p   Jonathan Miller

pc   BBC/Time-Life Films
tx **(GB)**   4 October 1981 (BBC2)
tx **(US)**   12 October 1981 (PBS)
sc ed   David Snodin
lght   John Treays
cost   Raymond Hughes
des   Colin Lowrey
m   Stephen Oliver

NFTVA viewing copy
16mm col sd c7,500ft 210mins

■ **CAST**

Anthony Pedley . . . . *Roderigo*
Bob Hoskins . . . . *Iago*
Geoffrey Chater . . . . *Brabantio*
Joseph O'Conor . . . . *Lodovico*
Alexander Davion . . . . *Gratiano*
Anthony Hopkins . . . . *Othello*
David Yelland . . . . *Cassio*
Peter Walmsley . . . . *Officer*
John Barron . . . . *Duke of Venice*
Seymour Green . . . . *First senator*
Howard Goorney . . . . *Second senator*
Penelope Wilton . . . . *Desdemona*
Rosemary Leach . . . . *Emilia*
Tony Steedman . . . . *Montano*
Max Harvey . . . . *First gentleman*
Terence McGinity . . . . *Second gentleman*
Nigel Nobes . . . . *Third gentleman*
Wendy Morgan . . . . *Bianca*

■ **DESCRIPTION** Television production of the play. A competent presentation, if little more, that at least tries to rethink the performances. Penelope Wilton's Desdemona, certainly the best thing in it, is strong-willed and passionate, and Hopkins becomes a light-skinned Arab, Miller being far more concerned with jealousy than racial stereotype. But Othello and Iago never interact; Hopkins is merely distracted, Hoskins too jovial. It might have paid off to reverse the roles; Hoskins bringing a fresh vigour to Othello, Hopkins – adept at saying one thing while thinking another – a superior Iago.

DRESSER, The

■ **GB • 1983**

d   Peter Yates
pc   Goldcrest/World Film Services

NFTVA preservation material

■ **DESCRIPTION** Feature film about an ageing actor (Albert Finney) and his dresser during the Second World War. Shows Finney blacking up for Othello when he should be playing King Lear, also views from the wings and on stage of the death of Othello. For full details of the film see entry under *King Lear*.

ZEFFIRELLI'S OTELLO: FROM STAGE TO SCREEN

■ **GB • 1986**

pc	BBC
tx	28 September 1986 (BBC2)
p	David Sweetman
ph	John Else

NFTVA preservation material
1" col sd 75mins

■ **DESCRIPTION** Television documentary on the making of Franco Zeffirelli's OTELLO (Italy 1986, not in NFTVA), a feature film adaptation of the Verdi opera, with Placido Domingo in the title role. The film crew followed Zeffirelli on location in Italy and Crete for a year. Interviews with Zeffirelli, Domingo and others involved in the production.

OTELLO

■ **GB/South Africa • 1988**

d	Janet Suzman
pc	Othello Productions/Focus Films/ Portobello Productions
tx	27 December 1988 (C4)
p	David Pupkewitz
ph	Dewalt Aukema

NFTVA viewing copy
½" col sd 199mins

■ **CAST**
John Kani . . . . *Othello*
Richard Haddon Haines . . . . *Iago*
Joanna Weinberg . . . . *Desdemona*
Dorothy Gould . . . . *Emilia*
Frantz Dobrowsky . . . . *Roderigo*
Neil McCarthy . . . . *Cassio*
Stuart Brown . . . . *Brabantio*

John Whiteley . . . . *Gratiano*
Peter Krummeck . . . . *Lodovico*
Gaynor Young . . . . *Bianca*
Martin Le Maitre . . . . *Montano*
Lindsay Reardon . . . . *Duke of Venice*

■ **DESCRIPTION** Television production of the play, based on Janet Suzman's Market Theatre of Johannesburg stage production. Miller's BBC version took the blackness out of Othello, Suzman puts it back again. With black African actor John Kani in the title role, the production's passion and political relevance caused a small sensation in South Africa. On the small screen, and taken out of its national context, much of this passion seems lost.

EVENING STANDARD DRAMA AWARDS 1989, The

■ **GB • 1989**

d/p	Mike Ward
pc	Thames Television
tx	14 November 1989 (ITV)
pres	Ned Sherrin

NFTVA viewing copy
½" col sd 51mins

■ **DESCRIPTION** Television awards ceremony for achievements in British stage drama over the year. Includes a specially filmed sequence of the Royal Shakespeare Company's production of *Othello* with Ian McKellen as Iago and Michael Grandage as Roderigo (A2S1). McKellen is presented with the Best Actor award, giving a speech in praise of Ian Charleson's Hamlet at the National Theatre. A full television version of the *Othello* production made in 1990 is given below.

■ **NOTES** Ian Charleson had recently died of AIDS. Felicity Kendal is presented with the Best Actress award for *Much Ado About Nothing*, but no extract is shown.

LATE SHOW SPECIAL

■ **GB • 1990**

d	Janet Fraser Crook
pc	BBC

tx   18 June 1990 (BBC2)
pres   Michael Ignatieff

NFTVA viewing copy
½" col sd 32mins

■ **DESCRIPTION** Television arts and media magazine. Michael Ignatieff interviews Trevor Nunn about his Royal Shakespeare Company production of *Othello* and the play in general. Includes sequences from the television version of the Nunn production (see below) and extracts from the 1922, 1952 and 1962 versions (all held by NFTVA).

OTHELLO

■ **GB • 1990**

■ *Theatre Night*

d   Trevor Nunn
pc   Primetime
tx   23 June 1990 (BBC2)
p   Greg Smith

NFTVA viewing copy
½" col sd 204mins

■ **CAST**
Michael Grandage . . . . *Roderigo*
Ian McKellen . . . . *Iago*
Clive Swift . . . . *Brabantio / Gratiano*
Willard White . . . . *Othello*
Sean Baker. . . . . *Cassio*
Brian Lawson . . . . *First senator / Second Cyprus soldier / Second Othello soldier*
David Hounslow . *Servant to the Senate / First Cyprus soldier / First Othello soldier*
John Burgess. . . . . *Duke of Venice / Lodovico*
Imogen Stubbs . . . . *Desdemona*
Phillip Sully . . . . *Montano*
Zoë Wanamaker . . . . *Emilia*
Marsha Hunt. . . . . *Bianca*
Jonathan Goldstein / Peter Rolinson . . . *Musicians*

■ **DESCRIPTION** Television adaptation of Trevor Nunn's 1989 Stratford and London production of the play. A highly acclaimed and highly popular stage production superbly reimagined as a television chamberpiece. Black opera singer Willard White indeed brings musicality as well as dignity

and strength to the title role, but the real centre and star performance is McKellen's poisoned and poisonous Iago. Stubbs manages to suggest both fragility and strength, Grandage is a most poignant Roderigo, while Wanamaker wholly revalues Emilia. Perhaps lacking some of the passion and televisual imagination of Nunn's 1979 MACBETH (qv), this is nevertheless deeply considered and expressed, a connoisseur's *Othello*.

PACKET OF 3

■ **GB • 1991**

d   John Stroud
pc   Jon Blair Film Company
tx   20 September 1991 (C4)

NFTVA viewing copy

■ **DESCRIPTION** Television comedy series. Programme on theme of Shakespeare, including a performance by the Reduced Shakespeare Company of their 'rap' *Othello* ('Now Othello got married to a chick named Desdemona / Took off for the wars and he left her alone-a'). Full details of the programme given in General section.

TRUE IDENTITY

■ **USA • 1991**

d   Charles Lane
pc   Touchstone Pictures
p   Carol Baum / Teri Schwartz
sc   Andy Breckman
ph   Tom Ackerman
m   Marc Mader

NFTVA preservation material
35mm col sd 8,386ft 93mins

■ **CAST**
Lenny Henry . . . . *Miles Pope*
Frank Langella . . . . . *Frank Luchino / Leland Carver*
Charles Lane . . . . *Duane*
James Earl Jones . . . . *Himself*
Shannon Holt. . . . . *Desdemona*
Lynne Griffin . . . . *Emilia*
Judson Scott. . . . . *Iago*
Richard Ganoung . . . . *Roderigo*

■ **DESCRIPTION** Feature film comedy. Miles Pope, a struggling black actor, dreams of playing Othello. He gets into trouble after discovering that a supposedly dead Mafia chief, Frank Luchino, is the patron of a new production of *Othello*. The Mafia pursue Miles, whose make-up artist friend Duane manages to disguise him as a white man. Further complications ensue, while Miles has landed the part of understudy to James Earl Jones in *Othello*. The Mafia attempt to run Jones over and Miles takes over from him. In the middle of his triumphant performance Miles denounces Luchino to the audience. Hit-and-miss comedy vehicle for black British comic Lenny Henry which allows him to run the gamut of his impersonations, centring on the changing attitudes he encounters as 'white'. 'There is an irritating simple-mindedness in the film's use of Shakespeare as a signifier of cultural respectability' (Ben Thompson, *Sight and Sound*).

SHAKESPEARE; OR, WHAT YOU WILL

■ **GB • 1992**

■ *Dark Horses / Without Walls*

pc	Wall to Wall Television
tx	13 October 1992 (C4)

NFTVA viewing copy

■ **DESCRIPTION** Television documentary on Shakespeare and homosexuality. Includes a reading from Iago's speech 'I lay with Cassio lately' (A3S3). For full details of the programme see entry in General section.

ENTERTAINMENT UK

■ **GB • 1993**

pc	Mentorn Films
tx	18 March 1993 (ITV)
p	John Needham / Jonathan Challis
pres	Toyah Willcox

NFTVA viewing copy
½" col sd 51mins

■ **CAST**
Jeffery Kissoon . . . . *Othello*

■ **DESCRIPTION** Television arts and entertainment magazine. Includes short item on a production of *Othello* by Birmingham Rep., interviewing actor Jeffery Kissoon and director Bill Alexander, plus three brief extracts from the production (A3S3).

■ **NOTES** The programme also includes a similar item on a production of *Macbeth* in Leicester (qv).

Mike Gwilym in PERICLES, PRINCE OF TYRE (1984)

PERICLES

PERICLES, PRINCE OF TYRE

■ **GB/USA 1984**

d	David Jones
pc	BBC/Time-Life Films
tx (GB)	8 December 1984 (BBC2)
tx (US)	11 June 1984 (PBS)
p	Shaun Sutton
sc ed	David Snodin
lght	Sam Barclay
cost	Colin Lavers
des	Don Taylor
m	Martin Best

NFTVA preservation material
1" col sd 180mins

■ **CAST**

Edward Petherbridge . . . . *Gower*
John Woodvine . . . . *Antiochus*
Edita Brychta. . . . . *Daughter to Antiochus*
Mike Gwilym . . . . *Pericles*
Robert Ashby . . . . *Thaliard*
Patrick Godfrey . . . . *Helicanus*
Amanda Redman . . . . *Marina*
Toby Salaman . . . . *Escanes / Pandar*
Norman Rodway. . . . . *Cleon*
Annette Crosbie . . . . *Dionyza*
Patrick Allen . . . . *Simonides*
Juliet Stevenson . . . . *Thaisa*
Valerie Lush . . . . *Lychorida*
Clive Swift . . . . *Cerimon*
Nicholas Brimble . . . . *Leonine*
Trevor Peacock . . . . *Boult*
Lila Kaye . . . . *Bawd*
Patrick Ryecart . . . . *Lysimachus*
Elayne Sharling . . . . *Goddess Diana*
Gordon Gostelow . . . . *First fisherman*
John Bardon. . . . . *Second fisherman*
Richard Derrington . . . . *Third fisherman*

■ **DESCRIPTION** Television production of the
play. An enjoyable production, well-cast and well-
performed. Particularly noteworthy are Mike
Gwilym in the title role and a menacing
Antiochus from the always excellent John
Woodvine. By not seeking to apologise for the
play's eccentricities, the producers did it the
greater service. Another example of the *BBC
Television Shakespeare* series appearing fresher
when tackling the lesser-known plays.

■ **REFERENCES** • Joan Hartwig, '*Pericles*: An
Unclaimed World', *Shakespeare on Film Newsletter*,
April 1985, pp. 1–2.

RICHARD II

SCARLET PIMPERNEL, The

■ **GB • 1935**

d   Harold Young

Maurice Evans in KING RICHARD II (1954)

pc	London Film Productions
p	Alexander Korda
sc	Lajos Biro / Sam Bermann / Robert Sherwood / Arthur Wimperis
ph	Harold Rosson
m	Arthur Benjamin

NFTVA viewing copy
35mm bw sd 8,768ft 97mins

■ **CAST**

Leslie Howard . . . . *Sir Percy Blakeney*
Merle Oberon . . . . *Lady Blakeney*
Raymond Massey . . . . *Chauvelin*

■ **DESCRIPTION** Feature film version of the
novel by Baroness Orczy. Hugely popular French
Revolution drama, a little faded now, though
Howard is still superb as the seeming dandy who
is really the mysterious 'Scarlet Pimpernel' who
rescues French aristocrats from the guillotine. At
the dramatic conclusion, when he encounters his
arch-rival Chauvelin, Blakeney quotes John of
Gaunt's speech 'This royal throne of kings, this
scepter'd isle' (A2S1).

■ **NOTES** A wartime 'sequel', 'PIMPERNEL'
SMITH (GB 1941, in NFTVA) has Howard as a
present-day historian, rescuing refugees from
Nazi Germany, with a fondness for quoting from
Shakespeare.

CROWN AND GLORY

■ **GB • 1937**

pc   Paramount British Productions

NFTVA viewing copy
35mm bw sd 3,988ft 44mins

■ **DESCRIPTION** Documentary compilation. A souvenir for the coronation of King George VI, released during coronation week, tracing the story of the British Empire from 1895 to his proclamation as King. It concludes with a shot of the new king and a recitation of John of Gaunt's speech, 'This royal throne of kings, this scepter'd isle' (A2S1).

KING RICHARD II

■ **USA • 1954**

■ *Hallmark Hall of Fame*

d   George Schaefer
pc   NBC
tx   24 January 1954 (NBC)
p   Albert McCleery
des   Richard Sylbert
cost   Noel Taylor
m   Herbert Menges

NFTVA preservation material
16mm bw sd 4,298ft 119mins

■ **CAST**
Maurice Evans . . . . *King Richard*
Sarah Churchill . . . . *Queen*
Kent Smith . . . . *Bolingbroke*
Bruce Gordon . . . . *Thomas Mowbray*
Richard Purdy . . . . *York*
Morton da Costa . . . . *Duke of Aumerle*
Louis Hector . . . . *Northumberland*
Jonathan Harris . . . . *Exton*
Fredric Worlock . . . . *John of Gaunt*

■ **DESCRIPTION** Television production of the play. A kinescope recording (i. e. telerecording) of a live broadcast, the second of the *Hallmark* Shakespeares. Loudly trumpeted as major cultural invasions into the world of commercial television,

in practice they were generally flat renditions with weak casts and little idea of poetry. Here the production values are comparatively lavish, but with the result that we see a pageant rather than a play.

■ **NOTES** Sarah Churchill, daughter of Sir Winston Churchill, was hostess for a number of *Hallmark Hall of Fame* programmes, often acting in them as well.

DARLING

■ **GB • 1965**

d   John Schlesinger
pc   Vic Films/Appia Films
p   Joseph Janni
sc   Frederic Raphael
ph   Ken Higgins
m   John Dankworth

NFTVA viewing copy
35mm bw sd 11,307ft 126mins

■ **CAST**
Julie Christie . . . . *Diana Scott*
Dirk Bogarde . . . . *Robert Gold*
Laurence Harvey . . . . *Miles Brand*

■ **DESCRIPTION** Feature film. Coldly observed morality tale about a young woman, a product of the 1960s, who falls victim to her own unscrupulousness. One scene has Julie Christie reading from John of Gaunt's speech 'This royal throne of kings, this scepter'd isle' (A2S1).

CAMPANADAS A MEDIANOCHE

■ **Spain/Switzerland 1966**

d   Orson Welles
pc   Internacional Films/Alpine

NFTVA preservation material

■ **DESCRIPTION** Feature film. The life of Shakespeare's Sir John Falstaff, with material taken from the plays *Richard II*, *1 Henry IV*, *2 Henry IV*, *Henry V* and *The Merry Wives of Windsor*. For full details see entry under *Henry IV*.

TRAGEDY OF KING RICHARD II, The

■ **GB • 1970**

d	Toby Robertson
pc	BBC
tx	30 July 1970 (BBC2)
p	Mark Shivas
lght	Jim Richards
cost	Juanita Watson
des	Tony Abbott

Prospect Theatre Company:

d	Richard Cottrell
cost	Tim Goodchild
m	Benjamin Pearce Higgins

NFTVA preservation material
2" col sd 125mins

■ **CAST**

Ian McKellen	*King Richard*
Timothy West	*Henry Bolingbroke*
Paul Hardwick	*John of Gaunt*
Robert Eddison	*Duke of York*
Peggy Thorpe-Bates	*Duchess of York*
Trevor Martin	*Earl of Northumberland*
Andrew Crawford	*Bishop of Carlisle*
James Laurenson	*Sir Pierce of Exton*
Lucy Fleming	*The Queen*
Charmian Eyre	*Duchess of Gloucester/*
	Lady in Waiting
Terence Wilton	*Duke of Aumerle*
Stephen Greif . .	*Thomas Mowbray, Duke of Norfolk/*
	Welsh Captain
David Calder	*Lord Ross/Groom*
Michael Spice	*Lord Willoughby*
Richard Morant	*Earl of Salisbury*
Luke Hardy	*Sir William Bagot*
Colin Fisher	*Sir John Bushy/Gardener's man*
Peter Bourne	*Sir Henry Green/*
	Abbott of Westminster
Myles Reithermann	*Henry Percy*
Michael Godfrey	*Gardener/Keeper*
Jeremy Nicholas	*Gardener's man*
David Nicholas	*Servant to York*
John Cording	*Servant to Exton*

■ **DESCRIPTION** Television presentation of the Prospect Theatre Company's production of the play. A careful attempt to transfer a popular stage production to the television screen and a 'semi-naturalistic' set. Its chief value is to preserve an intelligent and stimulating portrayal of Richard in a magnetic performance from Ian McKellen, then an exciting new Shakespearean star.

■ **NOTES** The Prospect Theatre Company produced the play for the 1969 Edinburgh Festival, before a countrywide tour, accompanying it with a production of Marlowe's *Edward II*, which was broadcast the following week (tx 6 August 1970, not in NFTVA). Television director Toby Robertson was 'closely involved in all stages' of both theatre productions as well.

RICHARD II

■ *GB/USA 1978*

■ *BBC Television Shakespeare*

d	David Giles
pc	BBC/Time-Life Films
tx (GB)	10 December 1978 (BBC2)
tx (US)	28 March 1979 (PBS)
p	Cedric Messina
sc ed	Alan Shallcross
des	Tony Abbott
cost	Robin Fraser-Payi

NFTVA preservation material
1" col sd 180mins

■ **CAST**

Derek Jacobi	*King Richard*
Jon Finch	*Bolingbroke, later Henry IV*
John Gielgud	*John of Gaunt, Duke of Lancaster*
Richard Owens .	*Thomas Mowbray, Duke of Norfolk*
Mary Morris	*Duchess of Gloucester*
Jeffrey Holland . .	*Duke of Surrey, the Lord Marshal*
Charles Keating	*Duke of Aumerle,*
	son to the Duke of York
Tim Brown/Mike Lewin	*Heralds*
Alan Dalton	*Green*
Damien Thomas	*Bagot*
Robin Sachs	*Bushy*
Charles Gray	*Duke of York*
Janet Maw	*Queen to Richard*
David Swift	*Earl of Northumberland*
David Dodimead	*Lord Ross*
John Flint	*Lord Willoughby*
Jeremy Bulloch	*Henry Percy,*
	son to Northumberland
Carl Oatley	*Earl Berkeley*
David Garfield	*Welsh captain*

John Barcroft . . . . *Earl of Salisbury*
Clifford Rose. . . . . *Bishop of Carlisle*
William Whymper . . . . *Sir Stephen Scroop*
Phillida Sewell / Sandra Frieze . . . . . *Queen's ladies*
Jonathan Adams . . . . *Gardener*
Alan Collins . . . . *Gardener's man*
John Curless . . . . *Lord Fitzwater*
Bruno Barnabe . . . . *Abbott of Westminster*
Wendy Hiller . . . . *Duchess of York*
Desmond Adams. . . . . *Sir Pierce of Exton*
Terry Wright . . . . *Murderer*
Joe Ritchie . . . . *Groom*
Paddy Ward . . . . *Keeper*
Ronald Fernee . . . . *Servant*

■ **DESCRIPTION** Television production of the play, the second title transmitted in the *BBC Television Shakespeare* series. After the populist effort of *Romeo and Juliet*, the BBC tried the Olivier approach, showing its theatrical muscle with a top-drawer cast one could never hope to see in the theatre. Alas, the play was a strange choice, being beautiful to hear but dangerously weak as drama unless approached with greater vigour than the BBC series generally displayed. The result is rather soporific. Nevertheless the verse is beautifully spoken, the action is properly framed for the small screen, and Jon Finch gives a fine sense of the ambitious Bolingbroke. But the mass audience began to switch off.

■ **REFERENCES** • Clive James, *The Crystal Bucket* (London: Jonathan Cape, 1981), pp. 157–9. • Pilkington, *Screening Shakespeare*, pp. 29–63.

RICHARD II

■ **GB • 1978**

■ *Shakespeare in Perspective*

d	Barbara Derkow
pc	BBC
tx	10 December 1978 (BBC2)
p	Victor Poole

NFTVA preservation material
16mm col sd c900ft 25mins

■ **DESCRIPTION** Talk given by Paul Johnson to accompany the screening of RICHARD II above. Johnson puts the play into its historical perspective, showing how it was seen as a threat to the throne when first produced in 1601.

■ **NOTES** The NFTVA holds two examples (the other is the 1984 *Coriolanus*, qv) of the series of short talks given to accompany each of the plays in the *BBC Television Shakespeare* series. The full list was Barry Took (*All's Well that Ends Well*), Anna Raeburn (*Antony and Cleopatra*), Brigid Brophy (*As You Like It*), Roy Hudd (*The Comedy of Errors*), General Sir John Hackett (*Coriolanus*), Dennis Potter (*Cymbeline*), Clive James (*Hamlet*), George Melly (*1 Henry IV*), Fred Emery (*2 Henry IV*), Lord Chalfont (*Henry V*), Michael Wood (*Henry VI* trilogy), Anthony Burgess (*Henry VIII*), Jonathan Dimbleby (*Julius Caesar*), Sir Peter Parker (*The Life and Death of King John*), Frank Kermode (*King Lear*), Emma Tennant (*Love's Labour's Lost*), Julian Symons (*Macbeth*), John Mortimer (*Measure for Measure*), Wolf Mankowitz (*The Merchant of Venice*), Jilly Cooper (*The Merry Wives of Windsor*), Roy Strong (*A Midsummer Night's Dream*), Eleanor Bron (*Much Ado About Nothing*), Susan Hill (*Othello*), P. J. Kavanagh (*Pericles, Prince of Tyre*), Paul Johnson (*Richard II*), Rosemary Anne Sisson (*Richard III*), Germaine Greer (*Romeo and Juliet*), Penelope Mortimer (*The Taming of the Shrew*), Laurens van der Post (*The Tempest*), Malcolm Muggeridge (*Timon of Athens*), Anthony Clare (*Titus Andronicus*), Sir David Hunt (*Troilus and Cressida*), David Jones (*Twelfth Night*), Russell Davies (*Two Gentlemen of Verona*) and Stephen Spender (*The Winter's Tale*).

Laurence Olivier in RICHARD III (1955)

RICHARD III

RICHARD III

■ **GB • 1911**

pc	Co-operative Cinematograph Company
ph	Will Barker [?]

NFTVA viewing copy
35mm bw st 1,324ft 15mins
English titles

■ **CAST OF ORIGINAL STAGE PRODUCTION**

James Berry . . . . *King Henry VI*
Alfred Brydone . . . . *King Edward IV*
Kathleen Yorke . . . . *Edward, Prince of Wales,*
afterwards King Edward V
Hetty Kenyon . . . . *Richard, Duke of York*
Murray Carrington . . . . . *George, Duke of Clarence*
F. R. Benson . . . . *Richard, Duke of Gloucester,*
afterwards King Richard III
Eric Maxon. . . . . *Henry, Earl of Richmond,*
afterwards King Henry VII
Moffat Johnston . . . . *Duke of Buckingham*
James Maclean. . . . . *Duke of Norfolk*
Victor McClure . . . . *Earl of Surrey, his son*
R. L. Conrick . . . . *Earl Rivers*
George Manship. . . . . *Earl of Oxford*
Harry Caine. . . . . *Lord Hastings*
Wilfred Caithness. . . . . *Lord Stanley*
L. Rupert. . . . . *Sir Richard Ratcliff*
H. James . . . . *Sir James Tyrrel*
Alfred Wild . . . . *Sir William Catesby*
Cecil Dighton . . . . *Sir James Blount*
John Howell . . . . *Sir Robert Brackenbury*
J. Victor . . . . *Lord Mayor of London*
H. O. Nicholson. . . . . *First murderer*
A. Wild . . . . *Second murderer*
Violet Farebrother . . . . *Elizabeth, Queen of*
King Edward IV
Elinor Aickin . . . . *Duchess of York, mother to*
King Edward IV, Clarence and Gloucester
Mrs [Constance] Benson . . . . *Lady Anne, widow of*
Edward, Prince of Wales, son to
King Henry VI, afterwards married
to the Duke of Gloucester

■ **DESCRIPTION** An abbreviated record of F. R. Benson's Stratford production, filmed at the Shakespeare Memorial Theatre, Stratford. In 1911 the Co-operative Cinematograph Company launched an ambitious series of Shakespearean films with the F. R. Benson Company: JULIUS CAESAR, MACBETH and THE TAMING OF THE SHREW are lost; the final film in the series, RICHARD III, is a fascinating record of a swaggering performance, but surely a crazy commercial proposition for 1911. The film is a literal recording with fixed camera and short explanatory titles from the play. Rachael Low gives a withering analysis of the film as film, Ball shows how it has no logical narrative at all. But one should not damn it for what it is not, a coherent, commercial film drama. It makes no pretensions to be anything other than a record of a performance, the camera subservient to the stage. Seen now, Benson's passionate, flailing acting certainly fixes the eye; maybe the contemporary audience was similarly transfixed. Pageantry and theatrical culture were considered good selling points, but the Co-operative Cinematograph Company never produced their promised versions of *The Merry Wives of Windsor* and *Twelfth Night*.

■ **NOTES** The opening scenes feature the Battle of Tewkesbury and the murder of Henry VI from *3 Henry VI*. The cast list given above comes from the F. R. Benson Company's performance at the Shakespeare Memorial Theatre, 21 April 1911; Queen Margaret was omitted. Not necessarily all of these people appeared in the film. British film producer Will Barker, himself responsible for two 'lost' Shakespeare films, the grandiose HENRY VIII (1911, a record of the Beerbohm Tree production) and the humbler HAMLET (1912, directed by and starring Charles Raymond, given as 1910 in some sources), later alleged that he was responsible for photographing the film. This is possible, but is not confirmed by contemporary sources. This seems odd, as Barker was not one to hide his light under a bushel.

■ **REFERENCES** • Ball, *Shakespeare in Silent Film*, pp. 84–8, 322–3. • Collick, *Shakespeare, Cinema and Society*, pp. 42–6 [a more generous assessment]. • Rachael Low, *History of the British Film 1906–1914* (London: George Allen & Unwin, 1949), pp. 224–8.

TOWER OF LONDON

■ **USA • 1939**

d/p	Rowland V. Lee
pc	Universal Pictures
sc	Robert N. Lee
ph	George Robinson
m	Frank Skinner

NFTVA viewing copy
35mm bw sd 8,311ft 92mins

■ **CAST**

Basil Rathbone . . . . *Richard III*
Boris Karloff . . . . *Mord the Executioner*
Barbara O'Neill . . . . *Queen Elizabeth*
Vincent Price . . . . *Duke of Clarence*
Ian Hunter . . . . *Edward IV*
Miles Mander . . . . *Henry VI*
Ralph Forbes . . . . *Henry Tudor*
Rose Hobart . . . . *Anne Neville*

■ **DESCRIPTION** Feature film. Shakespeare's interpretation of Richard III turned into a horror film, with the emphasis on the torture methods employed by Richard's executioner, Mord. Not strictly Shakespearean, though Clarence does drown in the butt of Malmsey wine. Wildly out as history, but plenty of shocks and thrills. They would have loved it at the Globe.

■ **NOTES** The film was remade in 1962 with Vincent Price now playing Richard (film not in NFTVA).

STRATFORD ADVENTURE

■ **Canada • 1954**

d	Morten Parker
pc	National Film Board of Canada
p	Guy Glover
sc	Gudrun Parker
ph	Donald Wilder
m	Lou Applebaum

NFTVA preservation material
16mm bw sd 1,414ft 40mins

Alec Guinness . . . . *Richard*
Irene Worth . . . . *Queen Margaret*

■ **DESCRIPTION** Documentary. A record of the 1953 Shakespeare festival held at Stratford, Ontario. The film shows how a small group of Stratford citizens devised the festival and built a theatre, the preparations for the festival, and *Richard III* with producer Tyrone Guthrie and actors Alec Guinness and Irene Worth, in rehearsal (the ghosts, A5S3) and briefly in production (the Battle of Bosworth, A5S4). Too little is seen of the play, but Guthrie dominates.

RICHARD III

■ **GB • 1955**

d/p	Laurence Olivier
pc	London Film Productions
assoc d	Anthony Bushell
text advisor	Alan Dent
ph	Otto Heller
art d	Carmen Dillon
p des	Roger Furse
m	William Walton

NFTVA viewing copy
16mm col sd 5,649ft 157mins

■ **CAST**

Laurence Olivier . . . . *Richard III*
John Gielgud . . . . *Clarence*
Ralph Richardson . . . . *Buckingham*
Cedric Hardwicke . . . . *Edward IV*
Claire Bloom . . . . *Lady Anne*
Mary Kerridge . . . . *Queen Elizabeth*
Pamela Brown . . . . *Jane Shore*
Alec Clunes . . . . *Hastings*
Michael Gough . . . . *Dighton*
Michael Ripper . . . . *Murderer*
Stanley Baker . . . . *Henry Tudor*
Norman Wooland . . . . *Catesby*
Helen Haye . . . . *Duchess of York*
Patrick Troughton . . . . *Tyrrel*
Clive Morton . . . . *Rivers*
Andrew Cruickshank . . . . *Brakenbury*
Andy Shine . . . . *Young Duke of York*
Paul Huson . . . . *Prince of Wales*
Nicholas Hannen . . . . *Archbishop*
Laurence Naismith . . . . *Lord Stanley*
Dan Cunningham . . . . *Lord Grey*
Douglas Wilmer . . . . *Lord Dorset*
Terence Greenidge . . . . *Scrivener*
George Woodbridge . . . . . *Lord Mayor of London*
Esmond Knight . . . . *Ratcliff*
John Laurie . . . . *Lovel*
John Philips . . . . *Norfolk*
Russell Thorndike . . . . *First priest*
Willoughby Gray . . . . *Second priest*

Stuart Allen . . . . *Page*
Wally Bascoe . . . . *First monk*
Norman Fisher . . . . *Second monk*
Peter Williams. . . . . *Messenger*
Anne Wilton . . . . *Scrubwoman*
Derek Prentice/Deering Wells . . . . . . *Clergymen*
Richard Bennett . . . . *Stanley*
Roy Russell . . . . *Abbott*
Timothy Bateson. . . . . *Ostler*
Bill Shine . . . . *Beadle*
Brian Nissen/Alexander Davion/
 Lane Meddick/Robert Bishop . . . . . *Messengers*

■ **DESCRIPTION** Feature film version of the play. 'Cor, look!', a young boy is reported by Raymond Durgnat to have said, 'Four sirs in one picture'. Faith in the cultural superiority of the British theatrical tradition is as strong here as it was with F. R. Benson in 1911, but nonetheless this is a superb movie in every way, the best of the Olivier trio. Free of contrivance or straining for effect, confident in keeping to its own pace; only the finally realistic battle scene (oddly filmed in Spain) disappoints. Building on Olivier's extraordinary stage creation, the film asks less what the cinema can do for the theatre (as with HENRY V and HAMLET) than what the theatre can give to the cinema. It is boldly and often exhilaratingly theatrical – Olivier's poses when inviting Buckingham to kiss his ring and his death throes are like nothing seen on the screen before. The colour is rich and the stagings pleasingly stylised. The performances match the grandeur of the presentation: Richardson's elliptical Buckingham, Gielgud's Clarence chilled to the marrow with horror, and of course Olivier's witty, ironic, splendidly wicked Richard. This is not the only way to film Shakespeare, certainly, but of its kind it is the best.

■ **NOTES** The film was premiered in the USA simultaneously in the cinema and on television, 11 March 1956, when it was broadcast in colour to an estimated (and rather improbable) 25,000,000 people – few of whom could receive colour pictures, and few of whom probably stayed watching to the end.

■ **REFERENCES** • Constance Brown, 'Olivier's Richard III: A Reevaluation', *Film Quarterly*, 20 no. 4, pp. 23–32 [reprinted in Eckert, *Focus on Shakespearean Films*, pp. 131–45]. • Davies, *Filming Shakespeare's Plays*, pp. 65–82. • *Variety*, 14 March 1956 [detailed review of the US television broadcast].

RICHARD III [TRAILER]

■ **GB • 1955**

NFTVA preservation material
35mm col sd 300ft 3mins

■ **DESCRIPTION** Trailer to the above.

MUSIC OF LENNON AND McCARTNEY, The

■ **GB • 1965**

d	Philip Casson
pc	Granada Television
tx	16 December 1965 (ITV)
p	John Hamp

NFTVA viewing copy
½" bw sd 44mins

■ **DESCRIPTION** Television programme in which Paul McCartney and John Lennon were joined by a number of artists each giving their versions of Beatles' songs, including Peter and Gordon, Lulu, Marianne Faithfull and Cilla Black. There is a comic *tour de force* from Peter Sellers, intoning 'A Hard's Day's Night' in the manner (and dress) of Laurence Olivier's portrayal of Richard III.

■ **NOTES** The NFTVA copy is an off-air recording from 30 December 1985.

RICHARD III

■ **GB • 1965**

■ *The Wars of the Roses*

d (RSC)	Peter Hall/John Barton
d (BBC)	Michael Hayes/Robin Midgley
pc	BBC
tx	22 April 1965 (BBC1)
p	Michael Barry
adapt	John Barton
lght	Robin Wright
cost/sets	John Bury
m	Guy Woolfenden

NFTVA viewing copy
¾" bw sd 145mins

CAST

Roy Dotrice . . . . *King Edward IV*
Susan Engel. . . . . *Queen Elizabeth*
Fergus McClelland . . . . *Prince Edward*
Paul Martin . . . . *Richard*
Katharine Barker . . . . *Princess Elizabeth*
Charles Kay . . . . *Clarence*
Ian Holm . . . . *Gloucester*
Madoline Thomas . . . . *Duchess of York*
Hugh Sullivan . . . . *Hastings*
Derek Waring . . . . *Rivers*
William Squire . . . . *Buckingham*
Charles Thomas . . . . *Catesby*
John Corvin . . . . *Ratcliff*
David Hargreaves . . . . *Norfolk*
Henry Knowles. . . . . *Tyrrel*
David Ellison. . . . . *First messenger*
Murray Brown . . . . *Second messenger*
Anthony Boden . . . . *Third messenger*
David Warner . . . . *King Henry VI*
Peggy Ashcroft . . . . *Margaret*
Alan Tucker. . . . . *Prince Edward*
Janet Suzman . . . . *Lady Anne*
Eric Porter . . . . *Richmond*
Maurice Jones . . . . *Oxford*
John Hussey . . . . *Derby*
Michael Rose . . . . *Bishop of Ely*
Ted Valentine . . . . *Lieutenant of the Tower*
Donald Burton . . . . *First murderer*
Philip Brack . . . . *Second murderer*
Malcolm Webster . . . . *Lord Mayor*
Marshall Jones. . . . . *First citizen*
Terence Greenidge . . . . *Second citizen*
Jeffery Dench . . . . *Third citizen*
David Morton . . . . *Messenger from Lord Derby*

DESCRIPTION Third of three-part adaptation by John Barton of the three *Henry VI* plays and *Richard III*, originally staged in 1963 as *The Wars of the Roses* by the Royal Shakespeare Company. The climax of a remarkable television event, chiefly of value for the quality and intensity of the performances, with Peggy Ashcroft and Ian Holm outstanding.

NOTES For details of the production and the first two parts of *The Wars of the Roses* see the entries for HENRY VI and EDWARD IV under *Henry VI*.

THEATRE OF BLOOD

GB • 1973

d   Douglas Hickox
pc   Cineman

NFTVA preservation material

CAST

Vincent Price . . . . *Edward Lionheart*
Robert Coote . . . . *Oliver Larding*

DESCRIPTION Feature film. An actor (Vincent Price) murders his critics in the manner of deaths from Shakespeare's plays. At a wine-tasting party, Oliver Larding is drowned, like Clarence, in a butt of wine. For full details of the film see entry in General section.

GOODBYE GIRL, The

USA • 1977

d   Herbert Ross
pc   Rastar
p   Ray Stark
sc   Neil Simon
ph   David M. Walsh
m   David Grusin

NFTVA viewing copy
35mm col sd 9,935ft 110mins

CAST

Richard Dreyfuss . . . . *Elliot Garfield*
Marsha Mason . . . . *Paula McFadden*
Quinn Cummings . . . . *Lucy McFadden*

RICHARD III CAST

Ray Berry
Powers Boothe
Tom Everett
Janice Fuller
Munson Hicks
Robert Kerman
Jeanne Lange
Robert Lesser
Fred McCarren
Nicholas Mele
Maureen Moore
Joseph Regalbuto
Peter Vogt

DESCRIPTION Feature film. An aspiring actor (Dreyfuss) and a dancer (Mason) share an apartment in New York. Sentimental Neil Simon comedy, featuring scenes from a hopeless off-Broadway homosexual interpretation of *Richard III*, in which Dreyfuss plays the title role.

RICHARD III

■ **GB • 1983**

■ *Shakespeare Lives*

d	Mary McMurray
pc	Quintet Films
tx	2 February 1983 (C4) [part one]
	9 February 1983 (C4) [part two]
p	Victor Glynn/Mike Ockrent

NFTVA preservation material
1" col sd c30+30mins

■ **CAST**
Clive Arrindell
Yvonne Bryceland
Joss Buckley
John Darrell
John Labanowski
Daniel Massey
Bill Wallis

■ **DESCRIPTION** Television theatre workshop, shown in two parts. Michael Bogdanov leads a group of National Theatre actors through various aspects of Shakespeare's play, in front of a studio audience, stressing its relevance to twentieth-century power politics. One of a lively and illuminating series.

■ **NOTES** Other plays covered in this series are *Hamlet, Measure for Measure, The Taming of the Shrew, The Tempest* and *Timon of Athens* (qqv).

LONDON STANDARD DRAMA AWARDS FOR 1985, The

■ **GB • 1985**

d	Jim Pople/George Sawford/
	Ian Little-Smith
pc	Thames Television
tx	19 November 1985 (ITV)
p	Jim Pople
pres	Ned Sherrin

NFTVA viewing copy
½" col sd 51mins

Antony Sher . . . . *Richard III*

■ **DESCRIPTION** Television awards ceremony for achievements in British stage drama over the year. Antony Sher receives the award for best actor from Lauren Bacall, followed by a filmed sequence of Sher in the Royal Shakespeare Company's *Richard III* at the Barbican, delivering the opening speech 'Now is the winter of our discontent' and the later 'Clarence hath not another day to live' (A1S1); the sequence shows Sher's distinctive use of crutches in his performance.

■ **NOTES** The filmed excerpt from *Richard III* is taken from the BBC arts and media review series *Saturday Review* (tx 15 June 1985).

TAKEAWAY

■ **GB • 1990**

■ *Nightingales*

d	Tony Dow
pc	Alomo Productions
tx	6 March 1990 (C4)
p	Esta Charkham
sc	Paul Makin

NFTVA viewing copy
½" col sd 24mins

■ **CAST**
Robert Lindsay . . . . *Carter*
David Threlfall . . . . *Bell*
James Ellis . . . . *Sarge*
Edward Burnham . . . . *Piper*

■ **DESCRIPTION** Television comedy series about night security staff. Pleasingly off-the-wall black comedy, interrupting everyday drudgery with surreal invention. Features a long sequence in which Carter and Bell consider getting rid of Sarge using passages from *Richard III* (mostly A1S4, the death of Clarence).

■ **NOTES** In the second series, the same idea was employed with reference to King Lear as KING LEAR II (qv).

RICHARD III

■ GB • 1992

d   Roger Jenkins
Royal National Theatre credits:
d   Richard Eyre
des   Bob Crowley
lght Jean Kalman
m   Dominic Muldowney

NFTVA preservation material
½" col sd 195mins

■ **CAST**

Bruce Purchase . . . *King Edward IV/Earl of Oxford*
David Collings . . . . *George, Duke of Clarence*
Ian McKellen . . . . *Richard, Duke of Gloucester*
Oliver Grig . . . . *Edward, Prince of Wales/Page*
Anthony Mellor . . . . *Richard, Duke of York*
Joyce Redman . . . . *Duchess of York*
Antonia Pemberton . . . . *Queen Margaret*
Helene Kvale . . . . *Lady Anne*
Sam Beazley . . . . *Ghost of Henry VI/*
Lord Mayor of London
Clare Higgins . . . . *Queen Elizabeth*
Crispin Redman . . . *Anthony Woodville, Earl Rivers*
Stephen Marchant. . . . . *Marquess of Dorset*
Derek Hutchinson . . . . *Lord Grey/*
Henry, Earl of Richmond
Richard Simpson . *Lord Hastings/Sir Walter Herbert*
Peter Jeffrey . . . . *Duke of Buckingham*
Richard Bremmer. . . . . *Lord Stanley*
Seymour Matthews. . *Bishop of Ely/Sir James Blunt*
David Beames . . . . *Sir William Catesby*
Peter Sullivan. . . . . *Sir Richard Ratcliffe*
Alan Perrin . . . . *James Tyrrel/Earl of Surrey*
Mark Strong . . . . *First Murderer/Lord Lovel/*
Duke of Norfolk
Phil McKee. . . . . *Second Murderer*
Simon Kunz . . . . *Sir Robert Brakenbury/*
Scrivener/Second Citizen
Ian Burfield . . . . *First Citizen*
Angela Clarke. . . . . *Maid/Nurse/Mistress*

■ **DESCRIPTION** Video recording of the Royal National Theatre production of *Richard III*. The first of the first two National Video Archive of Stage Performance recordings (along with HAMLET from 1993, qv), intended not as commercial entertainment but as a simple record and an invaluable tool for future researchers. The production itself was strikingly set in an imagined 1930s Fascist-ruled Britain and dominated by the powerful central performance of Ian McKellen.

■ **NOTES** Recorded on 26 May 1992. Filmed with three video cameras, one (fixed) giving a view of the full stage in long shot, the other two (controlled) giving closer shots of the players as seen from left and right. The intention is to create a video record of the stage performance without editorial interference, and the recordings are to be viewed simultaneously on three adjacent monitors, allowing the researcher to select the desired image. Viewing copies are held at the Theatre Museum, Covent Garden, with the master tapes held by the NFTVA. For further details see the entry for the National Video Archive of Stage Performance in the Archives and Libraries section.

■ **REFERENCES** • *Viewfinder*, February 1993, no. 17, pp. 11–13 [on the plans for the Archive].

Serge Reggiani and Anouk Aimée in LES AMANTS DE VERONE (1949)

ROMEO AND JULIET

ROMEO AND JULIET

■ USA • 1911

d/sc	Theodore Marston
pc	Thanhouser Film Corporation

NFTVA preservation material
16mm bw st 360ft 10mins
Incomplete – original length c2,000ft (35mm)

■ **CAST**

Julia M. Taylor . . . . *Juliet*
George Lessey . . . . *Romeo*
Mrs George W. Walton . . . . *Nurse*
William Garwood . . . . *Friar Laurence* [?]

■ **DESCRIPTION** Abbreviated version of the latter half of the play. The duel between Tybalt and Mercutio; Friar Laurence advises Romeo to flee; Romeo departs from Juliet's bed-chamber; Juliet's parents order her to marry Paris; Juliet and her nurse visit Friar Laurence; the Friar writes to Romeo; Juliet drinks poison and is lain in her tomb; Romeo learns of her death and purchases poison from the apothecary; Romeo kills Paris at Juliet's tomb; Romeo takes poison and dies at Juliet's side; Juliet wakes and kills herself; Friar Laurence enters the tomb [final sequence missing]. Commendably well presented and photographed, with judicious use of subtitles.

■ **NOTES** Originally distributed as two separate reels, each a complete story in itself, leaving exhibitors with the option of showing them singly or together (single-reel films were still most common at this period). The NFTVA holds a substantially complete second reel only. Some sources give Irma Taylor as Juliet. Ball credits Barry O'Neil as the director, Gertrude Thanhouser and Lloyd Lonergan as the script writers.

■ **REFERENCES** • Ball, *Shakespeare on Silent Film*, pp. 70–3, 317.

NICHOLAS NICKLEBY

■ **USA • 1912**

d	George O. Nicholls
pc	Thanhouser Film Corporation

NFTVA viewing copy
35mm bw st 1,872ft 21mins

■ **CAST**

Harry Benham . . . . *Nicholas Nickleby*
Justus D. Barnes . . . . *Ralph Nickleby*

■ **DESCRIPTION** Abbreviated adaptation of Charles Dickens's novel. Includes the sequences where Nicholas joins the Crummles's company and plays Romeo in their production of *Romeo and Juliet*.

■ **NOTES** As well as the film and television versions of Dickens's novel given below, the NFTVA also holds Biograph's NICHOLAS NICKLEBY (USA 1903); this, however, does not include the Crummles scenes.

SENTIMENTAL BLOKE, The

■ **Australia • 1919**

d	Raymond Longford
pc	Southern Cross Feature Film Company
sc	C. J. Dennis
ph	Arthur Higgins

NFTVA preservation material
35mm bw st 6,424ft 71mins

■ **CAST**

Arthur Tauchert . . . . . . *Bill, the Sentimental Bloke*
Gilbert Emery . . . . *Ginger Mick*
Lottie Lyell . . . . *Doreen*
Stanley Robinson . . . . *The Bloke*
Harry Young . . . . *The Stror 'At Coot*
Margaret Reid . . . . *Mar*

■ **DESCRIPTION** Feature film, based on the narrative poem *Songs of a Sentimental Bloke* by C. J. Dennis. Bill, an idler and a gambler, narrates the story of his courtship and marriage to Doreen, including a visit to the theatre to see a production of *Romeo and Juliet*. Bill explains the action to Doreen in his own distinctive style.

■ **NOTES** The film was remade in 1932 (not in NFTVA).

ALTE GESETZ, Das

■ **Germany • 1923**

d	E. A. Dupont
pc	Comedia-Film

NFTVA viewing copy

■ **CAST**
Ernst Deutsch. . . . . *Baruch / Romeo*

■ **DESCRIPTION** Feature film. In nineteenth-century Austria a young Jew struggles to become an actor, despite his rabbi father's disapproval. He plays Romeo in a humble performance of *Romeo and Juliet* put on by a travelling company. The audience laughs at his Jewish appearance, but he attracts the attention of the Archduchess Elisabeth Theresa. With her help he goes on to be famous and to play Hamlet. For full details of the film see entry under *Hamlet*.

BLUEBEARD'S SEVEN WIVES [TRAILER]

■ **USA • 1925**

NFTVA viewing copy
35mm bw st 52ft 1min

■ **CAST**
Ben Lyon . . . . *John Hart*
Blanche Sweet. . . . . *Juliet*

■ **DESCRIPTION** Trailer for feature film comedy about a timid film extra who accidentally becomes a star and a victim of the studio's publicity machine. The trailer includes a sequence from the balcony scene from *Romeo and Juliet* (A2S2) with Blanche Sweet as Juliet.

■ **NOTES** The feature film (not in NFTVA) was directed by Alfred Santell, production company First National Pictures, and included a sequence from the tomb scene.

■ **REFERENCES** • Ball, *Shakespeare on Silent Film*, pp. 270, 375.

CURED HAMS

■ **USA • c1927**

NFTVA viewing copy
35mm bw st 1,163ft 13mins

■ **CAST**
Jack Richardson

■ **DESCRIPTION** Comedy short. Feeble farce featuring the disastrous performance of two vaudeville actors (Will and Will Not) at a small town theatre. Among their acts is the balcony scene from *Romeo and Juliet*, during which the set collapses and the character playing Juliet loses his dress. This is followed by a title announcing 'A Midsummer Night's Dream – in January', but the playlet that follows is a Victorian melodrama in the snow with no other reference to Shakespeare.

■ **NOTES** No release information has been found about this film and it is not known if the title is its true one.

ROMEO E GIULIETTA

■ **GB • c1927**

pc   De Forest Phonofilms

NFTVA preservation material
35mm bw sd 543ft 6mins

■ **CAST**
Otakar Marak . . . . *Romeo*
Mary Cavanova . . . . *Juliet*

■ **DESCRIPTION** Musical short. An early sound film, using Lee De Forest's sound film process, featuring a song from Gounod's opera *Roméo et Juliette*, sung by Otakar Marak and Mary Cavanova.

■ **NOTES** For details of the De Forest Phonofilm sound films, see THE MERCHANT OF VENICE (1927).

DRAMA DE LUXE

■ **USA • 1927**

d/story   Norman Taurog
pc   Educational Pictures
ph   Leonard Smith

NFTVA preservation material
16mm bw sd 660ft 18mins

■ **CAST**
Lupino Lane. . . . . *J. Coddington Fish*

Wallace Lupino . . . . *Company manager*
Kathryn McGuire . . . . *Leading lady*

■ **DESCRIPTION** Comedy short. Knockabout comedy in which Lupino Lane joins a vaudeville company first as a bill sticker, and then as an actor after the leading man quits. Includes a scene from *Romeo and Juliet*, where Lane (playing Romeo) trips over his cloak into the orchestra pit, then destroys the set trying to climb up to Juliet. In the next scene he and the company manager fight one another with maces.

BROADWAY FEVER

■ **USA • 1928**

d	Eddie Cline
pc	Tiffany-Stahl
ph	John Boyle

NFTVA viewing copy
35mm bw st 4,692ft 52mins

■ **CAST**
Sally O'Neil . . . . *Sally McAllister*
Roland Drew . . . . *Eric Bryon*
Corliss Palmer . . . . *Lila LeRoy*
Calvert Carter . . . . *Butler*

■ **DESCRIPTION** Feature film comedy about a housemaid who impersonates the leading lady in rehearsal of a Broadway production and wins the producer's hand. Sally O'Neil is seen in one scene acting out lines from *Romeo and Juliet* while dusting.

■ **NOTES** Length on USA release 5,412ft.

HOLLYWOOD REVUE OF 1929, The

■ **USA • 1929**

d	Charles Riesner
pc	Metro-Goldwyn-Mayer
p	Harry Rapf
dial	Al Boasberg/Robert Hopkins
skit dial	Joe Farnham
ph	John Arnold/Irving Reis/ Maximilian Fabian
m	Arthur Lange

NFTVA viewing copy
35mm bw (col seq) sd 10,314ft 115mins

■ **CAST**
Jack Benny . . . . *Master of Ceremonies*
Conrad Nagel . . . . *Master of Ceremonies*
John Gilbert . . . . *Romeo*
Norma Shearer . . . . *Juliet*
Lionel Barrymore . . . . *Director*

■ **DESCRIPTION** Feature film. Jack Benny and Conrad Nagel host a musical revue of MGM acts, including Joan Crawford, Laurel and Hardy, Buster Keaton, Marie Dressler and an ensemble rendition of 'Singin' in the Rain'. Features a cheerful skit on *Romeo and Juliet*, where John Gilbert and Norma Shearer first play the balcony scene (A2S2) straight (filmed in black and white), then (in two-strip Technicolor) director Lionel Barrymore has a talk with them and they replay the scene in snappy modern dialogue.

■ **NOTES** Norma Shearer subsequently played Juliet in MGM's 1936 ROMEO AND JULIET (see below).

IMMORTAL GENTLEMAN, The

■ **GB • 1935**

d	Widgey R. Newman
pc	Bernard Smith

NFTVA preservation material
35mm bw sd 5,457ft 61mins

■ **CAST**
Terence de Marney . . . . *Romeo*
Rosalinde Fuller . . . . *Juliet*
Edgar Owen . . . . *Mercutio*
Derrick de Marney . . . . *Tybalt*

■ **DESCRIPTION** Feature film. Shakespeare and his friends meet in a Southwark tavern and their reminiscences give rise to sequences from Shakespeare's plays. Includes excerpts from the balcony scene (A2S2), the duel between Romeo and Tybalt (A3S1) and Romeo and Juliet parting at dawn (A3S5). For full details of the film see entry in General section.

ROMEO AND JULIET

■ **USA • 1936**

d	George Cukor
pc	Metro-Goldwyn-Mayer
p	Irving Thalberg
adapt	Talbot Jennings
ph	William Daniels
cost	Oliver Messel/Adrian
art d	Cedric Gibbons
m	Herbert Stothart

NFTVA viewing copy
35mm bw sd 11,102ft 123mins

■ **CAST**

Norma Shearer . . . . *Juliet*
Leslie Howard . . . . *Romeo*
Edna May Oliver. . . . . *Nurse*
John Barrymore . . . . *Mercutio*
Basil Rathbone . . . . *Tybalt*
C. Aubrey Smith . . . . *Lord Capulet*
Violet Kemble. . . . . *Lady Capulet*
Andy Devine . . . . *Peter*
Henry Kolker . . . . *Friar Laurence*
Ralph Forbes . . . . *Paris*
Reginald Denny. . . . . *Benvolio*
Maurice Murphy . . . . *Balthazar*
Conway Tearle. . . . . *Prince of Verona*
Robert Warwick . . . . *Lord Montague*
Virginia Hammond . . . . *Lady Montague*
Vernon Downing . . . . *Samson Capulet*
Ian Wolfe . . . . *Apothecary*
Anthony Kemble-Cooper . . . . . . *Gregory Capulet*
Anthony March. . . . . *Mercutio's page*
Howard Wilson . . . . *Abraham Montague*
Carlyle Blackwell Jr . . . . *Tybalt's page*
John Bryan . . . . *Friar John*
Katherine De Mille . . . . *Rosaline*
Wallis Clark . . . . *Town Watch*

■ **DESCRIPTION** Feature film adapation of the play. Celebrated and sumptuous version, a pet project of producer Irving Thalberg (Norma Shearer's husband), with the full MGM machine working behind an unshakeable faith in star power and the worthiness of the whole operation. Lavish, reverential and more fascinating than entertaining as such, the film mostly lacks passion. Shearer (31) and Howard (49) are a rather elderly couple, but rather surprisingly the seemingly miscast Shearer comes into her own in the latter half and gives a performance of great feeling. Rathbone is excellent, Barrymore a ham.

■ **NOTES** The film cost over $2,000,000 to produce and lost money heavily. The following year, in the comedy IT'S LOVE I'M AFTER (not in the NFTVA), Howard plays a celebrated stage actor and in the opening scene is seen playing the tomb scene with Bette Davis as his Juliet. Norma Shearer had already played Juliet in the Romeo and Juliet skit in THE HOLLYWOOD REVUE OF 1929 (qv).

■ **REFERENCES** • Graham Greene, *The Pleasure-Dome* (London: Secker & Warburg, 1972), pp. 109–11.

SHAKESPEARIAN SPINACH

■ **USA • 1940**

■ *Popeye the Sailor*

d	Dave Fleischer
pc	Paramount Pictures
p	Max Fleischer
anim	Roland Crandall/Ben Solomon

NFTVA preservation material
35mm bw sd 600ft 6mins

■ **DESCRIPTION** Cartoon short. A spoof on *Romeo and Juliet*, with Popeye the sailor as Romeo and Olive Oyl as Juliet.

PLAYMATES

■ **USA • 1941**

d	David Butler
pc	RKO

NFTVA preservation material

■ **DESCRIPTION** Feature film. Kay Kyser and his swing band team up with John Barrymore to put on updated Shakespeare. Includes the excruciating swing number 'Romeo Smith and Juliet Jones' performed by Kyser and his Orchestra. For full details of the film see entry in General section.

ONE DAY IN SOVIET RUSSIA

■ **Soviet Union • 1941**

d	M. Slutski/R. Karmen
pc	Central Newsreel Studio, Moscow
sc	V. Yagling/M. Zeitlin
ph	P. Karmen/M. Oshurkov
m	A. Gran

English version:

sup	Herbert Marshall
ed	Sidney Cole
nar	Quentin Reynolds

NFTVA viewing copy
35mm bw sd 5,084ft 56mins

■ **CAST**
Galina Ulanova . . . . *Juliet*

■ **DESCRIPTION** Documentary. Aspects of life in various parts of the Soviet Union on 24 August 1940. Includes short sequence showing Ulanova dancing in Prokofiev's *Romeo and Juliet* ballet at the Kirov Theatre, Leningrad.

■ **NOTES** English-language version.

TIME FLIES

■ **GB • 1944**

d	Walter Forde
pc	Gainsborough Pictures
p	Edward Black
sc	J. O. C. Orton/Ted Kavanagh/ Howard Irving Young
ph	Basil Emmott
m	Louis Levy/Bretton Byrd

NFTVA preservation material
35mm bw sd 7,945ft 88mins

■ **CAST**
Tommy Handley . . . . *Tommy*
Evelyn Dall . . . . *Susie Barton*
Moore Marriott . . . . *Soothsayer*
Graham Moffatt . . . . *Nephew*
John Salew . . . . *Shakespeare*
Leslie Bradley . . . . *Walter Raleigh*
Olga Lindo . . . . *Queen Elizabeth*

■ **DESCRIPTION** Feature film comedy. Cheerful if rather obvious romp in which Tommy Handley and friends are transported back in time to the reign of Queen Elizabeth. Among various encounters with the Elizabethans, Susie Barton enters the Globe theatre and finds William Shakespeare struggling with the composition of *Romeo and Juliet*. She suggests the lines for the balcony scene (A2S2) which they enact together.

■ **NOTES** Tommy Handley was primarily known as a radio comedian, star of the immensely successful BBC radio show ITMA.

NICHOLAS NICKLEBY

■ **GB • 1947**

d	Alberto Cavalcanti
pc	Ealing Studios
p	Michael Balcon
sc	John Dighton
ph	Gordon Dines
m	Lord Berners

NFTVA viewing copy
35mm bw sd 9,683ft 108mins

■ **CAST**
Derek Bond . . . . *Nicholas Nickleby*
Cedric Hardwicke . . . . *Ralph Nickleby*
Sally Ann Howes . . . . *Kate Nickleby*
Stanley Holloway . . . . *Vincent Crummles*
Vera Pearce . . . . *Mrs Crummles*
Aubrey Woods . . . . *Smike*
June Elvin . . . . *Miss Snevellicci*

■ **DESCRIPTION** Feature film. An unexceptional adaptation of Charles Dickens's novel, with some interesting incidents but fatally weakened by a dull central performance. Includes the Crummles's theatrical troupe's version of *Romeo and Juliet*, with Nicholas playing Romeo and Miss Snevellicci Juliet.

SOME HIGHLIGHTS OF MONTY'S MOSCOW VISIT

■ **GB • 1947**

■ *British Movietone News No. 922A*

pc   British Movietone News
rel date   7 February 1947

NFTVA preservation material
35mm bw sd 231ft 2mins

■ **CAST**

Galina Ulanova . . . . *Juliet*
Mikhail Gabovic. . . . . *Romeo*

■ **DESCRIPTION** Newsreel item. Viscount Montgomery of Alamein's visit to Moscow (6–12 January 1947), including his visit to the Bolshoi Theatre to see a production of Prokofiev's *Romeo and Juliet* ballet.

AMANTS DE VERONE, Les

English title LOVERS OF VERONA

■ **France • 1949**

d   André Cayatte
pc   CICC
p   Raymond Borderie
sc   André Cayatte/Jacques Prévert
ph   Henri Alekan
m   J. Kosma

NFTVA viewing copy
35mm bw sd 9,187ft 102mins [see note below]

■ **CAST**

Pierre Brasseur . . . . *Raffaele*
Serge Reggiani. . . . . *Angelo*
Anouk [Aimée]. . . . . *Georgia*
Louis Salou . . . . *Ettore Maglia*
Dalio. *Amadeo Maglia*
Marianne Oswald . . . . *Laetitia*

■ **DESCRIPTION** Feature film. One of the most successful attempts to transfer a Shakespearean story to a modern setting. In modern Venice and Verona a film company is making *Romeo and Juliet*. The stand-ins for the leading players are Angelo, a young glassblower, and Georgia, the daughter of a former Fascist official, and they feel that their own lives are mirrored by the parts they see in the film production. Georgia's malevolent fiancé tries to get a group of gangsters to murder Angelo, and when this fails persuades Georgia's family to murder him. The lovers die together on Juliet's tomb in the film studio. Expertly written by the prime architect of French cinema's doomed romanticism, Jacques Prévert, complemented by Alekan's expressive photography. Although ostensibly a tragic love story, the real centre of the film is the crumbling, bitter Maglia family, poisoned by its Fascist past.

■ **NOTES** The NFTVA has two viewing copies, one nitrate with English subtitles (9,308ft, 103mins) and the safety copy given above, which has no English subtitles.

ROMEO AND JULIET

■ **Italy/GB 1954**

d/adapt   Renato Castellani
pc   Verona Productions
p   Sandro Ghenzi
ph   Robert Krasker
m   Roman Vlad

NFTVA preservation material
35mm col sd 12,447ft 138mins

■ **CAST**

Laurence Harvey . . . . *Romeo*
Susan Shentall . . . . *Juliet*
Flora Robson . . . . *Nurse*
Mervyn Johns . . . . *Friar Laurence*
Bill Travers . . . . *Benvolio*
Enzo Fiermonte . . . . *Tybalt*
Aldo Zollo . . . . *Mercutio*
Giovanni Rota . . . . *Prince of Verona*
Sebastian Cabot . . . . *Capulet*
Lydia Sherwood. . . . . *Lady Capulet*
Norman Wooland. . . . . *Paris*
Giulio Garbinetti . . . . *Montague*
Nietta Zocchi . . . . *Lady Montague*
Dagmar Josipovich. . . . . *Rosaline*
Lucian Bodi . . . . *Friar John*
Prologue spoken by John Gielgud

■ **DESCRIPTION** Feature film adaptation of the play. An attempt to wed Shakespeare to the Italian neo-realist school of film-making, with much location photography, naturalistic crowd scenes and the expected cinematic gestures, requiring a considerable amount of the text to be cut, sometimes at the loss of sense. Beautiful to look at, the film's chief failing is to combine such ambitions with unsuitable British leads; an unknown

ROMEO AND JULIET

amateur as Juliet and an uncomfortably actorly Laurence Harvey as Romeo. In style and ambition something of a dry-run for the 1968 version below.

■ **REFERENCES** • Paul A. Jorgensen, 'Castellani's Romeo and Juliet: Intention and Response', *Film Quarterly*, Fall 1955, pp. 1–10 [reprinted in Eckert, *Focus on Shakespearean Films*, pp. 108–15].

ROMEO AND JULIET [TRAILER]

■ **GB • 1954**

NFTVA viewing copy
35mm col sd 335ft 4mins

■ **DESCRIPTION** Trailer to the above. Presenting 'the greatest love story of all time' in sweeping epic fashion, with a commentary that tends to unintentional parody, the overall effect being to emphasise the picture's absurdities.

ROMEO I DZHULYETA

English title ROMEO AND JULIET

■ **Soviet Union • 1954**

d/p	Lev Arnshtam/Leonid Lavrovsky
pc	Mosfilm
ph	Aleksandr Shelenkov/Yu-leng Cheng
m	Sergei Prokofiev (ed V. Shebalin)

NFTVA preservation material
35mm col sd 5,450ft 60mins
Incomplete – original length 8,396ft

■ **CAST**
Galina Ulanova . . . . *Juliet*
Yuri Zhdanov. . . . . *Romeo*
Sergei Koren. . . . . *Mercutio*
Alexei Yermolayev . . . . *Tybalt*
V. Kidryashov . . . . *Benvolio*
A. Lapauri. . . . . *Paris*

■ **DESCRIPTION** Ballet. Feature film adaptation of the Bolshoi Theatre Ballet's production of

Prokofiev and Lavrovsky's *Romeo and Juliet*, following substantially the action of the play, and extensively restaged for the cameras. Reasonably successful blend of ballet and film, aided by some imaginative location photography and Ulanova's passionate interpretation.

YOUNG LOVERS, The

■ **GB • 1954**

d	Anthony Asquith
pc	Group Film Productions
p	Anthony Havelock-Allan
sc	George Tabori/Robin Estridge
ph	Jack Asher
m	Peter Tchaikovsky

NFTVA viewing copy
16mm bw sd 3,470ft 96mins

■ **CAST**
Odile Versois. . . . . *Anna Szobek*
David Knight . . . . *Ted Hutchens*
David Kossoff . . . . *Szobek*

■ **DESCRIPTION** Feature film. Ted, a young Intelligence officer working at the US Embassy in London, meets Anna, the daughter of a minister from an unnamed communist country, at the ballet. Falling in love, they try to keep this secret from their respective powers. Anna becomes pregnant and she and Ted eventually escape the country by sea. One of any number of film plots using a *Romeo and Juliet* theme, this is included here for its Cold War associations and its mood of gloomy romanticism. The lovers meet at a performance of *Swan Lake*; the producers could have chosen *Romeo and Juliet*, but perhaps having an actress named Odile could not be overlooked.

■ **NOTES** Peter Ustinov's play *Romanoff and Juliet* covers a similar theme, with greater Shakespearean parallels (USA 1960, film version not in NFTVA).

ROMEO AND JULIET

■ **GB • 1956**

d/ph	John de Vere Loder, 2nd Baron Wakehurst

NFTVA preservation material
16mm col mu 94ft 2mins

■ **CAST**
Galina Ulanova . . . . *Juliet*
Christova
Zidanova
Kosen

■ **DESCRIPTION** Amateur ballet film. Scenes from the Bolshoi Theatre Ballet's production of *Romeo and Juliet* at Covent Garden, October 1956. *Pas de deux* by Christova and partner, a lute-player; entrance of Juliet's mother; Romeo gains admission to the ball; *pas de deux* by Juliet and Paris; the balcony scene – *pas de deux* by Romeo and Juliet.

■ **NOTES** Lord Wakehurst filmed a large number of ballet productions in the 50s and 60s. His film collection is held by the NFTVA.

THIS WAS THE FUTURE

■ **GB • 1957**

d/ed	Geoffrey Baines
pc	BBC
tx	31 December 1957 (BBC)
nar	Robert Donat

NFTVA preservation material
35mm bw sd 5,040ft 56mins

■ **CAST**
Tony Britton . . . . *Romeo*
Virginia McKenna . . . . *Juliet*

■ **DESCRIPTION** Television documentary compilation. A survey of the first twenty-one years of the BBC television service. Includes a short extract from the 1955 production of *Romeo and Juliet* (tx 22 May 1955, not otherwise in NFTVA), directed by Dallas Bower.

MARJORIE MORNINGSTAR

■ **USA • 1958**

d	Irving Rapper
pc	Beachwold Pictures/Warner Bros.
p	Milton Sperling
sc	Everett Freeman
ph	Harry Stradling
m	Max Steiner

NFTVA preservation material
35mm bw sd 4,679ft 52mins
Incomplete – original length 11,021ft

■ **CAST**
Gene Kelly . . . . *Noel Airman*
Natalie Wood . . . . *Marjorie Morgenstern*
Rad Fulton . . . . *Romeo*

■ **DESCRIPTION** Feature film, based on the novel by Herman Wouk. An ambitious New York Jewish girl falls for a second-rate musical performer. In a brief scene Marjorie is seen triumphing as Juliet in her college production of *Romeo and Juliet* (A5S3, the tomb scene).

ROMEO I JULIJA

English title ROMEO AND JULIET

■ **Yugoslavia • 1958**

d	Ivo Vrbanic
pc	Zagreb Film
des/anim	Borivoj Dovnikovic
m	Andjelko Klobucar

NFTVA preservation material
35mm col sd 939ft 10mins

■ **DESCRIPTION** Animated short. The *Romeo and Juliet* story from caveman days to modern times.

CARRY ON TEACHER

■ **GB • 1959**

d	Gerald Thomas
pc	Beaconsfield Film Productions
p	Peter Rogers
sc	Norman Hudis
ph	Reginald Wyer
m	Bruce Montgomery

NFTVA viewing copy
35mm bw sd 7,771ft 86mins

■ **CAST**

Ted Ray . . . . *William Wakefield*
Kenneth Williams . . . . *Edwin Milton*
Hattie Jacques . . . . *Grace Short*
Joan Sims . . . . *Sarah Allcock*
Kenneth Connor . . . . *Gregory Adams*
Charles Hawtrey . . . . *Michael Bean*
Leslie Phillips . . . . *Alistair Grigg*
Richard O'Sullivan . . . . *Robin Stevens/Romeo*
Diana Beevers . . . . *Penelope Lee/Juliet*

■ **DESCRIPTION** Feature film. Tame comedy, richly performed, from the early period of the *Carry On* series, featuring Ted Ray as the headmaster of an unruly school. Includes a riotous performance of the school play, *Romeo and Juliet*, with deadly accompaniment from the school orchestra, featuring sequences from the opening scene, the balcony scene (A2S2) and final scene. After numerous calamities, the set eventually collapses about the performers. The film also features an embarrassed teacher (Williams) fielding questions from his class about why their text of the play has been bowdlerised, and another teacher (Connor) wooing a school inspector with lines from the sonnets.

ROMEO, JULIE A TMA

GB title ROMEO, JULIET AND DARKNESS
USA title SWEET LIGHT IN A DARK ROOM

■ **Czechoslovakia • 1960**

d   Jirí Weiss
pc   Ceskoslovensky Film
sc   Jirí Weiss/Jan Otcenásek
ph   Václav Hanus
m   Jirí Srnka

NFTVA preservation material
35mm bw sd 8,686ft 96mins

■ **CAST**

Ivan Mistrik . . . . *Pavel*
Dana Smutná . . . . *Hana*

■ **DESCRIPTION** Feature film, based on the novel by Jan Otcenásek. The love between Pavel and Hana, a Jewish schoolgirl he hides and cares for in his mother's storeroom during the Nazi occupa-

tion of Czechoslovakia. Discovered by a collaborator, Hana walks out to be shot by the Nazis so that Pavel's actions will remain secret.

WEST SIDE STORY

■ **USA • 1961**

d   Robert Wise/Jerome Robbins
pc   Mirisch/Seven Arts/Beta
p   Robert Wise
sc   Ernest Lehman [based on stage production of Robert E. Griffith and Harold Prince]
book   Arthur Laurents
lyrics Stephen Sondheim
ph   Daniel L. Fapp
m   Leonard Bernstein

NFTVA preservation material
70mm col sd 17,437ft 155mins

■ **CAST**

Natalie Wood . . . . *Maria*
Richard Beymer . . . . *Tony*
George Chakiris . . . . *Bernardo*
Russ Tamblyn . . . . *Riff*
Rita Moreno . . . . *Anita*

■ **DESCRIPTION** Feature film adaptation of the Jerome Robbins stage musical, which updated *Romeo and Juliet* to a story of rival teenage gangs in New York. Tony, a member of the Jets gang, falls in love with Maria, whose brother Bernardo is the leading figure in the Puerto Rican Sharks gang. At Maria's behest, Tony tries to halt a fight between Bernardo and Jets member Riff, but when Bernardo kills Riff, Tony stabs Bernardo and is forced into hiding. Bernado's girlfriend Anita takes a message from Maria to Tony, but an encounter with the Jets along the way leads her to tell Tony that Maria is dead. Distraught, Tony is killed by one of the Sharks. Exhilarating production, with stylised dance routines (and an artificial storyline) strikingly placed in real New York locations.

(LORD WAKEHURST BALLET FILM COLLECTION REEL 13)

■ **GB • 1962–65**

d/ph John de Vere Loder,
2nd Baron Wakehurst

NFTVA preservation material
16mm col mu 498ft 14mins

■ **CAST**
Frank Schaufuss . . . . *Romeo*
Jacqueline Ivings . . . . *Juliet*
Jeremy Blanton . . . . *Paris*

■ **DESCRIPTION** Amateur ballet film. Includes
film of three minutes of dress rehearsal of John
Cranko's version of Prokofiev's *Romeo and Juliet* by
the Canadian National Ballet, January 1965.
Romeo watches *pas de deux* by Juliet and Paris at
the ball; *pas de deux* by Romeo and Juliet, Paris
intervening; dance by ensemble, Juliet's mother
intervening between her and Romeo.

PANIC BUTTON

■ **USA • 1964**

d	George Sherman
pc	Yankee Productions
p/story	Ron Gorton
sc	Hal Biller
adapt	Stephen Longstreet
ph	Enzo Serafin
m	Georges Garvarentz

NFTVA preservation material
35mm bw sd c8,100ft 90mins

■ **CAST**
Maurice Chevalier . . . . *Philippe Fontaine*
Eleanor Parker . . . . *Louise Harris*
Jayne Mansfield . . . . *Angela*
Michael Connors . . . . *Frank Pagano*
Akim Tamiroff . . . . *Pandowski*

■ **DESCRIPTION** Feature film comedy. A busi-
nessman (Connors), faced with an income tax
demand of $500,000, decides to invest in a delib-
erately bad movie. He employs a has-been French
actor (Chevalier) and a glamorous, talentless
actress (Mansfield) to appear in a television pilot
version of the *Romeo and Juliet* story. He takes the
film to the Venice Film Festival where it
unexpectedly gains huge acclaim and a prize.
A lively and agreeable comedy, with a plot
remarkably similar to Mel Brooks's 1967 THE
PRODUCERS.

(ROMEO: ROWNTREES POLO MINT)

■ **GB • 1965**

spon J. Walter Thompson

NFTVA preservation material
35mm bw sd c50ft+50ft 1min

■ **DESCRIPTION** Two television commercials for
Rowntrees polo mints.

SHAKESPEARE WALLAH

■ **India • 1965**

d	James Ivory
pc	Merchant-Ivory Productions

NFTVA viewing copy

■ **CAST**
Partap Sharma . . . . *Romeo*
Felicity Kendal . . . . *Juliet*
Geoffrey Kendal . . . . *Friar Laurence*

■ **DESCRIPTION** Feature film about a troupe of
English actors in India. Includes a performance of
the scene in Friar Laurence's cell from *Romeo and
Juliet* (A2S6) during which Juliet's appearance
gives rise to a fight between some young men in
the audience. The audience makes for the exits
and the play comes to a halt. For full details of
film see entry in General section.

ROMEO AND JULIET

■ **GB • 1966**

d/p	Paul Czinner
pc	Poetic Films
ph	S. D. Onions
chor	Kenneth MacMillan
sets/cost	Nicholas Georgiadis
m	Sergei Prokofiev

NFTVA viewing copy
16mm col sd 4,468ft 124mins

■ **CAST**
Margot Fonteyn . . . . *Juliet*

Rudolf Nureyev . . . . *Romeo*
David Blair . . . . *Mercutio*
Desmond Doyle . . . . *Tybalt*
Anthony Dowell . . . . *Benvolio*
Derek Rencher . . . . *Paris*
Michael Somes. . . . . *Lord Capulet*
Julia Farron . . . . *Lady Capulet*
Leslie Edwards . . . . *Escalus, Prince of Verona*
Georgina Parkinson . . . . *Rosaline*
Gerd Larsen . . . . *Nurse*
Ronald Hynd. . . . . *Friar Laurence*
Christopher Newton . . . . *Lord Montague*
Betty Kavanagh. . . . . *Lady Montague*

■ **DESCRIPTION** Ballet. Feature film version of Kenneth MacMillan's ballet, with Prokofiev's music played by the Orchestra of the Royal Opera House, Covent Garden, filmed as a stage production with a number of cameras and subsequently edited into a whole. An invaluable record of a famous production, but suffering inevitably from the mechanical method of its production. Most of the action of the play is represented.

■ **NOTES** Paul Czinner, who in 1936 filmed AS YOU LIKE IT (qv) with Elisabeth Bergner and Laurence Olivier, later in his career chose to specialise in filmed productions of ballets with the minimum of cinematic intrusion.

ROMEO AND JULIET

■ **Italy/GB 1968**

d	Franco Zeffirelli
pc	BHE/Dino De Laurentiis Cinematografica/Verona Productions
p	Anthony Havelock-Allan/ John Brabourne
sc	Franco Brusati/Masolino D'Amico
ph	Pasquale De Santis
m	Nino Rota

NFTVA preservation material
35mm col sd 13,680ft 152mins

■ **CAST**
Leonard Whiting . . . . *Romeo*
Olivia Hussey . . . . *Juliet*
Milo O'Shea . . . . *Friar Laurence*
Michael York . . . . *Tybalt*
John McEnery. . . . . *Mercutio*
Pat Heywood . . . . *Nurse*

Natasha Parry . . . . *Lady Capulet*
Paul Harwick . . . . *Lord Capulet*
Robert Stephens . . . . *Prince of Verona*
Keith Skinner . . . . *Balthazar*
Richard Warwick . . . . *Gregory*
Roberto Bisacco . . . . *Count Paris*
Bruce Robinson. . . . . *Benvolio*
Dyson Lovell . . . . *Sampson*
Ugo Barbone . . . . *Abraham*
Antonio Pierfederici . . . . *Lord Montague*
Esmeralda Ruspoli . . . . *Lady Montague*
Roy Holder . . . . *Peter*
Aldo Miranada . . . . *Friar John*
Dario Tanzini . . . . *Page to Tybalt*
Prologue and epilogue spoken by Laurence Olivier

■ **DESCRIPTION** Feature film adaptation of the play. Successful attempt to break away from more reverential Shakespearean productions of the past, deliberately aimed at the mainstream, young film audience. Romeo and Juliet were played by actors aged 17 and 15 respectively. As with the 1954 version (also an Anglo-Italian production), much of the text has been cut and broken up with cinematic gestures, and extensive location photography employed to make Shakespeare 'realistic'. Dropping the poetry can put too heavy a reliance on the plot, and some of the more implausible aspects of the story are readily apparent. Youthful vigour and some tasteful nudity made the film a considerable success.

■ **REFERENCES ♦** Jorgens, *Shakespeare on Film*, pp. 79–91, 261–5.

THEATRE OF BLOOD

■ **GB • 1973**

d	Douglas Hickox
pc	Cineman

NFTVA preservation material

■ **CAST**
Vincent Price . . . . *Edward Lionheart*
Ian Hendry . . . . *Peregrine Devlin*

■ **DESCRIPTION** Feature film. An actor (Vincent Price) murders his critics in the manner of deaths from Shakespeare's plays. Echoing the duel scene from *Romeo and Juliet*, Lionheart fences with

Peregrine Devlin using untipped blades, but although he wounds Hendry badly, he chooses to save him for a worse fate derived from *King Lear* (qv). For full details of film see entry in General section.

ROMEO OF THE SPIRITS

■ **GB • 1976**

d/sc	Nikolas L. Janis
pc	Thorntip
p	Roberts Aarons
ph	Stan Mestel
m	Sergei Prokofiev

NFTVA preservation material
35mm col sd 1,866ft 21mins

■ **CAST**
Michael Gough

■ **DESCRIPTION** Fiction short. A London tramp, a former actor, living around Charing Cross station, recalls lines from *Romeo and Juliet* which underline his own situation.

TURNING POINT, The

■ **USA • 1977**

d	Herbert Ross
pc	Hera Productions
p	Herbert Ross/Arthur Laurents
sc	Arthur Laurents
ph	Robert Surtees
m	John Lanchbery

NFTVA viewing copy
35mm col sd 10,728ft 119mins

■ **CAST**
Shirley MacLaine . . . . *Deedee Rogers*
Anne Bancroft . . . . *Emilia Jacklin*
Mikhail Baryshnikov . . . . *Yuri*

■ **DESCRIPTION** Feature film. Emotional drama set in the world of American ballet. Among a number of ballet sequences is a scene from Prokofiev's *Romeo and Juliet*, with choreography by Kenneth MacMillan.

ROMEO AND JULIET

■ **GB/USA 1978**

■ *BBC Television Shakespeare*

d	Alvin Rakoff
pc	BBC/Time-Life Films
tx (GB)	3 December 1978 (BBC2)
tx (US)	14 March 1979 (PBS)
p	Cedric Messina
des	Stuart Walker
m	James Tyler

NFTVA viewing copy
½" col sd 170mins

■ **CAST**
Rebecca Saire . . . . *Juliet*
Patrick Ryecart . . . . *Romeo*
Celia Johnson . . . . *Nurse*
Michael Hordern . . . . *Capulet*
Anthony Andrews . . . . *Mercutio*
Alan Rickman . . . . *Tybalt*
Christopher Northey . . . . *Paris*
Christopher Strauli . . . . *Benvolio*
Jacqueline Hill . . . . *Lady Capulet*
John Paul . . . . *Montague*
Zulema Dene . . . . *Lady Montague*
Joseph O'Conor . . . . *Friar Laurence*
David Sibley . . . . *Sampson*
Jack Carr. . . . . *Gregory*
Bunny Reed . . . . *Abraham*
Alan Bowerman . . . . *First Citizen*
Jeremy Young . . . . *First Watch*
Jeffrey Chiswick . . . . *Second Watch*
Laurence Naismith. . . . . *Escalus*
Paul Henry . . . . *Peter*
Gary Taylor. *Potpan*
Robert Burbage . . . . *Tybalt's page*
Esmond Knight. . . . . *Old Capulet*
Danny Schiller . . . . *Musician*
Roger Davidson . . . . *Balthasar*
Vernon Dobtcheff. . . . . *Apothecary*
John Savident . . . . *Friar John*
Mark Arden . . . . *Paris's page*
Marguerite Young . . . . *Citizen*
John Gielgud. . . . . *Chorus*

■ **DESCRIPTION** Television production of the play. The opening production in the BBC's ambitious complete cycle of the plays, and revealing many of the virtues and vices of the series as a whole. Conventional settings and a heavy reliance on celebrated stage names leads to an unexciting production, though with the inevitable felicities to be expected from such a cast. Clearly with the 1968 feature film version in mind, a young and untried actress was chosen to play Juliet, but without the sumptuous style to back this up the decision is less successful.

■ **REFERENCES** ● Clive James, *The Crystal Bucket* (London: Jonathan Cape, 1981), pp. 153–4.

ROMEU E JULIETA

■ **Brazil ● 1980**

d	Paulo Afonso Grisolli
pc	TV Globo
p/asst d	Maria Carmem Barbosa
sc	Walter George Durst

NFTVA preservation material
¾" col sd 94mins

■ **CAST**
Lucelia Santos . . . . *Julieta*
Fabio Junior . . . . *Romeu*
Ruth De Souza
Francisco Milani
Thereza Amayo
Daniel Dantas
Wellington Botelho
J. D'Angelo
Buza Ferraz

■ **DESCRIPTION** Television film. A modernised version of *Romeo and Juliet* set in the town of Ouro Preto, Brazil, among rival student fraternities. An intelligent, accurate translation of the settings of Shakespeare's imagination to an appropriate modern locale. Unlike so many attempts to borrow the *Romeo and Juliet* theme, here both plot and passions convince.

■ **NOTES** Portuguese dialogue with English subtitles. First transmitted in GB 31 August 1983 (C4). Brazilian transmission date not known.

LIFE AND ADVENTURES OF NICHOLAS NICKLEBY; PART 2, The

■ **GB ● 1982**

d	Jim Goddard
pc	Primetime Television
tx	14 November 1982 (C4)
p	Colin Callender
sc	David Edgar
m	Stephen Oliver

NFTVA viewing copy
½" col sd 109mins

■ **CAST**
Roger Rees . . . . *Nicholas Nickleby*
John Woodvine . . . . *Ralph Nickleby*
Emily Richard . . . . *Kate Nickleby*
Jane Downs . . . . *Mrs Nickleby*
Christopher Benjamin . . . . *Vincent Crummles*
Lila Kaye . . . . *Mrs Crummles*
Suzanne Bertish . . . . *Miss Snevellicci*

■ **DESCRIPTION** Television version of the original Royal Shakespeare Company production by Trevor Nunn and John Caird, adapted by David Edgar from the novel by Charles Dickens. An exhilarating record of a famous production, featuring in this episode Nicholas's time with the Crummles's company, playing Romeo in their triumphant version of *Romeo and Juliet*, with happy endings and surprise revivifications all round.

■ **NOTES** Originally broadcast as second episode of four; subsequently broadcast also as two double episodes. The NFTVA copy was recorded off-air 30 December 1987.

FROG PRINCE, The

■ **GB ● 1984**

d	Brian Gilbert
pc	Enigma Productions
p	Iain Smith
sc	Posy Simmonds
ph	Clive Tickner
m	Enya Ni Bhraonain

NFTVA preservation material
35mm col sd 8,093ft 90mins

■ **CAST**
Jane Snowden . . . . *Jenny*
Alexandre Sterling . . . . *Jean-Philippe*

■ **DESCRIPTION** Feature film. Thin romance between an English and a French student in Paris, 1961. Jenny angers Jean-Philippe when she says she will sleep with him only if he learns a passage from *Romeo and Juliet* (A2S2). He subsequently recites the speech to her on the Métro.

MISHIMA: A LIFE IN FOUR CHAPTERS

■ **USA/Japan 1985**

d	Paul Schrader
pc	Zoetrope/Filmlink International
p	Mata Yamamoto/Tom Luddy
sc	Paul Schrader/Leonard Schrader/
	Chieko Schrader
ph	John Bailey
m	Philip Glass

NFTVA preservation material
35mm col sd 10,883ft 120mins

■ **CAST**
Ken Ogata . . . . *Yukio Mishima*
Kenji Sawada. *Osamu*
Tsutomu Harada . . . . *Romeo*
Mami Okamoto. . . . . *Juliet*

■ **DESCRIPTION** Feature film. The life and works of controversial Japanese author Yukio Mishima. In the section 'Kyoko's House', dramatising a Mishima story about an actor, there is a brief sequence from an acted *Romeo and Juliet*.

■ **NOTES** Filmed in Japanese with English subtitles.

LEONARD BERNSTEIN'S WEST SIDE STORY

■ **GB • 1985**

■ *Omnibus*

d	Christopher Swann
pc	BBC
tx	10 May 1985 (BBC1)
p	Humphrey Burton
ph	John Else

NFTVA viewing copy
½" col sd 88mins

■ **CAST**
Kiri Te Kanawa . . . . *Maria*
José Carreras. . . . . *Tony*
Tatiana Troyanos . . . . *Anita*
Kurt Ollmann. . . . . *Riff*

■ **DESCRIPTION** Television arts documentary series. Fascinating look at a studio recording of *West Side Story*, with Leonard Bernstein conducting a top-notch cast of opera singers and clashing memorably with José Carreras.

■ **NOTES** The recording, for a record release, took place over four days in September 1984. NFTVA copy recorded off-air 23 February 1993 as part of series of classic *Omnibus* programmes celebrating their 25th anniversary.

JOHN GIELGUD: AN ACTOR'S LIFE: 1. EARLY STAGES

■ **GB • 1988**

d	Dave Heather
pc	TVS
tx	31 July 1988 (C4)
p	John Miller

NFTVA viewing copy
½" col sd 52mins

■ **CAST**
John Gielgud. *Romeo*
Gwen Ffrangcon-Davies . . . . *Juliet*

■ **DESCRIPTION** Television documentary. John Gielgud, in conversation with John Miller, looks back over his career as an actor, his working relationships with other actors and the techniques of his art. Includes an extract from a 1924 cinemagazine, showing Gielgud and Gwen Ffrangcon-Davies in the balcony scene from *Romeo and Juliet* (A2S2).

■ **NOTES** The first of two interviews with John Gielgud (the second, LATER STAGES, tx 7 August 1988, is also held by the NFTVA). The 1924 *Romeo and Juliet* is an excerpt from the play as produced by H. K. Ayliff and put on at the Regent's Theatre, King's Cross in May 1924. The same piece of film, which comes from an edition of Pathé's women's cinemagazine *Eve's Film Review*, appears in the programme on Gwen Ffrangcon-Davies below.

GWEN - A JULIET REMEMBERED

■ GB • 1988

■ *Omnibus*

d	David Spenser
pc	Saffron Productions
tx	7 October 1988 (BBC1)
p	Victor Pemberton

NFTVA viewing copy
½" col sd 59mins

■ **DESCRIPTION** Television documentary. The career of 97-year-old actress Gwen Ffrangcon-Davies, with special emphasis on her favourite Shakespearean role, Juliet. Includes contributions from her fellow actors, Nigel Hawthorne in conversation with her, and a specially staged master-class at the Aldwych Theatre on the role of Juliet. The film also includes the 1924 film of her with John Gielgud in *Romeo and Juliet* (see entry above).

LUBITSCH AUS BERLIN

■ Germany • 1992

d/nar	Enno Patalas
pc	Westdeutscher Rundfunk
p	Werner Dütsch
sc	Frieda Grafe
m	Aljoscha Zimmermann

NFTVA preservation material
½" col sd 44mins

■ **DESCRIPTION** Documentary compilation. The early Berlin years of film director Ernst Lubitsch, consisting entirely of archive material and film clips. Includes an extract from a *Romeo and Juliet* derivative directed by Lubitsch, ROMEO UND JULIA IM SCHNEE (Germany 1920), not otherwise held by the NFTVA.

ENTERTAINMENT UK

■ GB • 1993

pc	Mentorn Films
tx	18 February 1993 (ITV)
p	Jonathan Challis

NFTVA viewing copy
½" col sd 51mins

■ **CAST**
Joe Dixon . . . . *Romeo*

■ **DESCRIPTION** Television arts and entertainment magazine. Includes a two-minute item on the English Shakespeare Company's touring production of *Romeo and Juliet*, showing A3S5 with comments from actor Joe Dixon.

Stanley Lupino and Thelma Todd in YOU MADE ME LOVE YOU (1933)

TAMING OF THE SHREW

TAMING OF THE SHREW, The

■ GB • 1923

d	Edwin J. Collins
pc	British and Colonial Kinematograph Company
p	Edward Godal

NFTVA viewing copy
35mm bw st 939ft 10mins
Incomplete — preservation copy complete at
  2,022ft
English titles

■ CAST

Dacia Deane . . . . *Katharina*
Lauderdale Maitland . . . . *Petruchio*
M. Gray Murray . . . . *Baptista*
Cynthia Murtagh . . . . *Bianca*
Roy Beard. . . . . *Lucentio*

■ DESCRIPTION Condensed version of Shakespeare's play, concentrating chiefly on the wooing and winning of Katharina by Petruchio. Simply but quite adequately produced, this is a superior example of the cheap literary short favoured by many British producers of the 1920s who could not finance full features. The action is sensibly put over, there are generous chunks of the original text in the intertitles, and the performances are adequate. There is little cinematic inventiveness, certainly, but as a simple guide to the play it is faithful and might have been welcomed as an educational tool had schools taken notice of the cinema at that time.

■ NOTES The NFTVA's viewing copy is of the second reel only, showing the action from Petruchio agreeing to marry Katharina (A2S1) to the end of the play. This was one of a series of such two-reelers based on literary works, which included one other Shakespearean title, FAL-STAFF THE TAVERN KNIGHT (not in NFTVA), with Roy Byford as Falstaff. Byford appears as a Falstaff-figure in THE IMMORTAL GENTLE-MAN (qv). In 1915 British and Colonial had made a short 'sound' film of *The Taming of the Shrew* (not in NFTVA) using the Voxograph process, whereby offstage reciters spoke in synchronisation with the filmed scenes. It starred Arthur and Constance Backner.

■ REFERENCES ● Ball, *Shakespeare on Silent Film*, pp. 284–6, 377.

TAMING OF THE SHREW, The

■ USA ● 1929

d/adapt	Sam Taylor
pc	Pickford Corporation/ Elton Corporation
ph	Karl Struss
art d	William Cameron Menzies/ Laurence Irving

NFTVA preservation material
35mm bw sd 5,698ft 63mins
German titles and dialogue

■ CAST

Mary Pickford. . . . . *Katharina*
Douglas Fairbanks. . . . . *Petruchio*
Edwin Maxwell . . . . *Baptista*
Joseph Cawthorn. . . . . *Gremio*
Clyde Cook . . . . *Grumio*
Geoffrey Wardwell . . . . *Hortensio*
Dorothy Jordan . . . . *Bianca*

■ DESCRIPTION Feature film version of the play. The first sound film to attempt a full version of one of the plays, and rather too early to be attempting such an ambitious project. The emphasis is on the farcical knockabout, and as with the 1966 Burton and Taylor version, the audience is supposed to see parallels with the stars' own marriage. Seen now it seems quite engaging, with some fine sets, neat visual gags and exuberant playing. But despite drastic cutting of the text it failed heavily with audiences at the time.

■ NOTES The NFTVA copy is a German release version with the on-screen title DER WIDER-SPENSTIGEN ZÄHMUNG. The film appeared in both silent and sound versions, the latter also carrying many intertitles. Original American release length 6,116ft (68mins). This was the only film in which Douglas Fairbanks and Mary Pickford starred together.

ELSTREE CALLING

■ GB ● 1930

d	Adrian Brunel
sketches	Alfred Hitchcock

pc	British International Pictures
p	Walter C. Mycroft
sc	Val Valentine/Adrian Brunel/ Walter C. Mycroft
ph	Claude Friese-Greene
m	Reg Casson/Vivian Ellis/ Chick Endor/Ivor Novello/ Jack Strachey

NFTVA viewing copy
35mm bw (col seq) 7,783ft 86mins

■ **CAST**
Donald Calthrop . . . . . . *Himself/Doug/Petruchio*
Anna May Wong . . . . *Mary/Katharina*
Gordon Begg . . . . *William Shakespeare*

■ **DESCRIPTION** Feature film variety revue. A creaky but fascinating and often highly entertaining collection of party pieces by a host of British variety stars (Will Fyffe, Cicely Courtneidge, Jack Hulbert, Tommy Handley). Throughout the film there is a running gag with Donald Calthrop, who is trying to raise the tone of the show by putting on Shakespeare. Having been interrupted several times throughout the picture, while sneaking in extracts from *Hamlet* and *Henry V* (both qv), towards the end Calthrop gets to put on a spoof of the Douglas Fairbanks/Mary Pickford THE TAMING OF THE SHREW (USA 1929). Calthrop (Doug/Petruchio) arrives by motorbike to ask for Mary/Katharina, played by Anna May Wong. She responds by throwing the furniture at him, then a succession of custard pies, one of which hits Shakespeare (Gordon Begg) as he enters. The humour is somewhat laboured.

■ **NOTES** Alfred Hitchcock is credited on screen with 'sketches and other interpolated items'. In practice this meant the linking 'television' sketch with Gordon Harker, the 'Thriller' sketch and the *Taming of the Shrew* parody. This was apparently originally filmed in somewhat subtler form by Brunel, only to be rejected by the producers.

STAR IMPERSONATIONS

■ **GB • 1930**

d	Harry Hughes
pc	British International Pictures
p	Herbert Thompson

NFTVA preservation material
35mm bw sd 753ft 8mins

■ **CAST**
William Freshman
Vanda Greville
Mickey Brantford
Mabel Poulton
Donald Calthrop

■ **DESCRIPTION** Cinema advertisement for *Film Weekly* magazine. British actors impersonate Hollywood stars in scenes from recent films; the audience is invited to compete for a prize of £100 by naming the best impersonation. Included is an impersonation of Mary Pickford in THE TAMING OF THE SHREW (USA 1929) by Mabel Poulton. The winner was Donald Calthrop, impersonating George Arliss in DISRAELI (USA 1929).

YOU MADE ME LOVE YOU

■ **GB • 1933**

d	Monty Banks
pc	British International Pictures
sc	Frank Launder/Stanley Lupino
ph	John J. Cox
m	Harry Acres

NFTVA viewing copy
35mm bw sd 6,338ft 70mins

■ **CAST**
Stanley Lupino . . . . *Tom Daly*
Thelma Todd . . . . *Pamela Berne*
John Loder . . . . *Harry Berne*
Gerald Rawlinson . . . . *Jerry*
James Carew . . . . *Oliver Berne*

■ **DESCRIPTION** Feature film. Noisy musical comedy which modernises the plot of *The Taming of the Shrew*. Tom Daly is a songwriter who sees a girl in a traffic jam and writes a song about her ('What's Her Name?', featured to death throughout). Daly pays a visit to the girl, Pamela Berne, who is rich and spoilt, and through a trick of her father's they end up married. Daly's attempts to tame her are met with fury, then she gradually starts to fall for him, but becomes completely tamed only when he offers her a divorce. Not an entirely pleasant theme, but put over with gusto and boasting some splendidly violent scenes of domestic disharmony. Thelma Todd brings striking glamour to an otherwise standard British musical comedy of its day.

IMMORTAL GENTLEMAN, The

■ GB • 1935

d   Widgey R. Newman
pc   Bernard Smith

NFTVA viewing copy

■ CAST
Laidman Browne. . . . . *Petruchio*

■ **DESCRIPTION** Feature film. Shakespeare and his friends meet in a Southwark tavern and their reminiscences give rise to sequences from Shakespeare's plays. Includes an abridged scene from *The Taming of the Shrew* where Petruchio tells Katharina that he intends to marry her (A2S1). For full details of the film see entry in General section.

SECOND BEST BED

■ GB • 1938

d   Tom Walls
pc   Capitol Productions
p   Max Schach
sc   Ben Travers
ph   Jack Cox
m   Van Phillips

NFTVA preservation material
35mm bw sd 7,500ft 83mins

■ CAST
Tom Walls. . . . . *Victor Garnett*
Jane Baxter. . . . . *Patricia Lynton*
Veronica Rose . . . . *Jenny Murdoch*
Carl Jaffe . . . . *Georges Dubonnet*
Greta Gynt. . . . . *Yvonne*

■ **DESCRIPTION** Feature film. Risqué comedy, updating *The Taming of the Shrew*. Victor Garnett, a wealthy bachelor, marries the rich, spoilt and fiery-tempered Patricia Lynton. He then attempts to turn Patricia into his ideal of the perfect and obedient wife. Victor's too gallant behaviour with other women infuriates Patricia and she runs off to Monte Carlo, but they are eventually reconciled, if scarcely tamed. First-rate suggestive comedy in Ben Travers' best manner, with Tom Walls ideally cast as the worldly sophisticate with a roving eye. He does indeed give his wife the second best bed, and the line from Shakespeare's will is quoted in the opening titles.

QUIET MAN, The

■ USA • 1952

d   John Ford
pc   Republic/Argosy
p   John Ford/Merian C. Cooper/
        Michael Killanin
sc   Frank S. Nugent/Richard Llewellyn
ph   Winton C. Hoch
m   Victor Young

NFTVA viewing copy
35mm col sd 11,615ft 129mins

■ CAST
John Wayne . . . . *Sean Thornton*
Maureen O'Hara. . . . . *Mary Kate Danaher*
Barry Fitzgerald . . . . *Michaeleen Flynn*
Ward Bond . . . . *Father Lonergan*
Victor McLaglen . . . . *'Red' Will Danaher*
Mildred Natwick . . . . *Mrs Tillane*

■ **DESCRIPTION** Feature film. Sean Thornton, after a life as a boxer in America, returns to his native Galway. He falls out with his neighbour 'Red' Will Danaher, but falls in love with his sister Mary Kate. Through trickery Thornton gets her brother's permission for their marriage, but there is no dowry. Mary Kate unleashes her temper on Thornton when he declines to fight for the dowry. Thornton eventually challenges Danaher and a massive fight ensues which Sean wins, gaining the respect of both brother and sister. The spirit, if not quite the plot, of *The Taming of the Shrew*.

■ **NOTES** A later John Wayne feature, McLINTOCK! (USA 1963, see trailer below) takes its lead from THE QUIET MAN but is closer to the plot of Shakespeare's play.

KISS ME KATE [TRAILER]

■ **USA • 1953**

NFTVA preservation material
35mm col sd 40ft 1min

■ **DESCRIPTION** Trailer for the 1953 feature film (not in the NFTVA) of Cole Porter's musical update of *The Taming of the Shrew*.

TAMER TAMED, The

■ **GB • 1956**

pc	BBC
tx	7 February 1956 (BBC)
p	Anthony Pelissier
sc	Elaine Morgan
des	Roy Oxley

NFTVA preservation material
35mm bw sd 4,090ft 45mins

■ **CAST**

Bruno Barnabé . . . . *Christopher Sly/Hortensio*
Aubrey Dexter . . . . *Baptista*
John Gatrell. . . . . *Antonio*
Annabel Maule . . . . *Bianca*
Hugh Latimer . . . . *Lucentio*
Avice Landone. . . . . *Wife to Hortensio*
Robert Urquhart . . . . *Petruchio*
Judy Campbell . . . . *Katharina*
Marjorie Gresley. . . . . *Nurse*

■ **DESCRIPTION** Television play. A witty 'sequel' to *The Taming of the Shrew* from accomplished scriptwriter Elaine Morgan, showing how Petruchio and Katharina have fared after a year of marriage. Baptista has recalled his daughters to Padua, and on the journey both Bianca and Katharina are rather less tame than their husbands would have them be.

TAMING OF THE SHREW, The

■ **USA • 1956**

■ *Hallmark Hall of Fame*

d	George Schaefer

pc	NBC
tx	18 March 1956 (NBC)
p	Maurice Evans
adapt	Michael Hogan/William Nichols
lght	William Knight
des	Rouben Ter-Arutunian
cost	Rouben Ter-Arutunian/James Glenn
m	Lehman Engel

NFTVA preservation material
16mm bw sd 3,225ft 90mins

■ **CAST**

Maurice Evans . . . . *Petruchio*
Lilli Palmer . . . . *Katharina*
Diane Cilento . . . . *Bianca*
Philip Bourneuf . . . . *Baptista*
Jerome Kilty . . . . *Grumio*
Douglas Watson. . . . . *Hortensio*
John Colicos . . . . *Lucentio*
Robinson Stone . . . . *Vincentio*
Jack Fletcher . . . . *Tailor*
Ronald Long . . . . *Biondello*
Will B. Able . . . . *Curtis*

■ **DESCRIPTION** Television adaptation of the play. Despite some rough edges, the play is put over with a little more imagination and zest than was usually the case with the *Hallmark* series. The knockabout air (literally so when Petruchio and Katharina's first meeting takes place in a boxing ring) is initially fresh but outstays its welcome. Design and performances reflect the *commedia dell'arte* tradition.

■ **NOTES** Originally broadcast in colour (though most could only receive it in black and white) but preserved only in a black and white 'kinescope' (telerecording).

McLINTOCK! [TRAILER]

■ **USA • 1963**

NFTVA preservation material
35mm col sd c90ft 1min

■ **DESCRIPTION** Trailer for the 1963 feature film (not in NFTVA) starring John Wayne as a cattle baron with a tempestuous wife named Katherine (Maureen O'Hara). In part a tribute to THE QUIET MAN (see above) but closer in theme than the earlier film to *The Taming of the Shrew*.

TAMING OF THE SHREW, The

■ USA/Italy 1966

d	Franco Zeffirelli
pc	Royal Films/FAI
p	Richard Burton/Elizabeth Taylor/ Franco Zeffirelli
adapt	Paul Dehn/Suso Cecchi d'Amico/ Franco Zeffirelli
ph	Oswald Morris/Luciano Trasatti
p des	John de Cuir
art d	Giuseppe Mariani/Elven Webb
cost	Irene Sharaff/Danilo Donati
m	Nino Rota

NFTVA viewing copy
35mm col sd 10,859ft 121mins

■ CAST
Richard Burton. . . . . *Petruchio*
Elizabeth Taylor . . . . *Katharina*
Michael Hordern . . . . *Baptista*
Cyril Cusack . . . . *Grumio*
Michael York. . . . . *Lucentio*
Alfred Lynch . . . . *Tranio*
Natasha Pyne. . . . . *Bianca*
Alan Webb . . . . *Gremio*
Victor Spinetti . . . . *Hortensio*
Mark Dignam. . . . . *Vincentio*
Giancarlo Cobelli . . . . *Priest*
Vernon Dobtcheff . . . . *Pedant*
Roy Holder . . . . *Biondello*
Gianni Magni . . . . *Curtis*
Alberto Bonucci . . . . *Nathaniel*
Lino Capolicchio . . . . *Gregory*
Roberto Antonelli. . . . . *Philip*
Anthony Garner . . . . *Haberdasher*
Ken Parry . . . . *Tailor*
Bice Valori . . . . *Widow*

■ DESCRIPTION
Feature film adaptation of the play. Boisterous, vulgar interpretation which cuts the text down to the Petruchio-Katharina romance and has scant respect for such words as remain. There is little poetry here, but there was little enough of that to lose anyway, and the film is intended to be a bawdy, lively and colourful piece of historical slapstick (and an obvious exploitation of public perception of the Burton-Taylor romance). In this it is successful.

■ REFERENCES
● Jorgens, *Shakespeare on Film*, pp. 66–78, 258–61.

TAMING OF THE SHREW, The

■ West Germany • 1978

pc	ZDF
tx (GB)	20 May 1978 (BBC2)
p	Herbert Junkers
p/chor	John Cranko
sets/cost	Elisabeth Dalton
m	Karl-Heinz Stolze

NFTVA viewing copy
½" col sd 83mins

■ CAST
Marcia Haydée . . . . *Katharina*
Birgit Keil. . . . . *Bianca*
Gerd Praast . . . . *Petruchio*
Jan Stripling . . . . *Lucentio*
Egon Madsen . . . . *Gremio*
Jiri Kylian . . . . *Hortensio*
Leigh-Ann Griffiths/Ruth Papendick . . . . *Harlots*

■ DESCRIPTION
Ballet. John Cranko's ballet recorded in the Württemberg State Theatre by the Stuttgart Ballet with the Stuttgart State Theatre Orchestra, musical director Bernard Kontarsky.

■ NOTES
The programme was made in the German Federal Republic and broadcast in Britain as part of the 'Dance Month' series.

TAMING OF THE SHREW, The

■ GB/USA • 1980

■ *BBC Television Shakespeare*

d/p	Jonathan Miller
pc	BBC/Time-Life Films
tx (GB)	23 October 1980 (BBC2)
tx (US)	26 January 1981 (PBS)
sc ed	David Snodin
lght	John Treays
des	Colin Lowrey
cost	Alun Hughes
m	Stephen Oliver

NFTVA viewing copy
¾" col sd 125mins

■ **CAST**

Simon Chandler . . . . *Lucentio*
Anthony Pedley . . . . *Tranio*
John Franklyn-Robbins . . . . *Baptista*
Frank Thornton . . . . *Gremio*
Sarah Badel . . . . *Katharina*
Jonathan Cecil . . . . *Hortensio*
Susan Penhaligon . . . . *Bianca*
Harry Waters . . . . *Biondello*
John Cleese . . . . *Petruchio*
David Kincaid . . . . *Grumio*
Bev Willis . . . . *Baptista's servant*
Angus Lennie . . . . *Curtis*
Harry Webster . . . . *Nathaniel*
Gil Morris . . . . *Philip*
Leslie Sarony . . . . *Gregory*
Derek Deadman . . . . *Nicholas*
Denis Gilmore . . . . *Peter*
John Bird . . . . *Pedant*
Alan Hay . . . . *Tailor*
David Kinsey . . . . *Haberdasher*
John Barron . . . . *Vincentio*
Joan Hickson . . . . *Widow*

■ **DESCRIPTION** Television presentation of the play. The most popular of the BBC series, on account of Cleese, and one of the most successful, on account of Cleese (and Miller). Jonathan Miller took over the production of the *BBC Television Shakespeare* series in 1980 and revitalised it with this highly enjoyable, playful interpretation. John Cleese, greatly popular through the comedy series *Fawlty Towers*, nicely balances Petruchio with Basil Fawlty. Miller's view of the play was actually quite a sombre one (he suggested to the actors that there was a connection between Petruchio and Oliver Cromwell) and running this puritan viewpoint alongside the more obvious comedy pays dividends.

TAMING OF THE SHREW

■ **GB • 1983**

■ *Shakespeare Lives*

d	Mary McMurray
pc	Quintet Films
tx	5 January 1983 (C4) [part one]
	12 January 1983 (C4) [part two]
p	Victor Glynn/Mike Ockrent

NFTVA preservation material
1" col sd c30+30mins

■ **CAST**

Daniel Massey . . . . *Petruchio*
Suzanne Bertish . . . . *Katharina*
Clive Arrindell
Joss Buckley
John Darrell
Caroline Langrische
Bill Wallis
Meg Wynn Owen

■ **DESCRIPTION** Television theatre workshop, broadcast in two parts. Michael Bogdanov leads a group of National Theatre actors through aspects of *The Taming of the Shrew* in front of a studio audience. The first in a lively and engaging series. Bogdanov asks if the play does not so much debase women as show how women are debased.

■ **NOTES** Other plays covered in this series are *Hamlet*, *Measure for Measure*, *Richard III*, *The Tempest* and *Timon of Athens* (qqv).

Toyah Willcox as Miranda in THE TEMPEST (1979)

TEMPEST

TEMPEST, The

■ **GB • 1908**

d	Percy Stow
pc	Clarendon Film Company
sc	Langford Reed

NFTVA viewing copy
35mm bw st 708ft 8mins
English titles

■ **DESCRIPTION** Abbreviated version of the play. A delightful, skilful and adroitly simple interpretation. Sailors on board ship hand down the infant Miranda to Prospero standing in a boat. Gonzalo hands him a book. Prospero carries Miranda onto the island, where they encounter Caliban eating grass. Prospero leads him away at sword point. Prospero releases Ariel (played by a girl) from a tree. Ten years later Caliban creeps up on Miranda, but Ariel rescues her by turning into a monkey and chasing Caliban away. In his cave Prospero conjures up a tempest, and he and Miranda look through a gap in the cave to see a ship at sea sinking. Antonio and Ferdinand wander separately on the island. Miranda pleads with Prospero and gives instructions to Ariel. Ariel leads Ferdinand on, disappearing and reappearing, until he comes up to Miranda. They fall in love. Prospero comes up, secretly grateful, and angrily separates them. Prospero disarms Ferdinand and sets him to moving logs. Miranda joins him and Prospero gives them his blessing. Ariel taunts Antonio's party with visions of food. Prospero arrives and they kneel before him. Ferdinand, Miranda and Ariel arrive and Antonio greets his son. Prospero releases Ariel. On the rocks where Prospero was first set down everyone climbs into the ship, but Caliban is pushed away by one of the sailors. Possibly the only Shakespearean film from the early cinema period that both did the original justice and served the contemporary audience as expected entertainment. The play is judiciously handled; the titles alone are a model of simple clarity (see opening essay where they are given in full). For its time, this is a model Shakespearean film.

■ **NOTES** Presumably missing from this copy, along with its main title, is an explanation of why Prospero is marooned on the island. The length on release was 780ft. Filmed in both countryside and studio. The cast is not known.

FOUR FEATHERS, The

■ **GB** • **1939**

d	Zoltan Korda
pc	Alexander Korda Productions
p	Alexander Korda
sc	R. C. Sherriff
ph	Georges Périnal
m	Miklos Rosza

NFTVA viewing copy
35mm col sd 11,180ft 124mins

■ **CAST**
John Clements . . . . *Harry Faversham*
Ralph Richardson . . . . *Captain John Durrance*
C. Aubrey Smith . . . . *General Burroughs*
June Duprez . . . . *Ethne Burroughs*

■ **DESCRIPTION** Feature film, based on the novel by A. E. W. Mason. Splendid view of the British Empire through Hungarian eyes as the seemingly cowardly Harry Faversham proves himself a hero in the Sudan. The picture is stolen by Ralph Richardson, on invincible form, who is blinded in the desert (Clements rescues him); he gives a reading from the speech beginning 'Be not afeard; the isle is full of noises' (A3S2) from Braille.

YELLOW CANARY, The

■ **GB** • **1943**

d/p	Herbert Wilcox
pc	Imperator
sc	Miles Malleson/DeWitt Bodeen
ph	Mutz Greenbaum
m	Clifford Parker

NFTVA viewing copy
35mm bw sd 8,815ft 98mins

■ **CAST**
Anna Neagle . . . . *Sally Maitland*
Richard Greene . . . . *Jim Garrick*

■ **DESCRIPTION** Feature film. Anna Neagle is a supposed Nazi sympathiser who is really British through-and-through and helps foil a German plot to blow up the harbour in Halifax, Nova Scotia. The impossibility of being fooled even for a minute by the central premise kills a dreary film. The film opens with two British air-raid wardens discussing the Shakespeare-Bacon controversy. One of them ties Shakespeare to the

Blitz by quoting the lines beginning 'Be not afeard; the isle is full of noises' (A3S2).

LOVE STORY

USA title LADY SURRENDERS, A

■ **GB • 1944**

d	Leslie Arliss
pc	Gainsborough Pictures
p	Harold Huth
sc	Leslie Arliss/Doreen Montgomery/ Rodney Ackland
ph	Bernard Knowles
m	Hubert Bath

NFTVA viewing copy
35mm bw sd 10,133ft 113mins

■ **CAST**

Margaret Lockwood . . . . *Lissa Cambell*
Stewart Granger . . . . *Kit Firth*
Patricia Roc . . . . *Judy Martin*
Vincent Holman . . . . *Prospero*
Joan Rees . . . . *Ariel*

■ **DESCRIPTION** Feature film. The romance between a dying concert pianist and a half-blind pilot, a cast-iron commercial property of its day. Lockwood, Granger, Cornish settings and the 'Cornish Rhapsody' on the soundtrack all make for a highly professional weepie. The third member of the love triangle, Patricia Roc, is involved in the rehearsals for a production of *The Tempest* at Cornwall's open-air Minnack Theatre. Scenes from these rehearsals feature throughout.

YELLOW SKY

■ **USA • 1948**

d	William A. Wellman
pc	Twentieth Century-Fox Film Corporation
p/sc	Lamar Trotti
ph	Joe MacDonald
m	Alfred Newman

NFTVA viewing copy
35mm bw sd 8,873ft 99mins

■ **CAST**

Gregory Peck . . . . *Stretch*
Anne Baxter . . . . *Mike*
Richard Widmark . . . . *Dude*
James Barton . . . . *Grandpa*

■ **DESCRIPTION** Feature film Western, based on a story by W. R. Burnett. A superior Western, strikingly photographed and emphasising character over action, with intriguing parallels to *The Tempest*. Following a bank robbery Stretch and his band of outlaws escape into the desert and come across a ghost town, inhabited by a 'he-girl' named Mike and her prospector grandfather. The cynical Stretch finds himself mellowing under the influence of the humble prospector and the brave new world promised by the independent, gun-toting Mike. The outlaws fall out through the obsessive lust for gold of Dude, one of the gang. A shoot-out follows in which Stretch and those who have sided with him survive, and Dude and the others die. Stretch returns the money to the bank and rides off with Mike. The ghost town here becomes a moral testing ground for the outlaws. Stretch literally becomes a new man (he washes and shaves after Mike is repelled by his smell), his change marking a break-up in the solidarity of evil.

■ **NOTES** The film was remade in 1967 as THE JACKALS (not in NFTVA) with Vincent Price and Dana Ivarson and the action transferred to South Africa.

■ **REFERENCES** • Harlan Kennedy, 'Prospero's Flicks', *Film Comment*, Jan-Feb 1992, pp. 45–8.

FORBIDDEN PLANET

■ **USA • 1956**

d	Fred McLeod Wilcox
pc	MGM
p	Nicholas Nayfack
sc	Cyril Hume
ph	George Folsey
electronic tonalities	Louis and Bebe Barron

NFTVA viewing copy
35mm col sd 8,662ft 96mins

■ **CAST**

Walter Pidgeon . . . . *Dr Morbius*
Anne Francis . . . . *Altaira Morbius*
Leslie Nielsen . . . . *Commander Adams*
Warren Stevens . . . . *Lt 'Doc' Ostrow*
Earl Holliman . . . . *Cook*

■ **DESCRIPTION** Feature film. 2,000 AD – Commander Adams lands his spaceship on the planet Altair-4 in search of the lost spaceship 'Bellerophon'. His team find the two survivors, Dr Morbius and his daughter Altaira. They live in a luxurious home with a robot servant Robby. Morbius is cold towards Adams and his crew, informing them that all other survivors from the 'Bellerophon' died in mysterious circumstances. Morbius shows Adams the scientific marvels left behind by the Krells, the race who previously inhabited the planet, including a 'brain booster'. One of the crew dies in bizarre circumstances. Fighting off an invisible monster with laser beams, the crew briefly see a huge, hideous creature. Ostrow learns through the brain booster, but at the cost of his life, that the creature is a 'monster from the Id', the force that destroyed the Krell civilisation. Adams tells Morbius that the creature has arisen out of his own mind, and Morbius dies trying to defy his own subconscious, the creature dying with him. A first-rate piece of science fiction, witty and wooden in the manner of the best *Star Trek* episodes, with an amazing monster and some appealing *Tempest* parallels: Morbius as Prospero, Altaira as Miranda, Adams as Ferdinand, Robby as Ariel, the Id monster Caliban, even the drunken comedy of the cook can be equated with Stephano.

■ **NOTES** Robby the Robot proved a great hit and the following year appeared in his own starring vehicle, THE INVISIBLE BOY (not in NFTVA). This has no Shakespearean connection.

■ **REFERENCES** • Harlan Kennedy, 'Prospero's Flicks', *Film Comment*, Jan-Feb 1992, p. 47.

TEMPEST, The

■ **GB • 1956**

d/p	Ian Atkins/Robert Atkins
pc	BBC
tx	14 October 1956 (BBC)
des	Barry Learoyd
cost	Olive Harris
m	Hans Heimler

NFTVA viewing copy
35mm bw sd 9,978ft 111mins

■ **CAST**

Robert Eddison . . . . *Prospero*
Anna Barry . . . . *Miranda*
Patti Brooks. . . . . *Ariel*
Robert Atkins . . . . *Caliban*
Laidman Browne . . . . *Alonso*
Douglas Wilmer. . . . . *Antonio*
Charles Lloyd Pack . . . . *Gonzalo*
Olaf Pooley. . . . . *Sebastion* [sic]
Bernard Brown . . . . *Ferdinand*
Jonathan Meddings. . . . . *Trinculo*
Russell Thorndike. . . . . *Stephano*
Dennis Chinnery . . . . *Boatswain*
Patricia Kneale. . . . . *Iris*
Sylvia Beamish. . . . . *Ceres*
Jean Grayston. . . . . *Juno*

■ **DESCRIPTION** Television production of the play. Pedestrian single-set presentation with some rudimentary superimposed spirits, a cast who seem generally unaware of the finer points of what they say, and the creaking floorboards of live television. There are some small pleasures and some imaginative gestures (a piping Ariel yearning for freedom, a feral Caliban) and excellent music (notably Ceres and Juno's song). A typical example of the stodgy television productions that existed before more sophisticated production techniques and a greater awareness of the medium's potential changed things for the better in the 1960s.

■ **NOTES** Robert and Ian Atkins were father and son. Robert Atkins began acting with Beerbohm Tree in 1906; he appears in the 1913 HAMLET (qv), and directed a number of early BBC Shakespeare broadcasts, often recordings of his productions at the open-air theatre in Regent's Park. The NFTVA film is a telerecording of the live broadcast.

MICHAEL HORDERN

■ **GB • 1968**

■ *Tempo – the Actor and the Role*

d	Helen Standage
pc	ABC Television
tx	14 April 1968 (ITV)
p	John Irwin
pres/int	Derek Hart

NFTVA viewing copy
½" bw sd 25mins

■ **CAST**

Michael Hordern . . . . *Prospero*
Jane Asher . . . . *Miranda*
Freda Dowie . . . . *Ariel*

■ **DESCRIPTION** Television arts documentary. Michael Hordern talks about the role of Prospero: the challenge he finds in the role, the temptation of wallowing in the beauty of the verse, Prospero's humanity and compassion, and his dislike of the 'intellectual' approach. Passages from A1S2, A4S1 and the epilogue are performed in the studio.

AGE OF CONSENT

■ **Australia • 1969**

d	Michael Powell
pc	Nautilus Productions
p	James Mason/Michael Powell
sc	Peter Yeldham
ph	Hannes Staudinger
m	Stanley Myers

NFTVA viewing copy
35mm col sd 8,791ft 98mins

■ **CAST**

James Mason . . . . *Bradley Morahan*
Helen Mirren. *Cora*
Jack MacGowran . . . . *Nat Kelly*
Neva Carr-Glyn . . . . *Ma Ryan*
Antonia Katsaros . . . . *Isabel Marley*

■ **DESCRIPTION** Feature film, adapted from the novel by Norman Lindsay. Michael Powell spent much of his later years as a film-maker trying to raise the finance for his version of *The Tempest*, in the light of which this must be seen as a *Tempest* variation. Brad Morahan, a disenchanted artist, hides himself away on the Great Barrier Reef, where he encounters the drunken Ma Ryan and

her attractive daughter Cora. Morahan takes Cora as a model, he delighting in a new enthusiasm for his art, she delighting in new-found sexual desire. An acquaintance of Brad's, the coarse Nat Kelly, helps spoil the idyll. In a fight between Cora and Ma Ryan over money the latter falls to her death. A verdict of accidental death is returned, Kelly is arrested and Brad and Cora are left to themselves. Or Prospero stumbles on Miranda/Ariel and Sycorax, with intrusions from Caliban. Sometimes Powell is rather too interested in underwater shots of a naked Mirren, and the normally delightful MacGowran is sadly over the top, but this is an intriguing and undervalued work.

■ **NOTES** James Mason was to have been Powell's Prospero in *The Tempest*, with Mia Farrow as Ariel. See also the 1992 LATE SHOW SPECIAL on Powell below. The NFTVA's print is the British release version, with six minutes cut (mostly of an early art gallery sequence) and a new music track replacing Peter Sculthorpe's original.

■ **REFERENCES** • Robert Murphy, *Sixties British Cinema* (London: BFI, 1992), pp. 99–100.

TEMPEST, The

■ **GB • 1969**

d	Nicholas Young/David Snasdell
pc	A Rafters Players Production
exec p	Roger Sherman
ph	David Snasdell
m	John Deathridge

NFTVA preservation material
16mm bw sd 3,060ft 85mins

■ **CAST**

Christopher Scoular . . . . *Prospero*
Michael Menaugh. . . . . *Ferdinand*
Vanessa Blackmore. . . . . *Miranda*
Richard Phethean. . . . . *Ariel*
Johnny Eccles. . . . . *Caliban*
Richard Hermitage . . . . *Stefano*
David Alleyn . . . . *Antonio*
Christopher Temple . . . . *Sebastian*

■ **DESCRIPTION** Amateur feature film. A self-financed recording by the Rafters Players of their stage production of *The Tempest*. A brave effort, filmed over three weeks in Cornwall, on a minimal budget, all of which unfortunately shows. The production itself was only average and comes over as very poor in a badly lit and badly recorded film that uses none of the resources of the cinema for a play that demands them. Even the Cornish locations are used far too sparingly. As with the similar 1966 effort THE WINTER'S TALE (qv), one applauds the initiative, but it is hard to see why they bothered.

TEMPEST, The

Alternative title SKETCHES FOR THE TEMPEST

■ GB • 1974/9

d/anim/sc	George Dunning
pc	TV Cartoons

NFTVA preservation material
35mm col sd c700ft 8 mins
Contained within A TRIBUTE TO GEORGE DUNNING (1979)

■ **DESCRIPTION** Animation. Still images and animated fragments from George Dunning's unfinished version of *The Tempest*. Dunning, a visionary animator best known for YELLOW SUBMARINE (GB 1968), had been working on THE TEMPEST, his most ambitious solo project, for five years before his death in 1979. Intended to be of feature length; these surviving images and knowledge of Dunning's extraordinary other work from this period indicate that a uniquely beautiful Shakespearean film has been lost.

■ **REFERENCES** • John Canemaker, 'The Dunning Touch', *Sightlines*, Winter 1986/87, pp. 26–8.

YOUR NATIONAL THEATRE

■ GB • 1976

d/p	Derek Bailey
pc	London Weekend Television
tx	21 August 1976 (ITV)
nar	Albert Finney

prologue sc	Tony Harrison
m	William Walton

NFTVA preservation material
16mm col sd 3,155ft 87mins

■ **CAST**
John Gielgud.................... *Prospero*
Denis Quilley.................... *Caliban*
Julian Orchard................. *Trinculo*
Arthur Lowe .... *Stephano*

■ **DESCRIPTION** Television documentary celebrating the opening of the National Theatre on London's South Bank. Containing a large amount of archival material, it shows the history of the National Theatre project from the laying of the foundation stone in 1951 to the opening of the Lyttleton. Among the interviewees are Laurence Olivier (including his farewell speech to the company), Peter Hall, Denys Lasdun, Raymond Mander, Joe Mitchenson and Kenneth Tynan. There is unique film of the Olivier Theatre's revolving 'drum' before its installation. Shows scenes from the last night at the Old Vic, with Peggy Ashcroft, Ralph Richardson and John Gielgud (from the 1963 FAREWELL TO THE VIC, qv under *Measure for Measure*), and extracts from past productions, including Peter Hall's 1973 production of *The Tempest* with John Gielgud.

TEMPEST, The

■ GB • 1979

d/adapt	Derek Jarman
pc	Boyd's Company
p	Guy Ford/Mordecai Schreiber
ph	Peter Middleton
art d	Ian Whittaker/Steven Mehea
p des	Yolanda Sonnabend
cost	Nicolas Ede
m	Brian Hodgson/John Lewis

NFTVA preservation material
35mm col sd 10,382ft 115mins

■ **CAST**
Heathcote Williams .... *Prospero*
Karl Johnson .... *Ariel*
Toyah Willcox.................... *Miranda*
Peter Bull .... *Alonso*

Richard Warwick . . . . *Antonio*
Elisabeth Welch . . . . *Goddess*
Jack Birkett . . . . *Caliban*
Ken Campbell . . . . *Gonzalo*
David Meyer . . . . *Ferdinand*
Neil Cunningham . . . . *Sebastian*
Christopher Biggins. . . . . *Stephano*
Peter Turner . . . . *Trinculo*
Claire Davenport . . . . *Sycorax*
Kate Temple. . . . . *Young Miranda*
Helen Wallington-Lloyd/
 Angela Whittington . . . . *Spirits*

■ **DESCRIPTION** Feature film adaptation of the play. Derek Jarman's vision of *The Tempest* is one of the most strikingly original of Shakespearean films, wholly faithful to the spirit of the play, though difficult for some to accept. Set on the Scottish coast, with the few exterior scenes shot in eerie tints. Prospero (played by poet and 'real magician' Heathcote Williams) is a romantic, Byronic figure, half the age of all previous Prosperos, Miranda (played by punk singer Willcox) is playful, questioning, credibly adolescent, Ariel is petulant in a boiler suit or tuxedo, Caliban a truly revolting figure dressed as a butler with a taste for raw eggs. Jarman's deep love and understanding of the text sees the play rearranged brilliantly to serve as cinematic narrative. Perhaps the most impressive aspect of the film is the dialogue, which in this world out of time is both naturalistic and wholly appropriate – and beautifully spoken by an accomplished cast. Jarman is aware not only of the play's beauty and fantasy, but of its political intelligence. For some it has appeared wilfully eccentric, and this aspect has to be accepted. The dazzling appearance at the end of Elisabeth Welch singing 'Stormy Weather' is either a foolish pun or a perfect rounding off, according to taste.

■ **REFERENCES** • Derek Jarman, *Dancing Ledge* (London: Quartet, 1984), pp. 186–206.

TEMPEST, The [TRAILER]

■ **GB • 1979**

NFTVA preservation material
35mm col sd 110ft 1min

■ **DESCRIPTION** Trailer to the above.

TEMPEST, The

■ **GB/USA 1980**

■ *BBC Television Shakespeare*

d	John Gorrie
pc	BBC/Time-Life Films
tx (GB)	27 February 1980 (BBC2)
tx (US)	7 May 1980 (PBS)
p	Cedric Messina
sc ed	Alan Shallcross
lght	Clive Thomas
des	Paul Joel
cost	Alun Hughes
m	Joseph Horovitz

NFTVA preservation material
1" col sd 125mins

■ **CAST**

Michael Hordern . . . . *Prospero*
Derek Godfrey . . . . *Antonio*
David Waller . . . . *Alonso*
Warren Clarke . . . . *Caliban*
Nigel Hawthorne . . . . *Stephano*
David Dixon . . . . *Ariel*
Andrew Sachs . . . . *Trinculo*
John Nettleton . . . . *Gonzalo*
Alan Rowe. . . . . *Sebastian*
Pippa Guard . . . . *Miranda*
Christopher Guard. . . . . *Ferdinand*
Kenneth Gilbert . . . . *Boatswain*
Edwin Brown . . . . *Master*
Paul Greenhalgh . . . . *Francisco*
Christopher Bramwell . . . . *Adrian*
Gwyneth Lloyd . . . . *Juno*
Elizabeth Gardner . . . . *Ceres*
Judith Rees . . . . *Iris*

■ **DESCRIPTION** Television production of the play. It was unfortunate that this lifeless, traditional studio version should appear at roughly the same time as Derek Jarman's complete re-imagining of the same play. An elderly Prospero, an insipid Miranda, no feeling for magic or fantasy, in essence a blind denial of the play's imaginative power. There is an audience for those who want a simple, undemanding reading of the play, but really such television productions should now be a thing of the past.

TEMPEST, The

■ GB • 1983

■ *Shakespeare Lives*

d	Mary McMurray
pc	Quintet Films
tx	16 February 1983 (C4) [part one]
	23 February 1983 (C4) [part two]
p	Victor Glynn/Mike Ockrent

NFTVA preservation material
1" col sd c30+30mins

■ **CAST**

Michael Bryant . . . . *Prospero*
Clive Arrindell
Suzanne Bertish
Joss Buckley
John Darrell
John Labanowski
Dinsdale Landen
Bill Wallis

■ **DESCRIPTION** Television theatre workshop, broadcast in two parts. Michael Bogdanov guides a group of National Theatre actors through aspects of *The Tempest* with contributions from a studio audience. One of a lively and stimulating series; Bogdanov asks if the play is merely a magical fantasy or an exploration of illusion and reality, a dream of political and sexual power.

■ **NOTES** Other plays covered in this series are *Hamlet*, *Measure for Measure*, *The Taming of the Shrew* and *Timon of Athens* (qqv).

KNOT GARDEN, The

■ GB • 1985

d	Derek Bailey/David Freeman
stage d	David Freeman
pc	Landseer
tx	6 October 1985 (C4)
m	Michael Tippett

NFTVA viewing copy
½" col sd 93mins

■ **CAST**

Tom McDonnell . . . . *Faber*

Christine Botes . . . . *Thea*
Janis Kelly . . . . *Flora*
Marie Angel . . . . *Denise*
Omar Ebrahim . . . . *Mel*
Nigel Robson . . . . *Dov*
Philip Doghan . . . . *Mangus*

■ **DESCRIPTION** Television production of Sir Michael Tippett's opera, with the London Sinfonietta conducted by Howard Williams. Intense, austere work which, in fragmented scenes, shows the strained inter-relationships between seven characters. Ultimately they discover acceptance and reconciliation after the central figure Mangus suggests they perform a series of charades, based on the characters from *The Tempest*. Following this scheme, Mangus is Prospero, Flora Miranda, Mel Caliban, Dov Ariel, and Faber Ferdinand.

(SIR PETER HALL DIRECTS SHAKESPEARE'S LAST PLAYS)

■ GB • 1988

■ *South Bank Show*

d/p	Chris Hunt
pc	London Weekend Television
tx	24 April 1988 (ITV)
ed/pres	Melvyn Bragg

NFTVA viewing copy
½" col sd 55mins

■ **CAST**

Michael Bryant . . . . *Prospero*
Jennifer Caron Hall . . . . *Miranda*
Tony Haygarth . . . . *Caliban*
Tim Pigott-Smith . . . . *Trinculo*
John Bluthal . . . . *Stephano*

■ **DESCRIPTION** Television arts documentary. Engrossing account of Sir Peter Hall's final productions as director of the National Theatre, *Cymbeline*, *The Winter's Tale* and *The Tempest*, using the same group of actors throughout and showing preparations from first read-through to final dress rehearsal. From *The Tempest*, rehearsals for scenes A2S2 and A3S2, plus the epilogue, are shown in some detail, with comments from actors and director. There are also brief extracts from Hall's

1973 production of *The Tempest* derived from material taken for the 1976 television programme YOUR NATIONAL THEATRE (see above). For further details of programme see entries under *Cymbeline* and *The Winter's Tale*.

PROSPERO'S BOOKS

■ **GB/Netherlands/France/Italy • 1991**

d/sc	Peter Greenaway
pc	Allarts/Camera One/Cinéa/Penta
p	Kees Kasander
ph	Sacha Vierny
p des	Ben van Os/Jan Roelfs
art d	Eljo Embregts/Wilma Schuemie
m	Michael Nyman

NFTVA viewing copy
½" col sd 120mins

■ **CAST**

John Gielgud . . . . *Prospero*
Michael Clark . . . . *Caliban*
Michel Blanc . . . . *Alonso*
Erland Josephson . . . . *Gonzalo*
Isabelle Pasco . . . . *Miranda*
Tom Bell . . . . *Antonio*
Kenneth Cranham . . . . *Sebastian*
Mark Rylance . . . . *Ferdinand*
Gérard Thoolen . . . . *Adrian*
Pierre Bokma . . . . *Francisco*
Jim van der Woude . . . . *Trinculo*
Michiel Romeyn . . . . *Stephano*
Orphéo/Paul Russell/James Thierree/
    Emil Wolk . . . . *Ariel*
Marie Angel . . . . *Iris*
Ute Lemper . . . . *Ceres*
Deborah Conway . . . . *Juno*

■ **DESCRIPTION** Feature film. A bold re-imagining of *The Tempest* based around speculative notions of the contents of Prospero's books and the establishment theatrical figure of Sir John Gielgud, and making use of some dazzling computer-generated imagery. Gielgud speaks all the parts to begin with, but gradually, as matters are resolved, the characters regain their own voices. An extraordinary re-ordering and interpretation of the play. Or a pretentious, foolish and shallow nonsense that has none of the insight its multi-layered style seeks to suggest, a dull embarrassment which only works when the music takes over.

■ **NOTES** According to Greenaway, Prospero's books (the twenty-four books given to him by Gonzalo before his exile) were: *The Book of Water*, *A Book of Mirrors*, *A Book of Mythologies*, *A Primer of the Small Stars*, *An Atlas Belonging to Orpheus*, *A Harsh Book of Geometry*, *The Book of Colours*, *The Vesalius Anatomy of Birth*, *An Alphabetical Inventory of the Dead*, *A Book of Travellers' Tales*, *The Book of the Earth*, *A Book of Architecture and Other Music*, *The Ninety-Two Conceits of the Minotaur*, *The Book of Languages*, *End-plants*, *A Book of Love*, *A Bestiary of Past, Present and Future Animals*, *The Book of Utopias*, *The Book of Universal Cosmography*, *Love of Ruins*, *The Autobiographies of Pasiphae and Semiramis*, *A Book of Motion*, *The Book of Games*, and *Thirty-Six Plays* (the latter volume with nineteen pages left blank at the front for the inclusion of the first play, *The Tempest*).

■ **REFERENCES** • Peter Greenaway, *Prospero's Books: A Film of Shakespeare's The Tempest* (London: Chatto & Windus, 1991).

PETER GREENAWAY: ANATOMY OF A FILM-MAKER

■ **GB • 1991**

■ *Omnibus*

pc	BBC
tx	13 September 1991 (BBC1)
p	David Thompson

NFTVA viewing copy
½" col sd 50mins

■ **DESCRIPTION** Television arts documentary. Documentary on film-maker Peter Greenaway, with special reference to his recently released feature film PROSPERO'S BOOKS, a bold re-interpretation of *The Tempest* (see above) with John Gielgud as Prospero. The programme covers Greenaway's unique approach to film construction and narrative, showing how computer technology was employed in PROSPERO'S BOOKS and how the film was built around Gielgud's abilities and reputation.

■ **NOTES** The NFTVA also holds the complete Greenaway interview rushes for the programme.

TEMPEST

LATE SHOW SPECIAL

■ **GB • 1992**

pc	BBC
tx	24 September 1992 (BBC2)
p	David Thompson
pres	Tracey MacLeod

NFTVA viewing copy
½" col sd 39mins

■ **CAST**
Brian Pettifer. . . . . *Prospero*
Mark Hadfield . . . . *Galileo*

■ **DESCRIPTION** Television arts and media magazine. Documentary on the career of British filmmaker Michael Powell to coincide with the posthumous publication of the second volume of his memoirs. Covers Powell's career from THE RED SHOES (1948) onwards, including the period in the 1970s when he tried in vain to raise finance for his version of *The Tempest*. Illustrating this is a short, flat, dramatised sequence from the script prepared by Powell, featuring Prospero and Galileo (!).

■ **NOTES** Michael Powell first contemplated a film of *The Tempest* in 1952 with John Gielgud as Prospero and Moira Shearer as Ariel. The idea came up again during the production of AGE OF CONSENT (1969, see above), when James Mason was proposed as Prospero and Mia Farrow as Ariel, but the necessary finance was never forthcoming.

■ **REFERENCES** • Michael Powell, *Million-Dollar Movie* (London: Heinemann, 1992), pp. 515–20.

TIMON OF ATHENS

TIMON OF ATHENS

■ **GB • 1983**

■ *Shakespeare Lives*

d	Mary McMurray

Daniel Massey as Timon in the TIMON OF ATHENS edition of *Shakespeare Lives* (1981)

pc	Quintet Films
tx	19 January 1983 (C4) [part one]
	26 January 1983 (C4) [part two]
p	Victor Glover/Mike Ockrent

NFTVA preservation material
1" col sd c30+30mins

■ **CAST**
Daniel Massey . . . . *Timon*
Clive Arrindell
Joss Buckley
John Darrell
John Labanowski
Bill Wallis

■ **DESCRIPTION** Television theatre workshop, broadcast in two parts. Michael Bogdanov guides a group of National Theatre actors through aspects of *Timon of Athens*, with contributions from a studio audience. One in a lively, stimulating series; Bogdanov analyses a neglected play, showing that behind the seeming barrier of the language are timeless themes of betrayal and the corruption that money brings.

■ **NOTES** Other plays covered in this series are *Hamlet, Measure for Measure, Richard III, The Taming of the Shrew* and *The Tempest* (qqv).

Vincent Price as Lionheart forcing Robert Morley's Merridew to eat his pet poodles in THEATRE OF BLOOD (1973)

TITUS ANDRONICUS

THEATRE OF BLOOD

■ GB • 1973

d	Douglas Hickox
pc	Cineman

NFTVA preservation material

■ **CAST**

Vincent Price . . . . *Edward Lionheart*
Robert Morley . . . . *Meredith Merridew*

■ **DESCRIPTION** Feature film. An actor (Vincent Price) murders his critics in the manner of deaths from Shakespeare's plays. In a parody of Tamora's eating of her children, Meredith Merridew, imagining that he is taking part in the programme *This is Your Dish*, is served up his own poodles. He is then choked to death with the food. For full details of the film see entry in General section.

TITUS ANDRONICUS

■ **GB/USA** • 1985

■ *BBC Television Shakespeare*

d	Jane Howell
pc	BBC/Time-Life Films
tx (GB)	27 April 1985 (BBC2)
tx (US)	19 April 1985 (PBS)
p	Shaun Sutton
lght	Sam Barclay
des	Tony Burrough
cost	Colin Lavers
m	Dudley Simpson

NFTVA preservation material
1" col sd 150mins

■ **CAST**

Paul Davies-Prowles . . . . *Young Lucius*
Edward Hardwicke . . . . *Marcus*
Walter Brown . . . . *Aemilius*
Brian Protheroe . . . . *Saturninus*
Nicholas Gecks . . . . *Bassianus*
Derek Fuke . . . . *Captain / Third Goth*
Eileen Atkins . . . . *Tamora*
Neil McCaul . . . . *Demetrius*
Michael Crompton . . . . *Chiron*
Hugh Quarshie . . . . *Aaron*
Gavin Richards . . . . *Lucius*
Crispin Redman . . . . *Quintus*
Tom Hunsinger . . . . *Martius*
Michael Packer . . . . *Mutius*
Trevor Peacock . . . . *Titus*
Anna Calder-Marshall . . . . *Lavinia*
Paul Kelly . . . . *Publius / Second Goth*
Deddie Davies . . . . *Nurse*
Tim Potter . . . . *Clown*
John Benfield . . . . *First Goth / Caius*
Peter Searles . . . . *Fourth Goth / Valentine*

■ **DESCRIPTION** Television production of the play. One of the finest titles from the BBC series, bringing a little known work to full attention and doing it full justice in the presentation. Accurately pinpointing both the horror and the humour, a well-chosen cast play their parts with relish while never making the play seem ridiculous. Most impressive is Hugh Quarshie's wholly villainous Aaron. Fast-moving and genuinely horrific, it also finds space for poetry.

■ **REFERENCES** • Mary Z. Maher, 'Production Design in the BBC's *Titus Andronicus*', in Bulman and Coursen, *Shakespeare on Television*, pp. 144–50. • Willis, *The BBC Shakespeare Plays*, pp. 292–313.

EVENING STANDARD DRAMA AWARDS 1988, The

■ GB • 1988

d/p	Daniel Wiles/Paddy Haycocks
pc	London Weekend Television
tx	18 November 1988 (ITV)
pres	Melvyn Bragg

NFTVA viewing copy
½" col sd 52mins

■ CAST
Brian Cox . . . . *Titus Andronicus*
Sonia Ritter . . . . *Lavinia*
Jim Hooper . . . . *Saturninus*
Estelle Kohler . . . . *Tamora*

■ **DESCRIPTION** Television coverage of drama awards for the best in British drama over the past year. Includes a specially filmed extract on the Barbican stage from the Royal Shakespeare Company's production of *Titus Andronicus* (A5S3), directed by Deborah Warner (who receives the award for Best Director).

AT LEISURE

■ GB • 1993

■ *Sign On*

d/p	Rob Cowley
pc	Tyne Tees
tx	27 March 1993 (C4)

NFTVA viewing copy
½" col sd 24mins

■ **DESCRIPTION** Television programme offering information for the deaf. Includes a five-minute item reporting on a production of *Titus Andronicus* at the Octagon Theatre, Bolton, put on by a deaf and hearing cast. Brief interviews with artistic director Lawrence Till, other production staff, and actresses Paula Garfield (wholly deaf) and Julie Finlay (partially deaf), plus scenes of the play in rehearsal.

■ **NOTES** The production ran at the Octagon from 25 March to 10 April 1993. The pro-

gramme commentary is given in subtitles and voice-over, with British Sign Language from the presenters.

Anton Lesser as Troilus in TROILUS AND CRESSIDA (1981)

TROILUS AND CRESSIDA

THEATRE OF BLOOD

■ GB • 1973

d	Douglas Hickox
pc	Cineman

NFTVA preservation material

■ CAST
Vincent Price . . . . *Edward Lionheart*
Dennis Price . . . . *Hector Snipe*

■ **DESCRIPTION** Feature film. An actor (Vincent Price) murders his critics in the manner of deaths from Shakespeare's plays. Hector Snipe is lured to a theatre, fooled into believing that he is with friends, then like Hector is stabbed through by a spear and dragged down a road by a horse. For full details of the film see entry in General section.

TROILUS AND CRESSIDA

■ **GB/USA 1981**

■ *BBC Television Shakespeare*

d/p	Jonathan Miller
pc	BBC/Time-Life
tx (GB)	7 November 1981 (BBC2)
tx (US)	17 May 1982 (PBS)
sc ed	David Snodin
lght	Dennis Channon
des	Colin Lowrey
cost	Alun Hughes
m	Stephen Oliver

NFTVA viewing copy
16mm col sd c6,500ft 180mins

■ **CAST**

Charles Gray	Pandarus
Anton Lesser	Troilus
Tony Steedman	Aeneas
Suzanne Burden	Cressida
Max Harvey	Alexander
Peter Walmsley	Servant to Troilus
Vernon Dobtcheff	Agamemnon
Geoffrey Chater	Nestor
Benjamin Whitrow	Ulysses
Bernard Brown	Menelaus
Anthony Pedley	Ajax
The Incredible Orlando [Jack Birkett]	Thersites
Kenneth Haigh	Achilles
Simon Cutter	Patroclus
Esmond Knight	Priam
John Shrapnel	Hector
Elayne Sharling	Cassandra
David Firth	Paris
Paul Moriarty	Diomedes
David Kinsey	Servant to Paris
Ann Pennington	Helen
Peter Whitbread	Calchas
Merelina Kendall	Andromache
Cornelius Garrett	Margarelon
Tony Portacio	Helenus
Peter J. Cassell	Deiphobus

■ **DESCRIPTION** Television production of the play. Satisfactory presentation of a difficult play, with some rich characterisations from a well-chosen cast. Lesser and Burden make an effective pair of lovers and the outrageous Jack Birkett (Caliban in Derek Jarman's 1979 THE TEMPEST, qv) is unforgettable.

■ **REFERENCES** • Willis, *The BBC Shakespeare Plays*, pp. 229–59.

Richard Briers as Malvolio in TWELFTH NIGHT (1988)

TWELFTH NIGHT

TWELFTH NIGHT

■ **USA • 1910**

d	Charles Kent
pc	Vitagraph Company of America
p	J. Stuart Blackton

NFTVA viewing copy
35mm bw st 735ft 8mins
Incomplete – original length 970ft
English titles

■ **CAST**

Florence Turner	Viola
Charles Kent	Malvolio
Julia Swayne Gordon	Olivia
Tefft Johnson	Orsino
Edith Storey [?]	Sebastian
Marin Sais [?]	Maria
William Humphrey [?]	Toby Belch
James Young [?]	Andrew Aguecheek

DESCRIPTION Abbreviated version of the play. A charming interpretation, as with the other Vitagraph Shakespeares cluttered with too much plot, but with some strong individual scenes, notably Malvolio's reading of the letter. There are three very good performances: Florence Turner's perky Viola, an unidentified actress (Maris Sais?) having considerable fun as Maria, and Charles Kent in his every movement epitomising Malvolio's pomposity. As in Vitagraph's A MID-SUMMER NIGHT'S DREAM (1909, qv) the outside settings are refreshing.

NOTES The NFTVA's print has some scenes missing and some apparently out of order, as detailed by Ball. Identification of some of the actors is uncertain.

REFERENCES • Ball, *Shakespeare on Silent Film*, pp. 56–60, 314.

TWELFTH NIGHT

GB • 1916

■ *Gaumont Graphic 555*

pc	Gaumont
rel date	17 July 1916

NFTVA preservation material
35mm bw st 53ft 1min
English titles

DESCRIPTION Newsreel item. Nurses and wounded soldiers at Bournbrook Military Hospital in Birmingham watch an open air performance of *Twelfth Night*.

IMMORTAL GENTLEMAN, The

GB • 1935

d	Widgey R. Newman
pc	Bernard Smith

NFTVA viewing copy

CAST
Basil Gill . . . . *Malvolio*
Laidman Browne . . . . *Feste*

Dennis Hoey . . . . *Toby Belch*
Ivan Berlyn . . . . *Aguecheek*
Anne Bolt . . . . *Maria*

DESCRIPTION Feature film. Shakespeare and his friends meet in a Southwark tavern and their reminiscences give rise to sequences from Shakespeare's plays. Includes a discussion on drunkenness which leads to the kitchen scene from *Twelfth Night* (A2S3) with Feste, Belch, Aguecheek and Maria; Feste sings 'O Mistress Mine!' and Malvolio comes to admonish them. For full details of the film see entry in General section.

THIS IS CHARLES LAUGHTON

USA • 1953

pc	Sherman Harris
p	Gregory Paul

NFTVA preservation material
16mm bw sd 2,798ft 77mins

CAST
Charles Laughton . . . . *Orsino*

DESCRIPTION Television programme. Charles Laughton recites from the Bible and other texts, reads some poetry, tells stories and jokes. Includes a reading from *Twelfth Night* with Laughton as Orsino speaking to Viola. Transmission date not known.

NOTES The original television series (first tx 13 January 1953) was broadcast in 15-minute segments.

TWELFTH NIGHT

USA • 1957

■ *Hallmark Hall of Fame*

d	David Greene
pc	NBC
tx	15 December 1957 (NBC)
p	Robert Hartung
adapt	William Nichols
lght	William Knight

des   Rouben Ter-Arutunian
m   Lehman Engel

NFTVA preservation material
16mm bw sd 3,212ft 89mins

■ **CAST**

Maurice Evans . . . . *Malvolio*
Rosemary Harris . . . . *Viola*
Dennis King . . . . *Sir Toby Belch*
Denholm Elliott . . . . *Sebastian*
Max Adrian . . . . *Sir Anthony Aguecheek*
Frances Hyland . . . . *Olivia*
Howard Morris . . . . *Feste*
Alice Ghostley . . . . *Maria*
Gregory Morton . . . . *Antonio*
William Cottrell . . . . *Sea captain*

■ **DESCRIPTION** Television production of the
play. A rather more boldly imaginative production from the *Hallmark* series, with deliberately
artificial sets, Feste turned into a mime, and
Malvolio succumbing to an explosion when he
promises his revenge at the end. The programme
enjoys all the virtues and vices of live television
drama, and the telerecording is out of sync, but it
remains exciting to watch and Rosemary Harris is
charming.

TWELFTH NIGHT; NO. 1: HIS VERY GENIUS

■ **GB • 1959**

d   Peter Robinson
pc   Rediffusion
tx   21 January 1959 (ITV)
sc   Martin Worth
education
officer   Alan Nicholson
pres   John Westbrook

NFTVA preservation material
16mm bw sd 940ft 26mins

■ **CAST**

George A. Cooper . . . . *Sir Toby*
Geoffrey Bayldon . . . . *Sir Andrew*
Gillian Raine . . . . *Olivia*
Prunella Scales . . . . *Maria*
Terence Soall . . . . *Feste*
Peter Vaughan . . . . *Malvolio*

■ **DESCRIPTION** Television schools programme.
'We see how William Shakespeare, living and
working in Elizabethan London, conceived a
group of characters who are as real and lively now
as the day *Twelfth Night* was first presented, more
than 350 years ago' (*TV Times*). First in an imagi-
natively produced series of eight programmes,
this shows the kitchen scene (A2S3) where
Malvolio interrupts the revellers.

■ **NOTES** Subsequent programmes in the series
(not in the NFTVA) were 2: THIS IS ILLYRIA,
LADY; 3: O SPIRIT OF LOVE; 4: CAKES AND
ALE; 5: A KIND OF PURITAN; 6: PER-
CHANCE HE IS NOT DROWNED; 7: THE
WIND AND THE RAIN; and 8: PLAYED
UPON A STAGE. Richard Gale played Orsino,
Gillian Raine played Olivia and Sally Home
played Viola. The series was then followed by a
production of an abridged version of the play (tx
18 March 1959, not in NFTVA) directed by
Roger Jenkins with an entirely different cast,
except for Sally Home as Viola; John Wood was
Malvolio and Emrys James was Feste.

SHAKESPEARE WALLAH

■ **India • 1965**

d   James Ivory
pc   Merchant-Ivory Productions

NFTVA viewing copy

■ **CAST**

Laura Liddell . . . . *Gertrude*
Geoffrey Kendal . . . . *Malvolio*
Felicity Kendal . . . . *Maria*
Prayag Raaj . . . . *Feste*

■ **DESCRIPTION** Feature film about a troupe of
English actors in India. Includes a performance of
the cross-gartering scene from *Twelfth Night*
(A3S4), plus Feste's final song seen from the
wings. For full details of the film see entry in
General section.

PREPARING A PLAY; NO. 3: MOVEMENT

■ **GB • 1966**

d   Richard Gilbert

pc	Rediffusion
tx	5 October 1966 (ITV)
p	Charles Warren
sc	Alexander Franklin
des	Sylva Nadolny
education officer	Fernau Hall
pres	Mike Hall

NFTVA preservation material
16mm bw sd 957ft 26mins

■ **CAST**
Trevor Martin . . . . *Sir Toby Belch*
Jonathan Elsom . . . . *Sir Andrew Aguecheek*
William Ingram . . . . *Feste*
Kate Lansbury . . . . *Maria*
Christopher Benjamin . . . . *Malvolio*
Terence Woodfield . . . . *Fabian*

■ **DESCRIPTION** Television schools programme. Third in a series of five programmes 'for 13-year-olds and over' on the preparations involved for a production of *Twelfth Night*, from read-through to performance in front of an audience. This programme shows how actors employ movements to establish characterisation and the mood of a scene.

■ **NOTES** The other programmes in the series (not in NFTVA) were 1: THE STAGE; 2: FIRST STEPS; 4: SETTING THE PACE; and 5: DRESS REHEARSAL. Viola, Orsino and Olivia do not appear. The series then continued covering subjects other than Shakespeare.

PHOENIX AND THE TURTLE, The

■ **GB • 1972**

d/ed/m/p	Luigi V. R. Chiappini
pc	Milon Films
sc	David Pownall
ph	Alec Sheridan/ Trevor Wrenn/Ken Coles

NFTVA viewing copy
16mm col sd 2,160ft 60mins

■ **DESCRIPTION** Documentary showing the work of the Century Theatre Company as they tour the north-west of England with their mobile playhouse. Includes rehearsals for a production of *Twelfth Night* at Richmond, Yorkshire. Actors are seen dressing, some in American Indian costume, in dress rehearsal (with one man on a swing), and being addressed by director Nicholas Kent and artistic director Peter Oyston. Outside rehearsals of the swordfight between Viola and Aguecheek (A3S4) intercut with the dress rehearsals. Other plays shown in rehearsal and production as part of the tour are *How to Grow a Guerilla* and *Moby Dick*.

(KEN DODD: COMEDIAN)

■ **GB • 1978**

■ *South Bank Show*

d/p	Tony Cash
pc	London Weekend Television
tx	11 March 1978 (ITV)
ed/pres	Melvyn Bragg

NFTVA viewing copy
½" col sd 30mins

■ **CAST**
Ken Dodd . . . . *Malvolio*

■ **DESCRIPTION** Television arts documentary. A profile of comedian Ken Dodd, who talks to Melvyn Bragg about his career and his theories of humour. Includes Dodd in performance at the Manchester Palace Theatre, and reproducing his one 'straight' role as Malvolio specially for the programme, where Malvolio finds the letter (A2S5). Dodd comments on playing the role.

■ **NOTES** The NFTVA's copy was recorded 14 March 1992 as part of the *TV Heaven* series and does not include the general arts review from the second half of the programme.

TWELFTH NIGHT: OR, WHAT YOU WILL

■ **GB/USA 1980**

■ *BBC Television Shakespeare*

d	John Gorrie

pc	BBC/Time-Life Films
tx (GB)	6 January 1980 (BBC2)
tx (US)	27 February 1980 (PBS)
p	Cedric Messina
sc ed	Alan Shallcross
lght	John Summers
des	Don Taylor
cost	Alun Hughes

NFTVA preservation material
1" col sd 130mins

■ **CAST**

Alec McCowen . . . . *Malvolio*
Felicity Kendal . . . . *Viola*
Sinead Cusack . . . . *Olivia*
Annette Crosbie . . . . *Maria*
Robert Hardy . . . . *Sir Toby Belch*
Clive Arrindell . . . . *Orsino*
Ryan Michael . . . . *Curio*
Malcolm Reynolds . . . . *Valentine*
Ric Morgan . . . . *Sea captain*
Ronnie Stevens . . . . *Sir Andrew Aguecheek*
Trevor Peacock . . . . *Feste*
Robert Lindsay . . . . *Fabian*
Daniel Webb . . . . *Servant*
Jean Channon . . . . *Waiting woman*
Michael Thomas . . . . *Sebastian*
Maurice Roëves . . . . *Antonio*
Andrew Maclachlan . . . . *First officer*
Peter Holt . . . . *Second officer*
Arthur Hewlett . . . . *Priest*

■ **DESCRIPTION** Television production of the play. Wholly delightful and perfectly cast, the very best of the *BBC Television Shakespeare* series. Three of the leading players (Kendal, Hardy, Lindsay) were fresh from popular television series, providing a hopeful lure for the mass audience, but the good humour, the warm, happy characterisations and the melancholic undertone throughout would hold anybody. The outstanding figure, however, is Alec McCowen's text-book Malvolio, narcissistic, proud, and greatly pitiable. Filmed in the studio in a country house setting, the production suggests both Elizabethan England and a place out of time. Overall, it achieves that optimum stage performance that the BBC series sought so often to reproduce, so often failing. The only blot on all this is that the stage stairs creak. First broadcast on Twelfth Night itself, and a perfect celebration.

CAUGHT IN THE ACT

■ **GB • 1988**

d/p	Mary Gwatkin
pc	Reconnaissance Films/MV Films
tx	26 December 1988 (C4)

NFTVA viewing copy

■ **DESCRIPTION** Television documentary on the work of Kenneth Branagh's Renaissance Theatre Company, in particular its three touring productions of *As You Like It*, *Hamlet* and *Much Ado About Nothing*. Also includes references to the Riverside Studios production of *Twelfth Night*, directed by Branagh, televised four days after this programme (see below). For full details of the programme see entry in General section.

TWELFTH NIGHT

■ **GB • 1988**

d/p	Paul Kafno
pc	Thames Television
tx	30 December 1988 (C4)
Original stage production:	
d	Kenneth Branagh
p	David Parfitt
des	Bunny Christie
m	Paul McCartney/Pat Doyle

NFTVA viewing copy
½" col sd 156mins

■ **CAST**

Richard Briers . . . . *Malvolio*
Frances Barber . . . . *Viola*
Caroline Langrishe . . . . *Olivia*
Anton Lesser . . . . *Feste*
Tim Barker . . . . *Sea captain/Antonio*
Christopher Ravenscroft . . . . *Orsino*
Christopher Hollis . . . . *Curio/Sebastian*
Julian Gartside . . . . *Valentine*
James Saxon . . . . *Sir Toby Belch*
Abigail McKern . . . . *Maria*
James Simmons . . . . *Andrew Aguecheek*
Shaun Prendergast . . . . *Fabian*

■ **DESCRIPTION** Television version of the Renaissance Theatre Company's production of the play, originally directed by Kenneth Branagh at the Riverside Studios. A wintry studio setting determines the tone for this production, with melancholy and Richard Briers' sad Malvolio to the fore. The cast is not as strong as the BBC production above, and where that revealed the play's riches to the full, here the play is made to seem somewhat less than it is, a catalogue of opportunities only half taken. Briers, best known for his light comedy roles and adept at playing Ayckbourn and Shaw, does not quite provide the depth at its centre that the play needs. Anton Lesser's sober Feste is striking, but appears to have never been happy.

■ **NOTES** The production was first staged at the Riverside Studios, Hammersmith. The programme CAUGHT IN THE ACT (1988, see above and General section) documents the period when the Renaissance Theatre Company produced this play and the touring productions of *As You Like It*, *Hamlet* and *Much Ado About Nothing*.

Tessa Peake-Jones as Julia in TWO GENTLEMEN OF VERONA (1983)

TWO GENTLEMEN OF VERONA

TWO GENTLEMEN OF VERONA

■ **GB/USA 1983**

■ *BBC Television Shakespeare*

d	Don Taylor
pc	BBC/Time-Life Films
tx (GB)	27 December 1983 (BBC2)
tx (US)	23 April 1984 (PBS)
p	Shaun Sutton
lght	Sam Barclay
des	Barbara Gosnold
cost	Dinah Collin
m	Anthony Hooley

NFTVA preservation material
1" col sd 135mins

■ **CAST**
Frank Barrie . . . . *Sir Eglamour*
Tessa Peake-Jones . . . . *Julia*
Hetta Charnley . . . . *Lucetta*
Tyler Butterworth . . . . *Proteus*
John Hudson . . . . *Valentine*
Nicholas Kaby . . . . *Speed*

Michael Byrne . . . . *Antonio*
John Woodnutt . . . . *Panthino*
Joanne Pearce . . . . *Silvia*
Tony Haygarth . . . . *Launce*
Bella . . . . *Crab*
David Collings . . . . *Thurio*
Paul Daneman . . . . *Duke of Milan*
Daniel Flynn . . . . *Servant*
Charlotte Richardson/Jonathan Taylor . . . *Cupids*
Bill Badley/Tom Finucane/Robin Jeffrey *Lutenists*
Adam Kurakin . . . . *First outlaw*
John Baxter . . . . *Second outlaw*
Andrew Burt . . . . *Third outlaw*
Michael Graham Cox . . . . *Host*

■ **DESCRIPTION** Television production of the play. Adequate presentation of an unfamiliar work. Few tricks are played to make it more presentable, and in this instance the plain BBC style is best suited to giving the play its due. Lighting and music similarly sugar the pill, and Joanne Pearce delights as Silvia.

WINTER'S TALE

TRAGEDIA ALLA CORTE DI SICILIA, Una

Jeremy Kemp as Leontes in THE WINTER'S TALE (1981)

Alternative title NOVELLA D'INVERNO: UNA NOVELLA DI SHAKESPEARE
GB title WINTER'S TALE, The
GB re-issue title LOST PRINCESS, The

■ Italy • 1914

d	Baldassare Negroni
pc	Milano Films

NFTVA viewing copy
35mm bw st 2,900ft 32mins
English titles

■ CAST
Pina Fabbri . . . . *Paulina*
V. Cocchi . . . . *Leontes, King of Sicilia*

■ DESCRIPTION
Abbreviated version of the play. William Shakespeare reads *The Winter's Tale* to a group of friends. The plot and intertitles which follow are given in detail by Ball. The story is substantially that of the play, but Autolycus is cut out, there is no pursuit by a bear (Antigonus is instead thrown into a volcano) and Hermione is shown to be seemingly dead and not a statue, an unfortunate omission as it would have been an ideal gesture for a silent cinema version. The film concludes with Shakespeare's audience applauding him. An admirably clear interpretation, using some impressively large sets and attractive location work. There is enough romance and poetry to have pleased the contemporary audience with something a little out of the ordinary.

■ NOTES
The NFTVA's copy is the 1919 British re-issue. The various titles under which the film may have been known are detailed by Ball; the two British titles given above are for the British releases of 1914 and 1919. Aldo Bernardini, in his *Archivio del Cinema Italiano: Volume 1 — Il Cinema Muto* (1991), gives the original Italian title as UNA TRAGEDIA ALLA CORTE DI SPAGNA without further explanation.

■ REFERENCES
Ball, *Shakespeare on Silent Film*, pp. 170–6, 347.

WINTER'S TALE, The

■ GB • 1966

d	Fred Dunlop
pc	Cressida Film Productions/ Hurst Park
p	Peter Snell
ph	Oswald Morris
p des	Carl Toms
m	Jim Dale/Anthony Bowles

NFTVA preservation material
35mm col sd 13,581ft 151mins

■ CAST
Laurence Harvey . . . . *Leontes*
Jane Asher . . . . *Perdita*
Diana Churchill . . . . *Paulina*
Moira Redmond . . . . *Hermione*
Jim Dale . . . . *Autolycus*
Esmond Knight . . . . *Camillo*
Richard Gale . . . . *Polixenes*
David Weston . . . . *Florizel/Archidamas*
John Gray . . . . *Clown*
Edward Dewsbury . . . . *Old Shepherd/Gaoler*
Michael Murray . . . . *Paulina's steward*
Allan Foss . . . . *Antigonus*
Cherry Morris . . . . *Emilia*
Monica Maughan . . . . *Lady*
Joy Ring . . . . *Mopsa*
Joanna Wake . . . . *Dorcas*

Dan Caulfield . . . . *Lord*
Terry Palmer . . . . *Cleomines*
Frank Barry . . . . *Mamillius*
Charmian Eyre . . . . *Shepherd servant*

■ **DESCRIPTION** Feature film. A literal recording of Frank Dunlop's 1966 'Pop Theatre' Edinburgh Festival production. Why it was considered worthwhile to record such a mundane production in a manner that suggests the recording of a unique theatrical experience is hard to fathom. It is gloomily lit, the colour is poor, the film technique basic to the point of crudeness. The indifferent performances give no further clue.

WINTER'S TALE, The

■ **GB/USA • 1981**

■ *BBC Television Shakespeare*

d	Jane Howell
pc	BBC/Time-Life Films
tx (GB)	8 February 1981 (BBC2)
tx (US)	8 June 1981 (PBS)
p	Jonathan Miller
sc ed	David Snodin
lght	Sam Barclay
des	Don Homfray
cost	John Peacock
m	Dudley Simpson

NFTVA preservation material
1" col sd 185mins

■ **CAST**
John Welsh . . . . *Archidamus*
David Burke . . . . *Camillo*
Robert Stephens . . . . *Polixenes*
Jeremy Kemp . . . . *Leontes*
Anna Calder-Marshall . . . . *Hermione*
Jeremy Dimmick . . . . *Mamillius*
Merelina Kendall . . . . *Emilia*
Susan Brodrick . . . . *Second lady*
Leonard Kavanagh/John Bailey/
  William Relton . . . . *Lords to Leontes*
Cyril Luckham . . . . *Antigonus*
Margaret Tyzack . . . . *Paulina*
John Benfield . . . . *Jailer/Mariner*
Cornelius Garrett . . . . *Servant to Leontes*
John Curless . . . . *Cleomenes*
Colin McCormack . . . . *Dion*

Emrys Leyshon . . . . *Court official*
Arthur Hewlett . . . . *Shepherd*
Paul Jesson . . . . *Clown*
Harold Goldblatt . . . . *Time*
Rikki Fulton . . . . *Autolycus*
Robin Kermode . . . . *Florizel*
Debbie Farrington . . . . *Perdita*
Janette Legge . . . . *Dorcas*
Maggie Wells . . . . *Mopsa*
Peter Benson . . . . *Clown's servant*
George Howe . . . . *Paulina's steward*

■ **DESCRIPTION** Television production of the play. The BBC series, which failed so signally with *The Tempest*, a year later got everything right with that play's companion piece *The Winter's Tale*. Filmed in the studio with very spare, abstract sets, yet still evoking a strong sense of the pastoral, this is a beautifully judged production. Comedian Rikki Fulton revels in his role in particular. In one funny sequence a player addresses the camera in the standard form for asides, leaving a baffled Autolycus wondering just to whom is he talking. Such witty gestures should have been more in evidence in the series.

(SIR PETER HALL DIRECTS SHAKESPEARE'S LAST PLAYS)

■ **GB • 1988**

■ *South Bank Show*

d/p	Chris Hunt
pc	London Weekend Television
tx	24 April 1988 (ITV)
ed/pres	Melvyn Bragg

NFTVA viewing copy
½" col sd 55mins

■ **CAST**
Tim Pigott-Smith . . . . *Leontes*
Sally Dexter . . . . *Hermione*
Peter Woodward . . . . *Polixenes*
Eileen Atkins . . . . *Paulina*
Basil Henson . . . . *Camillo*

■ **DESCRIPTION** Television arts documentary. Engrossing account of Sir Peter Hall's final productions as director of the National Theatre,

Cymbeline, *The Winter's Tale* and *The Tempest*, using the same group of actors throughout and showing preparations from first read-through to final dress rehearsal. From *The Winter's Tale*, rehearsals for scenes A1S2, A3S2 and A5S5 are shown in some detail, with comments from actors and director. For further details of the programme see entries under *Cymbeline* and *The Tempest*.

ENTERTAINMENT UK

■ **GB** • **1992**

pc	Mentorn Films
tx	25 August 1992 (ITV)
p	Victoria Bridges

NFTVA viewing copy
½" col sd 56mins

■ **CAST**
Richard McCabe . . . . *Autolycus*
Graham Turner . . . . *Clown*

■ **DESCRIPTION** Television arts and entertainment magazine. Includes a three-minute item on Adrian Noble's production of *The Winter's Tale* at the Royal Shakespeare Theatre, Stratford, including an extract with Richard McCabe as Autolycus and Graham Turner as the Clown (A4S2). The actors are interviewed.

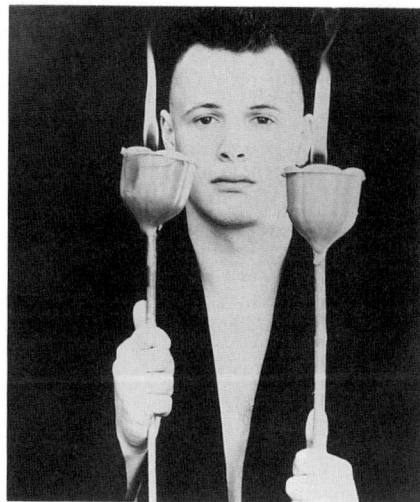

Derek Jarman's THE ANGELIC CONVERSATION (1985)

CHAPTER AND VERSE

■ **GB** • **1936**

d	Stanley Hawes
pc	Strand Film Company
spon	National Book Council
p	Paul Rotha
ph	George Noble

NFTVA viewing copy
35mm bw sd 1,467ft 16mins

■ **DESCRIPTION** Documentary. The history of writing and print, from cave paintings to William Morris; the production of paper; and the present-day production and distribution of books. The film ends with a recitation of the sonnet, 'Not marble, nor the gilded monuments' (55).

ANGELIC CONVERSATION, The

■ **GB** • **1985**

d/ph	Derek Jarman
pc	British Film Institute
p	James Mackay
ed	Cerith Wyn-Evans/Peter Cartwright
nar	Judi Dench
m	COIL

NFTVA viewing copy
35mm col sd 6,973ft 77mins

■ **CAST**
Paul Reynolds
Phillip Williamson

■ **DESCRIPTION** Experimental film accompanying readings of fourteen of the sonnets: 'Weary with toil I haste me to my bed' (27), 'When, in disgrace with Fortune and men's eyes' (29), 'When to the sessions of sweet silent thought' (30), 'When most I wink, then do mine eyes best see' (43), 'What is your substance, whereof you are made' (53), 'Not marble, nor the gilded monuments' (55), 'Sweet love, renew thy force; be it not said' (56), 'Being your slave, what should I do but tend' (57), 'Is it thy will thy image should keep open' (61), 'Then hate me when thou wilt; if ever, now' (90), 'They that have power to hurt, and will do none' (94), 'To me, fair friend, you never can be old' (104), 'O thou, my lovely boy, who in thy power' (126) and 'O me, what eyes hath Love put in my head' (148). The sonnets selected are mostly those addressed to a young man rather than the Dark Lady and the accompanying homoerotic imagery was filmed mostly on Super-8 and blown up to 35mm. Jarman's deep devotion to and understanding of Shakespeare is as evident here as in THE TEMPEST (GB 1979, qv), but this is a far more private work, abandoning narrative, often most interested in the texture of the image than its 'subject'; it is striking and just a little wearing after a while. Some of the images are literal echoes of the text, and the film works better when the correlations are more elusive. Similarly the choice of a female narrator provides a welcome ambiguity.

MIDSUMMER NIGHT'S MYSTERY, A

■ **GB • 1989**

■ *First Tuesday*

d/p	Kevin Sim
pc	Yorkshire Television
tx	4 July 1989 (ITV)

NFTVA viewing copy
½" col sd 51mins

■ **DESCRIPTION** Television documentary on the claims for Edward de Vere, Earl of Oxford to be the true author of Shakespeare's works. Evidence for this is sought among the sonnets, and Nicholas Gecks reads from 'My love is as a fever, longing still' (147). For full details of the programme see entry in General section.

SHAKESPEARE; OR, WHAT YOU WILL

■ **GB • 1992**

■ *Dark Horses / Without Walls*

pc	Wall to Wall Television
tx	13 October 1992 (C4)

NFTVA viewing copy

■ **DESCRIPTION** Television documentary on Shakespeare and homosexuality. Includes extracts from *Coriolanus* and *Othello* and a full reading of the sonnet 'A woman's face, with Nature's own hand painted' (20). For full details of the programme see entry in General section.

The puppet William Shakespeare from NEXT (1990)

GENERAL

SHAKESPEARE LAND

■ **GB • 1910**

pc	Kineto

NFTVA viewing copy
35mm bw st 329ft 4mins
English titles

■ **DESCRIPTION** Travelogue. Street scenes in Leamington Spa; Kenilworth Castle; Guys Cliff Mill; Warwick; Warwick Castle; travelling shot down drive to ornamental gateway; travelling shot along the road between Warwick and Stratford; three men clambering over a gate; Stratford church with the river Avon in the foreground; Anne Hathaway's cottage; Shakespeare's birthplace; Stratford Grammar School; the Shakespeare Memorial Theatre; author Marie Corelli's home; rowers, punters and swans on the river Avon.

OLD ACTOR, The

■ **USA** • **1912**

d	D. W. Griffith
pc	Biograph Company
sc	George Hennessy
ph	G. W. Bitzer

NFTVA viewing copy
35mm bw st 891ft 10mins [nitrate]
English titles

■ **CAST**

W. Chrystie Miller . . . . *The Old Actor*
Mary Pickford . . . . *His daughter*
Kate Bruce . . . . *His wife*
Charles West . . . . *The daughter's sweetheart*

■ **DESCRIPTION** Fiction short. A Shakespearean actor loses his part as the theatre manager believes that he is too old. Helping a beggar in the street, he is impressed to discover how much money the beggar has. Unable to find work, he disguises himself as a beggar. This disguise at first fools his family, but they trace him, bring him home, and a letter arrives offering him his part back. A gently effective character piece in Griffith's best manner; the actor's Shakespearean connections are revealed by his reading first from the 'All the world's a stage' speech (A2S7), then Macbeth's lines 'struts and frets his hour upon the stage/And then is heard no more' (A5S5), quoted in the intertitles. It is these lines that encourage him to disguise himself.

GLASTONBURY PAST AND PRESENT

■ **GB** • **1922**

pc	The Glastonbury Pageant Film Committee

p	H. O. Martinek
sc	Alys M. Buckton
ph	M. G. Benson

NFTVA preservation material
35mm bw st 4,024ft 45mins
English titles

■ **CAST FOR EPISODE FOUR**

Neil Curtis. . . . . *Will Shakespeare*
P. Mason . . . . *Sir Walter Raleigh*
Ethel D. Hanson . . . . *The Widow*
R. M. Stenner. . . . . *Farmer Jenkins*
Ada Hersey . . . . *Mrs Jenkins*
J. F. Barker . . . . *Collin*
M. Walker . . . . *Letty*
Sebastian Evans. . . . . *The Squire*
The Rev. L. S. Lewis . . . . *The Bishop*

■ **DESCRIPTION** Interest film in five episodes, each illustrating a time in the history of Glastonbury and based on the Glastonbury pageant for 1922. Episode one shows the legendary arrival of Joseph of Arimathea to preach Christianity to British tribes; episode two shows King Alfred's generosity in victory towards the Danes; episode three features King Edward III, the Black Prince and an accident to a young Jewish boy; episode four shows the Tor Fair at the time of Queen Elizabeth, including a small drama about a girl dressing as a boy so that she can be employed on the same farm as her lover, and a morality play which is watched by William Shakespeare and friends; in episode five Jack returns from the Colonies to join his foster parents at the Michaelmas Fair; he also takes part in the town pageant.

SHAKESPEARE RE-VISITS STRATFORD ON AVON

■ **GB** • **1922**

■ *Around the Town 110*

pc	Gaumont Film Company

NFTVA viewing copy
35mm bw st 318ft 3mins
English titles

■ **DESCRIPTION** Cinemagazine item. Members of the 'Will Shakespeare' company (identity unknown) at Stratford; dramatised scenes show Shakespeare wooing Anne Hathaway, bidding her farewell, and setting out for London with Philip Henslowe.

OLD BILL 'THROUGH THE AGES'

■ **GB • 1924**

d	Thomas Bentley
pc	Ideal Films
sc	Eliot Stannard
ph	Horace Wheddon

NFTVA viewing copy
35mm bw st 5,976ft 65mins
Incomplete – original length 7,800ft
English titles

■ **CAST**
Syd Walker . . . . *Old Bill*
Arthur Cleave. . . . . *Bert*
Jack Denton. . . . . *Alf*
Gladys ffolliott . . . . *Queen Elizabeth*
Austin Leigh . . . . *William Shakespeare*
Franzi Carlos . . . . *Anne Hathaway*
Bruce Bairnsfather . . . . *Himself*

■ **DESCRIPTION** Feature film comedy based on the characters created by Bruce Bairnsfather. Old Bill, in the trenches during the First World War, eats tinned lobster and dreams that he and his friends travel back in time to the time of William the Conqueror, to Runnymede for the signing of Magna Carta, to the time of Queen Elizabeth and lastly the Civil War. In the third section Old Bill is a courtier who is sent to Stratford to fetch William Shakespeare, whom he finds dictating a sonnet to a room full of typists. Shakespeare shows Old Bill his complete works (each volume ascribed to Francis Bacon), some of which are deemed unsuitable for the royal eyes, and Shakespeare, Anne Hathaway and Old Bill travel to court. There Shakespeare gives selected readings from the plays (including the *Hamlet* soliloquy, A3S1), gradually sending the court to sleep. Old Bill throws a Mills bomb at him, but he continues undeterred. Walter Raleigh introduces the court to tobacco, which goes down much better. Entertaining when described, somewhat tedious actually to view, with many obscure contemporary references and a general air of amateurishness. Nevertheless, in isolation the Shakespeare sequence is quite fun.

■ **NOTES** Bruce Bairnsfather was a cartoonist who created the highly popular character of Old Bill during the First World War. Other films based on the character were THE BETTER 'OLE (GB 1916 and USA 1926), based on Old Bill's best known phrase, and OLD BILL AND SON (GB 1940) (latter two films only in NFTVA). Bairnsfather appears as himself in this film, from which a whole sequence covering the Boston Tea Party is missing.

STRATFORD-ON-AVON

■ **GB • 1925**

pc	Hepworth Manufacturing Company

NFTVA viewing copy
35mm bw st 659ft 7mins
English titles

■ **DESCRIPTION** Travelogue. Scenes around Stratford, emphasising its links with Shakespeare: his birthplace, the Grammar School, a mulberry tree at 'New Place' said to have been planted by Shakespeare, Anne Hathaway's cottage, the Shakespeare Memorial Theatre, a public house called 'Shakespear's Hostelrie', John Harvard's house, and the church where Shakespeare is buried. The film concludes with superimposed figures of Shylock [?], Romeo and Juliet in the churchyard.

SHAKESPEARE'S COUNTRY

■ **GB • 1926**

■ *Wonderful Britain*

pc	British Screen Classics
p	Harry B. Parkinson

NFTVA viewing copy
35mm bw st 747ft 8mins
English titles

■ **DESCRIPTION** Travelogue of the Stratford-upon-Avon area.

SHAKESPEARE MEMORIAL THEATRE

■ **GB • 1926**

■ *Topical Budget 759–1*

pc Topical Film Company
rel date 11 March 1926

NFTVA viewing copy
35mm bw st 56ft 1min
English titles

■ **DESCRIPTION** Newsreel item. Various scenes inside and outside the fire-damaged Shakespeare Memorial Theatre at Stratford.

■ **NOTES** The Shakespeare Memorial Theatre was destroyed by fire on 6 March 1926. An appeal was soon launched and a new Shakespeare Memorial Theatre was opened by the Prince of Wales on Shakespeare's birthday in 1932 (see news items below).

SOVIET'S SALUTE TO SHAKESPEARE!

■ **GB • 1926**

■ *Topical Budget 765–2*

pc Topical Film Company
rel date 26 April 1926

NFTVA viewing copy
35mm bw st 58ft 1min
English titles

■ **DESCRIPTION** Newsreel item. Scenes in Stratford during the Shakespeare birthday celebrations, including flags of the various nations represented, and a visit from a Soviet delegation.

TO SHAKESPEARE'S MEMORY

■ **GB • 1927**

■ *Topical Budget 818–1*

pc Topical Film Company
rel date 28 April 1927

NFTVA viewing copy
35mm bw st 54ft 1min
English titles

■ **DESCRIPTION** Newsreel item. Scenes in Stratford during Shakespeare's birthday celebrations, including the unfurling of national flags and the visit of dignitaries to Shakespeare's birthplace.

SHAKESPEARE'S BIRTHDAY

■ **GB • 1927**

■ *Gaumont Graphic 1680*

pc Gaumont Film Company
rel date 28 April 1927

NFTVA preservation material
35mm bw st 82ft 1min
English titles

■ **DESCRIPTION** Newsreel item. Scenes in Stratford during Shakespeare's birthday celebrations.

STRATFORD-UPON-AVON PAGEANT OF 1927

■ **GB • 1927**

pc Pathé

NFTVA preservation material
35mm bw st 627ft 7mins
English titles

■ **CAST**
Fairfax Lucy . . . . *Queen Elizabeth*
Lewis Casson . . . . *Garrick*
Sybil Thorndike. . . . . *The Tragic Muse*
Irene Vanburgh . . . . *The Comic Muse*

■ **DESCRIPTION** Interest film. A record of the Stratford-upon-Avon pageant held in aid of the rebuilding of the Shakespeare Memorial Theatre. 'Queen Elizabeth's Progress', with participants in Elizabethan costume, is followed by the 'Garrick Pageant', with players in Regency costumes; the leading figures deliver speeches (given in the intertitles) and kneel before a bust of Shakespeare. A final title asks that a theatre should be built worthy of Shakespeare's name.

NOTES The pageant was directed by Randle Ayrton and took place on 9 July 1927. The film is probably a 'special' commissioned from the *Pathé Gazette* newsreel firm (see also SHAKESPEARE MEMORIAL THEATRE below, from 1929).

SHAKESPEARIAN RECITAL AND PAGEANT

■ **GB • 1927**

■ *Topical Budget 838–1*

pc Topical Film Company
rel date 15 September 1927

NFTVA preservation material
35mm bw st 47ft 1min
English titles

■ **DESCRIPTION** Newsreel item. Folk dancing and Shakespearean performance at Burley pageant in Yorkshire.

BRITISH AND BEST

■ **GB • 1928**

■ *Topical Budget 854–2*

pc Topical Film Company
rel date 9 January 1928

NFTVA preservation material
35mm bw st 33ft 1min
English titles

■ **DESCRIPTION** Newsreel item. The winning design for the Shakespeare Memorial Theatre by architect Elizabeth Scott.

■ **NOTES** Elizabeth Scott was the winner of an open competition to design the new Shakespeare Memorial Theatre after the fire in 1926. The new theatre opened in 1932.

SHAKESPEARE BIRTHDAY CELEBRATIONS AT STRATFORD

■ **GB • 1928**

■ *Empire News Bulletin 208*

pc British Pictorial Productions
rel date 26 April 1928

NFTVA preservation material
35mm bw st 38ft 1min
English titles

■ **DESCRIPTION** Newsreel item. Scenes in Stratford during Shakespeare's birthday celebrations.

TO THE IMMORTAL BARD

■ **GB • 1928**

■ *Topical Budget 870–1*

pc Topical Film Company
rel date 26 April 1928

NFTVA preservation material
35mm bw st 53ft 1min
English titles

■ **DESCRIPTION** Newsreel item. Ceremony held at Stratford to celebrate the 364th anniversary of Shakespeare's birthday.

BARD'S BIRTHDAY, The

■ **GB • c1929**

■ *British Screen News*

pc British Screen Productions

NFTVA preservation material
35mm bw st 92ft 1min
English titles

■ **DESCRIPTION** Newsreel item. Shakespeare's birthday celebrations at Stratford (exact year uncertain).

SHIVERING SHAKESPEARE

■ **USA • 1929**

■ *Our Gang*

d	Anthony Mack
pc	MGM
p/story	Robert F. McGowan
exec p	Hal Roach
ph	Art Lloyd

NFTVA preservation material
16mm bw sd c700ft 20mins

■ **CAST**
Jackie Cooper
Allen 'Farina' Hoskins
Norman 'Chubby' Chaney
Mary Ann Jackson
Bobby 'Wheezer' Hutchins

■ **DESCRIPTION** Comedy short. 'Our Gang' are forced into putting on a stage version of 'Quo Vadis', entitled *The Gladiator's Dilemma*, which degenerates into a huge pie-fight between performers and audience. Rather slow comedy with faltering early sound, which incidentally parodies Shakespearean language and the manner of the Roman plays.

■ **NOTES** 'Our Gang' were a group of children (with many changes of personnel) who starred in a long-running series of comedy shorts produced by Hal Roach. The film is a remake of a 1923 silent 'Our Gang' comedy, STAGE FRIGHT (not in NFTVA).

■ **REFERENCES** • Leonard Maltin and Richard W. Bann, *Our Gang: The Life and Times of the Little Rascals* (New York: Crown Publishers, 1977), pp. 108–10.

SHAKESPEARE MEMORIAL THEATRE, The

■ **GB • 1929**

pc	Pathé

NFTVA viewing copy
35mm bw st 1,066ft 12mins
English titles

■ **DESCRIPTION** Newsfilm. Extended scenes showing the laying of the foundation stone for the new Shakespeare Memorial Theatre on 2 July 1929 by Lord Ampthill. View of the old theatre; members of the Provincial Grand Lodge of Warwickshire and officers of the Grand Lodge of England walking through the streets to the site; Viscount Burham and Lord Ampthill make speeches; the foundation stone is laid; builders at work on the site.

■ **NOTES** A 'special' produced by the *Pathé Gazette* newsreel company. The NFTVA also holds the following similar but shorter newsreel items, all covering the same event: HOME FOR SHAKESPEARE'S DRAMA (*British Screen News*), SHAKESPEARE MEMORIAL THEATRE (*Empire News Bulletin 332*), SHAKESPEARE MEMORIAL THEATRE (*Gaumont Graphic 1908*) and TRIBUTE TO SHAKESPEARE (*Topical Budget 932–1*).

OFFICE STEPS

■ **USA • 1930**

d	George Hale
pc	Vitaphone Corporation
sc	Neville Fleeson/Harold Levey

NFTVA viewing copy
35mm bw sd 825ft 9mins

■ **CAST**
Jack Thompson
Gertrude McDonald
Harry McNaughton
The Phelps Sisters

■ **DESCRIPTION** Musical short. In the office of a Broadway musical promoter the boss, his secretary and the typists' pool all dance. Two tap dancers arrive for an audition, and then a Broadway actor of the old school (Harry McNaughton), who initially refuses to dance, delivers a monologue about 'the ring around the bath' peppered with Shakespearean quotations, then joins in the dance with everyone else.

■ **NOTES** One of the tap dancers appears to be George Raft.

SHAKESPEARE BIRTHDAY CELEBRATIONS 1930

■ **GB • 1930**

■ *Gaumont Graphic*

pc   Gaumont Film Company
rel date   April 1930

NFTVA preservation material
35mm bw st 138ft 1min
English titles

■ **DESCRIPTION** Newsreel item. Shakespeare's birthday celebrations in Stratford.

H. R. H. ON SHAKESPEARE

■ **GB • 1932**

■ *British Paramount News 121*

pc   British Paramount News
rel date   25 April 1932

NFTVA preservation material
35mm bw sd 144ft 2mins

■ **DESCRIPTION** Newsreel item. The Prince of Wales opens the new Shakespeare Memorial Theatre at Stratford and delivers a speech.

■ **NOTES** The new Shakespeare Memorial Theatre was opened on Shakespeare's birthday. The NFTVA also holds two silent newsreel items covering this story, STRATFORD ON AVON: 'SWEETEST SHAKESPEARE – FANCY'S CHILD' (*Pathé Gazette*) and SHAKESPEARE MEMORIAL (*Gaumont Graphic*).

SHAKESPEARE WITH TIN EARS

■ **USA • 1933**

d   Harry Sweet/Leslie Goodwins
pc   RKO
story   Harry Sweet/Hugh Cummins
ph   Jack Mackenzie

NFTVA preservation material
35mm bw sd 1,689ft 19mins

■ **CAST**
Harry Sweet . . . . *Fat*
Harry Gribbon . . . . *Rivets*

Tom Kennedy . . . . *The Boy*
Marjory Peterson . . . . *The Girl*
Dell Henderson . . . . *The Girl's Father*

■ **DESCRIPTION** Comedy short. 'Slapstick social comedy, with good gags, boisterously put over. Good entertainment for the masses' (*Kinematograph Weekly*, 21 September 1933, p. 23). No further information is available on this film, which is retained in the catalogue for its baffling title.

STRATFORD-ON-AVON: SHAKESPEARE'S BIRTHDAY

■ **GB • 1934**

■ *Universal Talking News 396*

pc   British Pictorial Productions
rel date   26 April 1934

NFTVA preservation material
35mm bw sd 950ft 10mins [full issue]

■ **DESCRIPTION** Newsreel item. Shakespeare's birthday celebrations in Stratford.

IMMORTAL GENTLEMAN, The

■ **GB • 1935**

d/p   Widgey R. Newman
pc   Bernard Smith
stage d   Maxwell Coborne
Shakespearian
   adviser   Terence de Marney
scen   John Quin
lght   Francis Brugiere
m   John Reynders

NFTVA viewing copy
35mm bw sd 5,457ft 61mins

■ **CAST**
Basil Gill . . . . *William Shakespeare/Malvolio*
Laidman Browne . . . . *Petruchio/Gambler/Feste*
Roy Byford . . . . *Squire*
Dennis Hoey . . . . *Soldier/Toby Belch*
Terence de Marney . *Harry Morton/Hamlet/Romeo*

Edgar Owen . . . . *Ben Jonson / Mercutio*
Ivan Berlyn . . . . *Father / Aguecheek*
J. Hubert Leslie . . . . *Michael Drayton*
Leo Genn. . . . . *Merchant / Shylock*
Derrick de Marney . . . . *James Carter / Tybalt*
Fred Rains . . . . *Miser*
Anne Bolt. . . . . *Jane / Maria*
Rosalind Fuller . . . . *Ophelia / Juliet / Lady*

■ **DESCRIPTION** Feature film. William Shakespeare, Ben Jonson and Michael Drayton meet at a tavern in Southwark. Shakespeare points out people in the tavern who each remind him of scenes from his plays. A wistful woman reminds him of Juliet, a melancholy old man reminds him of Hamlet, a miserly man argues with a Jewish pedlar who then becomes Shylock, two young men going out to fight a duel leads to the duel between Romeo and Tybalt, a turn in the conversation to nagging wives leads to *The Taming of the Shrew*. The soldier son of the landlord arrives and encourages Shakespeare himself to recite 'The Seven Ages of Man' (*As You Like It*). Ben Jonson then leads the company in singing 'Sigh no more, Ladies' (*Much Ado About Nothing*); the soldier and his cousin Jane sing 'It was a Lover, and his Lass' (*As You Like It*). The company's drunkenness leads Shakespeare to recall a scene from *Twelfth Night*. Jane comes across the sleeping poet and tells him that he looked to be dead; he assures her that on the contrary he will live forever. As dreadful a film as has ever been made, meanly produced, ill-lit, ill-staged, scarcely directed at all, with some howlingly bad excerpts from the plays, details of which are given under their individual titles. The nadir of filmed Shakespeare.

■ **NOTES** A Falstaff-like squire played by Roy Byford appears throughout the film but is never actually shown or described as being Falstaff.

(SHAKESPEARE CELEBRATIONS AT STRATFORD)

■ **GB • 1936**

■ *Gaumont-British News 243*

pc   Gaumont-British
rel date   27 April 1936

NFTVA preservation material
35mm bw mu 100ft 1min

■ **DESCRIPTION** Newsreel item. One of three items in the newsreel's 'Roving Camera' section, covering the Shakespeare birthday celebrations in Stratford.

WHO WAS THE BARD OF AVON?

■ **GB • 1938**

■ *British Paramount News 802*

pc   British Paramount News
rel date   3 November 1938

NFTVA preservation material
35mm bw mu 266ft 3mins

■ **DESCRIPTION** Newsreel item. A proposal to open Shakespeare's tomb in search of proof for the 'true' authorship of the plays.

ENGLAND'S SHAKESPEARE

■ **GB • 1939**

pc   Imperial Sound Studios
spon   London, Midland and Scottish
       Railway
sc   Neal Arden

NFTVA viewing copy
35mm bw sd 1,633ft 18mins

■ **DESCRIPTION** Travelogue on places of interest in and around Stratford-upon-Avon: the general countryside, Tudor costumes, Stratford-upon-Avon itself, the title pages of Shakespeare's plays, town houses, the Tudor home of John Harvard, Shakespeare's birthplace and school, New Place, Anne Hathaway's cottage, Warwick Castle, Kenilworth Castle, the Shakespeare Memorial theatre with people arriving for a performance, the inside of the theatre with the stage being set for a performance of *King Lear*, Holy Trinity Church and the statue of Shakespeare.

SHAKESPEARE'S COUNTRY

■ GB • c1940

■ *Gainsborough Miniatures*

pc   Gainsborough Pictures

NFTVA preservation material
35mm bw sd 1,000ft 11mins

■ **DESCRIPTION** Travelogue of Stratford-upon-Avon and its surroundings, including the Shakespeare Memorial Theatre and Anne Hathaway's cottage.

PLAYMATES

■ USA • 1941

d	David Butler
pc	RKO
p	Cliff Reid
sc	James V. Kern/Arthur Phillips
ph	Frank Redman
songs	Jimmy van Heusen/Johnny Burke

NFTVA preservation material
35mm bw sd 8,620ft 96mins

■ **CAST**
Kay Kyser . . . . *Himself*
John Barrymore . . . . *Himself*
Lupe Velez . . . . *Carmen de Torre*
Ginny Simms . . . . *Ginny*
Patsy Kelly . . . . *Lulu Monhan*
George Cleveland . . . . *Mr Pennypacker*
Alice Fleming . . . . *Mrs Pennypacker*
Kay Kyser's Orchestra . . . . *Themselves*

■ **DESCRIPTION** Feature film. In his last film, John Barrymore is reduced to self-parody, playing a temperamental, has-been actor who tries to revive his career by teaming up with the Kay Kyser swing orchestra to put on updated Shakespeare. As painful as it sounds; the assorted references to Shakespeare include a spoof *Julius Caesar* sequence, the swing number 'Romeo Smith and Juliet Jones', and Barrymore putting what remained of heart and soul into the *Hamlet* soliloquy (A3S1). For fans of the bizarre or minor swing bands only.

OUR MR SHAKESPEARE

■ GB • 1944

d/pc   Harold Baim

NFTVA viewing copy
35mm bw sd 3,299ft 37mins

■ **DESCRIPTION** Travelogue of Stratford-upon-Avon and the surrounding area, emphasising the Shakespearean connections.

SHAKESPEARE'S BIRTHDAY

■ GB • 1946

■ *British News 309*

pc   The Newsreel Association of Great Britain and Ireland
rel date   6 May 1946

NFTVA viewing copy
35mm bw sd 932ft 10mins [full issue]

■ **DESCRIPTION** Newsreel item. Shakespeare's birthday celebrations at Stratford.

STRATFORD CELEBRATES SHAKESPEARE'S BIRTHDAY

■ GB • 1948

■ *Television Newsreel 33*

pc   BBC
tx   30 April 1948 (BBC)

NFTVA viewing copy
35mm bw sd 308ft 3mins

■ **DESCRIPTION** Television news item. A tour of all the familiar Stratford landmarks during the Shakespeare birthday celebrations.

SHAKESPEARE RETURNS TO REGENT'S PARK

■ GB • 1949

■ *Television Rota Services 149*

pc   BBC
tx   6 June 1949 (BBC)

NFTVA preservation material
35mm bw sd 313ft 3mins

■ **DESCRIPTION** Television news item. Robert Atkins re-opens the Regent's Park Open Air Theatre and is seen in rehearsal with his company.

ROYAL VISITORS AT SHAKESPEARE'S BIRTHPLACE

■ **GB • 1950**

■ *Gaumont-British News 1701*

pc   Gaumont-British
rel date   24 April 1950

NFTVA preservation material
35mm bw sd 172ft 2mins

■ **DESCRIPTION** Newsreel item. King George VI and Queen Elizabeth, together with Princess Margaret, make their first visit to Stratford-upon-Avon. Lord Iliffe shows them round the Shakespeare Memorial Theatre.

DARK LADY OF THE SONNETS, The

■ **GB • 1955**

■ *Sunday-Night Theatre*

d/p   Douglas Allen
pc   BBC
tx   2 October 1955 (BBC)
des   Reece Pemberton

NFTVA viewing copy
35mm bw sd 2,442ft 27mins

■ **CAST**
Alan MacNaughtan . . . . *Shakespear*
Beatrix Lehmann . . . . *Queen Elizabeth*
Barbara Murray . . . . *The Dark Lady*
George Woodbridge . . . . *The Beefeater*

■ **DESCRIPTION** Television production of George Bernard Shaw's short play of 1910, in which Shakespear (in Shaw's spelling) has an assignation with the Dark Lady, but encounters Queen Elizabeth as well, to whom he puts an argument for a National Theatre.

■ **NOTES** The broadcast was immediately followed by the second half of THE MERRY WIVES OF WINDSOR (qv).

SHAKESPEARE BREATHES AGAIN!

■ **GB • 1956**

■ *British Paramount News 2627*

pc   British Paramount News
rel date   3 May 1956

NFTVA preservation material
35mm bw sd 106ft 1min

■ **DESCRIPTION** Newsreel item. The tomb of Sir Thomas Walsingham, in Chislehurst, opened at the request of an American seeking evidence that Christopher Marlowe was the author of Shakespeare's plays.

NIGHT IN THE CITY

■ **GB • 1957**

■ *Eye to Eye*

d/p/devised   Denis Mitchell
pc   BBC North Region Film Unit
tx   14 June 1957 (BBC)
m   Ewan MacColl

NFTVA preservation material
35mm bw sd 2,732ft 30mins

■ **DESCRIPTION** Television documentary. Impressions of life in a provincial city (Manchester) from evening to dawn, giving a memorable picture of the loneliness of people's lives. Among the various persons encountered is a busker who entertains a theatre queue with speeches from Shakespeare.

WILL SHAKESPEARE – GENT

■ GB • 1964

pc	BBC
tx	5 May 1964 (BBC1)
p	Derrick Amoore
ph	Peter Bartlett
pres	Fyfe Robertson

NFTVA preservation material
16mm bw sd 1,814ft 50mins

■ **DESCRIPTION** Television documentary. Fyfe Robertson investigates the various questions surrounding Shakespeare's identity, examining the known evidence, and showing him to have been very different from the usual image of 'the classic romantic poet of all time'.

■ **NOTES** Produced by the *Tonight* documentary series production team.

SHAKESPEARE'S 400TH ANNIVERSARY

■ GB • 1964

■ *Pathé News 64/36*

pc	Pathé
rel date	30 April 1964

NFTVA preservation material
35mm col sd 862ft 9mins

■ **DESCRIPTION** News item. Extended news coverage, 'in Techniscope and Technicolor', of the Shakespeare quatercentenary celebrations at Stratford.

SHAKESPEARE WALLAH

■ India • 1965

d	James Ivory
pc	Merchant-Ivory Productions
p	Ismail Merchant
sc	Ruth Prawer Jhabvala/James Ivory
ph	Subrata Mitra
m	Satyajit Ray

NFTVA viewing copy
½" col sd 124mins
English dialogue

■ **CAST**

Felicity Kendal	*Lizzie Buckingham*
Shashi Kapoor	*Sanju*
Geoffrey Kendal	*Tony Buckingham*
Laura Liddell	*Carla Buckingham*
Madhur Jaffrey	*Manjula*
J. D. Tytler	*Bobby*
Prayag Raaj	*Sharmaji*
Pincho Kapoor	*Guptaji*
Partap Sharma	*Aslam*

■ **DESCRIPTION** Feature film. A troupe of English and Indian actors led by Mr and Mrs Buckingham tour India, putting on performances of Shakespeare and other plays for dwindling audiences as British influence and interest in British culture gradually dies. The Buckinghams' daughter falls in love with Sanju, a young Indian who helps them when their car breaks down. Sanju's jealous former girl-friend, the film star Manjula, asks to see the troupe perform but she is recognised by the audience and the performance ends in uproar. The Buckinghams are unhappy about Lizzie's romance and decide to send her to England. Sanju has already told her that he cannot bring himself to marry an actress. A touching, thoughtful film, beautiful to look at, which takes an ironic look at British (and Shakespearean) cultural assumptions while still sadly acknowledging 'the victory of the motion picture over the theatre'. There are numerous sequences from the plays, cleverly selected to form a commentary on the action: those featured are *Antony and Cleopatra*, *Hamlet*, *Othello*, *Romeo and Juliet* and *Twelfth Night*. Details of these can be found under the individual plays.

■ **NOTES** Geoffrey Kendal and Laura Liddell ran a genuine theatrical troupe who toured India, the Shakespeareana Company, whose nature if not their exact experiences formed the basis of the film. The Shakespeare sequences within the film were as directed by the Kendals. Shashi Kapoor was married to the elder daughter Jennifer Kendal. In 1980 a straight documentary was made about the Kendal troupe, SHAKESPEARIS-TAN – EAST OF SUEZ (directed by Nicolaus Mackie, not in NFTVA).

■ **REFERENCES** • James Ivory, *Savages/Shakespeare Wallah* (London: Plexus, 1973) [published script] • Geoffrey Kendal, *The Shakespeare Wallah* (London: Sidgwick & Jackson, 1986) [autobiography].

MASKS AND FACES

■ **GB • 1969**

comp   Colin Ford
pc   British Film Institute

NFTVA viewing copy
35mm bw/col st/sd 8,168ft 91mins

■ **DESCRIPTION** Compilation of extracts from fiction films held in the then National Film Archive, showing changes in theatrical acting styles as recorded on film. Shakespearean titles (qqv) featured are RICHARD III (1911), HAMLET (1913), OTHELLO (1922), DER KAUFMANN VON VENEDIG (1923), ROMEO AND JULIET (1936) and RICHARD III (1955).

UNDERSTANDING SHAKESPEARE: HIS SOURCES

■ **GB • 1971**

d   W. Hugh Baddeley/George Murcell
pc   Gateway Film Productions
sc   W. Hugh Baddeley/
       Clement W. Bending
ph   Robin Ridgway/Peter Henton
nar   Richard Bebb

NFTVA preservation material
16mm col sd c700ft 20mins

■ **CAST**
James Bree . . . . *William Shakespeare*
Ishia Bennison

■ **DESCRIPTION** Educational film for secondary schools. An illustration of the background to Shakespeare's work, showing his childhood home life and influences, his discovery of the works of Plutarch and Holinshed, the plays of other authors and the work of a *commedia del arte* troupe. Various extracts from Shakespeare's plays are shown in a mock-up of the Globe Theatre.

■ **NOTES** See accompanying film below.

UNDERSTANDING SHAKESPEARE: HIS STAGECRAFT

■ **GB • 1971**

d   W. Hugh Baddeley/George Murcell
pc   Gateway Film Productions
sc   W. Hugh Baddeley/
       Clement W. Bending
ph   Robin Ridgway/Peter Henton
nar   Richard Bebb

NFTVA preservation material
16mm col sd c900ft 25mins

■ **CAST**
James Bree . . . . *William Shakespeare*
Colin Fisher
Henry Gilbert

■ **DESCRIPTION** Educational film for secondary schools. An illustration of how the contemporary stage affected Shakespeare's plays, from the physical nature of the theatre to such conventions as boys playing women's parts. Extracts from Shakespeare's plays illustrate how various features of the stage were used to represent the required settings and locations, along with the dramatic techniques of the period.

THEATRE OF BLOOD

■ **GB • 1973**

d   Douglas Hickox
pc   Cineman
p   John Kohn/Stanley Mann
sc   Anthony Greville-Bell
ph   Wolfgang Suchitzky
m   Michael J. Lewis

NFTVA preservation material
35mm col sd 9,223ft 102mins

■ **CAST**
Vincent Price . . . . *Edward Lionheart*
Diana Rigg . . . . *Edwina Lionheart*
Ian Hendry . . . . *Peregrine Devlin*
Harry Andrews . . . . *Trevor Dickman*
Coral Browne . . . . *Miss Chloe Moon*
Robert Coote . . . . *Oliver Larding*

Jack Hawkins . . . . *Solomon Psaltery*
Michael Hordern . . . . *George Maxwell*
Arthur Lowe . . . . *Horace Sprout*
Robert Morley . . . . *Meredith Merridew*
Dennis Price . . . . *Hector Snipe*
Diana Dors . . . . *Mrs Psaltery*
Joan Hickson . . . . *Mrs Sprout*
Renée Asherson . . . . *Mrs Maxwell*
Milo O'Shea . . . . *Inspector Boot*
Eric Sykes . . . . *Sergeant Dogge*

■ **DESCRIPTION** Feature film. Outrageous horror movie played as a bloody black joke; witty, though it could have been wittier, entertaining and often distasteful. Edward Lionheart is a hammy Shakespearean actor who decides to take murderous revenge on the theatre critics who denied him the Critics Circle award for the actor of the year. Making the punishment fit the crime, each murder is to be in the manner of a death from one of the Shakespeare plays in Lionheart's last repertory season. Aiding him in his crimes are his daughter Edwina and a group of London tramps who rescued Lionheart after he jumped into the Thames (quoting the *Hamlet* soliloquy beforehand), following his failure to win the award. Lionheart manages to acknowledge his debt to *Cymbeline*, *1 Henry VI*, *Julius Caesar*, *The Merchant of Venice*, *Othello*, *Richard III*, *Romeo and Juliet*, *Titus Andronicus* and *Troilus and Cressida* and is about to dispatch his final victim with reference to *King Lear* when the police arrive, Edwina is killed and Lionheart falls into a burning theatre. Details of the allusions are given in the entries under each play.

■ **NOTES** The opening title sequence features extracts showing bloody scenes from the NFTVA's prints of RICHARD III (1911), HAMLET (1913), OTHELLO (1922) and DER KAUFMAN VON VENEDIG (1923).

(WHITBREAD TROPHY: SHAKESPEARE)

■ **GB • 1978**

d   Stephen Frears
pc   Film Contracts

NFTVA preservation material
35mm col sd 3×c50ft 2mins

■ **DESCRIPTION** Three television commercials for Whitbread Trophy bitter.

FAME

■ **USA • 1980**

d   Alan Parker
pc   MGM
p   David de Silva/Alan Marshall
sc   Christopher Gore
ph   Michael Seresin
m   Michael Gore *et al.*

NFTVA viewing copy
35mm col sd 14,050ft 156mins

■ **CAST**
Irene Cara . . . . *Coco Hernandez*
Gene Anthony Ray . . . . *Leroy Johnson*
Frank X. Vitolo . . . . *Frankie*
Darrell Kirkman . . . . *Richard III*
Isaac Mizrahi . . . . *Touchstone*

■ **DESCRIPTION** Musical drama. The varying fortunes of some of the students at Manhattan's High School for the Performing Arts. During the auditions at the beginning of the film, several hopefuls recite Shakespeare: one delivers some of Richard's speech from A1S1 of *Richard III*, another quotes some of Touchstone's lines from A5S4 of *As You Like It*, and a third (Frankie, male) reads from Juliet's lines from the balcony scene of *Romeo and Juliet* (A2S2).

ORSON WELLES STORY, The

■ **GB • 1982**

■ *Arena*

pc   BBC
tx   18 May 1982 (BBC2) [part one]
        21 May 1982 (BBC2) [part two]
p   Leslie Megahey/Alan Yentob
nar/int   Alan Yentob

NFTVA preservation material
16mm col sd c5,600ft 105mins + 50mins

■ **DESCRIPTION** Two-part television interview with Orson Welles, covering the whole of his career with numerous illustrations from his films. A remarkable, inspiring two programmes; Welles is on prime form and gives one of the finest performances of his career. In the first part, covering his career in America, he stresses that his MACBETH (1948) was a B-picture quickie and talks about actors in the old French theatre who were 'king' actors – he himself is a 'king' actor. He praises Alexandre Trauner's art direction on OTHELLO (1952), saying that the production difficulties determined some of the cutting, but that some of the scenes are weak and he does not know what went wrong with the sound. In part two he describes CAMPANADAS A MEDIANOCHE (1966, GB title CHIMES AT MIDNIGHT) as a record of his preoccupation with the loss of innocence, talks of the idea of 'Merrie England', his interpretation of Falstaff, and the intentions behind the battle scene and the final rejection scene.

■ **NOTES** Among the interviewees contributing are John Huston, Anthony Perkins, Peter Bogdanovitch, Jeanne Moreau, Charlton Heston and Micheál MacLiammóir (archive film).

CAUGHT IN THE ACT

■ **GB • 1988**

d/p	Mary Gwatkin
pc	Reconnaissance Films/MV Films
tx	26 December 1988 (C4)
ph	Richard Harvey/Clive Gill

NFTVA viewing copy
½" col sd 50mins

■ **DESCRIPTION** Documentary on the Renaissance Theatre Company, as formed by Kenneth Branagh and David Parfitt, concentrating on the preparations for four productions. A complex mixture of extracts, rehearsals, interviews and general documentary footage, covering the creation of the Company, its aims and character, and detailing the progress of Derek Jacobi, Judi Dench and Geraldine McEwan as the directors of *Hamlet*, *Much Ado About Nothing* and *As You Like It* respectively, plus Branagh's own direction of *Twelfth Night* and its subsequent broadcast on television. For details of cast and contents as they relate to the respective plays, see entries for

CAUGHT IN THE ACT under those plays, also the 30 December 1988 broadcast of *Twelfth Night*.

■ **NOTES** The Renaissance Theatre Company toured from March 1988 with the three productions of *Hamlet*, *Much Ado About Nothing* and *As You Like It*, ending at London's Phoenix Theatre August-October 1988; *Twelfth Night* was produced at the Riverside Studios, Hammersmith, and then televised.

(SAVING THE ROSE THEATRE)

■ **GB • 1989**

■ *London Programme*

d/p	Nick Metcalfe
pc	London Weekend Television
tx	2 June 1989 (ITV)
pres	Trevor Phillips

NFTVA viewing copy
½" col sd 26mins

■ **DESCRIPTION** Television current affairs programme. The campaign to save the site of the Rose Theatre, recently discovered on London's South Bank during constructions for an office block. Protests resulted in a revised plan for a large span to be placed over the site, allowing public access, but with piles due to be driven through parts of the foundations the protests continued. Interviewees featured during the programme include Charlton Heston, James Fox, Vanessa Redgrave, Timothy Dalton, Ian McKellen and Peter Hall.

■ **NOTES** The NFTVA holds numerous television news items on the Rose Theatre story, mostly very brief, from 12 May to 17 July 1989. For details of holdings on recent television news programmes and Shakespeare, see the note at the end of this General section. See also TO DIG OR NOT TO DIG... below.

MIDSUMMER NIGHT'S MYSTERY, A

■ **GB • 1989**

■ *First Tuesday*

d/p	Kevin Sim
pc	Yorkshire Television
tx	4 July 1989 (ITV)
sc	Al Austin/Kevin Sim
nar	Paul Vaughan
m	Ernie Wood

NFTVA viewing copy
½" col sd 51mins

■ **CAST**
Nicholas Gecks . . . . *Hamlet*
Patrick O'Connell . . . . *Polonius/Macbeth*

■ **DESCRIPTION** Television documentary on the claims for Edward de Vere, Earl of Oxford to be the true author of Shakespeare's works. An engrossing questioning of the plays' authorship, with Charlton Ogburn, Enoch Powell and Charles Vere, Earl of Burford arguing against the standard view, and A. L. Rowse offering a weak defence. The arguments in favour of De Vere would have been stronger had they not chosen to read from one of his known poems. Excerpts from *Hamlet*, *Macbeth* and the sonnets are read by actors in Hedingham Castle, Essex, former seat of the Earls of Oxford.

LAURENCE OLIVIER 1907–1989: A TRIBUTE

■ **GB • 1989**

■ *Omnibus*

pc	BBC
tx	14 July 1989 (BBC1)
intro	Anthony Hopkins

NFTVA viewing copy
½" col sd 59mins

■ **DESCRIPTION** Television arts programme. Tribute to Laurence Olivier, broadcast on the day of his funeral. Hastily cobbled together hotch-potch of critical assessments and fleeting interviews with such luminaries as Trevor Griffiths, Michael Blakemore, Alan Bates, Claire Bloom, Michael Caine, Ian Holm, Jonathan Miller, Robert Stephens and Franco Zeffirelli. Much more interesting is the inclusion, in part two, of a 30-minute interview Olivier gave to Kenneth Tynan at the Old Vic in 1966. Supremely confi-

dent, Olivier discusses his major Shakespearean roles, with illustrations from the films.

■ **NOTES** The programme is divided into two parts, separated when broadcast by a screening of HENRY V (GB 1944). The Tynan interview is from LAURENCE OLIVIER, a programme in the *Great Acting* series (BBC2, tx 26 February 1966, not otherwise in NFTVA).

CHANNEL 4 NEWS

■ **GB • 1989**

pc	ITN
tx	12 October 1989 (C4)
rep	Kent Barker

NFTVA viewing copy
½" col sd 2mins [item length]

■ **DESCRIPTION** News item. Report on the discovery of the remains of the Globe Theatre by Museum of London archaeologists.

TO DIG OR NOT TO DIG …

■ **GB • 1989**

■ *Thames Reports*

d	Alison Kahn
pc	Thames Television
tx	11 December 1989 (ITV)
pres	Paul Greene

NFTVA viewing copy
½" col sd 11mins

■ **DESCRIPTION** Television current affairs programme. One of two items in programme, on the controversy over the excavations at the Globe and Rose Theatre sites, and the dispute arising between English Heritage and the Museum of London (which it funds) over who has control over archaeological surveys and digs in London. The programme includes scenes at the two sites, including the protests at the building plans at the Rose. Ian McKellen and Sam Wanamaker are among the interviewees.

■ **NOTES** Full-length of programme 25mins.

NEXT

■ **GB • 1990**

d/anim/sc	Barry Purves
pc	Aardman Animations
p	Sara Mullock
ph	David Alex Riddett/
	David Sproxton/
	Andy MacCormack

NFTVA viewing copy
½" col sd 5mins

■ **DESCRIPTION** Animation. A puppet William Shakespeare auditions as an actor by giving a five-minute performance of his complete works in dumbshow. An engaging and witty idea faultlessly executed, engrossing stuff for those attempting to recognise each fleeting reference to the plays.

BINGO: SCENES OF MONEY AND DEATH

■ **GB • 1990**

■ *Theatre Night*

d	Don Taylor
pc	BBC
tx	30 June 1990 (BBC2)
p	Tim Ironside Wood
des	Robert Hinds
m	Derek Bourgeois

NFTVA viewing copy
½" col sd 125mins

■ **CAST**

David Suchet	. . . .	*Shakespeare*
Brenda Bruce	. . . .	*Old woman*
Peter Jeffrey	. . . .	*William Combe*
Kenneth Haigh	. . . .	*Ben Jonson*
Ruth Mitchell	. . . .	*Judith*
George Malpas	. . . .	*Old man*
Greg Hicks	. . . .	*Son*
Madeline Church	. . . .	*Young woman*

■ **DESCRIPTION** Television production of Edward Bond's embittered play, set in 1615, showing an aged and weary William Shakespeare in retirement at Stratford. This is a portrait of a disillusioned man, who ponders on his life and fame and sees nothing but the hypocrisy and greed which drove him out of London but which he likewise finds in Stratford.

PACKET OF 3

■ **GB • 1991**

d	John Stroud
pc	Jon Blair Film Company
tx	20 September 1991 (C4)
p	Jon Blair

NFTVA viewing copy
½" col sd 26mins

■ **CAST**

Henry Normal
Jenny Eclair
Frank Skinner
The Reduced Shakespeare Company

■ **DESCRIPTION** Television comedy programme. Individual programme in series arranged around the theme of Shakespeare, with spoof performances including the duel scene from *Hamlet* performed by two accordionists playing 'Duelling Banjos', and the Reduced Shakespeare Company performing their versions of Shakespeare's plays: a 47-second version of *Hamlet* followed by one of 3 seconds, a 5-second performance of *Julius Caesar* as witnessed by the audience, a short version of *Macbeth* with heavy Scottish accents, a 'rap' version of *Othello*, and a rapid account of English history using all of Shakespeare's kings in the manner of a report on an American Football game. All a bit tired except for the duelling accordionists; the comedy links from the regular hosts are lamentable.

■ **NOTES** The Reduced Shakespeare Company (Adam Long, Reed Martin and Austin Tichenor) repeat their two versions of *Hamlet* and the American Football game in WHAT'S UP DOC? (tx 12 September 1992) below.

(SHAKESPEARE: THE ANIMATED TALES: PROMO REEL)

■ **GB • 1992**

NFTVA viewing copy
½" col sd 10mins

■ **DESCRIPTION** Promotional tape for the *Shakespeare: The Animated Tales* series of animated films based on the plays of Shakespeare. Over a montage of sequences from the films, the narration stresses the unique nature of the venture, its educational and entertainment value. Extracts follow from the first six titles in the series: HAMLET, THE TEMPEST, A MIDSUMMER NIGHT'S DREAM, ROMEO AND JULIET, TWELFTH NIGHT and MACBETH. The voiceover promises seven more titles in development. Credits are given for the series.

■ **NOTES** *Shakespeare: The Animated Tales* was a much-hyped series of 30-minute versions of the plays to adaptations by Leon Garfield. A co-production between S4C (Welsh Channel Four) and Soyuzmultfilm in Russia, the films (not in NFTVA) were recorded as dialogue only in Wales, the animated films produced in Russia (a different style of animation being devised for each film), then sold as tapes and initially broadcast on BBC2 in November/December 1992. Some of the films were ingeniously animated, others (using cel animation) were visually quite poor, but the real weakness was the failure to adapt the plays into 'thirty attention-grabbing minutes'. The ambitions and assumptions underlying the whole production are of greater interest. The intended audience was children, and picture books based on the programmes were published.

LAURENCE OLIVIER

■ **GB** • 1992

■ *J'Accuse/Without Walls*

d/p	Jeff Morgan
pc	Fulmar Television
tx	3 March 1992 (C4)
ph	Colin Skinner/Isobel Johnstone
pres	Russell Davies

NFTVA viewing copy
½" col sd 26mins

■ **DESCRIPTION** Television polemic. Russell Davies questions Laurence Olivier's position as the pre-eminent actor of his generation. A reasonable accusation is made, that Olivier's performances were all show and no substance, but it is badly compromised by using film clips as evidence of his acting abilities. In particular the 1965 OTHELLO, described as 'an apparently faithful record' of the stage production, comes in for much criticism, there being no suggestion made that a filmed record of a play might be a different experience to the play itself. The sobering thought is that Olivier will ultimately be judged thus, and probably not favourably, for performances that perfectly suited the tenor of their times.

■ **NOTES** Extracts are shown from MOSCOW NIGHTS (1935), WUTHERING HEIGHTS (1939), HENRY V (1944), HAMLET (1948), RICHARD III (1955), THE ENTERTAINER (1960) and OTHELLO (1965) (all held by NFTVA). Among the interviewees are Anthony Holden, Alan Brien, Hermione Lee and Snoo Wilson. *J'Accuse* is a series within the *Without Walls* slot where invited speakers denounce particular established figures in the arts.

WHAT'S UP DOC?

■ **GB** • 1992

d	Simon Pearce
pc	TVS
tx	12 September 1992 (ITV)

NFTVA viewing copy
½" col sd 112mins

■ **DESCRIPTION** Television magazine and entertainment programme for children. Includes a performance by the Reduced Shakespeare Company of their extremely abbreviated versions of *Hamlet* and their account of the history plays told in the manner of a report on an American Football game. The performance is much the same as that which they give in PACKET OF 3 (tx 20 September 1991) above.

SHAKESPEARE; OR, WHAT YOU WILL

■ **GB** • 1992

■ *Dark Horses / Without Walls*

pc   Wall to Wall Television
tx   13 October 1992 (C4)
pres   Simon Callow

NFTVA viewing copy
½" col sd 26mins

■ **DESCRIPTION** Television documentary on Shakespeare and homosexuality. Includes extracts from *Coriolanus* (A4S5 'O Marcius, Marcius!') and *Othello* (A3S3 'I lay with Cassio lately') spoken over images of writhing male bodies, and a full reading of Sonnet 20 ('A woman's face, with Nature's own hand painted'). Juliet Stevenson comments on the role of Rosalind in *As You Like It*, and Declan Donnellan discusses Cheek by Jowl's all-male production of the play. There are contributions from Stanley Wells, Alan Sinfield and Bruce R. Smith, outlining the likely acceptance of homosexuality in Shakespeare's time.

■ **NOTES** *Without Walls* is a arts programming slot on Channel Four; *Dark Horses* is a series within that slot on homosexual artists.

JOHN GIELGUD LOOKS BACK

■ **GB • 1993**

d   Andrew Holmes
pc   Holmes Associates
tx   3 January 1993 (C4)
p   Stephen Phillips

NFTVA viewing copy
½" col sd 62mins

■ **DESCRIPTION** Television interview. John Gielgud answers questions from a group of RADA students about his career and the views he has on his profession. An absorbing and informative programme, with Gielgud on prime form, covering the whole range of his career and offering some firm but kindly criticisms. On the subject of Shakespeare and film, he thought very little of the Hollywood A MIDSUMMER NIGHT'S DREAM (1935) and ROMEO AND JULIET (1936) and feels that Olivier's HENRY V (1944) was the first successful attempt. He expresses regret that Olivier was never able to film his *Macbeth*, praises Branagh's HENRY V (1989) and Branagh in general, and expresses his admiration for Peter Greenaway, who nevertheless gave him no direction at all for PROSPERO'S BOOKS (1991). He speaks of instructing Marlon Brando in JULIUS CAESAR (1953) and says he was disappointed at Brando's playing of the Forum scene where Brando followed his own inclinations.

CHANNEL 4 NEWS

■ **GB • 1993**

pc   ITN
tx   25 January 1993 (C4)
rep   Harry Smith

NFTVA viewing copy
½" col sd 2mins [item length]

■ **DESCRIPTION** News item. Report on the work of some English Shakespeare Company actors assisting with the teaching of Shakespeare in schools. Scenes of the actors at Wakefield Comprehensive using such devices as a chat show format to explain *Romeo and Juliet*, with comments on the experiment by some pupils.

Note

Since 1978 the NFTVA has been making off-air recordings of British television news broadcasts, initially infrequently but now covering the major news broadcasts each day. There are viewing copies for all ITV and C4 material from 1985 onwards. A few of the more substantial news items relating to Shakespeare have been included in this catalogue, but brief items have been excluded. NFTVA staff have dial-in access to the ITN Library database *Newsbase* (ITN produces the major news broadcasts for both ITV and C4) but the NFTVA does not subject-index such news broadcasts itself. Access tapes can also be made of all BBC news broadcasts recorded since 1 August 1990, but there is no subject-access available, and relevant items can only be traced by transmission date.

The Bard in Brooklyn: Vitagraph's Shakespearean Productions

Roberta E. Pearson and William Uricchio[1]

Charles Kent as Malvolio in
TWELFTH NIGHT (1910)

In 1910, Frank Dyer, the Vice-President of the Motion Picture Patents Company, addressed the moving picture's relationship to high culture. 'When the works of Dickens and Victor Hugo, the poems of Browning, the plays of Shakespeare and stories from the Bible are used as a basis for moving pictures, no fair-minded man can deny that the art is being developed along the right lines.'[2] The Vitagraph Company of America had already heeded Dyer's call and by 1910 had become the leading producer of the so-called 'quality films', that is, films based upon historical, biblical and literary subjects. Vitagraph also led other US studios in the production of Shakespearean adaptations. While the industry as a whole produced at least thirty-six fifteen-minute Shakespearean films between 1908 and 1913, Vitagraph alone turned out the following: 1908 – MACBETH, ROMEO AND JULIET, OTHELLO, RICHARD III, ANTHONY AND CLEOPATRA, JULIUS CAESAR, THE MERCHANT OF VENICE; 1909 – KING LEAR, A MIDSUMMER NIGHT'S DREAM, TWELFTH NIGHT; 1912 – CARDINAL WOLSEY (*Henry VIII*) and AS YOU LIKE IT, not to count parodies such as A COMEDY OF ERRORS (1908) and INDIAN ROMEO AND JULIET (1912).

Vitagraph, the largest of the pre-Hollywood studios, had extensive production facilities in Brooklyn, including three studios in operation by the end of 1908, with two more under construction. In 1908, Vitagraph turned out 'more new subjects each week than any other American concern.'[3] Vitagraph also exported more films to Europe than its competitors, opening its main European offices in Paris in 1906 and by 1908 building a complete film laboratory from which it sent prints to distribution offices in Italy, England and Germany.[4] Although surviving studio records are unfortunately scarce, Vitagraph publicity does support the inference that the scale of the studio's output, together with greater resources and more intensified division of labour, led to increased production of quality films, including the Shakespearean adaptations.

While Vitagraph undoubtedly sought to differentiate itself from the competition through the production of these films, the US film industry as a whole had strong motivations for filming Shakespeare. First, although Shakespeare was an English poet, the general reverence accorded his works in Europe practically guaranteed good sales of all Shakespearean films, a particularly compelling factor for Vitagraph. Second, in the wake of the 1907 BEN HUR copyright decision that forced producers to pay authors, studios were acutely aware of material in the public domain and knew that Shakespeare did not collect royalties. Third, as we have demonstrated elsewhere, Shakespeare may have been far more accessible to a diverse spectrum of viewers than may be apparent from a late-twentieth century perspective[5]. Fourth, Shakespeare provided as many thrills – duels, illicit romances, murders – as the rankest cheap melodrama. And fifth, if critics accused film-makers of excessive depiction of duels, etc., the industry could feign outraged innocence and wrap itself in the Bard's mantle.

While such factors undoubtedly entered into film producers' calculations, the desire for respectability provides the most powerful explanation for the production of quality films generally and of Shakespearean adaptations in particular. Around 1905, the concomitant rise of the nickelodeon, the fiction film and the working-class audience led to the industry's conflation with such despised cheap amusements as the low-priced melodrama, the penny arcade and the dance hall and to attacks from cultural arbiters such as ministers, state officials and journalists. The industry, seeking to reposition itself as a respectable, mainstream medium, employed many strategies, the production of quality films among them. Studio publicity and trade press reviews of Shakespearean adaptations specifically referenced the films' uplifting associations and benefits. In reviewing the Vitagraph Company's TWELFTH NIGHT, the *Moving Picture World* said:

> It elevates and improves the literary taste and appreciation of the greatest mass of the people, performing in this way a service which cannot be measured in material terms. Such work is the nature of an educational service which is deserving of the heartiest support of all who are working for the improvement of humanity.[6]

But while the industry sought to placate cultural arbiters and achieve respectability, in the process bringing new, middle-class viewers to the nickelodeons, it also desired to maintain its current audiences. Far from wishing to alienate its old customers in the quest for a 'better class' of patron, Vitagraph employed what we term a 'dual address' strategy, constantly insisting that the quality films had a broad appeal, and were, in fact, all things to all people. As with the other quality films, Vitagraph expected that Shakespearean adaptations would expand the audience. The *Vitagraph Bulletin* said of TWELFTH NIGHT, 'This release will attract Shakespearean students and dramatic societies . . . It will help you in making regular patrons out of casual visitors.'[7] But while studio publicity and trade press discourse implied that some viewers came to the nickelodeon with detailed knowledge of the Bard and his plays and enjoyed the films by virtue of the intertextual frame, it also emphasised the appeal of these adaptations to viewers not thus equipped. The *Vitagraph Bulletin* said of A MIDSUMMER NIGHT'S DREAM, 'Students of the great dramatist's works will thoroughly enjoy the careful pictorial presentation of the many scenes, while the whole play is so clearly portrayed that it will not fail to delight the spectator who is not familiar with the works of Shakespeare.'[8]

Vitagraph counted upon narrative simplification and photographic spectacle to ensure that the bulk of nickelodeon audiences would enjoy the Shakespearean films. 'Palladium', a columnist for the *Moving Picture World*, explained how the industry had adapted Shakespeare to suit allcomers.

> Shorn of intricacy of language, transposed into simply worked synopses at frequent intervals, abridged by rapid action, but retaining all their dramatic interest, 'Hamlet', 'Macbeth', 'Merchant of Venice', 'Richard III', 'Othello' etc., became absorbing epitomes of human interest within the comprehension and appreciation of all who saw. Emotion and temperament are the sole requirements to hold the interest of the poorest and most ignorant to the simplified dramas of Shakespeare. . . [9]

In addition to highly simplified plots that retained only the most familiar scenes and characters, the industry employed two other strategies to ensure narrative comprehension – accompanying lectures and copious intertitles that included the best-known of Shakespeare's lines. Said W. Stephen Bush of the *Moving Picture World*, 'Even with the short explanatory titles the plays have been enjoyed by all who ever had any acquaintance with Shakespeare at all, and many persons who had never read a line of Shakespeare have come away delighted after seeing the pictures and hearing them competently explained.'[10]

Vitagraph's JULIUS CAESAR exemplifies this narrative simplification, the film's fifteen shots omitting the six of the play's seventeen scenes that deal with the political intrigues of Marc Antony and his co-rulers, complexities that may have confused those not familiar with the play. Although the NFTVA print lacks original titles, Vitagraph's description indicates that the titles included four direct quotes and one paraphrase of some of the play's best-known lines.[11] The *New York Dramatic Mirror* appreciated Vitagraph's efforts to facilitate viewer understanding. 'By selecting only the vital scenes and inserting comprehensive explanatory titles in the film the story of the play is rendered fairly free from obscurity – the greatest obstacle to overcome in doing Shakespeare in moving pictures.'[12]

Caesar refusing the crown from Mark Antony in JULIUS CAESAR (1908)

Vitagraph simplified Shakespeare to meet the perceived needs of current audiences, but aimed photographic and staging spectacle at both these viewers and the better class of patron whom it wished to attract. These potential viewers would have been accustomed to a spectacular staging of Shakespeare that involved lavish and historically 'accurate' sets and costumes, the 'representation' of well-known paintings and the on-stage depiction of action Shakespeare himself had set off-stage. Vitagraph touted all its Shakespearean adaptations as consonant with this spectacular tradition, as in the case of RICHARD III. 'A grand spectacular reproduction of Shakespeare's *Richard III* a magnificent subject surpassing in every detail all previous efforts in this line.'[13] Reviewing Vitagraph's ANTHONY AND CLEOPATRA, the *New York Dramatic Mirror* referenced both clarity and spectacle. Comparing it to the favourably received RICHARD III, the reviewer said, 'It is clearer in telling the story, and even more elaborate in the spectacular features. The costumes and scenic effects are of the finest.'[14]

JULIUS CAESAR also exemplifies Vitagraph's spectacular approach to Shakespeare. The players in the Vitagraph film were alleged to have been garbed in the very costumes, presumably historically accurate, worn by their theatrical predecessors, Edwin Booth, Lawrence Barrett and Edward Loomis Davenport, all well known for their enactments of various roles in the play.[15] Period critics such as Stephen Bush pointed out that one shot reproduced the well-known painting by Gerome, 'The Death of Caesar'.[16] The on-screen depiction of off-stage action further illustrates Vitagraph's adherence to contemporary theatrical practice. In the play, during A1S2, Marc Antony thrice offers Caesar the crown offstage, while on stage Brutus and Cassius listen. The film's third shot, preceded by the intertitle, 'Marc Antony three times offers Caesar the crown,' shows Caesar seated in a grandstand, surrounded by a crowd of extras. While Caesar watches the race which Shakespeare's Casca only describes, Marc Antony presents the crown to him. The film's eleventh shot uses a cinematic device, superimposition, to emulate a moment of theatrical spectacle: the appearance of Caesar's ghost to Brutus at Philippi.

Did Vitagraph's Shakespearean adaptations achieve the desired respectability? The transformation of the film industry from despised cheap amusement to dominant mass medium is so overdetermined that the question permits of no easy answer. But we do know that those within the industry consistently pointed to Shakespearean adaptations as primary evidence of their cultural acceptability. After New York City's Mayor McClellan summarily revoked all nickelodeon licenses in 1908, exhibitors met to decide upon a course of action. Many referred ironically to cultural arbiters' objections to the assassination scene in JULIUS CAESAR, unable to believe that anyone could possibly find filmed Shakespeare immoral or objectionable. They pointed to JULIUS CAESAR as a primary example of film's contribution to culture. 'Several of the orators appealed to the shade of Julius Caesar to acclaim the moving picture as an artistic triumph of the century, a triumph which no devotee of the liberal arts could ignore and every true artist must celebrate.'[17]

Notes

1. The order of the authors' names was determined by a coin toss. The authors collaborated to such an extent that they could not themselves distinguish their 'individual' contributions. For more on the Vitagraph Shakespeares see William Uricchio and Roberta E. Pearson, *Reframing Culture: The Case of the Vitagraph Quality Films* (Princeton: Princeton University Press, 1993).
2. Frank L. Dyer, 'The Moral Development of the Silent Drama', *The Edison Kinetogram*, 15 April 1910, p. 11.
3. *New York Dramatic Mirror*, 14 November 1908, p. 10.
4. See chapter two of Kristin Thompson, *Exporting Entertainment: America in the World Film Market, 1907–34* (London: British Film Institute, 1985).
5. See Uricchio and Pearson, chapter 3.
6. *Moving Picture World*, 19 February 1910, p. 257.
7. *Vitagraph Bulletin*, 16–30 November 1909.
8. *Vitagraph Bulletin*, 1–15 December 1909.
9. Palladium, 'Moving Picture is an Uplifter: How it Reached the Multitudes', *Moving Picture World*, 28 May 1910, p. 887.
10. W. Stephen Bush, 'Shakespeare in Moving Pictures', *Moving Picture World*, 5 December 1908, pp. 446–7.

11. We viewed the National Film and Television Archive's German print which corresponds closely with the Vitagraph description.

12. 'Reviews of New Films', *New York Dramatic Mirror*, 12 December 1908, p. 6.

13. Letter from Vitagraph Company of America to film exchanges, 5 September 1908, Manufacturers Files, M-V, Box 5, Motion Picture Patents Company Papers, Edison National Historic Site, National Park Service, United States Department of the Interior.

14. *New York Dramatic Mirror*, 14 November 1908, p. 10.

15. 'Picture-Show Men Organize to Fight', *New York Times*, 27 December 1908.

16. *Moving Picture World*, 5 December 1908, p. 447.

17. 'Show Men Will Fight', *New York Daily Tribune*, 26 December 1908.

Roberta E. Pearson is Assistant Professor at the Annenberg School for Communication, University of Pennsylvania; William Uricchio is Professor of Film and Television History at the University of Utrecht. They have collaborated on *The Many Lives of the Batman: Critical Approaches to a Superhero and his Media* (1991) and *Reframing Culture: The Case of the Vitagraph Quality Films* (1993).

'When You Care Enough to Send the Best': Televised Shakespeare and the Hallmark Hall of Fame

Tise Vahimagi

Maurice Evans (Hamlet) and Ruth Chatterton (Gertrude) in HAMLET (1953)

It is generally regarded that the first full presentation of Shakespeare on American television was the *Hallmark Hall of Fame*'s production of HAMLET for NBC on 26 April 1953. Maurice Evans featured in the title role (which also marked his television debut), supported by Barry Jones (as Polonius), Sarah Churchill (Ophelia), Ruth Chatterton (Queen Gertrude) and Joseph Schildkraut (King Claudius). George Schaefer directed Albert McCleery's two-hour production.

The Sunday afternoon performance was reported, by trade journal *Variety*, as 'a stunning production, replete with many artistic assets in the way of performances, direction, music, scenery and costumes. Yet it remains primarily the great personal triumph of Maurice Evans' (*Variety* 29 April 1953). In his pseudo letter-to-the-bard piece as generally favourable review, the *Saturday Review*'s R. L. Shayon said, 'You will be pleasured, certes, to learn that *Hallmark Hall of Fame* commemorated the 389th anniversary of your baptism with a special two-hour television adaptation of HAMLET. It took two television adapters to cut the play: they did a lot of cutting. (Actually, only a hundred minutes were devoted to the play itself, the remaining quarter hour to the cause of the patron, a maker of greeting cards.)' (*Saturday Review* 16 May 1953)

This celebrated production marked (if not typecast) *Hallmark Hall of Fame* as the premier American television programme of craft and culture, a 'serious' television vessel, and a rare one at that, for the discriminating viewer to embark on in a virtual ocean of low-brow, primetime jetsam and flotsam (fast-buck game shows, noisy gangbuster series and inane situation comedies). Hallmark Greeting Cards were already an acknowledged leader in the industry when the company originated, via Hallmark's agency, Foote, Cone & Belding, the *Hallmark Hall of Fame* programme. Joyce Clyde Hall, who had founded Hallmark Cards, Inc., in 1910, was the driving force behind the company and later pioneer of the series of premier television presentations. In keeping with the company's well-established slogan, 'When You Care Enough to Send the Best', Hall opened his television series with full sponsorship of AMAHL AND THE NIGHT VISITORS and followed it up with the very best in name performers, producers and production values in American television at that time.

Before the Emmys and multiple other television awards came in, Hall and *Hallmark* made television history with HAMLET in 1953: they were also honoured as being the first American television show to present a colour transmission of a primetime programme[1] and the first colour production of Shakespeare (MACBETH) on US television. It may be said, perhaps, that it was Joyce Hall's vision of 'quality' that was to become the central factor behind *Hallmark Hall of Fame's* longevity of forty years on network television. Simply, Hall's feeling was: 'I'd rather make eight million good impressions than twenty-eight million bad ones. It's better to have eight million friends than twenty-eight million enemies.'

Hallmark Hall of Fame had started out in the latter part of the American 'Golden Age' of radio broadcasting under the title of *Hallmark Playhouse*, premiering in 1948 as an anthology series of dramatic presentations. The thirty-minute CBS Radio broadcasts, which included among their adaptations, for instance, James Hilton's *Random Harvest* with Joan Fontaine and Edna Ferber's *Cimarron* with Irene Dunne, developed into at first *Hallmark Presents Sarah Churchill* for thirteen weeks, then into *The Hallmark Television Playhouse* in January 1952 before (some three weeks later) adopting the long-running and now familiar programme title of *The Hallmark Hall of Fame*.

In 1951 the Hallmark company ventured into the developing television industry by sponsoring a weekly interview show hosted by actress Sarah Churchill, the daughter of Sir Winston Churchill,[2] in which prominent personalities were brought into the studio as guests for the fifteen-minute transmissions. The *Hallmark* television programme proper premiered in late 1951 with the first full-length opera ever presented on American television, Gian-Carlo Menotti's Christmas-themed AMAHL AND THE NIGHT VISITORS (NBC tx 24 December 1951), produced by Samuel Chotzinoff.[3] In his studies of early American television, Frank Sturcken extends the Hallmark background: 'It began rather humbly as a half-hour show. In 1952–53 it took on a slightly new format and there were intimations of the greatness to come. Sarah Churchill remained as the hostess and Albert McCleery became the producer-director. McCleery brought in an arena style of staging that he had had success with in 1949 in a production of *Romeo and Juliet* for NBC [tx 15 May 1949] and in a series called *Cameo Theatre*, although his settings had become more elaborate as his budget increased.'[4]

The two-hour HAMLET became an American television landmark, not only for the brilliance of its (1953) production values but also for the unprecedented commitment of a commercially minded network and the, usually, cost-conscious sponsor in presenting quality drama on primetime American television. Brian G. Rose elaborated in *Television and the Performing Arts*: 'Employing a cast of 28 (most of whom worked at minimum union scale) and five cameras and utilising three weeks of rehearsals, the show's final cost for NBC was a huge $180,000; Hallmark Greeting Cards contributed $100,000 as sole sponsor.'[5] Contemporary television critics hailed the presentation as (in the words of one reviewer) 'An experience belonging uniquely and indigenously to television itself.'[6] *Variety* journalist John Horn, contributing to the shower of praise that the programme attracted, observed the actors' use of the television setting: 'The sets by Richard Sylbert were spacious, capturing the expanse of a palace . . . particularly in the fluid movement of Evans in his "O what a rogue and peasant slave am I" soliloquy.' Horn was also impressed with the 'striking effects', the 'double-exposure appearance of the kingly ghost and his later reflection in a full-length mirror.' But he was cautious enough to note: 'Minor flaws were regrettable in such a high-calibre production – a stagehand cutting across the background during the "peasant slave" soliloquy; floor noise during Evans' "To be" speech' (*Variety* 29 April 1953).

A newcomer to television performance, Maurice Evans had difficulty adjusting to the intimacy of small-screen production: 'Accustomed to playing HAMLET in the wide spaces of the theatre, I found it excruciatingly difficult to deliver certain passages with the requisite vehemence without looking ridiculous at such close quarters. In rehearsal, we found the best way to scale the performance down to TV proportion was to have an assistant hold a piece of cardboard before the actors' faces. This represented the exact size of the image which would appear on the screen. This device helped me enormously.'[7]

During World War II Evans and George Schaefer had combined their talents to stage a variety of plays for American servicemen overseas, including what was to become known as 'G.I. *Hamlet*', a shortened version adapted specially for the military audience which later became the basis for the television production. 'We dreamed up a plan of setting it in a sort of Ruritania,' said director Schaefer. 'Getting away from tights, getting away from the Elizabethan flavour and almost giving it a *Prisoner of Zenda* look. In our production the soldiers saw a dashing court full of medals and military uniforms.'[8]

Hallmark's second Shakespearean production (also as a two-hour presentation) was KING RICHARD II (NBC tx 24 January 1954), for which enormous studio sets were constructed, featuring forty-foot castle walls, vast exteriors, and a huge, baroque-designed chamber hall. Despite the lavish production, originating from the reactivated Brooklyn studios of NBC, and Hallmark financing the whole $175,000 for production and time, the majority of the reviews were less than enthusiastic, perhaps in anticipation of *Hallmark* topping their previous production, and observed that the highly detailed scenery and elaborate sets were more distracting than spectacular. The *Hollywood Reporter*'s kinship with the industry, however, tended to colour that journal's review: 'Certainly here was a vast improvement over Evans' TV performance of *Hamlet* last season in achieving the near-perfect fusion of theatre and television in translating the Shakespearean brand of cunning, intrigue and double-cross into the intimate terms and exacting demands of home video viewing [in reference to the medium, not the technology].' (*Hollywood Reporter* 27 January 1954). It is significant at this stage to note that Maurice Evans' *Richard II* had won him his initial Broadway ovation back in 1937 and he revived it at the City Center Theatre, New York, in 1951.

KING RICHARD II, adapted for television by Evans himself, was once again the first full presentation of the classic on American television. Supporting Evans in his title role were Sarah Churchill (as the Queen), Frederic Worlock (John of Gaunt), Kent Smith (Bolingbroke), Bruce Gordon (Thomas Mowbray), and Richard Purdy (Duke of Aumerle). Schaefer co-directed for producer-director McCleery.[9] McCleery remembers that 'some of the critics didn't like the set and shooting [scenes] through the flame. So what, Evans takes direction beautifully – an artist who absorbs an idea and is so sensitive to direction. They laughed at me having to "direct" Maurice Evans but he was wonderful. I think the prison scene was the most exciting moment in the play – and on television ever.'[10]

The seemingly perfect working partnership of Evans and McCleery did involve some 'artistic' conflict when it came to planning future Shakespearean productions, following the success of HAMLET. 'When I was asked to do a second Shakespearean production for *Hallmark*,' said Evans, 'it was logical that I should pick *King Richard II*. For one thing, this is the play which brought me fame, if not fortune, in the United States and is the classic which I have played the greatest number of times.'[11] McCleery responds: 'He insisted on *Richard II*. I wanted to wait. I felt *Richard II* would be a good colour production if we could wait, but he absolutely insisted on doing it then. I still believe it would have been an ideal production for colour.'[12]

Hallmark's fourth television season (1954–55) combined their 132nd episode with their third Shakespearean production, MACBETH (NBC tx 28 November 1954). Evans again featured in the title role, with Staats Cotsworth (as Banquo), Judith Anderson (Lady Macbeth), House Jameson (King Duncan), and Richard Waring (Macduff). Hallmark had received by this time thousands of complimentary letters from viewers following their previous productions, so, naturally, when (as the NBC files recorded) 'so many of them asked that we do MACBETH next it seemed a logical choice, especially in view of the great success Mr Evans and Miss Anderson enjoyed with it in the theatre.'[13] Hallmark's press office confidently announced that 'We have been extremely pleased with the reception given Mr Evans' Shakespearean plays.'[14]

Owing to internal bad feeling that resulted in McCleery's departure from the *Hallmark* production team,[15] Evans' own television adaptation of MACBETH was co-directed by Schaefer for producer-director Hudson Faussett. Unlike traditional American cinema and stage directors, George Schaefer virtually celebrated television production: 'The greatest thing that television had was that ability to suddenly put you in a number of places at once. There it was – a little raw, maybe, but exciting.'[16] Along with the visual pleasures of Schaefer's intricate camera movement and unusual angles there was also the coming to terms with the new technology of colour television. 'The programme's most notorious feature,' observed Brian Rose in his reference guide, 'was its emphasis on bloodshed, opening with an extreme close-up of Macbeth's blood-soaked hands, followed by comparable shots of Lady Macbeth and later of the returned-from-the-grave Banquo, his face still covered with the marks of violence. Broadcast in vivid colour, the effect was, in those comparatively innocent times, shocking and gruesome.'[17] The reviewer for *Time* magazine shared a similar, albeit veiled, sense of discomfort: 'Except for the enforced shortage of cameras, colour TV worked no production hardship. "We just went ahead as though colour hadn't been invented," said Schaefer. One unfortunate result: after the murder of the King, the hands of Evans and Judith Anderson looked appropriately bloody on black-and-white; on colour TV they seemed to be literally dripping with gore' (*Time* 13 December 1954).

The colour production of MACBETH was considered a remarkable achievement nevertheless, with most of the kudos going to director George Schaefer. Where the HAMLET set had been constructed in a circle with the cameras positioned in the centre and radiating outward, MACBETH was like a stage setting. 'The camera work was so carefully plotted that, on the screen, the play had a novel air of extreme fluidity,' added *Time* magazine. Schaefer used only three cameras on the set and one on a platform, rather than the five cameras that handled the black-and-white transmission of HAMLET. Schaefer achieved a remarkable sense of mobility by keeping his camera moving into and out of the scene during each long sequence.

In 1955, HALLMARK changed its format from a regular hour-long (variously, half-hour/hour in 1954), weekly series to a limited run of special presentations during the following television seasons. Also, during the 1955–56 season the Evans-(executive)produced programmes for *Hallmark* were billed as *Maurice Evans Presents*. THE TAMING OF THE SHREW (NBC tx 18 March 1956) was one of these productions, a ninety-minute presentation directed by Schaefer from the television adaptation by Michael Hogan and William Nichols. Evans led the cast as Petruchio,[18] with Lilli Palmer (as Katharina), Diane Cilento (Bianca), Philip Bourneuf (Baptista), and Jerome Kilty (Grumio) supporting.

The set, the creation of Rouben Ter-Arutunian (who was also responsible for the costumes), was a large, virtually empty space 'with clowns carrying on props as needed'.[19] However, the lightweight tone in the presentation was ably suggested by the production's 'sense of playfulness', demonstrated by its 'placement of the opening 'sparring match between Kate and Petruchio in a boxing arena.'[20] Continuing a 'distancing effect', 'a pair of adagio dancers dressed like Kate and Petruchio re-create as part of the wedding entertainment the wooing, wedding and taming of Kate, whip and all – except this Kate makes the last move, breaking a paper hoop over her husband's head.'[21]

Although Schaefer's camerawork and editing made the most of it, full of unexpected angles, travelling shots and screen wipes, television had yet to achieve the depth of field of film; much more apparent during the 1950s when live programmes were lit, so it seemed, to suit the studio production process rather than the image the home viewing audience might experience. 'In emulating theatre, television has two choices,' comments author Bernice Kliman. 'Something equivalent to the proscenium arch, with its own version of reality, or the bare set, with actors alone providing the illusion of reality. The example of the four live Evans productions, however, seems clear: the bare set is best.'[22] Baptista's house was simply a raised scaffold between two enclosed boxes that represented the interior. The scaffold quickly became the boxing ring for Petruchio and Kate's first encounter, with 'bells, handlers and ringside audience'.[23] In Kliman's 1982 interview with Schaefer, the director recalled: 'Unfortunately, it is preserved only on black and white kinescope. It's the first time it had ever been done with a white floor and a white set and everything white, and these brilliant costume colours. Transitions were done with bright red chiffon scarves floating in front of the lens. For a live show, it was most extraordinary.'[24]

Variety, approaching it as 'Shakespeare played for laughs', considered the production a 'rich, resplendent show, with a fine example of compatible colour, and a great big tomfoolery showcase for Evans and Miss Palmer. Too bad,' as the reviewer realised, 'it failed to sustain interest throughout as it got bogged down in an overload of farce-within-a-farce. There is such a thing as padding out Padua' (*Variety* 21 March 1956). (A couple of years later *Hallmark* put on a version of the Cole Porter–Sam and Bella Spewack musical, *Kiss Me Kate* [NBC tx 20 November 1958], with Alfred Drake and Patricia Morison in the play-within-a-play roles performed by Evans and Palmer.)

The Hallmark people were spending upwards of $400,000 to transmit each of their plays around this time and if they were studying the audience-share ratings they could have found it a fairly discouraging experience. Their audience size during these years varied from 8 million to 18 million. (By way of comparison, a single sixty-minute episode of the newly launched Western series *Wagon Train* cost

Maurice Evans and Judith Anderson in MACBETH (1960)

around $227,000; the estimated audience was about 38 million.) Most sponsors would have demanded more for their money. Greeting cards have a low unit price, and Hallmark was assigning 75 per cent of its advertising budget to television. But since 1951, when it started the *Hall of Fame* series on television, the company's gross income had increased from an estimated $45 million a year to $90 million – 100 per cent. It was *TV Guide* magazine that later noted: 'Hallmark isn't too impressed by ratings. It is more interested in how many viewers like the plays and buy Hallmark cards. If more companies had that approach – which we believe is a realistic one – we'd see a lot better television.'[25]

Their following presentation of TWELFTH NIGHT (NBC tx 15 December 1957) had an audience of 8,650,000. The ninety-minute production, transmitted in colour, was adapted by William Nichols and directed by Canadian David Greene for producer Robert Hartung; Evans starred as Malvolio, with Rosemary Harris (Viola), Dennis King (Sir Toby Belch), Denholm Elliott (Sebastian) and Max Adrian (Aguecheek) supporting.

The *Daily Variety* and weekly *Variety* reviewers filed opposing opinions on the production. Weekly *Variety* reported that: 'The TV version did complicate matters a bit by the necessary cutting, but then it compensated by a beautiful production that, in its compatible tint version, was as rich and lavish as could be desired. The costumes were sheer opulence and the sets a fitting background; the music a delightful Elizabethan binder, and the dance sequences enchanting' (*Variety* 18 December 1957). While *Daily Variety* noted: 'Tastes change and a commercial comedy that laid 'em in the aisles in Elizabethan times doesn't necessarily hold up three-and-a-half centuries later. The antique nobility of language which has caused so much of Shakespeare to survive is only spasmodically present here. Unfortunately, the punning humour of which Shakespeare was so fond, and which so persistently remains a mystery to the modern ear, is very much present in TWELFTH NIGHT. Presentation was marred by two breakdowns during the [West] Coast transmission. Otherwise, black-and-white kine of the colour presentation from N.Y. was good' *(Daily Variety* 17 December 1957).

It was some three years before *Hallmark*'s sixth Shakespearean production: THE TEMPEST (NBC tx 3 February 1960). It was generally applauded as a 'handsome colour version', producer-director Schaefer, adaptor John Edward Friend and the fine cast (consisting of Evans as Prospero, Lee Remick as Miranda, Richard Burton as Caliban, Tom Poston and Ronald Radd as Trinculo and Stephano and Roddy McDowall as Ariel) keeping it sprightly and interesting. The sets, designed by Rouben Ter-Arutunian, were considered among the most imaginative seen on television, and composer-conductor Lehman Engel's score was generally hailed by reviewers as excellent. However, 'one must wonder at the choice of *Tempest* for telecast,' observed *Variety*, with its usual American cynicism. 'It's one of Shakespeare's hokier works, rather difficult to follow and is never quite merry enough for a real romp. Probably, it was the opportunity for spectacle which *Tempest* offered, but this was best realized on colour sets.' On Friend's television adaptation, *Variety* commented that the work 'basically was an editing job with one transplantation, the "Stuff That Dreams Are Made On" speech by Prospero used in the epilogue instead of midway through the play. Device tended to be a sort of disclaimer, with Prospero telling the audience the entire show was more or less of a fantasy' *(Daily Variety* 5 February 1960).

Perhaps the *Hallmark*/Shakespeare production to reach (eventually) the largest audience (worldwide) was their two-hour colour 'spectacle' of MACBETH (NBC tx 20 November 1960) which was filmed (by Freddie Young) in Scotland and was budgeted at nearly $1 million. This was not simply a restaging of their 1954 production. Producer-director Schaefer, using the facilities of Grand Prize Films Ltd in England, produced the play as a theatrical feature film, though tailored to TV dimensions. The Hallmark company paid roughly half the cost of the production and, with Schaefer's Compass Productions, held the TV and film rights to the movie. The mainly British cast featured Maurice Evans, Judith Anderson, Michael Hordern, George Rose, Ian Bannen, Felix Aylmer, Valerie Taylor, Jeremy Brett and Megs Jenkins. In a *TV Guide* piece about the production, George Schaefer detailed the filming: 'As soon as we arrived in Scotland, I drove out to look at Cawdor. It

ESSAY ● TISE VAHIMAGI

made me wince. People are living there now and they have modernised it, complete with fancy windows, central heating and telephone lines and modern roads outside the gates.'[26] The production unit then scouted other Highland locations and finally settled on another castle, Hermitage, which Schaefer had seen in an American travel magazine.

In Scotland, Schaefer hired some 250 local people and a few English to portray the troops. First he had to find enough Scottish pines for the men to use as camouflage. Then he filmed the sequence in three different locations to achieve the action he wanted. Schaefer also decided to hire eight shaggy sheepdogs to 'lend atmosphere' to the banquet scene in the castle where Macbeth first sees Banquo's ghost: 'I didn't expect those dogs to do tricks but I thought at least they'd be able to sit still. They did, too, all the time we were setting up a shot. The minute I yelled for quiet on the set and we started to shoot, though, they stood up and began to pace around. I finally had to fire the lot of them.'[27]

Following MACBETH's television premiere, *Hollywood Reporter*'s Hank Grant noted: 'To this reviewer, it was probably the best production from the works of Shakespeare to ever be presented on TV and it had an advantage over a legit stage version in that the realism afforded by the filming technique made it fascinatingly exciting even to viewers unable to fully digest the meanings in Shakespeare's beautiful but heavy prose.' Grant concluded: 'To Shakespeare buffs, it was an evening long to be remembered; to the average viewer, it was a rewarding excursion into a classic drama form that has not heretofore had the full advantage of bigtime production on TV.' *Variety* shared in the general applause. 'Network TV demonstrated, as did Hallmark, that when people care, they deserve the very best. In MACBETH they certainly had it, and the fact that it's permanently inscribed in celluloid for repeated use is to be applauded.' But on a negative note, *Variety*'s reviewer continued: 'Unfortunately, Maurice Evans' performance as Macbeth was spotty. His ordinary dialogue was delivered in such a declamatory tone that it left no room for growth for the more highly dramatic episodes. In the latter part of the play his soliloquies, being more tempered and controlled, carried greater conviction and force. But since the character of Macbeth is larger than life, some may prefer this rather stylized performance' (*Variety* 23 November 1960).

A decade later, *Hallmark* opened their twentieth (1970–71) season of what had by now become a limited mini-series of 'specials' with a two-hour 'telefilm' version of HAMLET (NBC tx 17 November 1970). Although this production was generally seen as 'touching the limits of TV as a medium for this play', this version was placed during the Regency period and (in typical 1970s flamboyant fashion) featured the players 'costumed à la turque and with sequined eyelids.' Peter Wood directed John Barton's adaptation for producer George LeMaire. The impressive cast included Richard Chamberlain, Sir Michael Redgrave, Margaret Leighton,

Richard Johnson, Sir John Gielgud and Ciaran Madden. 'There wasn't much poetry in this HAMLET,' said *Hollywood Reporter*'s Craig Fisher. 'Nor was there much pity and terror. But it was a swashbuckling, compelling version of the play, full of exciting details and interesting characterisations – a popularisation in the best sense of the word' (*Hollywood Reporter* 19 November 1970). Fisher also pointed out that 'At the centre of all this, however, was Richard Chamberlain as Hamlet; and the contrast between Chamberlain and the supporting cast was rather like the difference between the matinee idols in Hollywood costume epics of the forties and fifties and the clever casts with which they were surrounded.' The *Variety* reviewer remarked that 'John Barton's excisions from the play were usually adept but often eliminated important build-ups to the more famous soliloquies and dramatic byplay. Tinkering with Shakespeare's own dramatic economy is a danger-ous game, and Barton more than once fell into the trap of reducing the irreducible' (*Variety* 25 November 1970).

Though, curiously enough, *Hallmark Hall of Fame* hasn't presented a Shakespearean television adaptation since the 1970s the series remains a 'cultural landmark' in American television history. The programme has outdistanced all other television playhouses, theatres and drama showcases usually associated with prestigious tele-vision programming. During its time on air the programme's general application to small-screen artistry and quality (especially during its first decade of transmission) earned it over forty-nine Emmy awards, more than any other series on American television; including the first Emmy award ever presented to a sponsor. The *Hallmark* Shakespeares were worthy rather than exceptional examples of television theatre, but what is perhaps most striking about them is their very existence in 1950s American commercial television, a tribute to the intelligent and well-directed sponsorship of the Hallmark Greeting Cards company.

Notes

1. The third restaging of AMAHL AND THE NIGHT VISITORS (tx 20 December 1953) was the first sponsored network programme seen in colour and was transmitted just a few days after the Federal Communications Commission (FCC) approved NBC's patented 'colour tint' process [see also footnote 12]. NBC's *Kraft Television Theatre* (1947–58) later became the first primetime dramatic anthology series to be televised in 'compatible' colour (i.e. a monochrome receiver tuned to colour transmission); *Kraft*'s use of colour had begun intermittently in April 1954 and became permanent in July 1956 with the transmission of TEAR OPEN THE SKIES (tx 4 July 1956).
2. From a chorus line stage debut in 1936 through stage appearances (repertory and Broadway) and films to hosting as well as performing for *Hallmark Hall of Fame*, Sarah Churchill was generally regarded as the gossip-columnists' favourite 'flamboyant per-sonality'; perhaps simply because she was the actress-daughter of Sir Winston Churchill.
3. Samuel Chotzinoff was a lifelong musician and one-time accompanist for Jascha

Heifetz, subsequently his brother-in-law. He achieved fame as the man who negotiated for NBC chief David Sarnoff the signing of Arturo Toscanini to conduct the newly formed NBC Symphony in 1937. AMAHL AND THE NIGHT VISITORS was an original work specially commissioned by Hallmark. The prestigious production was restaged three times over the following years and became an American holiday season favourite.

4. Frank Sturcken, *Live Television: The Golden Age of 1946–1958 in New York* (Jefferson, North Carolina/London: McFarland & Company, 1990), p. 57.
5. Brian G. Rose, *Television and the Performing Arts: A Handbook and Reference Guide to American Cultural Programming* (Westport, Connecticut: Greenwood Press, 1986), p. 199.
6. Flora Schreibner, 'Television's *Hamlet*', *Quarterly of Film, Radio and Television*, vol. VIII no. 2, Winter 1953, p. 150.
7. Maurice Evans, *Hallmark Hall of Fame*, NBC files: Sturcken, p. 89.
8. Bernice W. Kliman, 'An Unseen Interpreter: Interview with George Schaefer', *Film Criticism*, vol. 7 no. 3, Spring 1983, p. 30.
9. Albert McCleery was the television and stage producer who had virtually pioneered theatre-in-the-round in 1939 and went on to head the famed Pasadena Playhouse. Celebrated for his productions of the classics for such early television anthologies as *Cameo Theatre*, *Firestone Theatre* and *Firestone Matinee Theatre*, McCleery made such an impact with his work on *Matinee Theatre* that name actors worked for scale because of the programme's professional cachet. It was said that from daytime television soap operas, released from home-bound viewers reacted with mail saluting the network for 'treating them with greater intelligence'.
10. Sturcken, p. 89.
11. Maurice Evans, *Hallmark Hall of Fame:* NBC files; Sturcken, p. 90.
12. Sturcken, p. 89. Following World War II, the television networks were concerned that the American public appeared to be more interested in new cars than 'with squinting at bad shows on the little picture tube', as Sturcken also notes (p. 15). Another problem that arose was over which band television should be assigned in the broadcast spectrum and whether it should be in black-and-white or colour. Finally, after a major colour controversy between CBS and NBC (during 1946–47) in which CBS's mechanical colour system was challenged by NBC's electronic colour system, the FCC ruled out colour and authorised black-and-white television in VHF range. It wasn't until 17 December 1953 that the FCC approved the start of colour television broadcasting based on the NTSC (National Television Standards Committee) recommended standards.
13. *Hallmark Hall of Fame*, NBC files: Sturcken, p. 90.
14. ibid. p. 90.
15. McCleery felt that Joyce Hall disliked his *Hallmark* productions of THE IMAGINARY INVALID (NBC tx 1 November 1953) and the $35,000 MOBY DICK (NBC tx 16 May 1954). McCleery's OF TIME AND THE RIVER (NBC tx 4 October 1953, restaged 15 November 1953) also got blasted by Hall, as well as the critics, which McCleery then used as his passport out of the Hallmark production team.
16. 'Art to Business: TV Then, TV Now', *Emmy*, vol. 3 no. 3, Summer 1981, p. 19.
17. Rose, p. 200.
18. 'Suddenly Evans, who in 1953 looked too old to be a credible Hamlet, in 1956 at fifty-five is as youthful a Petruchio as one would want, illustrating that perception is based

on style rather than form.' Bernice W. Kliman, 'Maurice Evans' Shakespeare Productions', in J. C. Bulman and H. R. Coursen (eds.), *Shakespeare on Television* (Hanover/London: University Press of New England, 1988), p. 99.

19. Kliman, 'Maurice Evans' Shakespeare Productions', p. 98.
20. Rose, p. 201.
21. Kliman, 'Maurice Evans' Shakespeare Productions', p. 98.
22. Kliman, 'Maurice Evans' Shakespeare Productions', p. 99.
23. Kliman, 'Maurice Evans' Shakespeare Productions', p. 98.
24. Kliman, 'An Unseen Interpreter', p. 30. Most of the anthology shows during the early part of the 1950s were transmitted live from New York studios, with kinescope films (a film photographed from a television tube, usually during a live broadcast), in pre-full network days, transported east-to-west by air for delayed local transmission on non-connected stations. When the nationwide link was eventually achieved in 1951 only the afternoon/evening schedules were staggered for shows emanating from New York; everything of course changed in the latter half of the 1950s when the television production base moved to Los Angeles and the Hollywood-studio filmed programmes began replacing live drama.
25. 'Success Despite Low Ratings', *TV Guide*, 20 February 1960, p. 3.
26. *TV Guide*, 19 November 1960, pp. 8–10.
27. ibid.

Tise Vahimagi is television researcher for BFI Publishing. He is co-author of *The American Vein: Directors and Directions in Television* (1979) and co-editor of *MTM: Quality Television* (1984). He has contributed to *Time Out, Australian Film Index, Film Dope, Sight and Sound, Primetime* and other publications. His illustrated history of British television for BFI Publishing/Oxford University Press will be published in Autumn 1994.

The BBC Television Shakespeare: Weary, Stale, Flat and Unprofitable?

Olwen Terris

John Cleese as Petruchio in THE TAMING OF THE SHREW (1980)

The British Broadcasting Corporation Television Shakespeare series began with ROMEO AND JULIET transmitted on 3 December 1978 and ended, more than six years later, with TITUS ANDRONICUS on 27 April 1985. Many felt that the televised canon told more about the cultural, political and economic role of the BBC and its conservative educational broadcasting policy than it enlightened its audience on the philosophical and moral concerns of Shakespeare, or illuminated the inventiveness of his dramatic technique through an exploration of the medium of television. Individual performances gave particular pleasure, and directorial flair and insight in some productions occasioned delight, but such moments were rare in the general feeling of apathy and weariness among both audiences and production teams, where finishing the series felt more like a dogged dedication to a commitment made long ago than an exuberant celebration of a major dramatic achievement.

The series was criticised for being too British in its conception and too corporate in its execution, while many reviewers challenged the wisdom of deciding to interpret Shakespeare through a broadcasting medium at all. Bland, dull, pedestrian, worthy are the adjectives most frequently found in the critical press, a feeling best summed up by Stanley Reynolds reviewing one play, THE TEMPEST, in *The Times*: 'There was little to find fault with ... that perhaps may be the most damning thing you could say about it ... There was nothing to stir the blood either to flashes of anger or the electric joy of a new experience. What we got was some more of the BBC's ghastly middle taste.'[1]

The sheer scope of the project and the challenges open to producers, directors, designers and actors dazzled the BBC's senior administration. Cedric Messina, veteran BBC producer, conceived the idea and vigorously championed it to the end, arguing that it should be produced, the BBC had a duty to do it and it would immeasurably enhance the teaching and study of Shakespeare in Britain and abroad, opening up his work to millions of viewers who might still be in ignorance. 'The Complete BBC Shakespeare' had a firm, authoritative ring, the series would be definitive and form a permanent library of plays for study for years to come. This defiant attitude, hovering uneasily between 'gung ho' and BBC maternalism, may have been the series' undoing. As critic Henry Fenwick noted in an article in the *Sunday Telegraph Magazine*, 'the project conceived by Cedric Messina, seemed gloriously British and gloriously BBC.'[2] The BBC was certainly concerned to endow the series with the full weight of authority and prestige which they believed was due to the Corporation as a disseminator of national culture, prefacing each programme with 'The British Broadcasting Corporation presents' as opposed to the more usual acronym BBC.

Messina's stated aim, made in part to reassure his American financial backers, was to make solid, straightforward televised accounts of Shakespeare's plays using well-known classical actors, to reach a wide audience and to enhance the teaching of Shakespeare. The plays would be set in Elizabethan England or in the historical period of the story (Ancient Rome for JULIUS CAESAR, Renaissance Verona for ROMEO AND JULIET). They were to be no more than 2½ hours long (the impracticalities of this stricture were soon realised and in later seasons several plays ran over three hours); there were to be no strong regional accents to confuse the foreign viewer or alienate the British one, and they were to have 'maximum acceptance to the widest possible audience'. Above all there were to be no 'monkey tricks'; but as Jonathan Miller (who took over from Messina as producer for the third and fourth seasons from 1980–2) noted, 'The brief was no monkey tricks and I think monkey tricks are at least 50 per cent of what interesting direction is about.'[3]

Televising Shakespeare has always occasioned suspicion and generated a great deal of critical debate, much of it repetitive, confused and inconclusive. There resides a fear, difficult to articulate, that the work's moral profundities are trivialised, the dramatic effects distorted and weakened, when perceived high culture is disseminated alongside the news, variety programmes and game shows delivered to millions of onlookers in their sitting rooms. Oddly, televising the work of other dramatists, Ayckbourn for example (another playwright/manager steeped in stage-craft) or the Restoration dramatists, has rarely stimulated such argument. George More O'Ferrall, writing of his production of *Hamlet* for the BBC in 1947, found no difficulty in adapting Shakespeare to the screen: 'Why should we claim that television is especially suited to Shakespeare? Because in its methods of presentation it comes nearer to the Elizabethan theatre for which the plays were written, than the modern theatre can do.'[4] He identified diverse acting spaces, rapid cutting between scenes, the intimacy between actor and audience as contributing to the continuous flow of broadcasting.

Cedric Messina was acutely conscious in the early productions of the expectations which he assumed his audience would bring to the televised plays. He felt the canon should be staged as naturalistically as possible. Of ROMEO AND JULIET he argued, 'You have to see a proper ballroom, a balcony, the garden, a piazza.'[5] An audience who saw reality in news and documentaries couldn't, it was supposed, make an imaginative leap, and invent for themselves the world of Verona with just a few stylistically strong visual prompts. This belief was held at a time when the Royal Shakespeare Company was regularly producing modern-dress versions of the plays and experimenting with minimal staging and televisual effects (two of these, *Antony and Cleopatra* and *Macbeth*, both directed by Trevor Nunn, were restaged for television and broadcast in 1974 and 1979 respectively to great critical acclaim). But it was thought that it was only sophisticated audiences, used to theatregoing, who would be refreshed by such innovation; audiences new to Shakespeare would only find confusion and uncertainty.

The fact that authenticity of setting offers no guarantee of success soon became apparent in the production of AS YOU LIKE IT (filmed at Glamis Castle), in which the heavily costumed actors were dwarfed by an excess of greenery in a production strangely at odds with the artifice of the play. HENRY VIII, by contrast, gained immeasurably by being filmed on location. It was shot at Hever Castle, Penshurst Place and Leeds Castle, taped during a cold winter, allowing the audience to see the condensed breath of the actors – an effect difficult to recreate in the studio.

Jonathan Miller's approach to televising Shakespeare was less conservative than Messina's. He tried to commission the most imaginative and creative directors working in the theatre at the time (Peter Brook, Ingmar Bergman, Richard Eyre) to work with him on the project and to try to revitalise the series which was by the end of Messina's production period already becoming jaded. None of these directors took up the offer and one can but assume that the restrictions which they felt would be placed on their directorial judgments proved unacceptable. Miller eventually chose Jane Howell, Elijah Moshinsky and Jack Gold and commissioned a fourth director, Michael Bogdanov, then working at the National Theatre. Bogdanov was known for his controversial Shakespearean productions, set firmly in the twentieth century as part of his conviction that Shakespeare can be made accessible to mass young audiences by providing contemporary references with which they can readily identify. Ignoring the guidelines forbidding modern dress, he began planning a modern-dress oriental interpretation of *Timon of Athens*. Miller, mindful of the agreement with the backers, took over casting and production just before rehearsals began and Bogdanov left, later condemning the series as 'the greatest disservice to Shakespeare in the last 25 years'.

Jonathan Miller, unlike Messina who had tended to assume a naïve audience, demanded a great deal from his. His approach was academic and scholarly. Miller's passionate belief at the time of producing the series was that the 'truth' in Shakespeare lay not, as Messina had believed, in a faithful reconstruction of historical location and costume, but a period verisimilitude founded upon a thorough study of the history, psychology and sociology of the Elizabethan age. He argued, uncontroversially, that any work of art reflects the concerns of the society which inspired it, so Shakespeare's plays must mirror the social, political and cultural beliefs of his day. Productions in the 1980s therefore should endeavour to reveal these truths by reflecting the attitudes in their visual design and intellectual rigour – they should be faithful to the Elizabethan picture of history.

Miller saw that a television screen is like a stage in that we see characters walking about and speaking, but its two-dimensional surface, shape and frame make it look like a painting. So he instructed his designers to create sets as if they had been painted by artists of the period, most notably the Dutch interiors of Vermeer (seen in THE TAMING OF THE SHREW) but also finding useful analogies in the work of Titian, Veronese and Rembrandt. These iconographic allusions became fundamental to a reading of the text and enabled Miller to maintain and preserve his insistence on theatrical artifice. The television screen was used as a canvas on which he painted pictures. Miller voiced his intentions in an interview with Tim Hallinan:

> Here was a writer who immersed himself in the themes and notions of his time. The only way you can unlock that imagination is to immerse yourself in the themes in which he was immersed. And the only way you can do that is by looking at the pictures which reflect the visual world of which he was a part and to acquaint yourself with the political and social issues with which he was preoccupied.[6]

The danger was that on occasions, in pursuing his academic beliefs to their logical limits, he lost the focus and passion of the play – in his OTHELLO, for example, race is denied as an issue (Othello, he argued, would have been seen as an Arab by the Elizabethans, and typically cited paintings to make his point).

Jonathan Miller's unpredictable casting proved to be one of the most interesting features of the series. Whereas Messina had preferred to cast classical actors who had played the role before, Miller cast John Cleese to play Petruchio, Warren Mitchell to play Shylock and Bob Hoskins for Iago. This desire to extend the talents of actors and actresses not accustomed to the classical stage continued into the final series with Leonard Rossiter as King John and Maureen Lipman as the Princess of France in LOVE'S LABOUR'S LOST. The writers of arts columns in the daily papers played on the curiosity value of wondering whether the hotelier of *Fawlty Towers* could make the transition to classical drama, and certainly the viewer's association with a performer's other roles provided a tension and enjoyment.

When Shaun Sutton, the third and final producer for the series, took over in 1982 he was left the renewed momentum of the series and a legacy of fourteen plays. He

Antigonus (Cyril Luckham) pursued by a bear in THE WINTER'S TALE (1981)

inherited Jane Howell and Elijah Moshinsky and added David Jones, James Cellan-Jones, Don Taylor and Stuart Burge to his team – all proven television directors. The number of different directors then working on the series created a range of styles more varied than had been the case with Miller and Messina. The move towards increased stylisation (first felt at the end of the second series with HENRY V) continued. Sutton, unlike Miller, was not a man of closely argued ideas and veered towards pragmatism, emphasising the technical demands of production:

> The director has also to understand how to use cameras to pace the production. Unique to television is the multi-camera. So the television director has to get to be a technician on top of everything else. Pictures, he's got to understand pictures – how to use the cameras.[7]

Messina's considerable skills of persuasion and dedication to fundraising for the series had resulted in £1.5 million in American backing for the project in co-production with Time-Life, based on grants from the Exxon Corporation, Metropolitan Life Insurance Company and Morgan Guaranty Trust Company of New York, with £5.5 million coming from Britain. It could be argued that the production of the BBC Television Shakespeare series owed less to Messina's ideas of a cultural heritage and more to the shrewdness of the American financiers in assessing the economic impact of the rapidly emerging video cassette market. By 1982 the series had already paid for itself and was making a profit from international sales – a remarkable achievement.

A further large-scale public relations exercise focused on educational sales and programming. In Britain the BBC organised an educational programme around the series based on books, television programmes and radio broadcasts to support the reading and interpretation of the plays. BBC Books published the texts as scripts, annotated with the cuts made by the directors and supplemented with critical essays. The first texts were published promptly to coincide with transmission, but when Alan Shallcross (Messina's script editor) and David Snodin (Miller's script editor) left to take up new posts there were considerable delays in copy preparation and four scripts were not published until a year after the series had ended.

From the very beginning of the project BBC Continuing Education had wanted to produce a series of short educational programmes to complement the plays. Authors, entertainers, politicians and critics were invited to speak for twenty-five minutes on what puzzled, disturbed, stimulated and delighted them about the play in the hope that their insights would capture the imagination of audiences unfamiliar with the work and prompt a viewing of the relevant production to come. Dennis Potter (on *Cymbeline*), George Melly (on *1 Henry IV*), General Sir John Hackett (on *Coriolanus*) and Malcolm Muggeridge (on *Timon of Athens*) were among the contributors to the *Shakespeare in Perspective* series, which gained a very respectable average audience of over a million.

The radio series *Prefaces to Shakespeare* featured well-known British actors and actresses commenting on a particular play and on their experiences of playing Shakespeare. Participants included Judi Dench, Dame Peggy Ashcroft and Michael Hordern. BBC Books published two paperback volumes entitled *Shakespeare in Perspective*, both edited by Roger Sales, which together provided an interesting and full account of the series.

Ironically the televised plays were not as accessible to the viewer for study. The series was broadcast before changes in copyright law gave educational institutions the right to record direct from television for teaching purposes or private research. At the end of the series the BBC still wished to maintain its idea of the coherent, unified product, consistent in quality, suggested by its title *The BBC Shakespeare Series*, and offered them for sale, through BBC Enterprises, as a complete library, selling at a price so high that it put them out of reach of many schools and other institutions. When it became clear through pressure from educators that the set was too expensive and not everyone required every play, six of the more popular plays (the ones found most often on the 'O' and 'A' level syllabuses) were sold more cheaply. Several years after the series ended some individual plays found their way into the high street video shops, retailing at about £10. At the time of writing

(Summer 1993) it was still not possible for individuals to see a less well-known (because less frequently performed) play – TITUS ANDRONICUS, TIMON OF ATHENS, THE LIFE AND DEATH OF KING JOHN – and no other performances of these plays made by other production companies were distributed commercially either. Negotiations are under way to sell all the plays for £25 each, but this deal will only be open to educational institutions through BBC Enterprises. It will not be available to individual students or the general public. Nor has the *Shakespeare in Perspective* series, regrettably, ever been available on low-cost video in the shops.

The *BBC Television Shakespeare* series may have lacked daring, there may have been an enervative, sanitised feel to the productions, the project itself may have been ill-conceived, but it did give millions of people the opportunity to see rarely performed plays, and not surprisingly perhaps these were often the most successful productions. They gave people who could not visit a theatre a chance to see the plays, perhaps for the first time. They gave performances to admire: Penelope Wilton's quiet, dignified strength as Desdemona, the muscular and graceful verse speaking of Alan Howard in CORIOLANUS, Claire Bloom's moving and haunting Queen Katharine in HENRY VIII, and the thoughtful, questioning directorial style revealed in the symbolic abstraction of Jane Howell's THE WINTER'S TALE, all offered new insights into ways of presenting Shakespeare on television. The technicians, designers and cameramen won many awards from the television industry for the excellence of their work.

At the close of the series Shaun Sutton commented cheerfully, confidently and unquestioningly on the project: 'It's all been enormous fun . . . never solemn, full of giggles, not too immersed in the intellectual content. It's the end of a great era, a great incident in the life of television.'[8]

Notes

1. *The Times*, 28 February 1980, p. 9, quoted in Susan Willis, *The BBC Shakespeare Plays: Making the Televised Canon* (Chapel Hill/London: University of North Carolina Press, 1991), p. 52.
2. Henry Fenwick, 'Transatlantic Row Breaks Over the BBC's Most Ambitious Drama Series', *Sunday Telegraph Magazine*, 24 September 1978, p. 25.
3. Henry Fenwick, 'To Be or Not to Be a Producer', *Radio Times*, 18–24 October 1980, p. 94.
4. George More O'Ferrall, 'Televising "Hamlet"', *Radio Times*, 5 December 1947, p. 30.
5. Henry Fenwick, 'The Production', in *BBC-TV Shakespeare: Romeo and Juliet* (London: BBC, 1978), pp. 20–1.
6. Tim Hallinan, 'Jonathan Miller on the Shakespeare Plays: Interview with Author', *Shakespeare Quarterly* 32 (1981), p. 134.
7. Mary Z. Maher, 'Shaun Sutton at the End of the Series', *Literature/Film Quarterly*, 14 no. 4 (1986), p. 190.

8.   'Exit Bard, Mayhem Stage Right', *Liverpool Daily Post*, 27 April 1985, p. 13. Quoted in Willis, p. 32.

Olwen Terris compiled and edited the first two editions of the British Universities Film & Video Council's *Shakespeare: A List of Audio-visual Materials Available in the UK* (now redesigned and expanded as *As You Like It: AudioVisual Shakespeare*). She is Honorary Librarian at the International Shakespeare Globe Centre and is Chief Cataloguer at the National Film and Television Archive.

BIRMINGHAM SHAKESPEARE LIBRARY
Chamberlain Square, Birmingham B3 3HQ
tel 021 235 4229 fax 021 233 4458

The Birmingham Shakespeare Library, founded in 1864, houses books, programmes, photographs, posters, sound recordings and production material files relating to Shakespearean performance in Great Britain and overseas. It contains more than 43,000 accessions and production material from over 600 productions. The videotape collection totals 76 titles (figure taken from 1991/2 Annual Report) and is being added to steadily. It concentrates mainly on videotapes such as the *BBC Television Shakespeare* series, which can be bought commercially. Appointments can be made to view the tapes on the Library's premises.

For further information contact the Head of Service, Fine and Performance Art.

BRITISH FILM INSTITUTE: LIBRARY AND INFORMATION SERVICES
21, Stephen Street, London WIP 1PL
tel 071 255 1444 fax 071 436 7950

The BFI's Library and Information Services maintains a large research library including books, periodicals, newspaper cuttings, unpublished scripts and a wide range of publicity materials. The Special Collections houses an extensive collection of papers donated by individuals and organisations. The BFI's database SIFT (Summary of Information on Film and Television) gives information on approximately half a million films, television programmes and videotapes.

The Library is open to members of the Institute. Contact the Information Services for details of subscription charges.

FOLGER SHAKESPEARE LIBRARY
201, East Capitol Street SE, Washington, DC 20003
tel 0101 202 544 4600

The Folger Shakespeare Library Film Archive was established in 1975 to acquire and preserve films and make these available to researchers for viewing. The study collection contains works from the silent period to Branagh's HENRY V (1989). Ballet and operatic versions of Shakespeare are held as are films containing brief Shakespearean sequences. A catalogue of their holdings has been published (see entry under Barry M. Parker in the Bibliography section).

For further information on holdings contact the Reference Librarian.

INTERNATIONAL SHAKESPEARE GLOBE CENTRE

Bear Gardens, Bankside, Liberty of the Clink, Southwark, London SE1 9EB
tel 071 928 7710 fax 071 928 7968

The Centre, founded by Sam Wanamaker, houses a collection of videotapes, slides, sound recordings and posters relating to Shakespearean performance. The archive also contains recordings of lectures given at the Globe as part of their educational programme and radio and television broadcasts discussing the history and development of the Globe Theatre, the current building project, the publicity campaigns and other material relating to the staging and acting of Shakespeare and his contemporaries. The Globe's holdings are currently being catalogued. When performances begin at the Globe it is the intention to record and preserve every performance for research and study. Material is stored in dust-proof metal cabinets but with no special facilities.

For further information contact Olwen Terris, Honorary Librarian, or Valery Aliez, Honorary Archivist.

NATIONAL FILM AND TELEVISION ARCHIVE

21 Stephen Street, London WIP 1PL
tel 071 255 1444 fax 071 580 7503

Formerly the National Film Archive, the NFTVA is a division of the British Film Institute. Information on the Archive's holdings of approximately 200,000 titles comprising feature films, shorts, documentaries, television programmes, newsreels, animation and amateur film can be obtained from the Cataloguing Department. The Archive also cares for the extensive collection of stills, posters and designs. All catalogues may be consulted free of charge (preferably by appointment). Enquiries by telephone or letter are also welcome.

BBC Access Scheme

From 1 August 1990, in addition to its regular off-air recordings of British commercial television, the NFTVA began to record the entire output of BBC1 and BBC2 for study access purposes. This was the result of an agreement whereby the BBC, which does not allow public access to its programme library, is contributing towards the Archive's provision of such a service. Records of individual programmes are not kept, so the researcher will be asked to provide details on titles and transmission dates. Examples of material available for viewing under this scheme include: BRIAN COX ON ACTING TRAGEDY (*Acting* series, tx 17 August 1990), LIVING SHAKESPEARE: A YEAR WITH THE RSC (*Omnibus* series, tx 6 December 1991), the 1992 *Shakespeare: The Animated Tales* series, episodes of *The Late Show* and other BBC arts programmes. Titles recorded as part of the Access scheme are not NFTVA acquisitions and are not included in this catalogue.

Contact Cataloguing Department ext 321/317/319. For information on stills contact the Stills, Posters and Designs department. All viewings must take place on the premises.

NATIONAL SOUND ARCHIVE
29 Exhibition Road, London SW7 2AS
tel 071 589 6603 fax 071 823 8970

The National Sound Archive holdings include all the London productions of the Royal Shakespeare Company and the Royal National Theatre from the mid-1960s. A free playback service is open to members of the public by appointment. Contact the Public Playback Service.

NATIONAL VIDEO ARCHIVE OF STAGE PERFORMANCE
Theatre Museum, 1E Tavistock Street, London WC2E 7PA
tel 071 836 7891 fax 071 836 5148

The National Video Archive of Stage Performance is in its infancy and at the time of writing has two recordings in its collection – a performance of Richard Eyre's production of *Richard III* for the Royal National Theatre with Ian McKellen as Richard and Adrian Noble's production of *Hamlet* for the Royal Shakespeare Company with Kenneth Branagh in the title role. The Museum has succeeeded in obtaining the co-operation of the Federation of Entertainment Unions in allowing certain productions to be videotaped. The intention is to record on three cameras using Super VHS and project all three tapes simultaneously in the viewing room so that researchers can look at whichever picture suits them best. The video recordings will be made in front of a live audience with no re-takes, re-rehearsals or lighting changes. In addition to recordings of performances, the Theatre Museum will be recording interviews, rehearsal sequences and documentary material for its Video Archive. Master tapes are kept with the NFTVA for preservation, viewing copies for access at the Theatre Museum in Covent Garden.

For further information contact the Head of the Theatre Museum.

SHAKESPEARE CENTRE LIBRARY
Henley Street, Stratford-upon-Avon CV37 6QW
tel 0789 204016 fax 0789 296083

In 1982 the Shakespeare Centre Library first set up video cameras at the Royal Shakespeare Theatre and its London base at the Barbican Theatre. Two plays were recorded in 1982 but from 1983 onwards all the productions in the two theatres and at The Pit have had an archive video made. When The Swan opened in 1986 all productions there were also covered. Space restrictions made it impossible to record at The Other Place but if a production transferred to the Pit then a recording was made. These recordings of a single performance are made by the theatre's technical staff as an unedited record for use by understudies, stage managers etc. They are made from fixed camera positions with no manual control and vary with regard to sound and picture quality. At the end of each season the master tapes are transferred to the theatre's archives at the Shakespeare Centre where they become available for use. The tapes may be used in the Library alongside other records such as prompt books, news cuttings and stills. No group viewing is allowed. Other videotapes are also kept, such as the *BBC Television Shakespeare* series and its associated *Shakespeare in Perspective* introductory talks.

THEATRE ON FILM AND TAPE ARCHIVE (TOFT)

TOFT, The Billy Rose Collection, The New York Public Library for the Performing Arts, 40 Lincoln Center Plaza, New York, NY 10023
tel 0101 212 870 1641 fax 0101 212 878 3852

TOFT forms part of the Billy Rose Theatre Collection of the New York Public Library for the Performing Arts at the Lincoln Center. Since 1970, TOFT has recorded Broadway, off-Broadway and regional theatre productions, and interviews with personalities from the theatre. The collection houses over 2,000 titles and viewings can be made by appointment on one of the Archive's nine monitors. Recordings are made usually with two cameras and no supplementary lighting. Editing is done live in the mobile video; there is no post-editing. New acquisitions have been listed in the *Shakespeare on Film Newsletter* (now incorporated in *Shakespeare Bulletin*).

Bibliography

This bibliography, while listing the key texts discussing Shakespeare on film and television, is selective and readers are urged also to take note of the book and journal references attached to entries in the main body of the catalogue. Where a book includes a filmography or bibliography this is stated. Biographical, autobiographical and critical accounts of actors and directors who have been involved in Shakespearean production on film and television are a valuable additional source of often anecdotal, historical and philosophical information. Peter Brook's *The Shifting Point: Forty Years of Theatrical Experience 1946–1987* (London: Methuen, 1988), for example, records his thoughts on the problems of filming Shakespeare in general and more specifically his experience of making KING LEAR (1970).

Indexes such as the *British Humanities Index* and the Fédération Internationale des Archives du Film (FIAF) publications edited by Michael Moulds, *International Index to Film Periodicals: An Annotated Guide* and *International Index to Television Periodicals: An Annotated Guide,* give information on articles appearing in journals and newspapers.

Aers, Lesley and Wheale, Nigel (eds.), *Shakespeare in the Changing Curriculum*, London, Routledge, 1991.
A collection of essays analysing the teaching of Shakespeare in schools. Two essays deal with the use of videotape: Peter Reynolds' article 'Unlocking the Door' (pp. 189–203) discusses how Shakespeare recorded on film or videotape can provide a stimulus to debate, and therefore good teaching, by challenging students to make their own connections between words on the page and images on screen. Nigel Wheale's essay 'Scratching Shakespeare: Videotaping the Bard' (pp. 204–21) suggests ways in which children might make their own videotapes stimulated by discussions of the plays.

Ball, Robert Hamilton, *Shakespeare on Silent Film: A Strange Eventful History*, London, George Allen and Unwin, 1968.
A detailed and authoritative work which furthered scholarship in Shakespearean films from the silent era. Discusses Shakespeare on film from 1899 until the beginning of sound in 1929. Ball's account includes excerpts from scenarios, reviews from contemporary journals and a rich variety of illustrations. The main text is a narrative treatment describing what was done with Shakespeare on silent film; the second section, 'Explanations and Acknowledgement', offers additional comment and and acknowledgment of other sources of information. Bibliography, filmography, film title and name indexes.

Buchman, Lorne M., *Still in Movement: Shakespeare on Screen*, New York, Oxford University Press, 1991.
Written from a background in film theory. Topics covered are conceptual – space, time and close-up. It is not always clear why Shakespearean film, as opposed to any other kind of film, is chosen to illustrate the theory.

Bulman, J. C. and Coursen, H. R. (eds.), *Shakespeare on Television: An Anthology of Essays and Reviews*, Hanover/London, University Press of New England, 1988.

Divided into three main sections. Part one contains general and theoretical essays which address Shakespeare on television from a variety of viewpoints – feminist, deconstructionist, political. Part two contains essays on individual productions made in Great Britain and the USA. Martin Banham's controversial essay 'BBC Television's Dull Shakespeares', in which he demanded excitement, delight, stimulation and enragement, none of which he experienced in watching the series, is included. Part three is a useful collection of reviews from major journals and newspapers on over seventy productions of Shakespeare's plays broadcast in Canada, America and Great Britain over the last forty years, ranging from TWELFTH NIGHT (NBC, tx 20 February 1949) with Marsha Hunt as Viola to the BBC's TITUS ANDRONICUS (PBS, tx 19 April 1985). Bibliography.

Collick, John, *Shakespeare, Cinema and Society*, Manchester, Manchester University Press, 1989 (Cultural Politics series).
Part one discusses British silent film (Collick's assessment of the *BBC Television Shakespeare* series argues provocatively that the aims behind the series, and the form and content of the final product, bore a marked resemblance to the Shakespeare films of the silent era). Part two discusses symbolism in Shakespearean films and the economic and cultural forces behind A MIDSUMMER NIGHT'S DREAM (1935). Part three looks at Kozintsev's GAMLET (1964) and KOROL LIR (1970). Part four discusses Kurosawa's KUMONOSU-JO (1957) and RAN (1985).

Coursen, H. R., *Shakespearean Performance as Interpretation*, Newark, University of Delaware Press, 1992.
A theatrical rather than a filmic approach to the plays. The author takes films or television programmes which exist in several versions and compares them; for example, his analysis of *Hamlet* ranges from the 1948 Olivier production, the 1961 Austrian Wirth/Schell made-for-television production with Dunja Movar as Ophelia, to the 1969 Tony Richardson film with Marianne Faithfull as Ophelia. He is sceptical of productions with 'bright ideas'; the 1986 Arena Theater production of *The Taming of the Shrew* is criticised for bringing its audience into a world midway between THE GODFATHER and *Miami Vice*.

Crowle, Samuel, *Shakespeare Observed: Studies in Performance on Stage and Screen*, Athens, Ohio University Press, 1992.
A study of film and stage productions looking at ways in which one production has influenced another; for example, the author argues that Polanski's MACBETH (1971) influenced Adrian Noble's 1986 stage production of *Macbeth* with Jonathan Pryce and Sinead Cusack. There is a chapter on Shakespearean comedies on film; individual films analysed include Welles's MACBETH (1948) and Branagh's HENRY V (1989). Crowle seems more at ease with writing about the theatre than he does when analysing film, and the observations are often written from a textual rather than a cinematic point of view. Notes and index.

Davies, Anthony, *Filming Shakespeare's Plays: The Adaptations of Laurence Olivier, Orson Welles, Peter Brook and Akira Kurosawa*, Cambridge, Cambridge University Press, 1988.
The study compares theatrical and cinematic space, arguing that the dramatic resources of cinema are essentially spatial. The central chapters discuss Olivier's HENRY V (1944), HAMLET (1948) and RICHARD III (1955); Orson Welles's MACBETH (1948), OTHELLO (1952) and CAMPANADAS A MEDIANOCHE (1966); Peter Brook's KING LEAR

(1970); and Akira Kurosawa's KUMONOSU-JO (1957). Davies discusses the dramatic problems which the plays pose for film-makers and examines how these films influenced later theatrical stagings. Concludes with an examination of the demands that distinguish the work of the Shakespearean stage actor from that of his counterpart in film. Contains stills from the films and a selected filmography of films reviewed.

Donaldson, Peter S., *Shakespearean Films/Shakespearean Directors*, London, Unwin Hyman, 1990.
The essays are drawn from the disciplines of film theory and psychoanalysis and are concerned with the ways in which the conventions and practices of the Elizabethan stage are refashioned in film. The seven films analysed are: Olivier's HENRY V (1944) and HAMLET (1948), Kurosawa's KUMONOSU-JU (1957), Jean-Luc Godard's KING LEAR (1987), Orson Welles's OTHELLO (1952), Liz White's OTHELLO (1980) and Zeffirelli's ROMEO AND JULIET (1968). Filmography.

Eckert, Charles W. (ed.), *Focus on Shakespearean Films*, Englewood Cliffs, Prentice-Hall, 1972.
A collection of critical essays on the well-known feature film adaptations of Shakespeare plays, including an excerpt from *Put Money in Thy Purse* by Micheál MacLiammóir on the filming of Welles's OTHELLO (1952), an interview with Peter Brook on filming Shakespeare, and P. M. Pasinetti on the role of Technical Advisor on Mankiewicz's JULIUS CAESAR (1953). Filmography. Bibliography.

France, Richard, *The Theatre of Orson Welles*, London, Associated University Presses, 1977.
A study of Welles's work for the theatre, which French argues provides significant insights for an understanding of his films. The Appendices give cast lists of stage productions and a selected list of radio credits. Bibliography. (Richard France's *Orson Welles on Shakespeare: The W. P. A. Mercury Theatre Playscripts*, London, Greenwood Press, 1990, a record of Welles's W. P. A. theatre productions, is also of interest).

Grant, Cathy (ed.), *As You Like It: AudioVisual Shakespeare*, London, British Universities Film & Video Council, 1992.
A redesigned and expanded edition of *Shakespeare: A List of Audio-visual Materials Available in the UK* (1987, ed. Olwen Terris). Lists over 550 videos, films, audiotapes, slide sets, computer programs, CD-ROMs and videodiscs available for hire or sale in Great Britain. Details are given of full-length performances, study extracts and critical studies; dance, musical and ballet versions of the plays are also included. Three essays discuss how film and video can be used in teaching Shakespeare. The directory concludes with a bibliography and a list of other archives with collections of Shakespeare on film.

Holderness, Graham, *The Shakespeare Myth*, Manchester, Manchester University Press, 1988.
An anthology of specially commissioned essays and interviews on Shakespeare's role in popular contemporary culture, examining such topics as sexual politics, psychoanalytic theories and post-structural linguistics. Some of the essays touch on Shakespeare on film and television; for example, an interview with Jonathan Miller on the *BBC Television Shakespeare*

and Holderness' essay on Shakespeare on television, 'Boxing the Bard', a political account of the relationship between culture and the broadcasters.

Holderness, Graham, *The Taming of the Shrew*, Manchester, Manchester University Press, 1989 (Shakespeare in Performance series).
Discusses John Barton's production for the RSC, 1960 (Peter O'Toole/Peggy Ashcroft), Franco Zeffirelli's 1966 film (Richard Burton/Elizabeth Taylor), Michael Bogdanov's production for the RSC, 1978 (Jonathan Pryce/Paola Dionisotti) and Jonathan Miller's *BBC Television Shakespeare* production, 1980 (Sarah Badel/John Cleese). The productions by Barton and Bogdanov were neither filmed nor televised. Bibliography.

James, Clive, *Clive James on Television: Criticism from the Observer 1972–1982*, London, Picador (Pan Books), 1991.
The omnibus edition of the three books of Clive James's television criticism – *Visions at Midnight* (London: Jonathan Cape, 1977), *The Crystal Bucket* (London: Jonathan Cape, 1981) and *Glued to the Box* (London: Jonathan Cape, 1983). Many of the reviews comment on the *BBC Television Shakespeare* series and other Shakespeare plays broadcast in this period. The accounts are humorous, sometimes irreverent, but always thoughtful, clear and intelligent. James's observations on speaking Shakespearean verse are particularly illuminating. Index by names, titles and subjects.

Jorgens, Jack J., *Shakespeare on Film*, London, Indiana University Press, 1977.
A detailed analysis of sixteen films: Max Reinhardt/William Dieterle's A MIDSUMMER NIGHT'S DREAM (1935), Peter Hall's A MIDSUMMER NIGHT'S DREAM (1968), Zeffirelli's THE TAMING OF THE SHREW (1966) and ROMEO AND JULIET (1968), Joseph Mankiewicz's JULIUS CAESAR (1953), Orson Welles's CAMPANADAS A MEDI-ANOCHE (1966), OTHELLO (1952) and MACBETH (1948), Olivier's HAMLET (1948), RICHARD III (1955) and HENRY V (1944), Roman Polanski's MACBETH (1971), Stuart Burge's OTHELLO (1965), Grigori Kozintsev's GAMLET (1964) and KOROL LIR (1970), Peter Brook's KING LEAR (1970), and Akira Kurosawa's KUMONOSU-JO (1957). Appendix includes credits, outlines of the films and extensive notes.

Kliman, Bernice W., *Hamlet: Film, Television and Audio Performance*, London, Associated Universities Presses, 1988.
The author's preface states that her book is aimed not only at those Shakespeare fans who 'would happily stay up until 4 a.m. to see a cut version of Olivier's HAMLET' but also at literary scholars and media critics. The text is divided into three parts: the first looks at the relationships between page, stage and screen; the second clarifies the particular nature of Shakespeare on television by examining the settings of productions from 1953–1984; and the third addresses interpretations of the play in silent films and sound recordings including an extensive essay on Sir Johnston Forbes-Robertson's HAMLET (1913). An appendix gives screen, stage and sound recording credits, a useful bibliography and a woefully inadequate index.

Kozintsev, Grigori, *Shakespeare: Time and Conscience*, London, Dennis Dobson, 1967.
Discusses the production and staging of Shakespeare's plays. Analyses in detail *King Lear* and

Hamlet. The final chapter deals with the chronicle plays with special reference to Prince Hal and Falstaff. The appendix is an extensive collection of notes made by Kozintsev during the filming of GAMLET (1964). (Kozintsev's *King Lear: The Space of Tragedy*, London, Heinemann, 1977, is a similar meditation on Shakespeare and cinema, and a diary of his 1970 film KOROL LIR.)

McLean, Andrew M., *Shakespeare: Annotated Bibliographies and Media Guide for Teachers*, Urbana, Illinois, National Council of Teachers of English, 1980.
Part one lists books and journal articles which discuss the teaching of Shakespeare; part two is a bibliography of criticism of Shakespeare on film; part three offers a guide to media resources available to teachers. It should be noted that some of the distribution information (relating chiefly to availability in the USA) will now be out of date.

Manvell, Roger, *Shakespeare and the Film*, London, J. M. Dent, 1971 (reprinted 1979 with new material).
A key work and one of the first books to examine the principal films which have been adapted from Shakespeare's plays. Discusses in particular the adaptations of Olivier, Welles and Kozintsev, and gives special attention to Kurosawa's KUMONOSU-JO (1957) and Peter Brook's KING LEAR (1970). Filmography and selected bibliography.

Miller, Jonathan, *Subsequent Performances*, London, Faber & Faber, 1986.
A learned account of Miller's work as a producer and director of stage, television and opera, concentrating on his belief that a work of art outlasts its creator, which with time creates subsequent problems of interpretation. The arguments and ideas expressed in the book were developed in the Clark Lectures at Trinity College, Cambridge and during the T. S. Eliot lectures at the University of Kent. A section of the book is devoted to Miller's productions for the *BBC Television Shakespeare* series, discussing matters of casting, interpretation and staging.

Parker, Barry M., *The Folger Shakespeare Filmography*, Folger Shakespeare Library, Department of Museum and Public Programs, 1979.
A clear and well-designed catalogue of the study collection of Shakespeare and Shakespeare adaptations on film held by the Folger Library. Includes feature-length versions, dance, musical or operatic versions of the plays and educational and abridged versions. The collection is regularly being added to and information on new acquisitions can be obtained from the Reference Librarian at the Folger Library. (See entry for the Folger Library in the Archives and Libraries section.)

Pilkington, Ace G., *Screening Shakespeare from Richard II to Henry V*, London, Associated Universities Presses, 1991.
Discusses in detail four plays in six films: RICHARD II, HENRY IV (parts 1 and 2) and HENRY V in the *BBC Television Shakespeare* series, Olivier's HENRY V (1944) and Welles's CAMPANADAS A MEDIANOCHE (1966). Argues that the financial and aesthetic restrictions placed on the BBC series helped to make new insights possible. The essays on CAMPANADAS A MEDIANOCHE and HENRY V (1944) are based upon a close examination of the shooting scripts. Extensive notes, filmography and bibliography.

Richmond, Hugh H., *King Richard III*, Manchester, Manchester University Press, 1989 (Shakespeare in Performance series).
Performances discussed include: Richard Burbage, Colley Cibber's productions from Garrick to Olivier, the RSC centennial (1964), Jane Howell's production for the *BBC Television Shakespeare* series (1982) (Ron Cook as Richard) and Bill Alexander's 1984 production at Stratford-upon-Avon (Antony Sher as Richard). Not all the productions discussed were filmed or broadcast, so the debate is written largely from a literary viewpoint concentrating on individual staged performances. Bibliography.

Rothwell, Kenneth S. and Melzer, Annabelle Henkin, *Shakespeare on Screen: An International Filmography and Videography*. London, Mansell, 1990.
A guide to films and videos based on Shakespeare's plays from KING JOHN (1899) to Kenneth Branagh's HENRY V (1989). Includes details of over 750 titles including major film adaptations, musical and dance versions, abridgments, travesties and excerpts. The holdings of some foreign archives are listed but the emphasis of the directory is on information held in the Folger Shakespeare Library, the Motion Picture Division of the Library of Congress, the then National Film Archive, London, and the BBC Written Archives Centre, Caversham. Many films have been viewed by Professor Rothwell and his critical comments form an interesting and informative part of the work. Distribution and availability details are given, although some of the information will now be out of date. Selected bibliography and indexes by personality, series and genre. The lack of an overall film title index is regrettable.

Shakespeare and Schools, ed. Rex Gibson, Shakespeare and Schools Project, Cambridge Institute of Education (1986 –).
The journal of the Shakespeare and Schools Project, published three times a year, which aims to encourage the teaching of Shakespeare in primary and secondary schools. Many of the articles report on initiatives in using film and video in the classroom to stimulate debate.

Shakespeare Bulletin, ed. James P. Luardi and June Schlueter, Lafayette College, Easton, PA (1982 –).
A quarterly journal of performance criticism and scholarship providing commentary on Shakespearean and Renaissance drama through feature articles, theatre reviews and book reviews. Its theatre coverage serves as a record of productions in New York, Canada and Great Britain. From 1992 it has incorporated the *Shakespeare on Film Newsletter*.

Shakespeare on Film Newsletter, ed. Bernice W. Kliman and Kenneth S. Rothwell, Burlington, University of Vermont (1976–1992).
Published in the spring and fall each academic year. Contains film and book reviews and notes courses and conferences debating Shakespeare on screen. Films and television programmes newly acquired by the Theater on Film and Tape (TOFT) Archive, Billy Rose Theater Collection at Lincoln Center's Library and the New York City Public Library are listed. (Note: From 1992 the Newsletter has been incorporated in *Shakespeare Bulletin*)

Shakespeare Survey: An Annual Survey of Shakespearean Study and Production, ed. Stanley Wells, No. 39, Cambridge, Cambridge University Press, 1987.
Essays from Shakespearean scholars, the majority discussing Shakespeare on film and tele-

vision. Articles include an essay by Andrew Davies on the critical literature on Shakespearean film, two accounts of the *BBC Television Shakespeare* series by Neil Taylor and Michèle Willems and an assessment of Shakespeare on radio by Stuart Evans. Graham Holderness and Christopher McCullough provide a filmography of 'complete, straightforward' versions of Shakespeare's plays on film, television and videotape. The filmography is valuable for its documentation of early television productions. It should be noted that the distribution information in the filmography will now be largely out of date.

Sinyard, Neil, *Filming Literature: The Art of Screen Adaptation*, London, Croom Helm, 1986. Chapter one, 'In My Mind's Eye', offers a lively account of Shakespeare on screen – 'RICHARD III (1955) is a splendid film, but it is a shame that the crowd scenes (where Richard is exhorted to take the crown for example) seem so sparsely populated, like friends gathering glumly for a thinly attended Equity meeting.' Olivier's HAMLET (1948) and OTHELLO (1965), Welles's OTHELLO (1952), Mankiewicz's JULIUS CAESAR (1953), Kurosawa's KUMONOSU-JO (1957), Polanski's MACBETH (1971) and Brook's KING LEAR (1970) are also discussed. Sinyard also makes some intriguing suggestions for feature film versions of the plays (PSYCHO as *Macbeth*, ONE-EYED JACKS as *Hamlet*).

Vardac, A. Nicholas, *Stage to Screen – Theatrical Origins of Early Film: David Garrick to D. W. Griffith*, Cambridge, Harvard University Press, 1949.
An analysis of how the melodrama and spectacle of nineteenth-century theatre anticipated the first films of the twentieth century. Includes an account of Henry Irving's Shakespearean productions (pp. 93–107) arguing that his emphasis on the visual marked a theatrical need for the motion picture. 'The words of Shakespeare had lost their necessity. Everything had been done visually with pictorial settings, descriptive business, and mass tableaux. The realistic-romantic phase of theatrical expression had come so far that, having climbed to the very doorstep of the motion picture, further progress seemed impossible without the motion-picture camera.' Extensive notes.

Warren, Roger, *Cymbeline*, Manchester, Manchester University Press, 1989 (Shakespeare in Performance series).
Productions discussed are: Peter Hall's production Stratford-upon-Avon, 1957 (Peggy Ashcroft as Imogen), William Gaskill's production Stratford-upon-Avon, 1962 (Vanessa Redgrave as Imogen), Elijah Moshinsky's *BBC Television Shakespeare* version, 1982 (Helen Mirren as Imogen), productions on the open stage by Jean Gascon (1970) and Robin Phillips (1986), Stratford, Ontario (Maureen O'Brien and Martha Burns respectively as Imogen), Bill Alexander's 1988 production for the National Theatre, London (Harriet Walter as Imogen) and Peter Hall's production for the National Theatre, 1988 (Geraldine James as Imogen). Not all these productions were filmed or broadcast, so the debate is written largely from a literary viewpoint concentrating on individual performances. Bibliography.

Willis, Susan, *The BBC Shakespeare Plays: Making the Televised Canon*, Chapel Hill/London, University of North Carolina Press, 1991.
A thorough history and analysis of the *BBC Television Shakespeare* series and an eyewitness account of the productions, from planning and rehearsal to taping and editing. Part one looks at the series as a phenomenon: its planning, production decisions, and critical recep-

tion in Great Britain and the USA, explaining how differences in transmission, tastes, educational efforts and critical responses shaped the differing reception. Part two examines the theories and styles of the major directors, and part three is production diaries based on the author's observations at the BBC during the making of TITUS ANDRONICUS, THE COMEDY OF ERRORS and TROILUS AND CRESSIDA. Bibliography.

This is a select index of names featured within the catalogue. Those indexed are actors playing the major roles in each of the plays (plus minor roles if the actor appears elsewhere), directors of major productions, directors of original stage productions, some further credits of interest, and for those films or television programmes with Shakespeare sequences, only the people involved in that sequence. Theatre, opera and ballet companies are also indexed. Page references will be found in the title index.

McDowall, Roddy
  CLEOPATRA (1963)
  MACBETH (1948)
McEnery, John
  MEASURE FOR MEASURE (1979)
  ROMEO AND JULIET (1968)
McEnery, Peter
  MIDSUMMER NIGHT'S DREAM, A (1981)
McEwan, Geraldine
  CAUGHT IN THE ACT (1988)
MacGinnis, Niall
  HAMLET (1948)
  HENRY V (1944)
McGoohan, Patrick
  ALL NIGHT LONG (1961)
MacGowran, Jack
  AGE OF CONSENT, The (1969)
MacGregor, Barry
  COMEDY OF ERRORS, The (1964)
McHugh, Frank
  MIDSUMMER NIGHT'S DREAM, A (1935)
MacKane, David
  OTHELLO (1946)
McKellen, Ian
  EVENING STANDARD DRAMA AWARDS 1989, The
  (1989)
  (IAN McKELLEN – DIARY OF A YEAR) (1985)
  MACBETH (1979)
  OTHELLO (1990)
  RICHARD III (1992)
  (SAVING THE ROSE THEATRE) (1989)
  TO DIG OR NOT TO DIG . . . (1989)
  TRAGEDY OF KING RICHARD II, The (1970)
McKenna, Virginia
  THIS WAS THE FUTURE (1957)
McKern, Abigail
  (DUSTIN HOFFMAN AND PETER HALL) (1989)
  TWELFTH NIGHT (1988)
McKern, Leo
  KING LEAR (1983)
Mackintosh, Kenneth
  OTHELLO (1965)
MacLiammóir, Micheál
  ORSON WELLES STORY, The (1982)
  OTHELLO (1952)
MacMillan, Kenneth
  ROMEO AND JULIET (1966)
  TURNING POINT, The (1977)
MacNaughtan, Alan
  DARK LADY OF THE SONNETS, The (1955)
McNaughton, Harry
  OFFICE STEPS (1930)
Madden, Ciaran
  HAMLET (1970)
Madsen, Egon
  TAMING OF THE SHREW, The (1978)
Maitland, Lauderdale
  TAMING OF THE SHREW, The (1923)
Makin, Paul
  KING LEAR II (1993)
  TAKEAWAY (1990)
Malleson, Miles
  MIDSUMMER NIGHT'S DREAM, A (1958)
  MIDSUMMER NIGHT'S DREAM, A (1964)

Mankiewicz, Joseph L.
  CLEOPATRA (1963)
  HOUSE OF STRANGERS (1949)
  JULIUS CAESAR (1953) [USA]
Mansfield, Jayne
  PANIC BUTTON (1964)
Marak, Otakar
  ROMEO E GIULIETTA (c1927)
Market Theatre of Johannesburg
  OTHELLO (1988)
Markowska, Elena
  AMLETO (1917)
Marowitz, Charles
  (HAMLET) (1989)
Marsh, Linda
  HAMLET (1964)
Marston, Theodore
  ROMEO AND JULIET (1911)
Martelli
  AMLETO (1917)
Martin, Keith
  DREAM, The (1967)
Martin, Trevor
  PREPARING A PLAY; NO. 3: MOVEMENT (1966)
  TRAGEDY OF KING RICHARD II, The (1970)
Mason, Brewster
  ALL'S WELL THAT ENDS WELL (1968)
  EDWARD IV (1965)
  HENRY VI (1965)
Mason, James
  AGE OF CONSENT, The (1969)
  DEADLY AFFAIR, The (1966)
  JULIUS CAESAR (1953) [USA]
Massey, Anna
  MIDSUMMER NIGHT'S DREAM, A (1964)
Massey, Daniel
  RICHARD III (1983)
  TAMING OF THE SHREW, The (1983)
  TIMON OF ATHENS (1983)
Massingham, Richard
  IN WHICH WE LIVE; BEING THE STORY OF A SUIT
  TOLD BY ITSELF (1943)
Mature, Victor
  MY DARLING CLEMENTINE (1946)
Maule, Annabel
  TAMER TAMED, The (1956)
Maw, Janet
  LIFE AND DEATH OF KING JOHN, The (1984)
  RICHARD II (1978)
Maxon, Eric
  RICHARD III (1911)
Maxwell, Edwin
  TAMING OF THE SHREW, The (1929)
Maxwell, James
  OTHELLO (1955)
Meddings, Jonathan
  TEMPEST, The (1956)
Mellor, Cherith
  MIDSUMMER NIGHT'S DREAM, A (1981)
Menaugh, Michael
  TEMPEST, The (1969)
Mercanton, Louis
  AMOURS DE LA REINE ELISABETH, Les
  (1912)

Nesbitt, Cathleen
  MACBETH (1945)
Nettleton, John
  TEMPEST, The (1980)
Newman, Widgey R.
  IMMORTAL GENTLEMAN, The (1935)
  MERCHANT OF VENICE, The (1927)
Newton, Robert
  HENRY V (1944)
Nicholls, Anthony
  KING LEAR (1975)
  OTHELLO (1965)
Nielsen, Asta
  HAMLET (1920)
Nielsen, Leslie
  FORBIDDEN PLANET (1956)
Nighy, Bill
  (KING LEAR) (1987)
Nimmo, Derek
  NIGHT OF COMIC RELIEF, A (1988)
Niven, David
  MATTER OF LIFE AND DEATH, A
  (1946)
Noble, Adrian
  ENTERTAINMENT UK (25/8/92)
  HAMLET (1993)
Nolan, Jeanette
  MACBETH (1948)
Normington, John
  EDWARD IV (1965)
  HENRY VI (1965)
Northey, Christopher
  ROMEO AND JULIET (1978)
Northrop, Louis
  MACBETH (1946)
Novelli, Amleto
  AMLETO (1910)
  CAJUS JULIUS CAESAR (1914)
Novelli, Ermete
  MERCANTE DI VENEZIA, Il (1910)
  RE LEAR (1910)
Novello, Ivor
  CARNIVAL (1921)
Nunn, Trevor
  ANTONY AND CLEOPATRA (1974)
  COMEDY OF ERRORS, The (1978)
  LATE SHOW SPECIAL (18/6/90)
  LIFE AND ADVENTURES OF NICHOLAS NICKLEBY;
  PART 2, The (1982)
  MACBETH (1979)
  OTHELLO (1990)
Nureyev, Rudolf
  ROMEO AND JULIET (1966)

O'Brien, Edmond
  JULIUS CAESAR (1953) [USA]
O'Connell, Patrick
  MIDSUMMER NIGHT'S MYSTERY, A
  (1989)
O'Conor, Joseph
  OTHELLO (1981)
  ROMEO AND JULIET (1978)
Ogburn, Charlton
  MIDSUMMER NIGHT'S MYSTERY, A (1989)

O'Hara, Maureen
  McLINTOCK! [TRAILER] (1963)
  QUIET MAN, The (1952)
O'Herlihy, Dan
  MACBETH (1948)
Okamoto, Hami
  MISHIMA: A LIFE IN FOUR CHAPTERS (1985)
Old Vic Theatre Company
  C. E. M. A. (1942)
  FAREWELL TO THE VIC (1963)
  KING OF DENMARK SEES HAMLET (1950)
  THREE SEASONS (1958)
Olive Oyl
  SHAKESPEARIAN SPINACH (1940)
Oliver, Edna May
  ROMEO AND JULIET (1936)
Olivier, Laurence
  AS YOU LIKE IT (1936)
  FAREWELL TO THE VIC (1963)
  GREAT MOMENTS FROM HAMLET (1950)
  HAMLET (1948)
  HENRY V (1944)
  HENRY V [TRAILER] (1944)
  KING LEAR (1983)
  LAURENCE OLIVIER (1992)
  LAURENCE OLIVIER 1907–1989: A TRIBUTE (1989)
  OTHELLO (1965)
  RICHARD III (1955)
  ROMEO AND JULIET (1968)
  ROYALTY HONOURS 'HAMLET' PREMIERE (1948)
  YOUR NATIONAL THEATRE (1976)
Ollmann, Kurt
  LEONARD BERNSTEIN'S WEST SIDE STORY
  (1985)
O'Neil, Sally
  BROADWAY FEVER (1928)
Orchard, Julian
  YOUR NATIONAL THEATRE (1976)
O'Shea, Milo
  ROMEO AND JULIET (1968)
O'Sullivan, Richard
  CARRY ON TEACHER (1959)
Our Gang
  SHIVERING SHAKESPEARE (1929)
Owen, Edgar
  IMMORTAL GENTLEMAN, The (1935)
Owen, Meg Wynn
  TAMING OF THE SHREW, The (1983)
Owens, Richard
  RICHARD II (1978)
Oxley, David
  MIDSUMMER NIGHT'S DREAM, A (1958)

Pack, Charles Lloyd
  HENRY VIII (1979)
  TEMPEST, The (1956)
Paget, F. M.
  KING JOHN (1899)
Paisey, Karen
  DREAM, The (1988)
Palmer, Geoffrey
  MIDSUMMER NIGHT'S DREAM, A (1981)
Palmer, Lilli
  TAMING OF THE SHREW, The (1956)

Note

William Shakespeare appears himself in the following:

This index gives all the titles within the catalogue, with the year of release and the name of the director (or otherwise producer) for common titles. There are also entries for series (in italics) with the individual titles held under that series. Where there is more than one entry in the catalogue for a film, and one of those entries gives greater details, the page number is given in bold.